.NET and XML

Other Microsoft .NET resources from O'Reilly

Related titles   Programming C#   Learning XML
C# in a Nutshell   Learning XSLT
Programming Visual Basic   .NET Framework Essentials
.NET   Mastering Visual Studio .NET
Programming ASP.NET
ASP.NET in a Nutshell

.NET Books   *dotnet.oreilly.com* is a complete catalog of O'Reilly's books on
Resource Center   .NET and related technologies, including sample chapters and
code examples.

ONDotnet.com provides independent coverage of fundamental, interoperable, and emerging Microsoft .NET programming and web services technologies.

Conferences   O'Reilly & Associates brings diverse innovators together to nurture the ideas that spark revolutionary industries. We specialize in documenting the latest tools and systems, translating the innovator's knowledge into useful skills for those in the trenches. Visit *conferences.oreilly.com* for our upcoming events.

Safari Bookshelf (*safari.oreilly.com*) is the premier online reference library for programmers and IT professionals. Conduct searches across more than 1,000 books. Subscribers can zero in on answers to time-critical questions in a matter of seconds. Read the books on your Bookshelf from cover to cover or simply flip to the page you need. Try it today with a free trial.

.NET and XML

Niel M. Bornstein

O'REILLY®

Beijing · Cambridge · Farnham · Köln · Sebastopol · Tokyo

.NET and XML
by Niel M. Bornstein

Copyright © 2004 O'Reilly Media, Inc. All rights reserved.
Printed in the United States of America.

Published by O'Reilly Media, Inc., 1005 Gravenstein Highway North, Sebastopol, CA 95472.

O'Reilly Media, Inc. books may be purchased for educational, business, or sales promotional use. On-line editions are also available for most titles (*safari.oreilly.com*). For more information, contact our corporate/institutional sales department: (800) 998-9938 or *corporate@oreilly.com*.

Editor:	Simon St.Laurent
Production Editor:	Reg Aubry
Cover Designer:	Ellie Volckhausen
Interior Designer:	David Futato

Printing History:

November 2003:	First Edition.

ISBN: 978-0-596-00397-5
[LSI]   [2011-09-09]

Table of Contents

Part I.   Processing XML with .NET

Preface

XML offers a flexible and standardized way to share data between programs running on disparate platforms. The .NET Framework is an exciting new platform for developing software that natively shares its data and processing across networks. It seems natural enough that XML and .NET fit together; indeed, Microsoft has provided a full suite of XML tools in the .NET Framework, and .NET relies heavily on XML for its vaunted remoting and web services capabilities.

This book is about .NET and XML. Now, there are plenty of books out there about .NET, and certainly there are quite a number about XML. However, as I set out to learn about using XML in .NET, I discovered a dearth of books about .NET *and* XML, especially ones that go into detail about the things that Visual Studio .NET can do behind the wizards.

This is a serious gap. The .NET framework provides deep support for the XML family of standards; not only does it use XML internally, but it also maks its XML tools available to you as a developer. There is a strong need for developers to know how .NET uses XML and to learn how they can use .NET to write their own XML-based applications.

In this book I hope to bridge this gap by providing details about how you can use .NET to write applications that use XML and by explaining some ways in which .NET uses XML to provide its advanced networked application features.

Organization of This Book

This book is organized into two major sections. The first eleven chapters cover a series of increasingly complex topics, with each chapter building on the previous one. These topics include:

- Reading XML using the standard XmlReader implementations
- Writing XML using the standard XmlWriter implementations
- Reading and writing formats other than XML by creating custom XmlReader and XmlWriter implementations

- Manipulating XML using the Document Object Model
- Navigating XML using XPath
- Transforming XML using XSLT
- Constraining XML using W3C XML Schema
- Serializing XML from objects using SOAP and other formats
- Using XML in Web Services
- Reading XML into, and writing XML from, databases with ADO.NET

Each of these chapters is organized in roughly the following manner. I begin each chapter with an introduction to the specification or standard the chapter deals with, and explain when it's appropriate to use the technology covered. Then I introduce the .NET assembly that implements the technology and give examples that illustrate how to use the assemblies.

The remaining nine chapters provide an API reference that gives an in-depth description of each assembly, its types, and their members.

Who Should Read This Book?

This book is intended for the busy developer who wants to learn how to use XML in .NET. You should know enough about C# and .NET to read the sample code, and you should be able to write enough C# to experiment and attempt variations on the examples.

However, even if you're not particularly familiar with C#, you may not be completely lost; the .NET features under discussion apply to all .NET-enabled languages, including Visual Basic .NET and C++ .NET.

While you don't need to know a lot about XML going in, you should know the basics: elements, attributes, namespaces, and how to create well-formed XML documents. I hope you'll have some specific areas you want to know more about by the time you're done.

About XML and Web Services

Everyone's been talking about .NET and XML Web Services lately, to the extent that I think a lot of developers new to XML think that XML and Web Services are synonymous. I'd like to make it very clear that this just isn't so.

Web Services could not exist without XML, but there's a whole lot more to XML than just SOAP, WSDL, and UDDI. While XML does provide the basic syntax for all the Web Services standards, it also has its own unique set of features that can be used in many interesting ways, from data interchange to web site content management.

While some books purport to teach XML in .NET, they all seem to skimp on the basics of XML processing. I hope this volume fills that gap.

About the Sample Code

I've always found that it's easiest to learn about a new technology by working on a simple project that uses that technology. To that end, in this book I use the example of a hardware store inventory system.

Angus Hardware is a retail operation whose customers include local consumers, as well as contractors and construction companies. Angus sells lots of little parts, such as screws and nails, and a few big-ticket items, such as a 15 amp, 3,500 RPM compound miter saw with a carbide blade and laser guide. For its high-volume bulk items, Angus tracks inventory once a month by inspecting the bins in the store, while for more exclusive items, inventory is tracked at the cash register as a sale is completed. Angus also publishes a mail-order catalog once a quarter and offers Internet sales in addition to its retail storefront operation. All these sales channels are based on the same inventory database, and it's very important that all the channels are kept updated with the latest list of items for sale and how many of those items are in stock.

This all makes a good demonstration of the power of XML in .NET. The hardware store needs to be able to handle a variety of different transactional scenarios: automated entry of vendors' parts lists, updates to inventory based on point of sale transactions, manual entry of monthly inventory numbers, batch printing of reports, and online sales and fulfillment. While a relational database management system still makes the best data store for such an inventory system, the need for interoperability maks a good case for XML. This book illustrates how .NET and XML work together to make a good platform for this kind of environment.

Although I refer to the Angus Hardware inventory system throughout the book, the actual code examples demonstrate the topic of each chapter in a relatively self-enclosed way. If you're reading chapters out of order, you won't be totally lost when it comes to the example code in each chapter. And, in addition to the running hardware store example, some chapters also contain standalone examples within the main text of how to use the technology.

Why C#?

Although many languages have access to the .NET runtime, C# is the native language of .NET. All but a few of the code examples in this volume are written in C#, because it is, frankly, the best language for the job.

From the standpoint of how .NET works with XML, though, remember that whatever the details of a language's syntax, the .NET Framework itself works in a consistent and predictable way. You should never fear that an XML document will be handled differently in C++ than in ASP.NET, for example.

Running the Examples

Many potential .NET developers are put off by the cost of Visual Studio .NET. There's no need to spend the big money to buy Visual Studio .NET to run the examples in this book—in fact, I've written all of them without using Visual Studio .NET. All of the C# code can be compiled and run for free by downloading the Microsoft .NET Framework SDK, either Version 1.0 or Version 1.1, from *http://msdn.microsoft.com/*.

Here's a simple "Hello, XML" example that you can try out using the C# compiler (as shown below):

```
using System;
using System.Xml;

public class HelloXML {
  public static void Main(string [] args) {
    XmlTextWriter writer = new XmlTextWriter(Console.Out);
    writer.WriteStartDocument();
    writer.WriteElementString("Hello", "XML");
    writer.WriteEndDocument();
    writer.Close();
  }
}
```

Once you have downloaded and installed the SDK, you can use the C# compiler, *csc.exe,* to compile any of the example C# code. The basic syntax for compiling a C# program called *HelloXML.cs* with the C# compiler is:

```
csc /debug /target:exe HelloXML.cs
```

This produces a .NET console executable called *HelloXML.exe*, which can then be run just like any Windows executable. The /debug option causes the compiler to produce an additional file, called *HelloXML.pdb*, which contains debugging symbols. The C# compiler can also be used to produce a .NET DLL with the command-line options /target:library.

The C# compiler can also compile multiple files at once by including them on the command line. At least one class in the source files on the command line must have a Main() method in order to compile an executable. If more than one class contains a Main() method, you can specify which one to use by including the /main:*classname* option on the command line.

Running the *HelloXML.exe* executable results in the following output:

```
<?xml version="1.0" encoding="IBM437"?><Hello>XML</Hello>
```

For more information on the C# compiler options, simply type csc /? or csc /help on the command line. The .NET Framework SDK Documentation, which comes with the .NET Framework SDK, provides more information on the other tools that come with the SDK. It's also a good first resource for information on any of the .NET assemblies.

Style Conventions

Items appearing in this book are sometimes given a special appearance to set them apart from the regular text. Here's how they look:

Italic
> Used for commands, email addresses, URIs, filenames, emphasized text, first references to terms, and citations of books and articles.

Constant width
> Used for literals, constant values, code listings, and XML markup.

Constant width italic
> Used for replaceable parameter and variable names.

Constant width bold
> Used to highlight the portion of a code listing being discussed.

 These icons signify a tip, suggestion, or general note.

 These icons indicate a warning or caution.

How to Contact Us

We have tested and verified the information in this book to the best of our ability, but you may find that features have changed (or even that we have made mistakes!). Please let us know about any errors you find, as well as your suggestions for future editions, by writing to:

O'Reilly & Associates, Inc.
1005 Gravenstein Highway North
Sebastopol, CA 95472
(800) 998-9938 (in the United States or Canada)
(707) 829-0515 (international/local)
(707) 829-0104 (fax)

You can also send us messages electronically. To be put on the mailing list or request a catalog, send email to:

info@oreilly.com

To ask technical questions or comment on the book, send email to:

bookquestions@oreilly.com

We have a web site for the book, where we'll list examples, errata, and any plans for future editions. You can access this page at:

http://www.oreilly.com/catalog/netxml/

For more information about this book and others, see the O'Reilly web site:

http://www.oreilly.com

Acknowledgments

Writing a book like this doesn't just happen. It takes encouragement and motivation, and I'd like thank my prime encourager, Dawn, and my prime motivator, Nicholas. Dawn, thanks for giving up so much of our time together and for keeping the household running while I was locked in my cave, basking in the eerie blue light of my computer monitor. Nicholas, who knew you'd be here before the book was finished? But here you are, making our lives interesting, and the book is finally done.

I have to thank my editors at O'Reilly: John Osborn, Brian MacDonald, and, most of all, Simon St.Laurent, who picked up the pieces when things looked darkest. I'd also like to thank Keyton Weissinger and Edd Dumbill for encouraging me to write, despite the months of pain and suffering involved. Thanks must also go to Kendall Clark, Bijan Parsia, and rest of the folks on #mf and #pants, for serving as a constant sounding board and for enduring my occasional griping.

I'd be remiss if I did not acknowledge my technical reviewers: Shane Fatzinger, Martin Gudgin, and David Sommers. Their input was invaluable in making this a book worthy of being published and read.

And finally, thanks to my bosses at Radiant Systems for giving me the opportunity to learn on the job. Nothing teaches like real-world experience, and in the past 18 months I've had enough experience with .NET and XML to make this, I hope, a really good book.

Processing XML with .NET

CHAPTER 1

Introduction to .NET and XML

The .NET framework, formally introduced to the public in July 2000, is the key to Microsoft's next-generation software strategy. It consists of several sets of products, which fulfill several goals Microsoft has targeted as being critical to its success over the next decade.

The Extensible Markup Language (XML), introduced in 1996 by the World Wide Web Consortium (W3C), provides a common syntax for data transfer between dissimilar systems. XML's use is not limited to heterogeneous systems, however; it can be, and often is, used for an application's internal configuration and datafiles.

In this chapter, I introduce the .NET Framework and XML, and give you the basic information you need to start using XML in the .NET Framework.

The .NET Framework

Unlike Windows (and operating systems generally), .NET is a software platform that enables developers to create software applications that are *network-native*. A network-native application is one whose natural environment is a standards-based network, such as the Internet or a corporate intranet. Rather than merely coexisting with the network, the network-native application is designed from the ground up to use the network as its playground. The alphabet soup of network standards includes such players as Internet Protocol (IP), Hypertext Transfer Protocol (HTTP), and others.

.NET enables *componentization* of software; that is, it allows developers to create small units of functionality, called *assemblies* in .NET, that can later be reused by other developers. These components can reside locally, on a standalone machine, or they can reside elsewhere on a network. Componentization is not new; previous attempts at building component software environments have included Common Object Request Broker Architecture (CORBA) and the Component Object Model (COM).

An important factor in the componentization of software is *language integration*. You may already be familiar with the concept of *language independence*, which means that you can develop software components in any of the languages that .NET supports and use the components you develop in any of those languages. However, language integration goes a step further, meaning that those languages support .NET natively. Using the .NET Framework from any of the .NET languages is as natural as using the language's native syntax.

Building on top of these basic goals, .NET also allows developers to use *enterprise services* in their applications. The .NET Framework handles common tasks such as messaging, transaction monitoring, and security, so that you don't have to. Enterprise services that .NET takes advantage of can include those provided by Microsoft SQL Server, Microsoft Message Queuing (MSMQ), and Windows Authentication.

Finally, .NET positions software developers to take advantage of the delivery of software functionality via *web services*. "Web services" is one of the latest buzzwords in the buzzword-rich world of information technology; briefly, a web service represents the delivery of application software functionality, over a network, on a subscription basis. This application functionality may be provided directly by a software vendor, as in a word processor or spreadsheet that runs within a web browser, or it may be provided in a business-to-consumer or business-to-business manner, such as a stock ticker or airline reservation system. Web services are built, in large part, on standards such as Simple Object Access Protocol (SOAP) and Web Services Description Language (WSDL).

Each of these goals builds on and relies on each of the others. For example, an enterprise service may be delivered via a web service, which in turn may rely upon the Internet for the delivery of data and components.

The .NET environment is composed of a group of products, each of which provides a piece of the total .NET puzzle. The .NET Framework is the particular set of tools that a developer can use to produce .NET applications and services. Figure 1-1 shows the .NET Framework architecture.

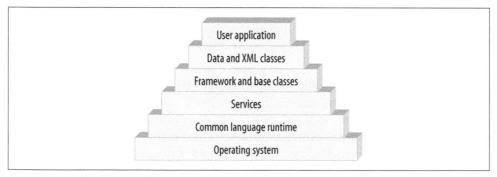

Figure 1-1. .NET Framework architecture

As Figure 1-1 suggests, the .NET Framework (which I'll often refer to simply as .NET throughout the rest of the book) has a layered structure that resembles a wedding cake. The bottom layer consists of the operating system, which is generally a member of the Windows family—although it doesn't need to be. Microsoft has provided .NET implementations for MacOS and FreeBSD, and there are open source efforts to implement it on other operating systems.

Above the operating system is the Common Language Runtime, (CLR), which is the actual execution environment in which .NET programs run. The CLR does exactly what its name implies; it provides a common set of constructs that all .NET languages have access to, and, in fact, they must provide language-specific implementations of these common constructs. (For further information, see *.NET Framework Essentials*, by Thuan Thai and Hoang Lam (O'Reilly).)

Above the OS and CLR are a series of framework classes, including the *data and XML classes*, which provide higher-level access to the framework services; *framework base classes*, which provide I/O, security, threading, and similar services; and *services classes*, such as web services and web forms. Finally, your custom applications make up the top layer.

To reiterate, here are some of the terms I've introduced in this discussion of the .NET Framework:

The Common Language Runtime
> The CLR is the layer of the .NET Framework that makes language independence work. Written mostly in Microsoft's new language, C#, the CLR provides services that any .NET program can use. Because of .NET's component architecture, software written in any language can call upon these services.
>
> Microsoft has also submitted a subset of the CLR to ECMA, the European information and communications standards organization. This subset is referred to as the Common Language Infrastructure (CLI).

The Framework Class Library
> The FCL contains the classes that allow you to build applications and services quickly and easily. These classes are used for file access, network socket communication, multithreading, database access, and a host of other functions.

Data and XML classes
> Although they are still a part of the FCL, the data and XML classes deserve to stand on their own in an introduction to .NET. These are the classes that enable you to work with data in a variety of formats.

Services
> The services layer makes up .NET's *remoting* and *web services* capabilities, which I'll talk about more in a minute. This layer also contains the user interface services, including Web Forms and Windows Forms.

Applications

Finally, your applications are at the top. These applications are not limited to accessing only the previous layer of services; applications can, and often do, make use of all the lower layers.

The XML Family of Standards

XML was specifically designed to combine the flexibility of SGML with the simplicity of Hypertext Markup Language (HTML). HTML, the markup language upon which the World Wide Web is based, is an application of an older and more complex language known as Standard Generalized Markup Language (SGML). SGML was created to provide a standardized language for complex documents, such as airplane repair manuals and parts lists. HTML, on the other hand, was designed for the specific purpose of creating documents that could be displayed by a variety of different web browsers. As such, HTML provides only a subset of SGML's functionality and is limited to features that make sense in a web browser. XML takes a broader view.

There are several types of tasks you'll typically want to perform with XML documents. XML documents can be read into arbitrary data structures, manipulated in memory, and written back out as XML. Existing objects can be written (or serialized, to use the technical term) to a number of different XML formats, including ones that you define, as well as standard serialization formats. The technologies most commonly used to perform these operations are the following:

Input

In order to read an XML Document into memory, you need to *read* it. There are a variety of XML parsers that can be used to read XML, and I discuss the .NET implementation in Chapter 2 .

Output

After either reading XML in or creating an XML representation in memory, you'll most likely need to *write* it out to an XML file. This is the flip side of parsing, and it's covered in Chapter 3.

Extension

You can use the same APIs you use to read and write XML to read and write other formats. I explore how this works in Chapter 4 .

DOM

Once it has been read into memory, you can *manipulate* an XML document's tree structure through the Document Object Model (DOM). The DOM specification was developed to introduce a platform-independent model for XML documents. The DOM is discussed in Chapter 5.

XPath

You will sometimes want to locate a particular element or attribute in the content of an XML document. The XPath specification provides the mechanism used to *navigate* an XML document. I talk about XPath in Chapter 6.

XSLT

Different organizations often develop different markup languages for the same problem domain. In those cases, it can be useful to *transform* an existing XML document in one format into another document in another format. XML Stylesheet Language Transformations (XSLT) was developed to enable you to convert XML documents into other XML and non-XML formats. XSLT is discussed in Chapter 7.

XML Schema

The original XML specification included the Document Type Description (DTD), which allows you to specify the structure of an XML document. The XML Schema standard allows you to *constrain* an XML document in a more formal manner than DTD. Using an XML Schema, you can ensure that a document structure and content fits the expected model. I discuss XML Schema in Chapter 8.

Serialization

In addition to the XML technologies listed above, there are specific XML syntaxes used for specific purposes. One such purpose is *serializing* objects into XML. Objects can be serialized to an arbitrary XML syntax, or they can be serialized to the Simple Object Access Protocol (SOAP). I discuss serialization in Chapter 9.

Web Services

Web Services allows for the *sharing* of resources on a network as if they were local through XML syntaxes such as SOAP, Web Services Definition Language (WSDL), and Universal Description, Discovery, and Integration (UDDI). Web Services provides the foundation for .NET remoting, although Web Services is, by its nature, an open framework that is operating system- and hardware-independent. Although Web Services as a topic can fill several volumes, I talk about it briefly in Chapter 10.

Data

Most modern software applications are concerned in some way with *storing* and accessing data. While XML can itself be used as a rudimentary data store, relational database management systems, such as SQL Server, DB2, and Oracle, are much better at providing quick, reliable access to large amounts of data. Like Web Services, database access is a huge topic; I'll try to give you a taste for XML-related database access issues in Chapter 11.

Since its invention, XML has gone far beyond the language for web site design that HTML is. It has acquired a host of related technologies, such as XHTML, XPath, XSLT, XML Schema, SOAP, WSDL, and UDDI, some of which are syntaxes of XML, and some of which simply add value to XML—and some of which do both.

I've just introduced a lot of acronyms, so look at Figure 1-2 for a visual representation of the relationships between some of these standards.

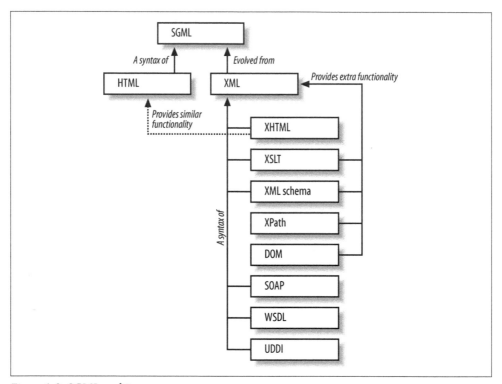

Figure 1-2. SGML and its progeny

Introduction to XML in .NET

Although many programming languages and environments have provided XML support as an add-on, .NET's support is integrated into the framework more tightly than most. The .NET development team decided to use XML extensively within the framework in order to meet its design goals. Accordingly, they built in XML support from the beginning.

The .NET Framework contains five main assemblies that implement the core XML standards. Table 1-1 lists the five assemblies, along with a description of the functionality contained in each. Each of these assemblies is documented in detail in Chapters 16 through 20.

Table 1-1. .NET XML assemblies

Assembly	Description
System.Xml	Basic XML input and output with XmlReader and XmlWriter, DOM with XmlNode and its subclasses, many XML utility classes
System.Xml.Schema	Constraint of XML via XML Schema with XmlSchemaObject and its subclasses
System.Xml.Serialization	Serialization to plain XML and SOAP with XmlSerializer
System.Xml.XPath	Navigation of XML via XPath with XPathDocument, XPathExpression, and XPathNavigator
System.Xml.Xsl	Transformation of XML documents via XSLT with XslTransform

In addition, the System.Web.Services and System.Data assemblies contain classes that interact with the XML assemblies. The XML assemblies used internally in the .NET Framework are also available for use directly in your applications.

For example, the System.Data assembly handles database operations. Its DataSet class provides a mechanism to transmit database changes using XML. But you can also access the XML generated by the DataSet and manipulate it just as you would any XML file, using classes in the System.Xml namespace.

Besides the .NET Framework's XML assemblies, there are several tools integrated into Visual Studio .NET and shipped with the .NET Framework SDK that can make your life easier when dealing with XML. These tools include *xsd.exe*, *wsdl.exe*, and *disco.exe*, among others.

There are also some tools shipped by Microsoft and other third parties that provide different ways to access and manipulate XML data. I describe some of them in Chapters 13 and 14.

.NET applications have access to system- and application-specific configuration files through the System.Configuration assembly. The System.Configuration assembly and the format of the XML configuration files, along with some examples of their use, are documented in Chapter 15.

As you can see, XML is deeply integrated into .NET. One entire layer of the .NET conceptual model shown in Figure 1-1 is devoted to XML. Although it shares the layer with data services, the XML and data assemblies are tightly integrated with each other.

Key Concepts

Before you can learn to work with XML in the .NET Framework, I have to introduce some of the key types you'll be using.

When using the DOM, as shown in Chapter 5, each node in an XML document is represented by an appropriately named class, starting with the abstract base class, XmlNode. Derived from XmlNode are XmlAttribute, XmlDocument, XmlDocumentFragment,

XmlEntity, XmlLinkedNode, and XmlNotation. In turn, XmlLinkedNode has a number of subclasses that serve specific purposes (XmlCharacterData, XmlDeclaration, XmlDocumentType, XmlElement, XmlEntityReference, and XmlProcessingInstruction). Several of these key types also have further subclasses. In each case, the final subclass of each inheritance branch has a name that is meaningful to one familiar with XML.

Figure 1-3 shows the XmlNode inheritance hierarchy.

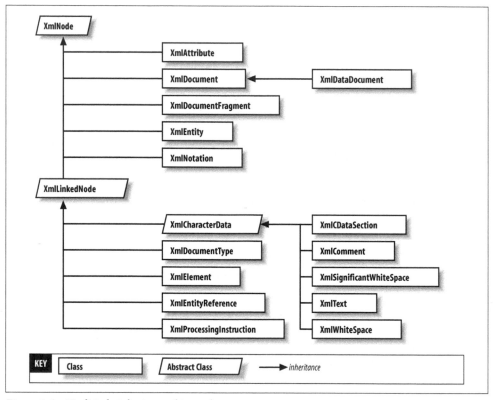

Figure 1-3. XmlNode inheritance hierarchy

Each of the concrete XmlNode subclasses are also represented by the members of the XmlNodeType enumeration: Element, Attribute, Text, CDATA, EntityReference, Entity, ProcessingInstruction, Comment, Document, DocumentType, DocumentFragment, Notation, Whitespace, and SignificantWhitespace, plus the special pseudo-node types, None, EndElement, EndEntity, and XmlDeclaration. Each XmlNode instance has a NodeType property, which returns an XmlNodeType that represents the type of the instance. An XmlNodeType value is also returned by the NodeType property of XmlReader, as discussed in Chapters 2, 3, and 4.

Moving On

In this chapter, I introduce the .NET Framework and the XML specification, and give you a flavor of how they work together. In the next chapter I show you how to read XML documents in .NET.

CHAPTER 2
Reading XML

Perhaps the simplest thing you can do with an existing XML document is to read it into memory. The .NET Framework provides a set of tools in the System.Xml namespace to help you read XML, whether you wish to deal with it as a stream of events or to load the data into your own data structures. In this chapter we take a look at XmlReader, its subclasses, and the associated .NET types and interfaces. I also discuss when it is appropriate to use the XmlReader instead of other methods of reading XML, and describe the differences between pull parsers and push parsers.

You can read XML from a local file or from a remote source over a network. You'll see how to deal with various local and remote inputs, including reading through a network proxy. And you'll learn how to validate an XML document regardless of which sort of input source is used.

Throughout this chapter, I make use of a hypothetical Angus Hardware purchase order in XML and do some simple processing of its contents.

Reading Data

Before you learn about reading XML, you must learn how to read a file. In this section, I'll cover basic filesystem and network input in .NET. If you're already familiar with basic I/O types and methods in .NET, feel free to skip to the next section.

I/O classes in .NET are located in the System.IO namespace. The basic object used for reading and writing data, regardless of the source, is the Stream object. Stream is an abstract base class, which represents a sequence of bytes; the Stream has a Read() method to read the bytes from the Stream, a Write() method to write bytes to the Stream, and a Seek() method to set the current location within the Stream. Not all instances or subclasses of Stream support all these operations; for example, you cannot write to a FileStream representing a read-only file, and you cannot Seek() to a position in a NetworkStream. The properties CanRead, CanWrite, and CanSeek can be interrogated to determine whether the respective operations are supported by the instance of Stream you're dealing with.

Table 2-1 shows the Stream type's subclasses and the methods each type supports.

Table 2-1. Stream subclasses and their supported members

Type	Length	Position	Flush( )	Read( )	Seek( )	Write( )
System.IO.BufferedStream	Yes	Yes	Yes	Yes	Yes	Yes
System.IO.FileStream	Yes	Yes	Yes	Yes	Yes	Yes
System.IO. IsolatedStorage. IsolatedStorageFileStream	Yes	Yes	Yes	Yes	Yes	Yes
System.IO.MemoryStream	Yes	Yes	Yes (does nothing)	Yes	Yes	Yes
System.Net.Sockets. NetworkStream	No (throws exception)	No (throws exception)	Yes (does nothing)	Yes	No (throws exception)	Yes
System.Security. Cryptography.CryptoStream	Yes	Yes	Yes	Yes	Yes	Yes

After Stream, the most important .NET I/O type is TextReader. TextReader is optimized for reading characters from a Stream, and provides a level of specialization one step beyond Stream. Unlike Stream, which provides access to data at the level of bytes, TextReader provides string-oriented methods such as ReadLine( ) and ReadToEnd( ). Like Stream, TextReader is also an abstract base class; its subclasses include StreamReader and StringReader.

Most .NET XML types receive their input from Stream or TextReader. You can often pass filenames and URLs directly to their constructors and Load( ) methods; however, you'll sometimes find it necessary to manipulate a data source before dealing with its XML content. For that reason, I talk first about handling Files and Streams before delving into XML.

Filesystem I/O

.NET provides two types that allow you to deal directly with files: File and FileInfo. A FileInfo instance represents an actual file and its metadata, but the File object contains only static methods used to manipulate files. That is, you must instantiate a FileInfo object to access the contents of the file as well as information about the file, but you can call File's static methods to access files transiently.

The following C# code snippet shows how you can use FileInfo to determine the length of a file and its latest modification date. Note that both Length and LastAccessTime are properties of the FileInfo object:

```
// Create an instance of File and query it
FileInfo fileInfo = new FileInfo(@"C:\data\file.xml");
```

```
long length = fileInfo.Length;
DateTime lastAccessTime = fileInfo.LastAccessTime;
```

 Since the `FileInfo` and `File` types are contained in the `System.IO` namespace, to compile a class containing this code snippet you must include the following using statement:

```
using System.IO;
```

I skip the using statements in code snippets, but I include them in full code listings.

You can also use the `File` type to get the file's last access time, but you cannot get the file's length this way. The `GetLastAccessTime()` method returns the last access time for the filename passed to it, but there is no `GetLength()` method equivalent to the `FileInfo` object's `Length` property:

```
// Get the last access time of a file transiently
DateTime lastAccessTime = File.GetLastAccessTime(@"C:\data\file.xml");
```

 In C#, as in many programming languages, the backslash character (\) has special meaning within a string. In C#, you can either double up on the backslashes to represent a literal backslash within a string, or precede the string with an at sign character (@), as I've done, to indicate that any backslashes within the string are to be treated literally.

In general, you should use the `File` class to get or set the attributes of a file that can be obtained from the operating system, such as its creation and last access times; to open a file for reading or writing; or to move, copy, or delete a file. You may want to use the `FileInfo` class when you wish to open a file for reading or writing, and hold on to it for a longer period of time. Or you may just skip the `File` and `FileInfo` classes and construct a `FileStream` or `StreamReader` directly, as I show you later.

You may read the contents of a file by getting a `FileStream` for it, via the `File` or `FileInfo` classes' `OpenRead()` methods. `FileStream`, one of the subclasses of `Stream`, has a `Read()` method that allows you to read characters from the file into a buffer.

The following code snippet opens a file for reading and attempts to read up to 1024 bytes of data into a buffer, echoing the text to the console as it does so:

```
Stream stream = File.OpenRead(@"C:\data\file.xml");
int bytesToRead = 1024;
int bytesRead = 0;
byte [] buffer = new byte [bytesToRead];

// Fill up the buffer repeatedly until we reach the end of file
do {
  bytesRead = stream.Read(buffer, 0, bytesToRead);
  Console.Write(Encoding.ASCII.GetChars(buffer,0, bytesRead));
} while (bytesToRead == bytesRead);
stream.Close();
```

The Encoding class is contained in the System.Text namespace. Encoding provides several useful methods for converting strings to byte arrays and byte arrays to strings. It also knows about several common encodings, such as ASCII. I'll talk more about encodings in Chapter 3.

Another way to access the data from a file is to use TextReader. File.OpenText( ) returns an instance of TextReader, which includes methods such as ReadLine( ), which lets you read an entire line of text from Stream at a time, and ReadToEnd( ), which lets you read the file's entire contents in one fell swoop. As you can see, TextReader makes for much simpler file access, at least when the file's contents can be dealt with as text:

```
TextReader reader = File.OpenText(@"C:\data\file.xml");

// Read a line at a time until we reach the end of file
while (reader.Peek( ) != -1) {
  string line = reader.ReadLine( );
  Console.WriteLine(line);
}
reader.Close( );
```

The Peek( ) method reads a single character from the Stream without moving the current position. Peek( ) is used to determine the next character which would be read without actually reading it, and it returns -1 if the next character is the end of the Stream. Other methods, such as Read( ) and ReadBlock( ), allow you to access the file in chunks of various sizes, from a single byte to a block of user-defined size.

So far, I've used types from the System, System.IO, and System.Text namespaces without specifying the namespaces, for the sake of brevity. In reality, you'll need to either specify the fully-qualified namespace for each class as it's used, or include a using statement in the appropriate place for each namespace.

Network I/O

Network I/O is generally similar to file I/O, and both Stream and TextReader types are used to access to data from a network connection. The System.Net namespace contains additional classes that are useful in dealing with common network protocols such as HTTP, while the System.Net.Sockets namespace contains generalized classes for dealing with network sockets.

To create a connection to a web server, you will typically use the abstract WebRequest class and its Create( ) and GetResponse( ) methods. Create( ) is a static factory method that returns a new instance of a subclass of WebRequest to handle the URL passed in to Create( ). GetResponse( ) returns a WebResponse object, which provides a method called GetResponseStream( ). The GetResponseStream( ) method returns a

Stream object, which you can wrap in a TextReader. As you've already seen, you can use a TextReader to read from an I/O stream.

The following code snippet shows a typical sequence for creating a connection to a network data source and displaying its contents to the console device. StreamReader is a concrete implementation of the abstract TextReader base class:

```
WebRequest request = WebRequest.Create("http://www.oreilly.com/");
WebResponse response = request.GetResponse();
Stream stream = response.GetResponseStream();
StreamReader reader = new StreamReader(stream);

// Read a line at a time and write it to the console
while (reader.Peek() != -1) {
  Console.WriteLine(reader.ReadLine());
}
```

 A network connection isn't initiated until you call the GetResponse() method. This gives you the opportunity to set other properties of the WebRequest right up until the time you make the connection. Properties that can be set include the HTTP headers, connection timeout, and security credentials.

This pattern works fine when the data source is a URL that adheres to the file, http, or https scheme. Here's an example of a web request that uses a URL with a file scheme:

```
WebRequest request = WebRequest.Create("file:///C:/data/file.xml");
```

Here's a request that has no URL scheme at all:

```
WebRequest request = WebRequest.Create("file.xml");
```

In the absence of a valid scheme name at the beginning of a URL, WebRequest assumes that you are referring to a file on the local filesystem and translates the filename to *file://localhost/path/to/file*. On Windows, the path *C:\data\file.xml* thus becomes the URL *file://localhost/C:/data/file.xml*. Technically, a URL using the file scheme does not require a network connection, but it behaves as if it does, as far as .NET is concerned. Therefore, your code can safely treat a file scheme URL just the same as any other URL. (For more on the URL file scheme, see *http://www.w3. org/Addressing/URL/4_1_File.html*.)

Don't try this with an ftp URL scheme, however. While there's nothing to stop you from writing your own FTP client using the Socket class, Microsoft does not provide a means to access an FTP data source with a WebRequest.

 One difference between file URLs and http URLs is that a file on the local filesystem can be opened for writing, whereas a file on a web server cannot. When using file and http schemes interchangeably, you should try to be aware of what resources your code is trying to access.

Network Access Through a Web Proxy

Another useful feature of the WebRequest class is its ability to read data through a web proxy. A *web proxy* is a server located on the network between your code and a web server. Its job is to intercept all traffic headed for the web server and attempt to fulfill as many requests as it can without contacting the web server. If a web proxy cannot fulfill a request itself, it forwards the request to the web server for processing.

Web proxies serve two primary purposes:

Improving performance

A proxy server can cache data locally to speed network performance. Rather than sending two identical requests from different clients to the same web resource, the results of the first request are saved, and sent back to any other clients requesting the same data. Typical web proxies have configurable parameters that control how long cached data is retained before new requests are sent on to the web server. The HTTP protocol can also specify this cache refresh period. Many large online services, such as America Online, use caching to improve their network performance.

Filtering

A proxy server can be used to filter access to certain sites. Filtering is usually used by businesses to prevent employees from accessing web sites that have no business-related content, or by parents to prevent children from accessing web sites that may have material they believe is inappropriate. Filters can be as strict or loose as necessary, preventing access to entire IP subnets or to single URLs.

The .NET Framework provides the WebProxy class to help you incorporate the use of web proxy servers into your application. WebProxy is an implementation of IWebProxy, and can only be used to proxy HTTP and HTTPS (secure HTTP) requests. It's important that you know the type of URL you are requesting data from: casting a FileWebRequest to an HttpWebRequest will cause an InvalidCastException to be thrown.

To make use of a proxy server that is already set up on your network, you first create the WebRequest just as before. You can then instantiate a WebProxy object, set the address of the proxy server, and set the Proxy() property of WebRequest to link the proxy server to the web server. The WebProxy constructor has many overloads for many different situations. In the following example, I'm using a constructor that lets me specify that the host name of the proxy server is *http://proxy.mydomain.com*. Setting the constructor's second parameter, BypassOnLocal, to true causes local network requests to be sent directly to the destination, circumventing the proxy server:

```
HttpWebRequest request = (HttpWebRequest) WebRequest.Create("http://www.oreilly.com/
");
request.Proxy = new WebProxy("http://proxy.mydomain.com",true);
```

Any data that goes through WebRequest to a destination external to the local network will now use the proxy server.

Why is this important? Imagine that you wish to read XML from an external web page, but your network administrator has installed a web proxy to speed general access and prevent access to some specific sites. Although the XmlTextReader has the ability to read an XML file directly from a URL, it does not have the built-in ability to access the web through a web proxy. Since XmlTextReader can read data from any Stream or TextReader, you now have the ability to access XML documents through the proxy. In the next section, I'll tell you more about the XmlReader class.

XmlReader

XmlReader is an abstract base class that provides an event-based, read-only, forward-only XML pull parser (I'll discuss each of these terms shortly). XmlReader has three concrete subclasses, XmlTextReader, XmlValidatingReader, and XmlNodeReader, which enable you to read XML from a file, a Stream, or an XmlNode. You can also extend XmlReader to read other, non-XML data formats, and deal with them as if they were XML (you'll learn how to do this in Chapter 4).

The base XmlReader provides only the most essential functionality for reading XML documents. It does not, for example, validate XML (that's what XmlValidatingReader does) or expand XML entities into their respective character data (though XmlTextReader does). This does not mean that XML read from a text file cannot be validated at all; you can validate XML from any source by using the XmlValidatingReader constructor that takes an XmlReader object as a parameter, as I'll demonstrate.

Here are those four terms I used to describe XmlReader again, with a little explanation.

Event-based
> An event in a stream-based XML reader indicates the start or end of an XML node as it is read from the data stream. The event's information is delivered to your application, and your application takes some action based on that information. In XmlReader, events are delivered by querying XmlReader's properties after calling its Read( ) method.

Read-only
> XmlReader, as its name implies, can only read XML. For writing XML, there is an XmlWriter class, which I will discuss in Chapter 3.

Forward-only
> Once a node has been read from an XML document, you cannot back up and read it again. For random access to an XML document, you should use XmlDocument (which I'll discuss in Chapter 5) or XPathDocument (which I'll discuss in Chapter 6).

Pull parser
> Pull parsing is a more complex concept, which I'll describe in detail in the next section.

Pull Parser Versus Push Parser

In many ways, XmlReader is analogous to the Simple API for XML (SAX). They both work by reporting events to the client. There is one major difference between XmlReader and a SAX parser, however. While SAX implements a *push parser* model, XmlReader is a *pull parser*.

 SAX is a standard model for parsing XML, originally developed for the Java language in 1997, but since then applied to many other languages. The SAX home page is located at *http://www.saxproject.org/*.

In a push parser, events are *pushed* to you. Typically, a push parser requires you to register a callback method to handle each event. As the parser reads data, the callback method is dispatched as each appropriate event occurs. Control remains with the parser until the end of the document is reached. Since you don't have control of the parser, you have to maintain knowledge of the parser's state so your callback knows the context from which it has been called. For example, in order to decide on a particular action, you may need to know how deep you are in an XML tree, or be able to locate the parent of the current element. Figure 2-1 shows the flow of events in a push parser model application.

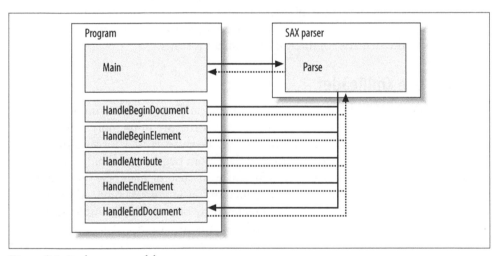

Figure 2-1. Push parser model

In a pull parser, your code explicitly *pulls* events from the parser. Running in an event loop, your code requests the next event from the parser. Because you control the parser, you can write a program with well-defined methods for handling specific events, and even completely skip over events you are not interested in. Figure 2-2 shows the flow of events in a pull parser model application.

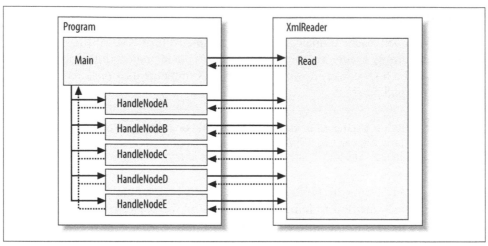

Figure 2-2. Pull parser model

A pull parser also enables you to write your client code as a *recursive descent parser*. This is a top-down approach in which the parser (XmlReader, in this case) is called by one or more methods, depending on the context. The recursive descent model is also known as *mutual recursion*. A neat feature of recursive descent parsers is that the structure of the parser code usually mirrors that of the data stream being parsed. As you'll see later in this chapter, the structure of a program using XmlReader can be very similar to the structure of the XML document it reads.

When to Use XmlReader

Since XmlReader is a read-only XML parser, you should use it when you need to read an XML file or stream and convert it into a data structure in memory, or when you need to output it into another file or stream. Because it is a forward-only XML parser, XmlReader may be used only to read data from beginning to end. These qualities combine to make XmlReader very efficient in its use of memory; only the minimum amount of data required is held in memory at any given time. Although you can use XmlReader to read XML to be consumed by one of .NET's implementations of DOM, XML Schema, or XSLT (each of which is discussed in later chapters), it's usually not necessary, as each of these types provides its own mechanism for reading XML—usually using XmlReader internally themselves!

On the other hand, XmlReader can be a useful building block in an application that needs to manipulate XML data in ways not supported directly by a .NET type. For example, to create a SAX implementation for .NET, you could use XmlReader to read the XML input stream, just as other .NET XML types, such as XmlDocument, do.

You can also extend XmlReader to provide a read-only XML-style interface to data that is not formatted as XML; indeed, I'll show you how to do just that in Chapter 4.

The beauty of using XmlReader for non-XML data is that once you've written the code to respond to XmlReader events, handling a different format is a simple matter of dropping in a specialized, format-specific XmlReader without having to rewrite your higher-level code. This technique also allows you to use a DTD or XML Schema to validate non-XML data, using the XmlValidatingReader.

Using the XmlReader

The .NET Framework provides three implementations of XmlReader: XmlTextReader, XmlValidatingReader, and XmlNodeReader. In this section, I'll present each class one at a time and show you how to use them.

XmlTextReader

XmlTextReader is the most immediately useful specialization of XmlReader. XmlTextReader is used to read XML from a Stream, URL, string, or TextReader. You can use it to read XML from a text file on disk, from a web site, or from a string in memory that has been built or loaded elsewhere in your program. XmlTextReader does not validate the XML it reads; however, it does expand the general entities <, >, and & into their text representations (<, >, and &, respectively), and it does check the XML for well-formedness.

In addition to these general capabilities, XmlTextReader can resolve system- and user-defined entities, and can be optimized somewhat by providing it with an XmlNameTable. Although XmlNameTable is an abstract class, you can instantiate a new NameTable, or access an XmlReader's XmlNameTable through its NameTable property.

> An XmlNameTable contains a collection of string objects that are used to represent the elements and attributes of an XML document. XmlReader can use this table to more efficiently handle elements and attributes that recur in a document. An XmlNameTable object is created at run-time by the .NET parser every time it reads an XML document. If you are parsing many documents with the same format, using the same XmlNameTable in each of them can result in some efficiency gains—I'll show you how to do this later in this chapter.

Like many businesses, Angus Hardware—the hardware store I introduced in the preface—issues and processes purchase orders (POs) to help manage its finances and inventory. Being technically savvy, the company IT crew has created an XML format for Angus Hardware POs. Example 2-1 lists the XML for *po1456.xml*, a typical purchase order. I'll use this document in the rest of the examples in this chapter, and some of the later examples in the book.

Example 2-1. A purchase order in XML format

```
<?xml version="1.0"?>

<po id="PO1456">

  <date year="2002" month="6" day="14" />

  <address type="shipping">
    <name>Frits Mendels</name>
    <street>152 Cherry St</street>
    <city>San Francisco</city>
    <state>CA</state>
    <zip>94045</zip>
  </address>

  <address type="billing">
    <name>Frits Mendels</name>
    <street>PO Box 6789</street>
    <city>San Francisco</city>
    <state>CA</state>
    <zip>94123-6798</zip>
  </address>

  <items>
    <item quantity="1"
          productCode="R-273"
          description="14.4 Volt Cordless Drill"
          unitCost="189.95" />
    <item quantity="1"
          productCode="1632S"
          description="12 Piece Drill Bit Set"
          unitCost="14.95" />
  </items>

</po>
```

Example 2-1 and all the other code examples in this book are available at the book's web site, *http://www.oreilly.com/catalog/netxml/*.

Angus Hardware's fulfillment department, the group responsible for pulling products off of shelves in the warehouse, has not yet upgraded, unfortunately, to the latest laser printers and hand-held bar-code scanners. The warehouse workers prefer to receive their pick lists as plain text on paper. Since the order entry department produces its POs in XML, the IT guys propose to transform their existing POs into the pick list format preferred by the order pickers.

Here's the pick list that the fulfillment department prefers:

```
Angus Hardware PickList
=======================
```

```
PO Number: PO1456

Date: Friday, June 14, 2002

Shipping Address:
Frits Mendels
152 Cherry St
San Francisco, CA 94045

Quantity Product Code Description
======== ============ ===========
       1        R-273  14.4 Volt Cordless Drill
       1        1632S  12 Piece Drill Bit Set
```

You'll note that while the pick list layout is fairly simple, it does require some formatting; Quantity and Product Code numbers need to be right-aligned, for example. This is a good job for an XmlReader, because you really don't need to manipulate the XML, but just read it in and transform it into the desired text layout. (You could do this with an XSLT transform, but that solution comes later in Chapter 7!)

Example 2-2 shows the Main( ) method of a program that reads the XML purchase order listed in Example 2-1 and transforms it into a pick list.

Example 2-2. A program to transform an XML purchase order into a printed pick list

```csharp
using System;
using System.IO;
using System.Xml;

public class PoToPickList {

  public static void Main(string[] args) {

    string url = args[0];

    XmlReader reader = new XmlTextReader(url);

    StringBuilder pickList = new StringBuilder( );
    pickList.Append("Angus Hardware PickList").Append(Environment.NewLine);
    pickList.Append("========================").Append(Environment.NewLine).
Append(Environment.NewLine);

    while (reader.Read( )) {
      if (reader.NodeType == XmlNodeType.Element) {
        switch (reader.LocalName) {
          case "po":
            pickList.Append(POElementToString(reader));
            break;
          case "date":
            pickList.Append(DateElementToString(reader));
            break;
          case "address":
            reader.MoveToAttribute("type");
```

```
        if (reader.Value == "shipping") {
          pickList.Append(AddressElementToString(reader));
        } else {
          reader.Skip( );
        }
        break;
      case "items":
        pickList.Append(ItemsElementToString(reader));
        break;
    }
  }
}

  Console.WriteLine(pickList);
  }
}
```

Let's look at the `Main( )` method in Example 2-2 in small chunks, and then we'll dive into the rest of the program.

```
XmlReader reader = new XmlTextReader(url);
```

This line instantiates a new `XmlTextReader` object, passing in a URL, and assigns the object reference to an `XmlReader` variable. If the URL uses the `http` or `https` scheme, the `XmlTextReader` will take care of creating a network connection to the web site. If the URL uses the `file` scheme, or has no scheme at all, the `XmlTextReader` will read the file from disk. Because the `XmlTextReader` uses the `System.IO` classes we discussed earlier, it does not currently recognize any other URL schemes, such as `ftp` or `gopher`:

```
StringBuilder pickList = new StringBuilder( );
pickList.Append("Angus Hardware PickList").Append(Environment.NewLine);
pickList.Append("========================").Append(Environment.NewLine) .
Append(Environment.NewLine);
```

These lines instantiate a `StringBuilder` object that will be used to build a string containing the text representation of the pick list. We initialize the `StringBuilder` with a simple page header.

 The `StringBuilder` class provides an efficient way to build strings. You could just concatenate several `string` instances together using the `+` operator, but there's some overhead involved in the creation of multiple strings. Using the `StringBuilder` is a good way to avoid that overhead. To learn more about the `StringBuilder`, see *Learning C#* by Jesse Liberty (O'Reilly).

```
while (reader.Read( )) {
  if (reader.NodeType == XmlNodeType.Element) {
```

This event loop is the heart of the code. Each time `Read( )`is called, the XML parser moves to the next node in the XML file. `Read( )` returns `true` if the read was successful, and `false` if it was not—such as at the end of the file. The expression within the if statement ensures that you don't try to evaluate an EndElement node as if it were an Element node; that would result in two calls to each method, one as the parser reads an Element and one as it reads an EndElement. XmlReader.NodeType returns an XmlNodeType.

Now that you have read a node, you need to determine its name:

```
switch (reader.LocalName) {
```

The LocalName property contains the name of the current node with its namespace prefix removed. A Name property that contains the name as well as its namespace prefix, if it has one, is also available. The namespace prefix itself can be retrieved with the XmlReader type's Prefix property:

```
case "po":
  pickList.Append(POElementToString(reader));
  break;
case "date":
  pickList.Append(DateElementToString(reader));
  break;
case "address":
  reader.MoveToAttribute("type");
  if (reader.Value == "shipping") {
    pickList.Append(AddressElementToString(reader));
  } else {
    reader.Skip();
  }
  break;
case "items":
  pickList.Append(ItemsElementToString(reader));
  break;
```

For each element name, the program calls a specific method to parse its subnodes; this demonstrates the concept of recursive descent parsing, which I discussed earlier.

One element of the XML tree, address, is of particular interest. The fulfillment department doesn't care who's paying for the order, only to whom the order is to be shipped. Since the Angus Hardware order pickers are only interested in *shipping* addresses, the program checks the value of the type attribute before calling AddressElementToString(). If the address is not a shipping address, the program calls Skip() to move the parser to the next sibling of the current node.

To read in the po element, the program calls the POElementToString() method. Here's the definition of that method:

```
private static string POElementToString(XmlReader reader) {

  string id = reader.GetAttribute("id");

  StringBuilder poBlock = new StringBuilder();
  poBlock.Append("PO Number: ").Append(id).Append(Environment.NewLine).
Append(Environment.NewLine);
  return poBlock.ToString();
}
```

The first thing this method does is to get the id attribute. The GetAttribute() method returns an attribute from the current node, if the current node is an element; otherwise, it returns string.Empty. It does not move the current position of the parser to the next node.

After it gets the id, POElementToString() can then return a properly formatted line for the pick list.

Next, the code looks for any date elements and calls DateElementToString():

```
private static string DateElementToString(XmlReader reader) {

    int year = Int32.Parse(reader.GetAttribute("year"));
    int month = Int32.Parse (reader.GetAttribute("month"));
    int day = Int32.Parse (reader.GetAttribute("day"));
    DateTime date = new DateTime(year,month,day);

    StringBuilder dateBlock = new StringBuilder();
    dateBlock.Append("Date: ").Append(date.ToString("D")).Append(Environment.NewLine) .
Append(Environment.NewLine);
    return dateBlock.ToString();
}
```

This method uses Int32.Parse() to convert strings as read from the date element's attributes into int variables suitable for passing to the DateTime constructor. Next, you can format the date as required. Finally, the method returns the properly formatted date line for the pick list:

```
private static string AddressElementToString(XmlReader reader) {

StringBuilder addressBlock = new StringBuilder();
addressBlock.Append("Shipping Address:\n");

    while (reader.Read() && (reader.NodeType == XmlNodeType.Element || reader.NodeType
== XmlNodeType.Whitespace)) {
        switch (reader.LocalName) {
            case "name":
            case "company":
            case "street":
            case "zip":
                addressBlock.Append(reader.ReadString());
                addressBlock.Append(Environment.NewLine);
                break;
            case "city":
                addressBlock.Append(reader.ReadString());
                addressBlock.Append(", ");
                break;
            case "state":
                addressBlock.Append(reader.ReadString());
                addressBlock.Append(" ");
                break;
        }
    }
```

```
        addressBlock.Append("\n");
        return addressBlock.ToString();
    }
```

Much like the Main() method of the program, AddressElementToString() reads from the XML file using a while loop. However, because you know the method starts at the address element, the only nodes it needs to traverse are the subnodes of address. In the cases of name, company, street, and zip, AddressElementToString() reads the content of each element and appends a newline character. The program must deal with the city and state elements slightly differently, however. Ordinarily, a city is followed by a comma, a state name, a space, and a zip code. Then, the program returns the properly formatted address line.

Now we come to the most complex method, ItemsElementToString(). Its complexity lies not in its reading of the XML, but in its formatting of the output:

```
    private static string ItemsElementToString(XmlReader reader) {

        StringBuilder itemsBlock = new StringBuilder();
        itemsBlock.Append("Quantity Product Code Description\n");
        itemsBlock.Append("======== ============ ===========\n");

        while (reader.Read() && (reader.NodeType == XmlNodeType.Element || reader.NodeType
== XmlNodeType.Whitespace)) {
            switch (reader.LocalName) {
              case "item":
                intquantity = Int32.Parse(
                reader.GetAttribute("quantity"));
                stringproductcode = reader.GetAttribute("productCode");
                stringdescription = reader.GetAttribute("description");
                itemsBlock.AppendFormat(" {0,6}   {1,11}   {2}",
                  quantity,productCode,description).Append(Environment.NewLine);
                break;
            }
        }

        return itemsBlock.ToString();
    }
```

The ItemsElementToString() method makes use of the AppendFormat() method of the StringBuilder object. This is not the proper place for a full discussion of .NET's string-formatting capabilities, but suffice it to say that each parameter in the format string is replaced with the corresponding element of the parameter array, and padded to the specified number of digits. For additional information on formatting strings in C#, see Appendix B of *C# In A Nutshell*, by Peter Drayton, Ben Albahari, and Ted Neward (O'Reilly).

This program makes some assumptions about the incoming XML. For example, it assumes that in order for the output to be produced correctly, the elements must appear in a very specific order. It also assumes that certain elements will always occur, and that others are optional. The XmlTextReader cannot always handle exceptions to these assumptions, but the XmlValidatingReader can. To ensure that an unusable pick list is not produced, you should always validate the XML before doing any processing.

XmlValidatingReader

XmlValidatingReader is a specialized implementation of XmlReader that performs validation on XML as it reads the incoming stream. The validation may be done by explicitly providing a Document Type Declaration (DTD), an XML Schema, or an XML-Data Reduced (XDR) Schema—or the type of validation may be automatically determined from the document itself. XmlValidatingReader may read data from a Stream, a string, or another XmlReader. This allows you, for example, to validate XML from XmlNode using XmlTextReader, which does not perform validation itself. Validation errors are raised either through an event handler, if one is registered, or by throwing an exception.

The following examples will show you how to validate the Angus Hardware purchase order using a DTD. Validating XML with an XML Schema instead of a DTD will give you even more control over the data format, but I'll talk about that topic in Chapter 8.

Example 2-3 shows the DTD for the sample purchase order.

Example 2-3. The DTD for Angus Hardware purchase orders

```
<?xml version="1.0" encoding="UTF-8"?>

<!ELEMENT po (date,address+,items)>
<!ATTLIST po id ID #REQUIRED>

<!ELEMENT date EMPTY>
<!ATTLIST date year CDATA #REQUIRED
              month (1|2|3|4|5|6|7|8|9|10|11|12) #REQUIRED
              day (1|2|3|4|5|6|7|8|9|10|11|
                  12|13|14|15|16|17|18|19|
                  20|21|22|23|24|25|26|27|
                  28|29|30|31) #REQUIRED>

<!ELEMENT address (name,company?,street+,city,state,zip)>
<!ATTLIST address type (billing|shipping) #REQUIRED>

<!ELEMENT name    (#PCDATA)>

<!ELEMENT company (#PCDATA)>

<!ELEMENT street  (#PCDATA)>

<!ELEMENT city    (#PCDATA)>

<!ELEMENT state   (#PCDATA)>
```

Example 2-3. The DTD for Angus Hardware purchase orders (continued)

```
<!ELEMENT zip     (#PCDATA)>

<!ELEMENT items (item)+>

<!ELEMENT item EMPTY>
<!ATTLIST item quantity CDATA #REQUIRED
               productCode CDATA #REQUIRED
               description CDATA #REQUIRED
               unitCost CDATA #REQUIRED>
```

 For more information on DTDs, see Erik Ray's *Learning XML*, 2nd Edition (O'Reilly) or Elliotte Rusty Harold and W. Scott Mean's *XML in a Nutshell*, 2nd Edition (O'Reilly).

To validate the XML with this DTD, you must make one small change to the XML document, and one to the code that reads it. To the XML you must add the following document type declaration after the XML declaration (`<?xml version="1.0"?>`) so that the validator knows what DTD to validate against.

```
<!DOCTYPE po SYSTEM "po.dtd">
```

 Remember that even if you insert the `<!DOCTYPE>` declaration in your target XML file, you must still explicitly use `XmlValidatingReader` to validate the XML. `XmlTextReader` does not validate XML, only `XmlValidatingReader` can do that.

In the code that processes the XML, you must also create a new `XmlValidatingReader` to wrap the original `XmlTextReader`:

```
XmlReader textReader = new XmlTextReader(url);
XmlValidatingReader reader = new XmlValidatingReader(textReader);
```

By default, `XmlValidatingReader` automatically detects the document's validation type, although you can also set the validation type manually using `XmlValidatingReader`'s `ValidationType` property:

```
reader.ValidationType = ValidationType.DTD;
```

Unfortunately, if you take this approach, you'll find that errors are not handled gracefully. For example, if you add an address of type="mailing" to the XML document and attempt to validate it, the following exception is thrown:

```
Unhandled Exception: System.Xml.Schema.XmlSchemaException: The 'type' attribute has
an invalid value according to its data type. An error occurred at file:///C:/
Chapter 2/po1456.xml(16, 12).
   at System.Xml.XmlValidatingReader.InternalValidationCallback(Object sender,
ValidationEventArgs e)
   at System.Xml.Schema.Validator.SendValidationEvent(XmlSchemaException e,
XmlSeverityType severity)
   at System.Xml.Schema.Validator.ProcessElement()
```

```
at System.Xml.Schema.Validator.Validate()
at System.Xml.Schema.Validator.Validate(ValidationType valType)
at System.Xml.XmlValidatingReader.ReadWithCollectTextToken()
at System.Xml.XmlValidatingReader.Read()
at PoToPickListValidated.Main(String[] args)
```

Obviously, you'd like to handle exceptions more cleanly than this. You have two options: you can wrap the entire parse tree in a try...catch block, or you can set the XmlValidatingReader object's ValidationEventHandler delegate. Since I assume that you already know how to write a try...catch block, let's explore a solution that uses a ValidationEventHandler.

ValidationEventHandler is a type found in the System.Xml.Schema namespace, so you'll need to first add this line to the top of your code:

```
using System.Xml.Schema;
```

Next, add the following line after you instantiate the XmlValidatingReader and set the ValidationType to ValidationType.DTD:

```
reader.ValidationEventHandler += new ValidationEventHandler(HandleValidationError);
```

This step registers the callback for validation errors.

Now, you're ready to actually create a ValidationEventHandler. The signature of the delegate as defined by the .NET Framework is:

```
public delegate void ValidationEventHandler(
  object sender, ValidationEventArgs e
);
```

Your validation event handler must match that signature. For now, you can just write the error message to the console:

```
private static void HandleValidationError(
  object sender, ValidationEventArgs e) {
  Console.WriteLine(e.Message);
}
```

Now, if you run the purchase order conversion program using the invalid XML file I talked about earlier, the following slightly more informative message will print to the console:

```
'mailing' is not in the enumeration list. An error occurred at file:///C:/Chapter 2/
po1456.xml(16, 12).
```

 By default, if a validation error is encountered, an exception is thrown and processing halts. However, with XmlValidatingReader, if there were more validation errors in the file, each one of them would be reported individually as processing continued.

I'm sure you can think of useful ways to use a validation event. Some examples of useful output that I've thought of include:

- If processing is being done interactively, present the user with the relevant lines of XML, so she can see the erroneous data.

- If processing is being done by an automated process, alert a system administrator by email or pager.

The entire revised program is shown in Example 2-4.

Example 2-4. Complete program for converting an Angus Hardware XML purchase order to a pick list

```
using System;
using System.IO;
using System.Text;
using System.Xml;
using System.Xml.Schema;

public class PoToPickListValidated {

  public static void Main(string[] args) {

    string url = args[0];

    XmlReader textReader = new XmlTextReader(url);
    XmlValidatingReader reader = new XmlValidatingReader(textReader);
    reader.ValidationType = ValidationType.DTD;
    reader.ValidationEventHandler += new ValidationEventHandler(HandleValidationError);

    StringBuilder pickList = new StringBuilder();
    pickList.Append("Angus Hardware PickList\n");
    pickList.Append("=======================\n\n");

    while (reader.Read()) {
      if (reader.NodeType == XmlNodeType.Element) {
        switch (reader.LocalName) {
          case "po":
            pickList.Append(POElementToString(reader));
            break;
          case "date":
            pickList.Append(DateElementToString(reader));
            break;
          case "address":
            reader.MoveToAttribute("type");
            if (reader.Value == "shipping") {
              pickList.Append(AddressElementToString(reader));
            } else {
              reader.Skip();
            }
            break;
          case "items":
            pickList.Append(ItemsElementToString(reader));
            break;
        }
      }
    }
```

Example 2-4. Complete program for converting an Angus Hardware XML purchase order to a pick list (continued)

```
      }

    Console.WriteLine(pickList);
  }

  private static string POElementToString(XmlReader reader) {

    string id = reader.GetAttribute("id");

    StringBuilder poBlock = new StringBuilder( );
    poBlock.Append("PO Number: ").Append(id).Append("\n\n");
    return poBlock.ToString( );
  }

  private static string DateElementToString(XmlReader reader) {

    int year = XmlConvert.ToInt32(reader.GetAttribute("year"));
    int month = XmlConvert.ToInt32(reader.GetAttribute("month"));
    int day = XmlConvert.ToInt32(reader.GetAttribute("day"));
    DateTime date = new DateTime(year,month,day);

    StringBuilder dateBlock = new StringBuilder( );
    dateBlock.Append("Date: ").Append(date.ToString("D")).Append("\n\n");
    return dateBlock.ToString( );
  }

  private static string AddressElementToString(XmlReader reader) {

    StringBuilder addressBlock = new StringBuilder( );
    addressBlock.Append("Shipping Address:\n");

    while (reader.Read( ) && (reader.NodeType == XmlNodeType.Element || reader.NodeType ==
XmlNodeType.Whitespace)) {
        switch (reader.LocalName) {
          case "name":
          case "company":
          case "street":
          case "zip":
            addressBlock.Append(reader.ReadString( ));
            addressBlock.Append("\n");
            break;
          case "city":
            addressBlock.Append(reader.ReadString( ));
            addressBlock.Append(", ");
            break;
          case "state":
            addressBlock.Append(reader.ReadString( ));
            addressBlock.Append(" ");
            break;
      }
    }
```

```
      addressBlock.Append("\n");
      return addressBlock.ToString();
  }

  private static string ItemsElementToString(XmlReader reader) {

      StringBuilder itemsBlock = new StringBuilder();
      itemsBlock.Append("Quantity Product Code Description\n");
      itemsBlock.Append("======== ============ ===========\n");

      while (reader.Read() && (reader.NodeType == XmlNodeType.Element || reader.NodeType ==
XmlNodeType.Whitespace)) {
          switch (reader.LocalName) {
            case "item":
              object [] parms = new object [3];
              parms [0] = XmlConvert.ToInt32(reader.GetAttribute("quantity"));
              parms [1] = reader.GetAttribute("productCode");
              parms [2] = reader.GetAttribute("description");
              itemsBlock.AppendFormat(" {0,6}  {1,11}  {2}\n",parms);
              break;
        }
      }

      return itemsBlock.ToString();
  }

  private static void HandleValidationError(object sender,ValidationEventArgs e) {
    Console.WriteLine(e.Message);
  }
}
```

XmlNodeReader

The XmlNodeReader type is used to read an existing XmlNode from memory. For example, suppose you have an entire XML document in memory, in an XmlDocument, and you wish to deal with one of its nodes in a specialized manner. The XmlNodeReader constructor can take an XmlNode object as its argument from anywhere in an XML document or document fragment, and perform its operations relative to that node.

For example, you might wish to construct an Angus Hardware XML purchase order in memory rather than reading it from disk. One reason you might choose to construct a PO in memory is if order entry is being done by an outside party in a non-XML format, and some other section of your program is taking care of converting the data into XML. The actual construction of an XmlDocument is covered in Chapter 5, but for now let's assume that you've been given a complete XmlDocument that constitutes a valid PO.

To print the pick list, you need only make one small change to Example 2-4: replace the XmlTextReader constructor with XmlNodeReader, passing in an XmlNode as its argument.

```
XmlReader reader = new XmlNodeReader(node);
```

The rest of the program continues as before, validating the XmlNode passed in and printing the pick list to the console. The only difference is in the type of inputs the program takes—in this case, the input comes directly from the XmlNode.

To recap the different XmlReader subclasses: XmlTextReader is used to read an XML document from some sort of file, whether it's on a local disk or on a web server; XmlNodeReader is used to read an XML fragment from an XmlDocument that's already been loaded some other way; XmlValidatingReader is used to validate an XML document that's being read using an XmlTextReader. The subclasses of XmlReader are mostly interchangeable, with a few exceptions discussed later.

Moving On

You've now seen how to access files on a local filesystem and a network. You have learned how to use the various XmlReader implementations. And I've discussed the pull parser pattern used by the .NET XML parser and how it differs from a push parser.

You should now be able to read any arbitrary XML file using XmlReader. In the next chapter, I'll show you the other side of the XML I/O picture by introducing XmlWriter.

CHAPTER 3

Writing XML

In the previous chapter, you saw that reading XML in .NET is a fairly simple proposition. In some ways, writing XML is even simpler. In this chapter, I'll start by covering common file and network output in .NET. Then I'll show you how to write XML to a local or remote file, including various ways to customize the appearance of the generated XML.

Writing Data

As with XmlReader, I'll start by taking a general look at how data is written in .NET. I've already covered input, and output is very similar in that most operations involve the Stream class. After a general introduction to how the writing process works, I'll show you a quick and simple way of writing text to a file.

Filesystem I/O

I covered the basics of opening and reading a file through the File and FileInfo objects in Chapter 2. In this section, I'll focus on writing to a file using the same objects.

To begin with, File has a Create( ) method. This method takes a filename as a parameter and returns a FileStream, so the most basic creation and writing to a file is fairly intuitive. Stream and its subclasses implement a variety of Write( ) methods, including one that writes an array of bytes to the Stream. The following code snippet creates a file named *myfile.txt* and writes the text .NET & XML to it:

```
byte [] buffer = new byte [] {46,78,69,84,32,38,32,88,77,76};
string filename = "myfile.txt";

FileStream stream;
stream = File.Create(filename);
stream.Write(buffer,0,buffer.Length);
```

That byte array is an awkward way to write a string to a Stream; ordinarily, you wouldn't hardcode an array of bytes like that. I'll show you a more typical way of encoding a string as a byte array in a moment.

If the file already exists, the previous code overwrites the files's current contents. You may not want to do that in practice; you may prefer to *append* to the file if it already exists. You can handle this very easily in .NET in several different ways. This snippet shows one way, with the changes highlighted:

```
byte [] buffer = new byte [] {46,78,69,84,32,38,32,88,77,76};
string filename = "myfile.txt";

FileStream stream;
if (File.Exists(filename)) {
  // it already exists, let's append to it
  stream = File.OpenWrite(filename);
  stream.Seek(0,SeekOrigin.End);
} else {
  // it does not exist, let's create it
  stream = File.Create(filename);
}

stream.Write(buffer,0,buffer.Length);
```

SeekOrigin is an enumeration in the System.IO namespace that indicates where the Seek( ) method should seek from. In this code, I'm seeking 0 bytes from the end, but you could also seek from the beginning of the Stream (SeekOrigin.Begin) or from the current position (SeekOrigin.Current).

File access and permissions

There are several other ways to open a file for writing. For example, this snippet shows several changes from the previous one. The changes are highlighted:

```
byte [] buffer = new byte [] {46,78,69,84,32,38,32,88,77,76};
string filename = "myfile.txt";

FileStream stream;
FileMode fileMode;
if (File.Exists(filename)) {
  // it already exists, let's append to it
  fileMode = FileMode.Append;
} else {
  // it does not exist, let's create it
  fileMode = FileMode.CreateNew;
}

stream = File.Open(filename,fileMode,FileAccess.Write,FileShare.None);
stream.Write(buffer,0,buffer.Length);
```

The `File.Open()` method has several overloads with additional parameters. The `FileMode` enumeration specifies what operations the file is to be opened for. Table 3-1 lists the `FileMode` enumerations.

Table 3-1. FileMode values

Value	Description
CreateNew	A new file will be created. If it already exists, an `IOException` is thrown.
Create	A file will be created, or, if it already exists, truncated and overwritten.
Open	An existing file will be opened. If it does not exist, a `FileNotFoundException` is thrown.
OpenOrCreate	If the file exists, it will be opened; if it does not, a new file will be created.
Truncate	An existing file will be opened and truncated to zero bytes long. An attempt to read a truncated file will result in an exception being thrown.
Append	If the file exists, it will be opened and data will be written at the end of the file. If the file does not exist, a new file will be created. Any attempt to `Seek()` to a position before the previous end of the file will result in an exception being thrown. An attempt to read from the file will result in an `ArgumentException` being thrown.

The `FileAccess` enumeration restricts the operations a program can exercise on the file, once it has been opened. Table 3-2 details the `FileAccess` enumerations.

Table 3-2. FileAccess values

Value	Description
Read	Data can be read from the file.
Write	Data can be written to the file.
ReadWrite	Data can be read from or written to the file. Equivalent to `FileAccess.Read | FileAccess.Write`.

`FileShare` restricts what operations *other* applications can exercise. Table 3-3 describes the `FileShare` enumerations.

Table 3-3. FileShare values

Value	Description
None	No other process may access the file as long as this process has it open.
Read	Subsequent requests to read from the file by other processes will succeed, if they have the other appropriate permissions.
Write	Subsequent requests to write to the file by other processes will succeed, if they have the other appropriate permissions.
ReadWrite	Subsequent requests to read from and write to the file by other processes will succeed, if they have the other appropriate permissions (equivalent to `FileShare.Read | FileShare.Write`).
Inheritable	The file handle is inheritable by child processes. This is not directly supported by Win32.

Some combinations of FileMode and FileAccess do not make sense and will cause an ArgumentException to be thrown. For example, opening a file with FileMode.Create and FileAccess.Read would mean that you wanted to create a file but then only be allowed to read from it.

Encodings and StreamWriter

Having to create an array of bytes to write with the Stream.Write( ) method is a bit tiresome. Luckily, there are at least two ways to work around this. The first is System.Text.Encoding. This class contains methods to convert strings to and from byte arrays, for a given number of standard encodings, including ASCII, UTF-8, and UTF-16. These encodings are provided as static properties of the Encoding class. Strings in .NET are stored in Unicode—while ASCII characters are each stored in a single byte, Unicode characters are stored in four bytes. The GetBytes( ) method takes a .NET string and returns an array of bytes in the appropriate encoding, suitable for use by Stream.Write( ):

Unicode is a standard that provides a unique four-byte representation of every character in every alphabet, on any computer operating system and platform. Happily, XML and .NET both use encodings of Unicode by default. For more information about Unicode, visit the Unicode Consortium's web site at *http://www.unicode.org/*.

```
string message = "Hello, world.";
byte [] buffer = Encoding.ASCII.GetBytes(message);
string filename = "myfile.txt";

FileStream stream;
FileMode fileMode;
if (File.Exists(filename)) {
  // it already exists, let's append to it
  fileMode = FileMode.Append;
} else {
  // it does not exist, let's create it
  fileMode = FileMode.CreateNew;
}

stream = File.Open(filename,fileMode,FileAccess.Write,FileShare.None);
stream.Write(buffer,0,buffer.Length);
```

Just to belabor the point, remember that a C# byte is the familiar eight-bit byte, but a C# char is a Unicode character. The encodings defined in the .NET Framework are shown in Table 3-4.

Table 3-4. Supported encodings

Class name	Property name	Description
ASCIIEncoding	Encoding.ASCII	7 bit ASCII, used in the snippet above. Support is required for XML processors.
UnicodeEncoding	Encoding. BigEndianUnicode	Big-endian Unicode.
	Encoding.Unicode	Little-endian Unicode.
	Encoding.Default	Represents the default encoding for the current system.
UTF7Encoding	Encoding.UTF7	UTF-7.
UTF8Encoding	Encoding.UTF8.	UTF-8. Support is required for XML processors.

In addition, any other encodings are accessible by calling Encoding.GetEncoding() and passing the code page or encoding name.

The other way to write a stream of characters is even simpler. A FileStream is a subclass of Stream, which can be used as a parameter to the StreamWriter's constructor. StreamWriter is analogous to StreamReader, and is a subclass of TextWriter, which is optimized to write textual data to a Stream. The TextWriter's Write() and WriteLine() methods take care of the encoding of various datatypes when writing to a Stream:

```
string textToWrite = "This is the text I want to write to the file.";
string filename = "myfile.txt";

FileStream stream;
FileMode fileMode;
if (File.Exists(filename)) {
  // it already exists, let's append to it
  fileMode = FileMode.Append;
} else {
  // it does not exist, let's create it
  fileMode = FileMode.CreateNew;
}

stream = File.Open(filename,fileMode,FileAccess.Write,FileShare.None);
StreamWriter writer = new StreamWriter(stream);
writer.Write(textToWrite);
writer.Flush();
writer.Close();
```

The last two lines of this code snippet cause the output buffer to be flushed, and the file to be closed. Every time you write to the file and you want the file on disk to reflect the changes immediately, it is important to call Flush() on the Stream or StreamWriter. You can also indicate that the contents of the file are to be flushed to disk automatically by setting AutoFlush to true:

```
StreamWriter writer = new StreamWriter(stream);
writer.AutoFlush = true;
writer.Write(textToWrite);
```

When you are completely done with a file, you should call Close( ) on the File or the Stream. If you don't call Close( ) yourself, the file will be closed when the garbage collector cleans up the method's local variables. Unfortunately, you don't know when that will happen, so it's always best to close files yourself.

 You can close the underlying file by calling Close( ) on the FileStream because, by default, when you instantiate a FileStream, it owns the underlying file. It's important to remember that the FileStream owns the underlying file handle in case you open several streams on the same file; closing any one of them will cause all of them to be closed.

There's an even quicker way to append to an existing file. The StreamWriter class has a constructor that takes a filename as a parameter. Since StreamWriter inherits from TextWriter, it implements the IDisposable interface, which allows you to use the using keyword to automatically close the Stream at the end of the using block.

All the code you wrote above could instead be simplified to five lines, if all you want to do is write a quick chunk of text to a file:

```
string textToWrite = "This is the text I want to write to the file.";
string filename = "myfile.txt";
using (StreamWriter writer = new StreamWriter(filename,true)) {
  writer.Write(textToWrite);
}
```

The second parameter to the StreamWriter constructor indicates that the text is to be appended to the file if the file already exists.

Network I/O

Just as with input, network output can use Socket, Stream, or WebRequest objects. The basic unit of network communication is the Socket. For higher-level network output, you can use the WebRequest class. Whether communicating over a Socket or a WebRequest, however, you'll be using a Stream to actually read and write data.

Writing data with Sockets

To communicate over a network using a Socket, there must be a server of some sort listening for requests at the other end. The construction of network application servers is beyond the scope of this book, but Example 3-1 shows you how to create a simple network client program.

Example 3-1. A simple network client program

```
using System;
using System.IO;
using System.Net.Sockets;

public class NetWriter {
```

Example 3-1. A simple network client program (continued)

```
public static void Main(string [] args) {

    string address = "example.com";
    int port = 9999;

    TcpClient client = new TcpClient(address,port);
    NetworkStream stream = client.GetStream( );

    StreamWriter writer = new StreamWriter(stream);

    writer.WriteLine("hello\r\n");
    writer.Flush( );

    using (StreamReader reader = new StreamReader(stream)) {
      while (reader.Peek( ) != -1) {
        Console.WriteLine(reader.ReadLine( ));
      }
    }
  }
}
```

The Main( ) method can be broken down into its major steps. The first step is to initialize some variables:

```
string address = "example.com";
int port = 9999;
```

TcpClient is a convenient specialization of a TCP/IP client Socket. The GetStream( ) method makes the connection and returns a Stream to communicate with the remote Socket:

```
TcpClient client = new TcpClient(address,port);
NetworkStream stream = client.GetStream( );
```

Next, you use a StreamWriter to write a single line directly to the remote Socket. Since you've connected to port 9999 of the server *example.com*, you can write the line hello, followed by an end-of-line marker, to the Socket, and receive back the data that the server wants to send. Once again, it's important to call Flush( ), so that the data is actually written to the Stream:

 This example assumes that there is some server at the domain address *example.com* listening for requests on port 9999. In reality, this service does not exist. A similar procedure could be used to connect to any network resource on any port, as long as you know what protocol (such as HTTP) to use to communicate with it.

```
StreamWriter writer = new StreamWriter(stream);

writer.WriteLine("hello\r\n");
writer.Flush( );
```

Now that you have written data to the Stream, you can read any data that the server sends back. This while loop checks that there is more data to read, and then echoes it to the console. Finally, the using statement automatically closes the Stream, which closes the underlying network Socket and releases any resources the Socket is holding, much like closing a FileStream:

```
using (StreamReader reader = new StreamReader(stream)) {
  while (reader.Peek( ) != -1) {
    Console.WriteLine(reader.ReadLine( ));
  }
}
```

Similar to the way the FileStream class owns its underlying file handle, the StreamWriter owns the underlying network stream. In Socket-based communication, you shouldn't close the StreamWriter until you're done with the entire conversation, because the same underlying Stream will be used to read the response. The Stream represents both sides of the conversation.

Writing data with WebRequest

As I mentioned in Chapter 2, the WebRequest class supports the http, https, and file URL schemes, so you could theoretically use a WebRequest to send data to a web server. However, the mechanism for writing files to a web server is not so clear cut; the options for writing data to URLs are limited to the methods that HTTP supports, namely GET, HEAD, POST, PUT, DELETE, TRACE, and OPTIONS. In Chapter 2, I used the default HTTP method, GET. Table 3-5 describes the other HTTP methods.

Table 3-5. HTTP methods

Method	Description
GET	A request for information located at the URI
HEAD	A request for header information about the data located at the URI
POST	A request for information located at the URI, which includes additional request parameters
PUT	A request to store the body of the request at the location specified by the URI
DELETE	A request to delete the information located at the URI
TRACE	A request to have the body sent back to the requester, usually used for debugging
OPTIONS	A request for information about the communication options available for the information located at the URI

There are at least two ways to write data to a web server. The first involves complicated URLs using the POST or GET methods and CGI or ASP.NET code on the server, all of which are outside the scope of this book. The second requires the server to support the HTTP PUT method, which may also require some custom setup on the server. Example 3-2 shows a simple program that constructs a WebRequest using the PUT method.

Example 3-2. Program to send an HTTP PUT request

```
using System;
using System.IO;
using System.Net;

public class HttpPut {

  public static void Main(string [] args) {

    string url = "http://myserver.com/file.txt";
    string username = "niel";
    string password = "secret";
    string data = "This data should be written to the URL.";

    HttpWebRequest request = (HttpWebRequest)WebRequest.Create(url);
    request.Method = "PUT";
    request.Credentials = new NetworkCredential(username, password);
    request.ContentLength = data.Length;
    request.ContentType = "text/plain";

    using (StreamWriter writer = new StreamWriter(request.GetRequestStream())) {
      writer.WriteLine(data);
    }

    WebResponse response = request.GetResponse();

    using (StreamReader reader = new StreamReader(response.GetResponseStream())) {
      while (reader.Peek() != -1) {
        Console.WriteLine(reader.ReadLine());
      }
    }
  }
}
```

If your web server does not support the PUT method, you will probably receive an HTTP (405) Method not allowed error, wrapped in a System.Net.WebException.

Let's look at this code in small pieces:

```
HttpWebRequest request = (HttpWebRequest)WebRequest.Create(url);
request.Method = "PUT";
request.ContentLength = data.Length;
request.ContentType = "text/plain";
request.Credentials = new NetworkCredential(username, password);
```

This code creates a new WebRequest to communicate with the server and sets the method to PUT. With a PUT request, you need to set the ContentLength property before writing to the Stream. If the PUT method is properly implemented, it should also require some sort of authentication to prevent improper access; that's what the NetworkCredential is for:

In an interactive application, you should not hardcode a username and password in your source code; you should prompt the user to enter them. The NetworkCredential class handles basic, digest, NTLM, and Kerberos authentication automatically. If you're concerned about writing secure code—and you should be!—check out *Secure Coding: Principles & Practices* by Mark G. Graff and Kenneth R. van Wyk (O'Reilly).

```
using (StreamWriter writer = new StreamWriter(request.GetRequestStream( ))) {
  writer.WriteLine(data);
}
```

This code writes the content of the file directly to the WebRequest's Stream. It's important to close the Stream (done here by virtue of the IDisposable interface and the using statement) to release the connection for reuse; otherwise, the application will run out of connections:

 The GET method does not allow any data to be written to the request body. If you attempt to write data to a WebRequest's Stream and WebRequest.Method is GET, the default, a ProtocolViolationException will be thrown.

```
WebResponse response = request.GetResponse( );

using (StreamReader reader = new StreamReader(response.GetResponseStream( ))) {
  while (reader.Peek( ) != -1) {
    Console.WriteLine(reader.ReadLine( ));
  }
}
```

Finally, data is read from the WebResponse. Typically, the data returned from a PUT request should include the URL of the file you created or updated.

Once you have a WebRequest, you can also set its WebProxy as I demonstrated in Chapter 2.

There is a whole world of detail to be examined when it comes to HTTP PUT. However, I just wanted to give you a taste of writing data across the network, because a Stream is a Stream as far as XmlWriter is concerned, and a local file may just as well be halfway across the planet.

XmlWriter and Its Subclasses

XmlWriter is an abstract base class that defines the interface for creating XML output programmatically. It contains methods such as WriteStartElement( ) and WriteEndElement( ) to write data. XmlWriter maintains the state of the XML document as it writes, so it knows which start element or attribute to close when you call WriteEndElement( ) or WriteEndAttribute( ).

`XmlTextWriter` is the subclass of `XmlWriter`, which provides support for output of XML to any `Stream`, filename, or `TextWriter`. In addition to all the required features of an `XmlWriter`, `XmlTextWriter` allows you to set the formatting of the output, using the `Formatting`, `Indentation`, `IndentChar`, `Namespaces`, and `QuoteChar` properties.

The `XmlTextWriter` formatting properties are described in Table 3-6.

Table 3-6. XmlTextWriter formatting properties

Property	Type	Description
Formatting	System. Xml. Formatting	Specify `Formatting.None` if the XML is to be produced without indentation, or `Formatting.Indented` to produce indented XML. `Formatting.Indented` makes for more readable output, but the canonical XML produced is identical.
Indentation	int	If `Formatting` is set to `Formatting.Indented`, `Indentation` specifies the number of characters by which to indent each successive level of markup.
IndentChar	char	If `Formatting` is set to `Formatting.Indented`, `IndentChar` specifies the character with which to indent each successive level of markup. To ensure valid XML, you should use any valid XML whitespace character.
Namespaces	bool	Specifies whether the `XmlTextWriter` supports W3C XML Namespaces.
QuoteChar	char	Specifies the character with which to quote attribute values. `QuoteChar` may be either a single quote or a double quote. Setting `QuoteChar` to any other character will cause an `ArgumentException` to be thrown.

With an `XmlTextWriter`, you always have access to the base `Stream` through the `BaseStream` property. This is useful for manipulating the `Stream` at runtime, such as calling `Seek( )` to reset the `Stream`'s position.

When to Use XmlWriter

You should use `XmlWriter` when you want to output data from your program to a file or `Stream` in XML format. Since `XmlTextWriter`'s constructors take a `Stream`, a filename, and a `TextWriter`, respectively, you can output to any common I/O target.

In addition, any .NET class that takes an `XmlWriter` to output its data as XML may use any `XmlWriter` subclass. This means, for example, that you may output a DOM tree in any of the supported formats. You may also send data to any other format, as long as an `XmlWriter` exists to produce that format.

Like `XmlReader`, you can extend `XmlWriter` to produce output in alternative XML syntaxes—or even syntaxes that have nothing whatsoever to do with XML, as long as the `XmlWriter` interface is supported.

Using the XmlWriter

XmlWriter contains methods to write any type of XML node to its output Stream. There is just one subclass in the .NET Framework, XmlTextWriter, which will handle most of your XML output needs.

Example 3-3 shows a short program that writes data to an XmlTextWriter.

Example 3-3. Program to write XML with XmlTextWriter

```
using System;
using System.IO;
using System.Text;
using System.Xml;

public class WriteXml {
  public static void Main(string [] args) {

    // Create the XmlWriter
    XmlTextWriter writer = new XmlTextWriter(Console.Out);

    // Set the formatting to something nice
    writer.Formatting = Formatting.Indented;

    // Write the XML declaration
    writer.WriteStartDocument(true);

    // Write a comment
    writer.WriteComment("the first element follows.");

    // Start the root element
    writer.WriteStartElement("root");

    // Write an attribute
    writer.WriteAttributeString("id","_1");

    // Write another attribute
    writer.WriteStartAttribute"name", "foo");
    writer.WriteString("bar");
    writer.WriteEndAttribute();

    // Write another element
    writer.WriteElementString("element1","some characters");

    writer.WriteStartElement("cdataElement");
    writer.WriteAttributeString("date",DateTime.Now.ToString());
    writer.WriteCData("<this contains some characters XML wouldn't like & would choke
on");
    writer.WriteString("<this contains some characters XML wouldn't like & so the
XmlWriter replaces them");
    writer.WriteEndElement();

    // Write an empty element
```

Example 3-3. Program to write XML with XmlTextWriter (continued)

```
    writer.WriteStartElement("emptyElement");
    writer.WriteEndElement( );

    // Write another empty element
    writer.WriteStartElement("emptyElement","foo");
    writer.WriteFullEndElement( );

    // Write some text
    writer.WriteString("One string ");
    writer.WriteEntityRef("amp");
    writer.WriteString(" another.");

    // Close the root element
    writer.WriteEndElement( );

    // End the document
    writer.WriteEndDocument( );

    // Flush and close the output stream
    writer.Flush( );
    writer.Close( );
  }
}
```

Let's walk through this code in small chunks:

```
    XmlTextWriter writer = new XmlTextWriter(Console.Out);
```

Console.Out is just like any other TextWriter, so you can pass it to the XmlTextWriter constructor. If you wanted, you could have instead created a new StreamWriter and written the XML to a file or an HttpWebRequest:

```
    writer.Formatting = Formatting.Indented;
```

This produces XML formatted with indenting, as described previously. It's easier to read, but doesn't affect the code at all:

```
    writer.WriteStartDocument(true);
```

This line writes the XML declaration. There are two overloads of WriteStartDocument( ); Example 3-3 uses the one that takes a bool parameter, indicating that the XML declaration should include standalone="yes". XmlWriter will determine the correct encoding from the underlying TextWriter. If I had chosen to write to a file, the encoding would be UTF8:

> My computer indicated that the encoding when writing to the console was IBM437, but since this is generated automatically by the operating system and .NET implementation, your mileage may vary.

```
    writer.WriteComment("the first element follows.");
```

This line writes an XML comment to the Stream. Although XML comments are enclosed in angle brackets (`<!-- ... -->`), all you have to pass to `WriteComment()` is the text of the comment:

```
writer.WriteStartElement("root");
```

Now I begin to write the first element. The `WriteStartElement()` method writes the opening angle bracket and the element name (`<root`) to the Stream; `XmlWriter` is smart enough to wait for any attributes before writing the closing angle bracket. There are several overloads of `WriteStartElement()`, providing the flexibility to specify a namespace and prefix. Here I'm just writing a plain element name:

```
writer.WriteAttributeString("id","_1");
```

Before moving on to the next element, this line adds an attribute to the root element. Like `WriteStartElement()`, `WriteAttributeString()` has several overloads, allowing you to specify the namespace and prefix, as well as the local name and value:

```
writer.WriteStartAttribute("name", "foo");
writer.WriteString("bar");
writer.WriteEndAttribute();
```

These lines use another method, `WriteStartAttribute()`, that has similar overloads. In this case, I have indicated the start of an attribute named name, whose namespace is foo. Because I did not specify a prefix, `XmlWriter` will automatically assign a prefix for the namespace. If I had previously used the same namespace in a different element or attribute, `XmlWriter` is smart enough to use the same prefix, whether I had assigned the prefix myself or had one assigned for me by `XmlWriter`.

After starting to write the attribute, I've used `WriteString()` to write the attribute's value, "bar", and finally closed the attribute with `WriteEndAttribute()`:

```
writer.WriteElementString("element1","some characters");
```

`WriteElementString()`, like `WriteAttributeString()`, writes the entire element with the specified text content. It also includes the closing angle bracket, so there is no need to call `WriteEndElement()`:

```
writer.WriteStartElement("cdataElement");
writer.WriteAttributeString("date",DateTime.Now.ToString());
writer.WriteCData("<this contains some characters XML wouldn't like & would choke
on");
writer.WriteString("<this contains some characters XML wouldn't like & so the
XmlWriter replaces them");
writer.WriteEndElement();
```

This step writes an element named cdataElement. This element has an attribute called date, but, more importantly, its content begins with a CDATA section. `XmlWriter` takes care of adding the `<![CDATA[...]]>` markup around the character data. The call to `WriteString()` writes a similar string; in this case, `XmlWriter` will replace the special characters with the appropriate entities:

```
writer.WriteStartElement("emptyElement");
writer.WriteEndElement();

writer.WriteStartElement("emptyElement","foo");
writer.WriteFullEndElement();
```

These four lines show two different ways to write empty elements. The first one will be written as <emptyElement/> because XmlWriter knows that the element is empty. In the second one, even though the element is empty, XmlWriter will write a full end element (<emptyElement></emptyElement>) because WriteFullEndElement() was specifically called.

In addition, in the second empty element, I specified the namespace foo. Because it is the same namespace used in an attribute earlier, XmlWriter automatically uses the same prefix, which it originally assigned when writing that attribute:

```
writer.WriteString("One string ");
writer.WriteEntityRef("amp");
writer.WriteString(" another.");
```

These lines write some text to the XML. WriteString() writes the text verbatim, while WriteEntityRef() writes an entity reference. WriteEntityRef() takes care of formatting the entity reference correctly; in this case & will be written to the Stream:

```
writer.WriteEndElement();
writer.WriteEndDocument();
```

The final call to WriteEndElement() closes the root element, because XmlWriter keeps track of its depth in the node tree. WriteEndDocument() closes the document:

```
writer.Flush();
writer.Close();
```

Finally, you should always remember to flush and close the Stream.

Compiling and running this program, the following output is written to the console:

```
<?xml version="1.0" encoding="IBM437" standalone="yes"?>
<!--the first element follows.-->
<root id="_1" d1p1:name="bar" xmlns:d1p1="foo">
  <element1>some characters</element1>
  <cdataElement date="7/1/2002 9:26:22 PM"><![CDATA[<this contains some characters
XML wouldn't like & would choke on]]>&lt;this contains some characters XML wouldn't
like &amp; so the XmlWriter replaces them</cdataElement>
  <emptyElement />
  <d1p1:emptyElement>
</d1p1:emptyElement>One string &amp; another.</root>
```

Remember the root element, with its name="bar" attribute? In the output, you can see that XmlWriter selected the prefix d1p1 for the namespace foo. It also remembered this prefix and used it for the emptyElement element later in the output. Remember that I could have assigned the prefix myself, with a different overload of WriteStartAttribute():

```
writer.WriteStartAttribute("baz", "name", "foo");
```

The output would then have changed to this:

```
<?xml version="1.0" encoding="IBM437" standalone="yes"?>
<!--the first element follows.-->
<root id="_1" baz:name="bar" xmlns:baz="foo">
  <element1>some characters</element1>
  <cdataElement date="7/1/2002 9:26:22 PM"><![CDATA[<this contains some characters
XML wouldn't like & would choke on]]>&lt;this contains some characters XML wouldn't
like &amp; so the XmlWriter replaces them</cdataElement>
  <emptyElement />
  <baz:emptyElement>
</baz:emptyElement>One string &amp; another.</root>
```

Notice that subsequent calls to `WriteStartElement( )` with the same name still properly pick up the prefix, whether you set it or `XmlWriter` sets it.

Moving On

You've now seen how to read and write XML using the `XmlReader` and `XmlWriter` types. The next chapter will show you how to read and write non-XML data as though it were XML.

CHAPTER 4

Reading and Writing Non-XML Formats

While more and more information is stored in XML, there are still lots of systems out there that use other formats. Both legacy integration and new non-XML formats are constant challenges for XML developers. Now that you've seen how to use the implementations of XmlReader and XmlWriter provided in the .NET class libraries, you're ready to learn how to implement your own custom types to handle some more complex scenarios. By combining XmlReader and XmlWriter, you can work with information stored in other formats as if it was XML, mixing and matching formats as you find appropriate for your projects.

For example, although the XmlReader class allows you to read standard XML syntax, there are alternative XML syntaxes that serve specialized purposes. There are XML syntaxes that do not use slashes and angle brackets, and some of these are considered to be more human-readable and less verbose than standard XML. Most of these alternative XML formats still retain all the functionality of standard XML. Other common non-XML formats contain structures you can treat as XML structures when convenient.

Reading Non-XML Documents with XmlReader

To read any sort of document using a non-XML format as though it were XML, you can extend XmlReader by writing a custom XmlReader subclass. Among the advantages of writing your own XmlReader subclass is that you can use your custom XmlReader wherever you would use any of the built-in XmlReaders. For example, even if the underlying data isn't formatted using standard XML syntax, you can pass any instance of a custom XmlReader to XmlDocument.Load( ) to load the XML document into a DOM (more on XmlDocument in Chapter 5). You could load a DOM tree from the data, use XPath to query the data, even transform the data with XSLT, all this even though the original data does not look anything like XML.

As long as an alternative syntax provides a hierarchical structure similar to XML, you can create an XmlReader for it that presents its content in a way that looks like XML. In this chapter you'll learn how to write a custom XmlReader implementation which will enable you to read data formatted in PYX, a line-oriented XML format, as if it were XML.

Reading a PYX Document

Before you can write an XmlPyxReader, you first need to understand PYX syntax. PYX is a line-oriented XML syntax, developed by Sean McGrath, which reflects XML's SGML heritage. PYX is based on Element Structure Information Set (ESIS), a popular alternative syntax for SGML.

 Unlike many of the terms in this book, *PYX* is not an acronym for anything. A *pyx* is is a container used in certain religious rites, and the PYX notation was developed mostly using the Python programming language.

In a *line-oriented* format, each XML node occurs on a new line. The XML nodes that PYX can represent include start element, end element, attribute, character data, and processing instruction. The first character of each line indicates what sort of node the line represents. Table 4-1 shows the prefix characters and what node type each represents.

Table 4-1. PYX prefix characters and their corresponding XmlNodeType values

PYX prefix character	XmlNodeType value
(	Element
)	EndElement
A	Attribute
-	Text
?	ProcessingInstruction

As you can see by the limited number of node types it contains, PYX represents only the *logical* structure of an XML document, not the *physical* structure. There are no DocumentType, EntityReference, Comment, or CDATA XmlNodeTypes in a PYX document. This lack of certain nodes is consistent with PYX's ESIS ancestry; in SGML, the separation between document structure and document content is enforced more rigidly than in XML.

None of this should stop you from using PYX to represent basic XML documents. In fact, PYX's structure makes it very easy to parse using the XmlReader model.

To test your XmlPyxReader, you'll need a file in PYX format. Example 4-1 shows the same purchase order we dealt with in Chapter 2, reformatted in PYX. A few lines are highlighted; I'll discuss these after the example.

Example 4-1. A purchase order expressed in PYX

```
(po
Aid PO1456
(date
Ayear 2002
Amonth 6
Aday 14
)date
(address
Atype shipping
(name
-Frits Mendels
)address
(street
-152 Cherry St
)street
(city
-San Francisco
)city
(state
-CA
)state
(zip
-94045
)zip
)address
(address
Atype billing
(name
-Frits Mendels
)name
(street
-PO Box 6789
)street
(city
-San Francisco
)city
(state
-CA
)state
(zip
-94123-6798
)zip
)address
(items
(item
Aquantity 1
AproductCode R-273
```

Example 4-1. A purchase order expressed in PYX (continued)

```
Adescription 14.4 Volt Cordless Drill
AunitCost 189.95
)item
(item
Aquantity 1
AproductCode 1632S
Adescription 12 Piece Drill Bit Set
AunitCost 14.95
)item
)items
)po
```

Notice that all the data matches the data from Example 2-1, although the format is clearly very different.

Each line that begins with (is a start element, as in the first highlighted line:

```
(po
```

This is equivalent to the <po> element start tag. The next highlighted line is an attribute:

```
Ayear 2002
```

This is equivalent to year="2002" in standard XML syntax. After the A, the next whitespace-delimited word is the name of the attribute, and the rest of the line contains the attribute value. Multiple attributes on the same element are just listed in order, on separate lines.

Although PYX doesn't really support XML namespaces, there's no reason you can't recognize them yourself. The following PYX fragment shows a way to represent namespaces in PYX:

```
(myElement
Axmlns http://www.mynamespaceuri.com/
Axmlns:foo http://www.anothernamespaceuri.com/
)myElement
```

That PYX fragment is equivalent to the following XML fragment:

```
<myElement xmlns="http://www.mynamespaceuri.com/" xmlns:foo="http://www.
anothernamespaceuri.com/" />
```

The next highlighted line in Example 4-1 is an EndElement node:

```
)date
```

The name of the element is given after the) prefix character. This is equivalent to the </date> end tag. Note that there is no PYX shorthand for an empty element, like <item />.

The last highlighted line is text:

```
-Frits Mendels
```

After the -, the rest of the line contains the element's text value. Because only the prefix character on any line is significant, the rest of the line can contain any characters, including the PYX prefix characters (, A, -,), and ?, and XML reserved characters <, >, and &. CDATA sections are thus irrelevant in PYX.

 PYX is a fairly simple format, and XmlPyxReader will be correspondingly simple. Writing a more complex XmlReader is certainly possible, but it would take several chapters' worth of examples to show all the details. If, after reading this chapter, you're interested in a considerably more complex model for writing XmlReader subclasses, I urge you to read Ralf Westphal's article, "Implementing XmlReader Classes for Non-XML Data Structures and Formats." You can view the article online at *http://msdn.microsoft.com/library/en-us/dndotnet/html/ Custxmlread.asp*.

Writing an XmlPyxReader

To read a PYX file, you need to write a subclass of XmlReader. The basic process for writing a subclass of XmlReader follows.

1. First, you'll want to write a skeleton class that implements all the abstract properties and methods of XmlReader. Initially, you'll want to stub them out so that you can make sure your code can always be compiled, even though it may not be fully functional yet. I recommend having the stub methods and properties throw a NotImplementedException rather than returning a default value, so that you don't depend on the some default value that the unfinished stub code returns. Returning a default value might fool you into thinking that the code is working properly when all it's doing is returning some hard-coded value!

2. Next, you need to define the underlying mechanism that your XmlReader subclass will use to traverse its data source. Although it appears to the user that the XmlReader.Read() method moves the node pointer to the next node, what that really means in terms of the XmlReader subclass's internal state may be completely different. This step may include defining a struct, a private class, or several data members to hold the reader's state.

3. You may find it useful to write some tests for the code so that you'll know how well your XmlReader subclass works. As part of your tests, you should read the equivalent data using XmlTextReader and your XmlReader subclass, to make sure they both behave in the same way.

4. Finally, you can fill in the stub properties and methods with real implementation code. Each time you implement a property or method, more and more tests should pass. Finally, when you've implemented all the properties and methods, all the tests should pass; thus you'll know that the implementation of your XmlReader subclass is complete.

I'll lead you through these steps in the sections that follow.

Writing the skeleton

The first step in writing any custom XmlReader is to create a class that derives from XmlReader and implements all of its abstract members. Example 4-2 shows a partial listing of the skeleton of an XmlPyxReader type. I've implemented the abstract properties and methods of XmlReader by causing each to throw a NotImplementedException. I'll go back and fill in this skeleton in a later step.

Example 4-2. The XmlPyxReader skeleton

```
using System;
using System.Xml;

public class XmlPyxReader : XmlReader {

  public override XmlNodeType NodeType {
    get { throw new NotImplementedException( ); }
  }

  public override string Name {
    get { throw new NotImplementedException( ); }
  }

  public override string LocalName {
    get { throw new NotImplementedException( ); }
  }

  public override string NamespaceURI {
    get { throw new NotImplementedException( ); }
  }

...

  public override string LookupNamespace(string prefix) {
    throw new NotImplementedException( );
  }

  public override void ResolveEntity( ) {
    throw new NotImplementedException( );
  }

  public override bool ReadAttributeValue( ) {
    throw new NotImplementedException( );
  }
}
```

 The full source code for the skeleton and the completed XmlPyxReader are available, along with all the other example files from the rest of the book, on the book's web site.

Defining the PYX traversal mechanism

Because XmlPyxReader reads PYX nodes, I've decided to define a private class that can be used to store the properties of each PYX node as it is read. The Node class in our implementation stores the name and value of each node read, its type, a list of its attribute names and their values, an index indicating which attribute has been read, and an indicator that shows whether the node represents an element whose close tag has been read. The last three fields of Node are referenced later in the program. They contain the values of three special attributes; xml:space, xml:lang, and xml:base.

The xml: prefix always maps to the URI *http://www.w3.org/XML/ 1998/namespace*.

Since Node uses IList and ArrayList types, you'll need to include a reference to the System.Collections and System.Collections.Specialized namespaces at the head of your source file. Here is the complete definition of the Node type:

```
private class Node {
   internal XmlNodeType nodeType = XmlNodeType.None;
   internal string name = string.Empty;
   internal string value = string.Empty;
   internal NameValueCollection attributes = new NameValueCollection( );
   internal int currentAttribute = -1;
   internal bool isEnd = false;
   internal XmlSpace xmlSpace = XmlSpace.Default;
   internal string xmlLang = System.Globalization.CultureInfo.CurrentCulture.
ThreeLetterISOLanguageName;
   internal string xmlBase = string.Empty;}
```

Storing the Node instance data

XmlPyxReader needs a way to read the data from a file and a place to store each PYX node in memory as it is read. When I define the constructors, I'll make sure that they all eventually funnel down to a TextReader, which I'll simply call reader:

```
private TextReader reader;
```

Because XML is hierarchical, it will be useful to have a Stack of Node objects to store the nodes. As a node is read from the PYX data, it is pushed onto the Stack, and when the node's end is reached, it is popped from the Stack:

```
private Stack nodes = new Stack( );
```

XmlPyxReader also requires a number of instance variables to store specific information that is returned by certain of the abstract methods derived from XmlReader. First, the ReadState enumeration is used to hold the state of the XmlReader:

```
private ReadState readState = ReadState.Initial;
```

Finally, the XmlNameTable, discussed in Chapter 2, holds atomized strings used to compare element and attribute names efficiently:

```
private XmlNameTable nameTable = new NameTable();
```

A couple of private methods will also be useful. Keep in mind that every time you call XmlPyxReader.Read(), you're reading another node from the underlying document. The next thing you'll want to do is to examine the properties of the node that's been read. Internally, you'll need a way to examine the node in order to return data to the user. For this purpose, a Peek() method will come in very handy. Calling Stack.Peek() on an empty Stack will cause an InvalidOperationException to be thrown, so this method should return a null instance to prevent that condition from arising:

```
private Node Peek() {
  Node node = null;
  if (nodes.Count > 0) {
    node = (Node)nodes.Peek();
  }
  return node;

}
```

Similarly, removing the current Node from the Stack can be done with a Pop() method:

```
private Node Pop() {
  Node node = null;
  if (nodes.Count > 0) {
    node = (Node)nodes.Pop();
  }
  return node;

}
```

The final private method, ReadAttributes(), reads all attributes for the current element. It uses the TextReader object's Peek() and ReadLine() methods to check the first character of each line, and read the entire line if the prefix is A. Once it has read the line, it uses the string type's Substring() method to read the attribute's name and value, and adds them to the Node object's ArrayList variables. If the attribute name is xml:space, xml:lang, or xml:base, the value is stored in the appropriately named field of the Node so that it can be accessed by an XmlReader property.

Once ReadAttributes() has read all the attributes, if the first character of the next line is), the element must be empty, and its Node's isEnd field can be set to true; a prefix of - or (would indicate that the element either had character content or subelements. Finally, the method calls ReadLine() one last time to consume the close tag:

```
private void ReadAttributes() {
  Node node = Peek();
  while (reader.Peek() == 'A') {
```

```
      string line = reader.ReadLine();
      string key = line.Substring(1, line.IndexOf(" ") - 1);
      string value = line.Substring(line.IndexOf(" ") + 1);
      node.attributes.Add(key,value);
      nameTable.Add(key);
      if (key == "xml:space") {
        if (value == "default") {
          node.xmlSpace = XmlSpace.Default;
        } else if (value == "preserve") {
          node.xmlSpace = XmlSpace.Preserve;
        }
      }
      if (key == "xml:lang") {
        node.xmlLang = value;
      }
      if (key == "xml:base") {
        node.xmlBase= value;
      }
    }
    if (reader.Peek() == ')') {
      node.isEnd = true;
      reader.ReadLine();
    }
  }
}
```

 The ReadAttributes() method is your first chance to see an
XmlNameTable in action. Although XmlPyxReader doesn't do anything
earth-shattering with its XmlNameTable, it does add attribute and element names to the table as they are encountered. You'll see another
use of the XmlNameTable shortly in the Read() method. As I mentioned
in Chapter 2, the XmlNameTable can be used by other XML classes in .
NET, so maintaining the table is worthwhile.

Writing the tests

There are several useful tests that I can think of to ensure that XmlPyxReader is working correctly. You could:

- Use the XmlPyxReader to load an XmlDocument and print it out to the console. The
  resulting XML document should be equivalent to the original PYX document,
  but in standard XML syntax. Since I won't introduce XmlDocument until
  Chapter 5, I won't use this one yet.

- Use the Microsoft.XmlDiffPatch.XmlDiff type to compare an original XML document, read with an XmlTextReader, to a PYX document, read with
  XmlPyxReader. To learn about XmlDiff and the Microsoft.XmlDiffPatch
  namespace, see Chapter 13.

- Simply read the PYX document and write it to the console in a simple-to-under-
  stand, non-XML format. This is the easiest way to test the code, and this is the
  method I use.

Example 4-3 shows a very simple test program that uses the third approach to read data from the PYX document, and write it to the console, one node at a time. I've highlighted some lines, and I'll discuss them in a moment.

Example 4-3. Source code for ReadToConsole test class

```
using System;
using System.IO;
using System.Xml;

public class ReadToConsole {

  public static void Main(string [] args) {

    string filename = args[0];
    using (TextReader textReader = File.OpenText(filename)) {
      XmlReader reader = null;
      string extension = Path.GetExtension(filename);
      switch (extension) {
        case ".pyx":
          reader = new XmlPyxReader(textReader);
          break;
        case ".xml":
          XmlTextReader xmlReader = new XmlTextReader(textReader);
          xmlReader.WhitespaceHandling = WhitespaceHandling.None;
          reader = xmlReader;
          break;
        default:
          Console.Error.WriteLine("unknown file type: {0}", extension);
          Environment.Exit(1);
          break;
      }
      while (reader.Read()) {
        Console.WriteLine("NodeType={0} Name=\"{1}\" Value=\"{2}\"",
          reader.NodeType, reader.Name, reader.Value);
      }
    }
  }
}
```

In the highlighted lines, I'm using Path.GetExtension( ) to get the 4-letter extension of the filename passed in to the Main( ) method. The program should behave exactly the same way no matter what sort of XmlReader subclass is used. I'm using the file extension to determine whether I'm reading a PYX document or a standard XML document, and instantiating the appropriate XmlReader subclass. In the case of standard XML, I'm additionally setting the WhitespaceHandling property to WhitespaceHandling.None so that any empty lines or carriage returns that might clutter the output aren't printed. The beginning of the expected output for the XML file *po1456.xml* is shown below:

```
NodeType=XmlDeclaration Name="xml" Value="version="1.0""
NodeType=DocumentType Name="po" Value=""
```

```
NodeType=Element Name="po" Value=""
NodeType=Element Name="date" Value=""
NodeType=Element Name="address" Value=""
NodeType=Element Name="name" Value=""
...
```

Filling in the stubs

Now that the infrastructure has been created and the test program has been written, you can begin to implement the public properties and methods required for an XmlReader.

The XmlReader base class does not require any particular constructors, but I want XmlPyxReader to be able to accept TextReader, Stream and string types as input. This requirement calls for three constructors: one that takes a TextReader, one that takes a Stream, and one that takes a string. These inputs give you the flexibility to read data from any source, whether it is a local file, a network resource, or a buffer in memory. In my implementation, each of the constructors initializes the reader instance variable. reader is then used to read data from the underlying data source. Here are the three constructors:

```
public XmlPyxReader(TextReader reader) {
  this.reader = reader;
}

public XmlPyxReader(Stream stream) {
  reader = new StreamReader(stream);
}

public XmlPyxReader(string source) {
  reader = new StringReader(source);
}
```

 The Stream and string constructors are interesting because they both still allow you to use the TextReader internally. The former creates a new StreamReader around the Stream, while the latter creates a new StringReader for the PYX content. Now the rest of the code doesn't care where the data came from originally; it's all a TextReader internally.

The next step is to implement some of the abstract XmlReader properties. NodeType should return the XmlNodeType of the current node. However, it's not quite as simple as returning the current Node object's NodeType; you must account for the attributes and the special XmlNodeType values EndElement and None. The NodeType property uses the Peek( ) method defined earlier.

Note that before it does anything, NodeType checks to make sure that the XmlPyxReader is in the Interactive ReadState. Many of the other properties and methods will also check the ReadState. The ReadState will be set later, in the Read( ) method:

```
public override XmlNodeType NodeType {
  get {
    if (readState != ReadState.Interactive || nodes.Count <= 0)
      return XmlNodeType.None;

    Node node = Peek( );
    XmlNodeType nodeType = node.nodeType;
    if (node.currentAttribute > -1 &&
      node.currentAttribute < node.attributes.Count) {
      nodeType = XmlNodeType.Attribute;
    } else if (node.value != null && node.value != string.Empty) {
        nodeType = XmlNodeType.Text;
      } else if (node.isEnd) {
        nodeType = XmlNodeType.EndElement;
    }
    return nodeType;
  }
}
```

The Name property returns the name of the current node, whether it's an element or an attribute:

```
public override string Name {
  get {
    if (readState != ReadState.Interactive || nodes.Count <= 0)
      return string.Empty;

    Node node = Peek( );
    string name = node.name;
    if (NodeType == XmlNodeType.Attribute) {
      name = node.attributes.AllKeys[node.currentAttribute];
    }
    return name;
  }
}
```

As I demonstrated earlier, PYX can support namespaces in a roundabout way. LocalName will just call Name, and determine if there is a namespace prefix using the string.IndexOf( ) and Split( ) methods. Prefix uses a similar method to return the current node's namespace prefix. Note that since these properties call the Name property, there's no need to check the ReadState; it'll be checked within the Name property:

```
public override string LocalName {
  get {
    int index = Name.IndexOf(':');
    if (index > -1) {
      return Name.Split(':')[1];
    } else {
      return Name;
    }
  }
```

```
  }

  public override string Prefix {
    get {
      int index = Name.IndexOf(':');
      if (index > -1) {
        return Name.Split(':')[0];
      } else {
        return string.Empty;
      }
    }
  }
```

Because of the unusual namespace handling in XmlPyxReader, the NamespaceURI property doesn't really need to return anything useful. In an XmlReader that handled namespaces properly, you'd want to return the real namespace URI here:

```
public override string NamespaceURI {
  get { return string.Empty; }
}
```

The BaseURI, XmlSpace, and XmlLang properties, which I described earlier, will return a default value, or the value of the relevant field for the current Node:

```
public override string BaseURI {
  get {
    if (readState == ReadState.Interactive && nodes.Count > 0) {
      return Peek().xmlBase;
    } else {
      return string.Empty;
    }
  }
}

public override XmlSpace XmlSpace {
  get {
    if (readState == ReadState.Interactive && nodes.Count > 0) {
      return Peek().xmlSpace;
    } else {
      return XmlSpace.Default;
    }
  }
}

public override string XmlLang {
  get {
    if (readState == ReadState.Interactive && nodes.Count > 0) {
      return Peek().xmlLang;
    } else {
      return System.Globalization.CultureInfo.CurrentCulture.
ThreeLetterISOLanguageName;
    }
  }
}
```

The `NameTable` and `ReadState` properties will simply return the values of the nameTable and readState instance variables, respectively:

```
public override XmlNameTable NameTable {
  get { return nameTable; }
}

public override ReadState ReadState {
  get { return readState; }
}
```

The `Depth` property returns the depth of the current node in the document. If the current node is an element, `Depth` will be the number of nodes in the stack. If, however, the current node is an attribute, you must add the current attribute's position to obtain the true depth. Conveniently, the current attribute's position is stored in the Node:

```
public override int Depth {
  get {
    if (readState != ReadState.Interactive)
      return 0;

    int depth = nodes.Count;
    Node node = Peek();
    if (node != null && node.currentAttribute != -1) {
      depth += node.currentAttribute;
    }
    return depth;
  }
}
```

The `Value` property returns the value of either a text node or an attribute. Since the Node type keeps track of its current attribute, you can use Node to determine whether the reader is currently positioned on an attribute, and return the value accordingly:

```
public override string Value {
  get {
    Node node = Peek();
    if (readState == ReadState.Interactive || node == null) {
      return string.Empty;
    }
    string value = node.value;
    if (node.currentAttribute > -1
        && node.currentAttribute < node.attributes.Count) {
      value = node.attributes[node.currentAttribute];
    }
  }
  return value;
}
```

The `HasValue` property simply indicates whether the current node has a value:

```
public override bool HasValue {
  get {
```

```
    if (readState != ReadState.Interactive)
      return false;

    Node node = Peek();
    return node.value != string.Empty;
  }
}
```

The IsEmptyElement property indicates whether the current node is an empty element; that is, an element of the form <element/>. In PYX, elements are never empty, so implementing IsEmptyElement is particularly easy:

```
public override bool IsEmptyElement {
  get { return false; }
}
```

The Node type's attributes collection holds the current element's attribute names and values, This means you can fill in the various attribute-related methods. The AttributeCount property simply returns the number of attributes for the current node:

```
public override int AttributeCount {
  get {
    if (readState != ReadState.Interactive)
      return 0;

    Node node = Peek();
    int count = 0;
    if (node != null) {
      count = node.attributes.Count;
    }
    return count;
  }
}
```

That takes care of XmlReader's abstract properties. Next I'll start implementing the methods.

The various GetAttribute() method overloads and the various indexers all do very similar things. Many of them can be factored out to their most basic level, which is to return one specific attribute value, based either on the attribute's name or its index. The NameValueCollection type is ideally suited for this sort of thing:

```
public override string GetAttribute(string name) {
  Node node = Peek();
  if (node == null || readState != ReadState.Interactive)
    return string.Empty;
  else
    return node.attributes[name];}

public override string GetAttribute(string name, string namespaceURI) {
  return GetAttribute(name);
}
```

```
public override string GetAttribute(int i) {
  Node node = Peek( );
  if (node == null || readState != ReadState.Interactive)
    return string.Empty;
  else
    return node.attributes[i];}

public override string this[int i] {
  get { return GetAttribute(i); }
}

public override string this[string name] {
  get { return GetAttribute(name); }
}

public override string this[string name, string namespaceURI] {
  get { return GetAttribute(name, namespaceURI); }
}
```

The this property is called an *indexer*. An indexer is a special sort of property that takes parameters. In C#, the parameters are enclosed in square brackets.

Indexers are used when the class contains a collection of some sort. In the case of an XmlReader, the indexers reference the collection of attributes for the current node. I included the indexers with the GetAttribute( ) methods because its behavior is more similar to a GetAttribute( ) method than to any of the other properties. In fact, you can see from the code that this really is just a proxy for GetAttribute( ).

The various MoveToAttribute( ), MoveToFirstAttribute( ), and MoveToNextAttribute( ) methods move the current attribute pointer to the specified attribute. If the attribute doesn't exist, some of these methods will return false:

```
public override bool MoveToAttribute(string name) {
  Node node = Peek( );
  if (node == null || readState != ReadState.Interactive)
    return false;

  string value = node.attributes[name];
  if (value != null) {
    MoveToAttribute(Array.IndexOf(node.attributes.AllKeys, name));
    return true;
  } else {
    return false;
  }
}

public override bool MoveToAttribute(string name, string namespaceURI) {
  return MoveToAttribute(name);
}
```

```
public override void MoveToAttribute(int i) {
  if (readState != ReadState.Interactive)
    return;

  Node node = Peek();
if (i < node.attributes.Count)
    node.currentAttribute = i;
}

public override bool MoveToFirstAttribute() {
  if (readState != ReadState.Interactive)
    return false;

  Node node = Peek();
  if (node.attributes.Count > 0) {
    MoveToAttribute(0);
    return true;
  } else {
    return false;
  }
}

public override bool MoveToNextAttribute() {
  if (readState != ReadState.Interactive)
    return false;

  Node node = Peek();
  if (node.attributes.Count > node.currentAttribute) {
    node.currentAttribute++;
    return true;
  } else {
    return false;
  }
}
```

If the current node is an attribute, the MoveToElement() method moves the
XmlReader's current node pointer to the element containing the current attribute and
returns true. Otherwise, MoveToElement() returns false:

```
public override bool MoveToElement() {
  if (readState != ReadState.Interactive)
    return false;

  Node node = Peek();
  if (node.currentAttribute != -1) {
    node.currentAttribute = -1;
    if (node.isEnd)
      node.isEnd = false;
    return true;
  } else {
    return false;
  }
}
```

Next is Read( ), one of the most complex methods in the XmlPyxReader class. This method reads a line from the PYX document, and takes various actions based on the first character of the line. I'll give the method definition, with comments interspersed:

```
public override bool Read( ) {
```

To begin with, you need to set the ReadState to Interactive, indicating that document reading is underway:

```
if (readState == ReadState.Initial) {
  readState = ReadState.Interactive;
}
```

The next step is to look at the previous Node on the Stack. If there is one, and it's been marked as having ended, and it either has text value or the next line in the TextReader is a start element, it should be removed from the Stack. This logic may seem strange, but the reason for it is that you need to know when NodeType should return EndElement; EndElement is only returned when a non-empty element is encountered. A non-empty element is one which has text value or a child element. By popping the current Node, you prevent an EndElement XmlNodeType from being returned:

```
Node node = Peek( );
if (node != null && node.isEnd &&
    (node.value != string.Empty || reader.Peek( ) == '(')) {
    Pop( );
}
```

only now can you begin reading lines from the TextReader using ReadLine( ):

```
string line = reader.ReadLine( );
```

As each line is read, you need to check to see if it's null or empty. If it's null, the TextReader has reached the end of the Stream. If the line is empty, there's something wrong with the PYX data, because every line in a PYX file must have at least a prefix. Either way, this signals the end of the file, as you're only interested in lines with content:

```
if (line != string.Empty && line != null) {
```

Now you need to examine the first character of each line. As noted in Table 4-1, an open parenthesis (() in the prefix indicates the beginning of an element; in this case, you can create a new element Node, set its name, and read its attributes using the private ReadAttributes( ) method I defined earlier. This is also a good place to add the element name to the XmlNameTable. Finally, don't forget to push the Node onto the stack:

```
switch (line[0]) {
  case '(':
    Node elementNode = new Node( );
    elementNode.nodeType = XmlNodeType.Element;
    elementNode.name = line.Substring(1).Trim( );
    nameTable.Add(elementNode.name);
```

```
nodes.Push(elementNode);
ReadAttributes();
break;
```

If the line's prefix is the close parenthesis ()), the line represents an element's closing tag. Because the element has ended, you can pop it off the Stack:

```
case ')':
  Pop();
  node = Peek();
  break;
```

A hyphen (-) in the line's prefix indicates a text node. You should create a text Node to hold it, and instantiate a StringBuilder to accumulate the text. Because a text line could be followed by any number of additional text lines, you should accumulate each of these text lines in the StringBuilder. Finally, when the first character of the next line is not a hyphen, you can set the text Node's value to the accumulated value of the StringBuilder and push the Node onto the stack:

```
case '-':
  Node textNode = new Node();
  textNode.nodeType = XmlNodeType.Text;
  StringBuilder text = new StringBuilder();
  text.Append(line.Substring(1));
  while (reader.Peek() == '-') {
    line = reader.ReadLine();
    text.Append(line.Substring(1));
  }
  node.isEnd = true;
  textNode.value = text.ToString();
  nodes.Push(textNode);
  break;
```

If the first character of the line is a question mark (?), the line represents a processing instruction. You should create a new Node, set its name and value, and push it onto the stack. For our purposes, the name or target of the PI is everything before the first whitespace, and the data is everything after it:

```
case '?':
  Node piNode = new Node();
  piNode.nodeType = XmlNodeType.ProcessingInstruction;
  piNode.name = line.Substring(1,line.IndexOf(' '));
  piNode.value = line.Substring(line.IndexOf(' '));
  nodes.Push(piNode);
  break;
```

Any other case is considered an error. You should set the XmlPyxReader's readState to ReadState.Error and return false. All the other cases are fine, and the Read() method should return true:

```
    default:
      readState = ReadState.Error;
      return false;
  }
  return true;
```

The last step is to handle the cases where a null or empty line was read from the PYX Stream. These cases should indicate the end of the Stream, so you should set the XmlPyxReader's readState to ReadState.EndOfFile and return false:

```
    } else {
      readState = ReadState.EndOfFile;
      return false;
    }
  }
```

The EOF property returns true if the XmlPyxReader is positioned at the end of the Stream. Since you already know that you've set readState to ReadState.EndOfFile if the reader is at the end of the Stream, you can use that knowledge here:

```
public override bool EOF {
  get { return readState == ReadState.EndOfFile; }
}
```

The Close() method closes the underlying TextReader and sets the readState instance variable to ReadState.Closed:

```
public override void Close() {
  reader.Close();
  readState = ReadState.Closed;
}
```

The ReadString() method has different behavior depending on the current Node's XmlNodeType. If the Node is an element, this method will read lines from the Stream as long as they begin with a hyphen. It then sets the Node's value instance variable to the value read in, in much the same way that the Read() method did.

If, on the other hand, the current Node is already a text node, ReadString() simply returns the node's value. In all other cases, the method returns an empty string:

```
public override string ReadString() {
  if (readState != ReadState.Interactive)
    return string.Empty;

  Node node = Peek();
  switch (node.nodeType) {
    case XmlNodeType.Element:
      StringBuilder text = new StringBuilder();
      while (reader.Peek() == '-') {
        string line = reader.ReadLine();
        text.Append(line.Substring(1));
      }
      node.value = text.ToString();
      if (reader.Peek() == ')') {
        string line = reader.ReadLine();
        Pop();
        node = Peek();
        if (node != null) {
          node.isEnd = true;
        }
```

```
        }
      return node.value;
    case XmlNodeType.Text:
      return node.value;
    default:
      return string.Empty;
    }
  }
}
```

Since all the attributes are read when Read( ) reads an element, this implementation of ReadAttributeValue( ) does not actually read anything. It returns true if the current Node has attributes, and false otherwise:

```
public override bool ReadAttributeValue( ) {
  if (readState != ReadState.Interactive)
    return false;

  Node node = Peek( );
  if (node.nodeType == XmlNodeType.Attribute) {
    return true;
  } else {
    return false;
  }
}
```

All the remaining abstract properties and methods listed in Example 4-2 have no real meaning in XmlPyxReader, so you can let them keep their current implementation, which is to throw the NotImplementedException.

Finally, XmlReader has virtual methods and properties which you may chose to override. HasAttributes simply indicates whether the current node has attributes:

```
public override bool HasAttributes {
  get {
    if (readState != ReadState.Interactive)
      return false;

    Node node = Peek( );
    return node.attributes.Count != 0;
  }
}
```

Skip( ) moves the XmlReader's current position to the next sibling of the most recent element node. This is done simply by popping the current node:

```
public override void Skip( ) {
  if (readState != ReadState.Interactive)
    return;
  Pop( );
}
```

And that's it, you've just written XmlPyxReader. Now you're ready to test it.

Testing XmlPyxReader

You could have been using the ReadToConsole program to test your work as you were going along, and I certainly encourage that practice. Now that XmlPyxReader is done, though, you definitely should test it. Here's the output I got when I ran it:

```
NodeType=Element Name="po" Value=""
NodeType=EndElement Name="date" Value=""
NodeType=Element Name="address" Value=""
NodeType=Element Name="name" Value=""
NodeType=Text Name="" Value="Frits Mendels"
NodeType=EndElement Name="name" Value=""
NodeType=Element Name="street" Value=""
NodeType=Text Name="" Value="152 Cherry St"
NodeType=EndElement Name="street" Value=""
NodeType=Element Name="city" Value=""
NodeType=Text Name="" Value="San Francisco"
NodeType=EndElement Name="city" Value=""
NodeType=Element Name="state" Value=""
NodeType=Text Name="" Value="CA"
NodeType=EndElement Name="state" Value=""
NodeType=Element Name="zip" Value=""
NodeType=Text Name="" Value="94045"
NodeType=EndElement Name="zip" Value=""
NodeType=EndElement Name="address" Value=""
NodeType=Element Name="address" Value=""
NodeType=Element Name="name" Value=""
NodeType=Text Name="" Value="Frits Mendels"
NodeType=EndElement Name="name" Value=""
NodeType=Element Name="street" Value=""
NodeType=Text Name="" Value="PO Box 6789"
NodeType=EndElement Name="street" Value=""
NodeType=Element Name="city" Value=""
NodeType=Text Name="" Value="San Francisco"
NodeType=EndElement Name="city" Value=""
NodeType=Element Name="state" Value=""
NodeType=Text Name="" Value="CA"
NodeType=EndElement Name="state" Value=""
NodeType=Element Name="zip" Value=""
NodeType=Text Name="" Value="94123-6798"
NodeType=EndElement Name="zip" Value=""
NodeType=EndElement Name="address" Value=""
NodeType=Element Name="items" Value=""
NodeType=EndElement Name="item" Value=""
NodeType=EndElement Name="item" Value=""
NodeType=EndElement Name="items" Value=""
NodeType=EndElement Name="po" Value=""
```

Except for the absence of the XML and document declarations (which don't exist in PYX), this output looks just like the output using XmlTextReader. Since everything is working as expected, it's time to use XmlPyxReader in a real application.

Using XmlPyxReader

Luckily, you already have just such an application. In Chapter 2, I showed you how to write PoToPickList, which generates the PO pick list from an XML file. You can now plug XmlPyxReader in to PoToPickList to generate a pick list from a PYX document. Example 4-4 shows the Main( ) method of PoToPickList again, with the change highlighted.

Example 4-4. Main( ) method of PoToPickList, using XmlPyxReader

```
public static void Main(string[] args) {

  string filename = args[0];

  TextReader textReader = File.OpenText(filename);
  XmlReader reader = new XmlPyxReader(textReader);

  StringBuilder pickList = new StringBuilder( );
  pickList.Append("Angus Hardware PickList").Append(Environment.NewLine);
  pickList.Append("========================").Append(Environment.NewLine).
Append(Environment.NewLine);

  while (reader.Read( )) {
    if (reader.NodeType == XmlNodeType.Element) {
      switch (reader.LocalName) {
        case "po":
          pickList.Append(POElementToString(reader));
          break;
        case "date":
          pickList.Append(DateElementToString(reader));
          break;
        case "address":
          reader.MoveToAttribute("type");
          if (reader.Value == "shipping") {
            pickList.Append(AddressElementToString(reader));
          } else {
            reader.Skip( );
          }
          break;
        case "items":
          pickList.Append(ItemsElementToString(reader));
          break;
      }
    }
  }

  Console.WriteLine(pickList);
}
```

If you run the PYX purchase order in Example 4-1 through PoToPicklist again, you'll see exactly the same results you saw in Chapter 2, reproduced here in Example 4-5.

Example 4-5. Output of PoToPickList, using XmlPyxReader

```
Angus Hardware PickList
========================

PO Number: PO1456

Date: Friday, June 14, 2002

Shipping Address:
Frits Mendels
152 Cherry St
San Francisco, CA 94045

Quantity Product Code Description
======== ============ ===========
       1        R-273  14.4 Volt Cordless Drill
       1        1632S  12 Piece Drill Bit Set
```

Writing an XmlPyxWriter

Using XmlTextWriter is very simple, if you want to write your XML in standard angle-brackets syntax. But since you learned how to read PYX in Chapter 3, you should learn how to write PYX here.

Because PYX does not handle many XML structural features, the implementation is quite simple. Example 4-6 shows a possible implementation of an XmlPyxWriter. After you look over the code, I'll highlight some important bits.

Example 4-6. XmlPyxWriter implementation

```
using System;
using System.Collections;
using System.Globalization;
using System.IO;
using System.Xml;

public class XmlPyxWriter : XmlWriter {

  // constructors

  public XmlPyxWriter(TextWriter writer) {
    this.writer = writer;
  }

  public XmlPyxWriter(Stream stream) {
    this.writer = new StreamWriter(stream);
  }

  public XmlPyxWriter(string filename) {
    this.writer = new StreamWriter(filename);
  }
```

Example 4-6. XmlPyxWriter implementation (continued)

```
// private instance variables

private TextWriter writer;
private WriteState writeState = WriteState.Start;
private XmlSpace xmlSpace = XmlSpace.Default;
private string xmlLang = CultureInfo.CurrentCulture.ThreeLetterISOLanguageName;
private Stack elementNames = new Stack();

// private instance methods

private void Write(string text) {
  writer.WriteLine("-{0}", text);
  if (writeState == WriteState.Element) {
    writeState = WriteState.Content;
  }
}

private void Write(char ch) {
  writer.WriteLine("-{0}", ch);
  if (writeState == WriteState.Element) {
    writeState = WriteState.Content;
  }
}

private void Write(char [] buffer, int index, int count) {
  writer.WriteLine("-{0}", buffer, index, count);
  if (writeState == WriteState.Element) {
    writeState = WriteState.Content;
  }
}

// properties from XmlWriter

public override WriteState WriteState {
  get { return writeState; }
}

public override XmlSpace XmlSpace {
  get { return xmlSpace; }
}

public override string XmlLang {
  get { return xmlLang; }
}

// methods from XmlWriter

public override void WriteEndDocument() {
  // no-op
}

public override void WriteComment(string text) {
```

Example 4-6. XmlPyxWriter implementation (continued)

```
    // no-op
  }

  public override void WriteStartDocument() {
    writeState = WriteState.Prolog;
  }

  public override void WriteStartDocument(bool standalone) {
    writeState = WriteState.Prolog;
  }

  public override void WriteDocType(string name, string pubid, string sysid, string
subset) {
    writeState = WriteState.Prolog;
  }

  public override void WriteStartElement(string prefix, string localName, string ns) {
    writer.WriteLine("({0} ", localName);
    elementNames.Push(localName);
    writeState = WriteState.Element;
  }

  public override void WriteEndElement() {
    writer.WriteLine("){0}", elementNames.Pop());
  }

  public override void WriteFullEndElement() {
    WriteEndElement();
  }

  public override void WriteStartAttribute(string prefix, string localName, string ns) {
    writer.Write("A{0} ",localName);
    writeState = WriteState.Attribute;
  }

  public override void WriteEndAttribute() {
    writer.WriteLine();
    writeState = WriteState.Element;
  }

  public override void WriteProcessingInstruction(string name, string text) {
    writer.WriteLine("?{0} {1}", name, text);
  }

  public override void WriteEntityRef(string name) {
    char ch = ' ';
    switch (name) {
      case "amp":
        ch = '&';
        break;
      case "lt":
        ch = '<';
```

Example 4-6. XmlPyxWriter implementation (continued)

```
      break;
    case "gt":
      ch = '>';
      break;
    case "quot":
      ch = '"';
      break;
    case "apos":
      ch = '\'';
      break;
  }
  Write(ch);
}

public override void WriteCData(string text) {
  Write(text);
}

public override void WriteCharEntity(char ch) {
  Write(ch);
}

public override void WriteWhitespace(string ws) {
  Write(ws);
}

public override void WriteString(string text) {
  if (writeState == WriteState.Attribute) {
    writer.Write("{0}", text);
  } else {
    Write(text);
  }
}

public override void WriteSurrogateCharEntity(char lowChar, char highChar) {
  Write(lowChar);
  Write(highChar);
}

public override void WriteChars(char [] buffer, int index, int count) {
  Write(buffer, index, count);
}

public override void WriteRaw(char [] buffer, int index, int count) {
  Write(buffer, index, count);
}

public override void WriteRaw(string data) {
  Write(data);
}

public override void WriteBase64(byte [] buffer, int index, int count) {
```

Example 4-6. XmlPyxWriter implementation (continued)

```
    Write(writer.Encoding.GetChars(buffer), index, count);
  }

  public override void WriteBinHex(byte [] buffer, int index, int count) {
    Write(writer.Encoding.GetChars(buffer), index, count);
  }

  public override void Close( ) {
    writer.Close( );
    writeState = WriteState.Closed;
  }

  public override void Flush( ) {
    writer.Flush( );
  }

  public override string LookupPrefix(string ns) {
    return string.Empty;
  }

  public override void WriteNmToken(string name) {
    writer.Write(name);
  }

  public override void WriteName(string name) {
    writer.Write(name);
  }

  public override void WriteQualifiedName(string localName, string ns) {
    writer.Write(localName);
  }
}
```

As you can see, it's not a terribly complicated class. Most of the code is just a matter of filling in the abstract methods defined in XmlWriter. Here's a run-down of what it does, beginning with the private instance variables:

```
    private TextWriter writer;
    private WriteState writeState = WriteState.Start;
    private XmlSpace xmlSpace = XmlSpace.Default;
    private string xmlLang = CultureInfo.CurrentCulture.ThreeLetterISOLanguageName;
    private Stack elementNames = new Stack( );
```

These five private instance variables maintain all the state information you'll need in order to write PYX. writer is the TextWriter instance to which you are writing data. writeState is an instance of the XmlWriteState enumeration, indicating the state of the XmlWriter. xmlSpace is an instance of the XmlSpace enumeration, indicating the current xml:space scope. xmlLang is a string, indicating the current xml:lang scope. Finally, elementNames is a Stack of element names, which you'll want to maintain so that you can write the appropriate element name when you close the element:

Since PYX has no concept of xml:space or xml:lang, xmlSpace is initialized to XmlSpace.Default and xmlLang is initialized to the current environment's language.

```
private void Write(string text) {
  writer.WriteLine("-{0}", text);
  if (writeState == WriteState.Element) {
    writeState = WriteState.Content;
  }
}

private void Write(char ch) {
  writer.WriteLine("-{0}", ch);
  if (writeState == WriteState.Element) {
    writeState = WriteState.Content;
  }
}

private void Write(char [] buffer, int index, int count) {
  writer.WriteLine("-{0}", buffer, index, count);
  if (writeState == WriteState.Element) {
    writeState = WriteState.Content;
  }
}
```

These three private instance methods proxy the TextWriter.Write( ) and WriteLine( ) methods in such a way as to maintain the WriteState correctly. When the method is called, it writes a start text character followed by the text. If the writeState is currently WriteState.Element, it sets the state to WriteState.Content. Otherwise, it can be assumed that you're either already writing content, or you're writing an attribute's value; you leave the state as it is and merely write the text:

```
public XmlPyxWriter(TextWriter writer) {
  this.writer = writer;
}

public XmlPyxWriter(Stream stream) {
  this.writer = new StreamWriter(stream);
}

public XmlPyxWriter(string filename) {
  this.writer = new StreamWriter(filename);
}
```

XmlPyxWriter has three constructors, one taking a TextWriter, one taking a Stream, and one taking a filename. Each of them initializes the writer instance variable in different ways, but the end result in each case is a TextWriter, ready to be written to.

The next section of code contains implementations of XmlWriter's abstract properties and methods:

```
public override WriteState WriteState {
  get { return writeState; }
```

```
  }

  public override XmlSpace XmlSpace {
    get { return xmlSpace; }
  }

  public override string XmlLang {
    get { return xmlLang; }
  }
```

These three properties simply return the values of their respective private instance variables, without any further trickery:

```
  public override void WriteEndDocument() {
    // no-op
  }

  public override void WriteComment(string text) {
    // no-op
  }
```

These two method bodies are empty, because although PYX does not actually include the concept of comments or an end document, there's no need to throw an exception if client code calls these methods. There is no data lost, because the start document is implied, and comments are not meaningful to an XML parser—especially not a PYX parser:

```
  public override void WriteStartDocument() {
    writeState = WriteState.Prolog;
  }

  public override void WriteStartDocument(bool standalone) {
    writeState = WriteState.Prolog;
  }

  public override void WriteDocType(string name, string pubid, string sysid, string
  subset) {
    writeState = WriteState.Prolog;
  }
```

These three methods do not actually write anything to a PYX file; however, they do affect the state of the XmlWriter. Calling one of these methods indicates that the parser is currently in the document's prolog. The XmlState.Prolog value is not used internally, but any of your client code that queries XmlState can use the information however you want to:

```
  public override void WriteStartElement(string prefix, string localName, string ns) {
    writer.WriteLine("({0} ", localName);
    elementNames.Push(localName);
    writeState = WriteState.Element;
  }
```

WriteStartElement(), like all methods in XmlPyxWriter, ignores any namespace and prefix information. It writes the element to the TextWriter, pushes the element name onto the Stack, and sets the state to WriteState.Element:

```
public override void WriteEndElement() {
  writer.WriteLine("){0}", elementNames.Pop());
}

public override void WriteFullEndElement() {
  WriteEndElement();
}
```

In PYX, both WriteEndElement() and WriteFullEndElement() do the same thing—and WriteFullEndElement() does it by simply calling WriteEndElement() directly. WriteEndElement() pops the current element name off the Stack and writes the PYX close element tag:

```
public override void WriteStartAttribute(string prefix, string localName, string ns)
{
  writer.Write("A{0} ",localName);
  writeState = WriteState.Attribute;
}
```

Similar to WriteStartElement(), WriteStartAttribute() writes the PYX start attribute tag to the TextWriter, ignoring namespace information. However, it does not push the attribute's name to the Stack; the Stack only contains element names:

```
public override void WriteEndAttribute() {
  writer.WriteLine();
  writeState = WriteState.Element;
}
```

WriteEndAttribute() finishes the attribute line and sets the writeState back to WriteState.Element to indicate that whatever comes next, whether it's element content or a close element tag, applies to an element and not an attribute:

```
public override void WriteProcessingInstruction(string name, string text) {
  writer.WriteLine("?{0} {1}", name, text);
}
```

WriteProcessingInstruction() writes a processing instruction, which is indicated by a line starting with a question mark, followed by the processing instruction name and its text:

```
public override void WriteEntityRef(string name) {
  char ch = ' ';
  switch (name) {
    case "amp":
      ch = '&';
      break;
    case "lt":
      ch = '<';
      break;
    case "gt":
```

```
        ch = '>';
        break;
      case "quot":
        ch = '"';
        break;
      case "apos":
        ch = '\'';
        break;
    }
    Write(ch);
}
```

 There is no WriteXmlDeclaration( ) method in XmlWriter, because the XML declaration is written by the WriteStartDocument( ) method.

Although PYX has no concept of entities and entity references, you can at least convert the known XML entities to their respective character representations. WriteEntityRef( ) does this, calling one of the private Write( ) methods to maintain the state and write a dash at the beginning of the line, if necessary:

```
public override void WriteCData(string text) {
  Write(text);
}

public override void WriteCharEntity(char ch) {
  Write(ch);
}

public override void WriteWhitespace(string ws) {
  Write(ws);
}

public override void WriteString(string text) {
  if (writeState == WriteState.Attribute) {
    writer.Write("{0}", text);
  } else {
    Write(text);
  }
}

public override void WriteSurrogateCharEntity(char lowChar, char highChar) {

  Write(lowChar);
  Write(highChar);
}

public override void WriteChars(char [] buffer, int index, int count) {
  Write(buffer, index, count);
}
```

```
public override void WriteRaw(char [] buffer, int index, int count) {
  Write(buffer, index, count);
}

public override void WriteRaw(string data) {
  Write(data);
}

public override void WriteBase64(byte [] buffer, int index, int count) {
  Write(writer.Encoding.GetChars(buffer), index, count);
}

public override void WriteBinHex(byte [] buffer, int index, int count) {
  Write(writer.Encoding.GetChars(buffer), index, count);
}
```

These methods, which write textual data in one form or another, all do more or less the same thing by delegating to the private Write( ) method. PYX has no concept of the different types of text these methods represent, so they are all treated the same way:

```
public override void Close( ) {
  writer.Close( );
  writeState = WriteState.Closed;
}

public override void Flush( ) {
  writer.Flush( );
}
```

These two methods simply delegate their work to the TextWriter. Additionally, Close( ) sets the writeState to WriteState.Closed:

```
public override string LookupPrefix(string ns) {
  return string.Empty;
}
```

LookupPrefix( ) returns an empty string because, again, PYX has no concept of namespaces:

```
public override void WriteNmToken(string name) {
  writer.Write(name);
}

public override void WriteName(string name) {
  writer.Write(name);
}

public override void WriteQualifiedName(string localName, string ns) {
  writer.Write(localName);
}
```

The previous three methods are intended to ensure that names written to XML files are valid according to the XML specification. PYX has no concept of valid names, so these methods just write the names to the Stream as is.

Now that XmlPyxWriter is complete, you can take the XmlWriter client code from Example 3-3 and make one small change to start writing the output in PYX:

```
public static void Main(string [] args) {

// Create the XmlWriter
  //XmlTextWriter writer = new XmlTextWriter(Console.Out);
  XmlPyxWriter writer = new XmlPyxWriter(Console.Out);

  // Set the formatting to something nice - not supported by XmlPyxWRiter
  //writer.Formatting = Formatting.Indented;

  // Write the XML declaration
  writer.WriteStartDocument(true);

  ...
```

You'll notice that I've deleted the line that set the XmlFormatting, as that is a property of XmlTextWriter, and has no meaning in the context of a PYX writer.

Here's the resulting PYX, representing the same data as the XML version:

```
(root
Aid _1
Aname bar
(element1
-some characters
)element1
(cdataElement
Adate 7/4/2002 1:38:42 PM
-<this contains some characters XML wouldn't like & would choke on
-<this contains some characters XML wouldn't like & so the XmlWriter replaces them
)cdataElement
(emptyElement
)emptyElement
(emptyElement
)emptyElement
-One string
-&
- another.
)root
```

Moving On

I've now shown you how to create XmlReader and XmlWriter types to read one particular alternative XML syntax, and how to use them in programs that think they're reading and writing XML. You can think of other applications; besides other alternative XML syntaxes, such as YAML (Yet Another Markup Language) and James

---

Clark's Compact Syntax for RELAX NG, you could read data from other formats completely unrelated to XML, such as CSV files, DBF files—even databases and file-systems.

The knowledge of how to read and write XML to and from a variety of physical and logical formats forms a good basis for what's to follow. You'll see the real power of `XmlReader` and `XmlWriter` as they are combined with higher-level XML functionality, starting with the Document Object Model.

CHAPTER 5

Manipulating XML with DOM

The first section of this book laid the groundwork for your XML education by showing you how to read and write XML and other data using the .NET Framework. In between reading and writing, however, you'll often need to work with the data in other ways. This section will introduce various W3C standards and the implementations of those standards in the .NET Framework.

The XmlReader allows you to access XML data in a read-only, forward-only manner, but sometimes you need to read XML in a non-sequential manner. For example, you may want to change the order of a couple of elements somewhere in the middle of the document tree. For this purpose, the World Wide Web Consortium developed the Document Object Model (DOM).

In this chapter, I'll discuss what the DOM is, how .NET implements it, and when it is appropriate to use the DOM in your own code. Finally, we'll look at some examples using the DOM in C#.

What Is the DOM?

The DOM is an interface for manipulating XML content, structure, and style in an object-oriented fashion. It provides a standardized way of manipulating XML documents, including accessing elements and other nodes, taking actions on an object tree based on events, applying styles to documents, loading documents into object trees and saving object trees to documents, and more.

The DOM is language- and platform-neutral, meaning that it can be applied to any programming language on any hardware platform or operating system. Since its start in 1997, the DOM Working Group has made it a specific goal to ensure the DOM's language- and platform-neutrality. They've been successful; you can easily find a DOM implementation in just about any modern programming language, on any modern hardware platform.

The DOM represents an XML document as a *tree* of objects. Each object in the tree is called a *node*. The types of nodes that the DOM specifies are Document, DocumentFragment, DocumentType, EntityReference, Element, Attr, ProcessingInstruction, Comment, Text, CDATASection, Entity, and Notation. Some of these node types can have subnodes, and the types of subnodes that a particular node type can have are specified. To handle collections of nodes, the DOM also specifies a NodeList object and, for dictionaries of nodes (keyed by their names), the NamedNodeMap object. Figure 5-1 shows the DOM inheritance hierarchy.

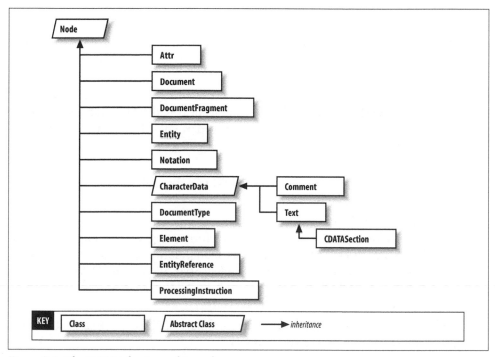

Figure 5-1. The DOM inheritance hierarchy

The DOM specifies a group of interfaces, not actual objects. This means that the implementation of the objects is not mandated, only the methods that must be accessible from a client of the DOM. Because the objects are specified by their interfaces, they cannot be created with traditional constructors; instead, factory methods are commonly used.

The DOM also specifies a number of lower-level types, such as DOMString and DOMTimeStamp. These are used internally in the DOM recommendation, but particular language bindings are free to use their own native formats for these types. In C#, these are string and DateTime, respectively.

A Brief Introduction to the DOM Specification

The DOM architecture is divided into several *modules*. Although there is no real meaning to the term, a module of the DOM can be thought of simply as a group of related functionality. The modules as defined by the W3C DOM Working Group are:

DOM Core
> DOM Core defines the actual tree-like object model you can use to navigate an XML document.

DOM XML
> The XML DOM extends the DOM Core to deal with XML 1.0-specific features and requirements, such as entities, processing instructions, and character data sections.

DOM HTML
> The HTML DOM extends the DOM Core to deal with HTML-specific requirements. These include the ability to identify a particular link in an HTML document.

DOM Events
> This module enables you to access the DOM tree through mouse, keyboard, and HTML-specific events.

DOM Cascading Style Sheets
> DOM CSS allows you to manipulate the formatting of documents through *Cascading Style Sheets* (*CSS*), as well as manipulating the style sheets themselves. For information on CSS, see *Cascading Style Sheets: The Definitive Guide*, by Eric A. Meyer (O'Reilly).

DOM Load and Save
> Loading and saving documents is an integral part of XML work, and this is the part of the DOM that allows you to do so.

Document Editing
> This module includes methods for manipulating a DOM tree while still maintaining its validity.

DOM XPath
> DOM XPath includes a set of functions for querying a DOM tree using XPath 1.0 expressions. Although we will use some XPath features in this chapter, XPath is discussed in detail in Chapter 6.

In addition, the DOM Working Group has defined several *levels* of functionality. The requirements for each level are formally documented by the W3C at *http://www. w3.org/DOM/DOMTR*.

Level 0

DOM Level 0 is not an official standard or recommendation of the W3C. Level 0 actually represents the object-oriented document functionality as implemented in Netscape Navigator 3.0 and Microsoft Internet Explorer 3.0.

HTML DOM is also sometimes referred to as DOM Level 0, although a DOM Level 0 is formally described in the DOM Level 1 documents.

Level 1

DOM Level 1 specifies the DOM Core and HTML DOM modules. The recommendation itself, like all the DOM recommendations, includes IDL (Interface Definition Language) definitions and Java and ECMAScript bindings. The DOM Level 1 Core specification includes such things as the actual tree structure, memory management, and naming conventions. The Level 1 HTML DOM includes naming conventions and HTML-specific elements.

Level 2

DOM Level 2 includes recommendations for DOM Core, Views, Events, Style, Traversal and Range, and HTML (still in progress as of this writing). The changes in DOM Level 2 Core include new types and changes to interfaces and exceptions, and the IDL version has been made more up-to-date.

Level 3

DOM Level 3 includes more changes to DOM Core and Events, as well as new Load and Save and XPath recommendations. As of this writing, all of the DOM Level 3 recommendations are still in the Working Draft stage, so there is no support for Level 3 in the .NET Framework.

Other Levels

The future holds any number of additional levels. Anything that you see in the list of DOM modules that is not listed in Levels 1 through 3 is fair game for some future level. Stay tuned to *http://www.w3.org/DOM/* for the latest news about DOM.

For more information on the DOM generally, refer to *XML in a Nutshell, 2nd Edition,* by Elliotte Rusty Harold and W. Scott Means (O'Reilly).

When to Use the DOM

Because the DOM represents an XML document as a tree in memory, it is best used for small documents or documents for which the memory footprint is known in advance, and when the application needs to manipulate the document's structure rather than just reading in the XML data.

One thing to keep in mind if you are considering using the DOM is that the entire document must be read into memory before any of it is available for use. This differs from the read-only, forward-only model of XmlReader, which allows you to read a single node at a time, and thus gives you the ability to deal with very large XML documents efficiently.

For this reason, the DOM is also appropriate when you need to access XML elements or attributes non-sequentially. The entire document is resident in memory, so searching for a particular node does not require disk access.

The .NET DOM Implementation

.NET implements only Levels 1 and 2 of the Core module of DOM. As such, the core DOM functionality is provided: standard node types and the object tree view of a document. .NET also provides some features specified in other modules that are not yet part of an official DOM level (such as loading and saving of a document, and document traversal via XPath). If these modules become official W3C Recommendations, it is expected that future .NET implementations will support them.

Example 5-1 lists a program you can run to demonstrate which features the .NET Framework's DOM implementation supports.

Example 5-1. A program to report DOM module support

```
using System;
using System.Xml;

class DomFeatureChecker {

  private static readonly string [] versions = new string [] {
    "1.0", "2.0" };

  private static readonly string [] features = new string [] {
    "Core", "XML", "HTML", "Views", "Stylesheets", "CSS",
    "CSS2", "Events", "UIEvents", "MouseEvents", "MutationEvents",
    "HTMLEvents", "Range", "Traversal" };

  public static void Main(string[] args) {
    XmlImplementation impl = new XmlImplementation( );

    foreach (string version in versions) {
      foreach (string feature in features) {
        Console.WriteLine("{0} {1}={2}", feature, version,
          impl.HasFeature(feature, version));
      }
    }
  }
}
```

The `HasFeature()` method of the `XmlImplementation` class returns true if the given feature is implemented. If you run this program with the .NET Framework version 1.0 or 1.1, you'll see the following output:

```
Core 1.0=False
XML 1.0=True
HTML 1.0=False
Views 1.0=False
Stylesheets 1.0=False
CSS 1.0=False
CSS2 1.0=False
Events 1.0=False
UIEvents 1.0=False
MouseEvents 1.0=False
MutationEvents 1.0=False
HTMLEvents 1.0=False
Range 1.0=False
Traversal 1.0=False
Core 2.0=False
XML 2.0=True
HTML 2.0=False
Views 2.0=False
Stylesheets 2.0=False
CSS 2.0=False
CSS2 2.0=False
Events 2.0=False
UIEvents 2.0=False
MouseEvents 2.0=False
MutationEvents 2.0=False
HTMLEvents 2.0=False
Range 2.0=False
Traversal 2.0=False
```

Although a particular DOM module may not be supported by the .NET Framework, that should not indicate that the functionality provided by that module is not available. All it actually means is that the standard way of providing the functionality is not implemented. In fact, in many cases, the standard is not defined yet, so it's not possible for *any* DOM implementation to support all of the modules!

The best place to start exploring the .NET DOM implementation is with the `XmlImplementation` type.

The XmlImplementation

`XmlImplementation` implements the `DOMImplementation` interface specification. The `DOMImplementation` is used as a place to keep certain methods that have no other logical home. Because the DOM is specified using IDL, there is no way to specify a constructor. Instead, you are expected to create a new DOM `Document` by calling `DOMImplementation.createDocument()`. In .NET, you can do this by either calling `XmlImplementation.CreateDocument()` or by using the `XmlDocument` constructor.

Remember that when I say that a .NET type implements a DOM interface, I'm not necessarily saying that it implements a C# interface. Rather, since DOM is specified in terms of IDL interfaces, the .NET types implement a DOM IDL interface specification.

DOMImplementation also requires a createDocumentType( ) method, which returns a DocumentType node. The DocumentType represents the contents of a DTD. .NET adds the method CreateDocumentType( ) to the XmlDocument class instead.

Finally, DOMImplementation requires the hasFeature( ) method. This method, which I used in Example 5-1, can be used to determine what features of the DOM are available for use in a given implementation.

The XmlNode Type Hierarchy

Because the .NET Framework provides a complete Level 2 Core implementation, the standard node inheritance tree is available. As you'll recall from Chapter 1, each node in an XML document is represented by an appropriately named class, starting with the abstract base class, XmlNode. Look at Figure 5-2 and compare the XmlNode inheritance hierarchy to the DOM Node inheritance hierarchy in Figure 5-1. You should see that every DOM type maps to exactly one .NET XmlNode subclass, although some XmlNode subclasses do not have an equivalent DOM type.

You can also see in Figure 5-2 that the .NET Framework inserts some additional levels of inheritance in the DOM hierarchy. These additional types provide a place for groupings of common functionality (XmlLinkedNode) as well as adding some functionality that is not required by the DOM specification (XmlWhitespace, XmlSignificantWhitespace).

The .NET DOM implementation provides intuitive names, similar enough to the relevant DOM interface to understand without further comment. In most cases, there is a one-to-one relationship between a DOM interface and the .NET implementation; however, Table 5-1 lists the exceptions to that rule.

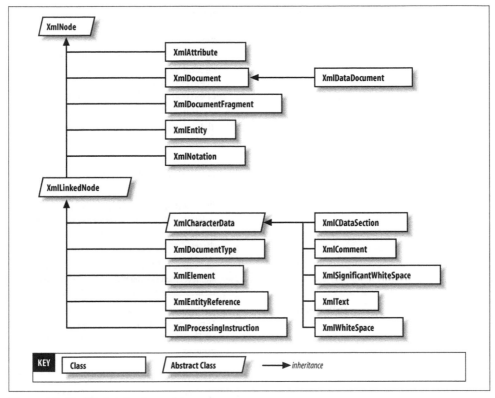

Figure 5-2. XmlNode inheritance hierarchy

Table 5-1. .NET DOM implementation exceptions

DOM interface	.NET implementation	Notes
DOMString	String	The DOM recommendation specifies that a language binding may use any type to represent a DOMString, as long as it supports UTF-16 encoding.
DOMTimeStamp	None	The DOM recommendation specifies that a language binding may use any type to represent a DOMTimeStamp, as long as it can hold the time in milliseconds. However, the Core module does not actually specify any use for the DOMTimeStamp type.
DOMException	XmlException	A DOMException is only raised when an error prevents operations from continuing. XmlException signals these conditions as well as framework-specific errors.
ExceptionCode	None	The ExceptionCode is not directly implemented in .NET. The DOM recommendation specifies that ExceptionCode is only necessary in language bindings that do not support exceptions natively.

Table 5-1. .NET DOM implementation exceptions (continued)

DOM interface	.NET implementation	Notes
DOMImplementation	XmlImplementation	.NET includes the CreateDocumentType( ) method on the XmlDocument class. The createDocument( ) and createDocumentType( )methods were added to DOMImplementation in DOM Level 2.
Document	XmlDocument	.NET adds the Document constructor and includes the CreateDocumentType( ) factory method here rather than on DOMImplementation.
Node	XmlNode	The DOM Level 2 methods isSupported( ) and hasAttributes( ) are not implemented.
NodeType	XmlNodeType	The DOM NodeType defines a list of codes for the various node types; the XmlNodeType enum defines six additional types to allow it to be used by other classes.
NodeList	XmlNodeList	XmlNodeList implements the IEnumerable interface, therefore individual nodes can be accessed via the standard IEnumerator methods.
NamedNodeMap	XmlNamedNodeMap	XmlNamedNodeMap implements the IEnumerable interface, therefore individual nodes can be accessed via the standard IEnumerator methods.

IEnumerable and IEnumerator are .NET interfaces that define methods that are used to move through a collection of objects. They are not DOM interfaces, although they are used in .NET DOM processing.

Another general exception is that when the DOM interface has a method named xxxNS( ), the corresponding .NET Xxx( ) method is simply overloaded to include the namespace URI parameter. The DOM interfaces are specified this way because IDL does not support overloaded methods.

Creating an XmlDocument

Although XmlNode sits at the top of the inheritance tree, XmlDocument is the top-level node in an actual document object tree. The XmlDocument has child nodes, which are accessible through the XmlNode type's various properties and methods. One of these child nodes, accessible through the DocumentElement property, is an ordinary XmlElement representing the root element of the tree. There may also be a document type node (such as <!DOCTYPE inventory SYSTEM "inventory.dtd">), represented by an XmlDocumentType, accessible through the DocumentType property. Finally, some XML documents will have an XML declaration (such as <?xml version="1.0"

encoding="utf-8" standalone="no">), represented by an XmlDeclaration, and accessible only as an ordinary child node of the XmlDocument. Figure 5-3 represents a typical XML document tree structure in memory.

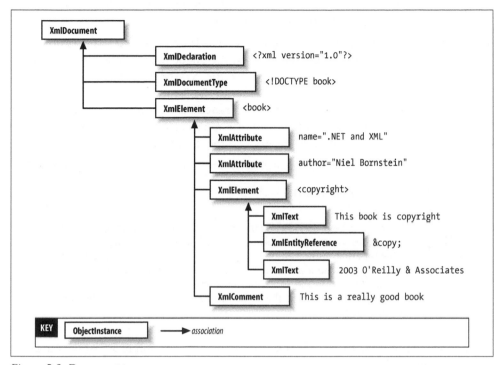

Figure 5-3. Document tree

You can create an XmlDocument in memory either by calling its constructor or by calling XmlImplementation.CreateDocument(). Both of these methods are overloaded to take an XmlNameTable, and the XmlDocument constructor is also overloaded to take an XmlImplementation.

 XmlNameTable is used to store atomized element and attribute names. It provides a more efficient way to compare the names than using strings. If you create two XmlDocument instances using the same XmlImplementation, they will share an XmlNameTable, making name comparisons more efficient.

Creating a new XmlDocument gives you an empty document.

```
XmlDocument document = new XmlDocument();
```

 Technically, the DOM says you shouldn't be able to instantiate a node by calling a constructor. However, .NET has provided an XmlDocument constructor for convenience.

Now that you have a document, you're free to start adding nodes to it. As specified by the DOM, in addition to serving as a representation of the XML document, XmlDocument also acts as a factory for the creation of new nodes. The first thing you might want to do is to create the XML declaration. XmlDocument has a CreateXmlDeclaration( ) method that does just that.

This method takes version, encoding, and standalone parameters. There are some constraints on the values of these parameters: the encoding parameter must be null or the name of an encoding supported by the System.Text.Encoding class; the standalone parameter must be null, "yes", or "no"; and, as of this writing, the version parameter must be "1.0". CreateXmlDeclaration( ) creates the XmlDeclaration node, but does not insert it into the tree; you must use AppendChild( ) or a similar method to actually add the node to the document:

```
XmlDeclaration declaration = document.CreateXmlDeclaration("1.0",Encoding.UTF8.
HeaderName,null);
document.AppendChild(declaration);
```

 This code snippet sets the document's encoding to Encoding.UTF8. In most cases you can safely use the default encoding of the XmlDeclaration. However, if you were to save the document to an XmlWriter that had a different encoding, the XmlWriter would discard the encoding set in the XmlDeclaration and use its own instead. This replacement ensures that the XML can be read back in with the correct encoding.

Next, you might wish to specify the document type. Example 5-2 shows a DTD named *inventory.dtd*.

Example 5-2. A DTD for warehouse inventory listings

```
<?xml version="1.0" encoding="UTF-8"?>

<!ELEMENT inventory (date,items)>

<!ELEMENT date EMPTY>
<!ATTLIST date year CDATA #REQUIRED
                month (1|2|3|4|5|6|7|8|9|10|11|12) #REQUIRED
                day (1|2|3|4|5|6|7|8|9|10|11|
                    12|13|14|15|16|17|18|19|
                    20|21|22|23|24|25|26|27|
                    28|29|30|31) #REQUIRED>

<!ELEMENT items (item)+>

<!ELEMENT item EMPTY>
<!ATTLIST item quantity CDATA #REQUIRED
                productCode CDATA #REQUIRED
                description CDATA #REQUIRED
                unitCost CDATA #REQUIRED>
```

The XmlDeclaration and XmlDocumentType nodes are optional, but if you choose to use them, they must appear in that order, and before the document element. If you can't add them sequentially in your code using AppendChild( ), you can use the XmlDocument type's methods InsertAfter( ), InsertBefore( ), or PrependChild( ) to ensure that the nodes are in the correct order. Note that PrependChild( ) is not a DOM Level 1 or Level 2 method, but a .NET-specific extension.

XmlDocument has a CreateDocumentType( ) method that, predictably, creates an XML document type. This method takes a name, a system ID, a public ID, and an internal subset as parameters, the last three of which can be null. Again, you must use AppendChild( ) to add the XmlDocumentType node to the tree:

```
XmlDocumentType docType = document.CreateDocumentType("inventory",
    null,"inventory.dtd",null);
document.AppendChild(docType);
```

If you try to create an XmlDocumentType node but the specified DTD does not exist, a FileNotFoundException will be thrown.

Next, you should create the document element. CreateElement( ) creates a new XmlElement but, again, does not insert it into the XML tree:

```
XmlElement documentElement = document.CreateElement("inventory");
document.AppendChild(documentElement);
```

If you inspect the XmlDocument instance's DocumentElement property, you'll see that the new XmlElement has automatically become the document element because it is the first XmlElement added to the tree:

```
XmlElement element = document.DocumentElement;
Console.WriteLine("DocumentElement is " + element.Name);
```

At any point, you might wish to examine the document tree as it would appear if serialized to XML. The following code snippet will do that for you with nice human-readable formatting.

```
XmlTextWriter writer = new XmlTextWriter(Console.Out);
writer.Formatting = Formatting.Indented;
document.WriteTo(writer);
```

Next, continue building your XmlDocument, one element at a time. The next required element is the date:

```
XmlElement dateElement = document.CreateElement("date");
dateElement.SetAttribute("year","2002");
dateElement.SetAttribute("month","6");
dateElement.SetAttribute("day","22");
document.DocumentElement.AppendChild(dateElement);
```

You'll notice that, in this case, you call `AppendChild()` on the document's `DocumentElement`, rather than the document itself. Besides being the right way to build a valid document for this DTD, this is necessary because a document is only allowed to have one child element. Attempting to append another child element directly to the document would cause the following exception to be thrown:

```
System.InvalidOperationException: This document already has a DocumentElement node.
```

Continuing, create the items and several item elements:

```
// create the items element
XmlElement itemsElement = document.CreateElement("items");
document.DocumentElement.AppendChild(itemsElement);

// create some item elements
XmlElement itemElement = document.CreateElement("item");
itemElement.SetAttribute("quantity","15");
itemElement.SetAttribute("productCode","R-273");
itemElement.SetAttribute("description","14.4 Volt Cordless Drill");
itemsElement.AppendChild(itemElement);

itemElement = document.CreateElement("item");
itemElement.SetAttribute("quantity","23");
itemElement.SetAttribute("productCode","1632S");
itemElement.SetAttribute("description","12 Piece Drill Bit Set");
itemsElement.AppendChild(itemElement);
```

By now, you should see that you've built the following XML document:

```
<?xml version="1.0" encoding="UTF-8"?>
<!DOCTYPE inventory SYSTEM "inventory.dtd">
<inventory>
  <date year="2002" month="6" day="22" />
  <items>
    <item quantity="1" productCode="R-273" description="14.4 Volt Cordless Drill" />
    <item quantity="1" productCode="1632S" description="12 Piece Drill Bit Set" />
  </items>
</inventory>
```

That looks fairly good, but is it valid? You can check with the `XmlValidatingReader` from Chapter 2. Remember that one of the `XmlValidatingReader` type's constructors takes a `Stream`. You can write the `XmlDocument` to a `MemoryStream`, flush the `Stream` to ensure that all the data has been written, set the `Stream` instance's pointer back to the beginning, and then pass it to the `XmlValidatingReader`. You can either let the `XmlSchemaException` be thrown and handle it in a try...catch, or register a `ValidationEventHandler` as I did in Chapter 2. In this case I'll just let the default `InternalValidationCallback` do the work:

```
Stream stream = new MemoryStream();
XmlTextWriter textWriter = new XmlTextWriter(new StreamWriter(stream));
document.WriteTo(textWriter);
textWriter.Flush();
stream.Seek(0,SeekOrigin.Begin);
```

```
XmlReader textReader = new XmlTextReader(stream);
XmlReader reader = new XmlValidatingReader(textReader);
try {
  while (reader.Read()) {
    // Validation only happens when you call Read()
  }
} catch (XmlSchemaException e) {
  Console.WriteLine(e);
} finally {
  stream.Close();
}
```

 You might think that you could use a combination of XmlNodeReader and XmlValidatingReader to validate the document. However, remember that although the XmlValidatingReader constructor takes an XmlReader, an ArgumentException will be thrown if it's not actually an XmlTextReader.

Now you can run the program and the XmlValidatingReader will tell you if you've forgotten anything:

```
System.Xml.Schema.XmlSchemaException: The required attribute 'unitCost' is missing.
An error occurred at (1, 140).
    at System.Xml.XmlValidatingReader.InternalValidationCallback(Object sender,
ValidationEventArgs e)
    at System.Xml.Schema.Validator.SendValidationEvent(XmlSchemaException e,
XmlSeverityType severity)
    at System.Xml.Schema.Validator.BeginChildren()
    at System.Xml.Schema.Validator.ProcessElement()
    at System.Xml.Schema.Validator.Validate()
    at System.Xml.Schema.Validator.Validate(ValidationType valType)
    at System.Xml.XmlValidatingReader.ReadWithCollectTextToken()
    at System.Xml.XmlValidatingReader.Read()
    at CreateInventory.Main(String[] args) in C:\Chapter 5\CreateInventory.cs:line 85
```

This exception indicates that an attribute required by the DTD is missing. You can go back and add the missing unitCost attributes to their respective elements. Because the DOM allows non-sequential access to the XML tree, you can actually go back to nodes that you created early in the program and assign the cost to each item at the end. This might be necessary in real life if the data were coming from disparate sources—maybe the list of items comes from a database, while the cost comes from a flat file; you don't want to have to scan the entire file as each row is read from the database.

Since you still have the items element in memory, you can simply iterate through its child nodes, looking up the productCode attribute, and adding the unitCost attribute with the appropriate value. If the code encounters an unknown productCode, it will throw an ApplicationException:

```
XmlNodeList elements = itemsElement.ChildNodes;
foreach (XmlElement currentElement in elements) {
  double cost = 0d;
```

```
    string productCode = currentElement.GetAttribute("productCode");
    switch (productCode) {
      case "R-273":
        cost = 189.95;
        break;
      case "1632S":
        cost = 14.95;
        break;
      default:
        throw new ApplicationException("Unknown productCode: "
          + productCode);
    }
    currentElement.SetAttribute("unitCost",cost.ToString());
  }
```

There are other ways you could navigate through the items element's child nodes. For example, if there were other types of child nodes besides elements, or other elements besides item, you could replace the first line of code with the following:

```
XmlNodeList elements = itemsElement.GetElementsByTagName("item");
```

Either way, you now have valid XML:

```
<?xml version="1.0" encoding="UTF-8"?>
<!DOCTYPE inventory SYSTEM "inventory.dtd">
<inventory>
  <date year="2002" month="6" day="22" />
  <items>
    <item quantity="15" productCode="R-273" description="14.4 Volt Cordless Drill"
unitCost="189.95" />
    <item quantity="23" productCode="1632S" description="12 Piece Drill Bit Set"
unitCost="14.95" />
  </items>
</inventory>
```

Finally, you should save the document to a file:

```
document.Save("inventory.xml");
```

The XmlDocument.Save() method has several overloads. The one used here takes a filename, creates all necessary FileInfo and/or XmlWriter instances, and serializes the document to the file. Other overloads take a Stream, a TextWriter, or an XmlWriter, respectively, so you can save the document not only to a variety of destinations, but even to alternative XML syntaxes, using, for example, the XmlPyxWriter I showed you in Chapter 4.

Reading an XmlDocument

An XmlDocument can easily be loaded from disk using the Load() method. It has overloads for a Stream, filename, TextReader, or XmlReader, and the LoadXml() method will load an XML string from memory. This provides great flexibility; you can load an XmlDocument from a file, a web site, standard input, a memory buffer, or any subclass of Stream or TextReader, as well as any subclass of XmlReader.

For example, suppose the inventory file were stored on a web server, at *http://www.angushardware.com/inventory.xml*. The following code would let you read it:

```
XmlDocument document = new XmlDocument( );
document.Load("http://www.angushardware.com/inventory.xml");
```

After reading the entire document into memory, you now have non-sequential access to the entire XML tree. For example, you could easily navigate down to the number of each item in stock using the XmlNode type's SelectNodes( ) method. SelectNodes( ) returns an XmlNodeList based on an XPath expression; in this case, you're selecting all nodes that match the expression //items/item, and writing them to the console:

```
XmlDocument document = new XmlDocument( );
document.Load("http://www.angushardware.com/inventory.xml");
XmlNodeList items = document.SelectNodes("//items/item");
foreach (XmlElement item in items) {
  Console.WriteLine("{0} units of product code {1} in stock",
    item.GetAttribute("quantity"),
    item.GetAttribute("productCode"));
}
```

 XPath is covered in Chapter 6.

Although you don't necessarily know in what order the items will appear in the inventory file, you might want to print out the inventory in some reasonable order, such as by product code. While an XML Schema can alert you if elements in an XML document are in the wrong order, it can't ensure that elements are ordered by an attribute *value*. To do this, you can create a private inner class called UnitInventory to hold a single product type's inventory information. This class will implement the IComparable interface to permit easy sorting, and you can override ToString( ) to use the same object to print the inventory:

```
private class UnitInventory : IComparable {
  private string productCode;
  private int quantity;
  private string description;
  private double unitCost;

  public UnitInventory(string productCode, string quantity,
    string description, string unitCost) {
    this.productCode = productCode;
    this.quantity = Int32.Parse(quantity);
    this.description = description;
    this.unitCost = Double.Parse(unitCost);
  }

  public int CompareTo(object other) {
    UnitInventory otherInventory = (UnitInventory)other;
    return productCode.CompareTo(otherInventory.productCode);
  }
```

```
    public override string ToString( ) {
      return quantity + " units of product code " +
        productCode + ", '" + description +
        "', in stock at $" + unitCost;
    }
  }
```

Now you can create an instance of `UnitInventory` for each row returned by `SelectNodes( )`, add each to an `ArrayList` and sort the list, and, finally, write each item to the console:

```
XmlDocument document = new XmlDocument( );
document.Load("http://www.angushardware.com/inventory.xml");
XmlNodeList items = document.SelectNodes("//items/item");

ArrayList list = new ArrayList(items.Count);

foreach (XmlElement item in items) {
  list.Add(new UnitInventory(item.GetAttribute("productCode"),
    item.GetAttribute("quantity"),
    item.GetAttribute("description"),
    item.GetAttribute("unitCost")));
}
list.Sort( );

foreach (UnitInventory inventory in list) {
  Console.WriteLine(inventory);
}
```

If you run the program, you'll see the list of inventory items sorted by the `productCode` attribute:

```
23 units of product code 1632S, '12 Piece Drill Bit Set', in stock at $14.95
15 units of product code R-273, '14.4 Volt Cordless Drill', in stock at $189.95
```

Changing an XmlDocument

In the previous example, you didn't actually change the underlying document. In fact, there's nothing there that you couldn't have done with an `XmlReader`. Unlike an `XmlReader`, however, the DOM allows you to change an existing XML document.

Suppose you decided to stop validating the inventory records. In order to make this change, you would need to remove the DOCTYPE node from all of the XML files. How would you go about doing this?

The short answer is `XmlNode.RemoveChild( )`. This method removes the node passed in from the object tree. You can read in all the XML files in the current directory, and remove the `XmlDocumentType` node. Then you can serialize the file back out (with the extension *.new* so you don't overwrite the original) and check that the DOCTYPE node is gone:

```
string currentDirectory = Environment.CurrentDirectory;
string [] files = Directory.GetFiles(currentDirectory, "*.xml");

foreach (string file in files) {
  XmlDocument document = new XmlDocument( );
  document.Load(file);
  XmlDocumentType documentType = document.DocumentType;
  document.RemoveChild(documentType);
  document.Save(file + ".new");
}
```

This process can be repeated with any type of XmlNode. For example, you could remove the inventory element, leaving an empty document, except for the XML declaration. Or you could use RemoveAll( ) to remove everything in the document entirely, while leaving the empty file in place:

```
document.Load(file);
document.RemoveAll( );
```

 If you remove the document element, the document is no longer well-formed. XmlDocument.Save( ) will throw an XmlException.

A more common case, given our example, would be to change the quantity of a particular item in stock. If you look back at the purchase order DTD from Chapter 2, you can see that the item elements are identical. You could write a small program to read in the store inventory and a purchase order, and decrement the inventory by the number of items sold in the PO.

Let's build the program, starting with a class called SellItems. To begin, because you're dealing with the same inventory file for all of the purchase orders, you can just store it as an instance variable:

```
private XmlDocument inventory;
```

In the Main( ) method, all you need do is instantiate a new SellItems object, passing the list of purchase order files that appeared on the command line:

```
static void Main(string [] args) {
  new SellItems(args);
}
```

The constructor creates the inventory XmlDocument and loads it from a file:

```
private SellItems(string [] files) {
  inventory = new XmlDocument( );
  inventory.Load("inventory.xml");
```

Next, loop through the purchase order file names, calling SellItemsFromPoFile( ) for each one:

```
foreach (string filename in files) {
  SellItemsFromPoFile(filename);
}
```

Finally, save the inventory document with all changes:

```
    inventory.Save("inventory.xml");
}
```

The `SellItemsFromPoFile()` method will create and load an individual purchase order from the list. For efficiency, each purchase order `XmlDocument` shares the same `XmlNameTable` with the others, and with the inventory `XmlDocument`:

```
private void SellItemsFromPoFile(string filename) {
    XmlDocument po = new XmlDocument(inventory.NameTable);
    po.Load(filename);
```

This XPath expression selects each `item` element from the purchase order:

```
    XmlNodeList elements = po.SelectNodes("//items/item");
```

This loop calls `SellItemsFromElement()` for each `item` element that the XPath expression returned:

```
    foreach (XmlElement element in elements) {
        SellItemsFromElement(element);
    }
}
```

Next is `SellItemsFromElement()` itself, the method that actually decrements the inventory. First, you get the product code and the quantity sold from the purchase order's item element:

```
private void SellItemsFromElement(XmlElement poItem) {
    string productCode = poItem.GetAttribute("productCode");
    int quantitySold = Int32.Parse(
      poItem.GetAttribute("quantity"));
```

Now, you search for the same product code in the inventory's item elements. Again, XPath is discussed in the next chapter; for now, don't worry too much about the XPath syntax:

```
    string xPathExpression =
      "//items/item[@productCode='" + productCode + "']";
    XmlElement inventoryItem =
      (XmlElement)inventory.SelectSingleNode(xPathExpression);
```

 If the XPath expression does not return a single matching node, a `NullReferenceException` will be thrown. It might be smart to wrap this call in a `try...catch` block to handle this better, and avoid abnormal termination of the program.

Here you're getting the quantity attribute from the inventory document, subtracting from it the amount in the purchase order document, and setting the inventory document's quantity attribute to the new decremented amount:

```
    int quantity = Int32.Parse(inventoryItem.GetAttribute("quantity"));
    quantity -= quantitySold;
    inventoryItem.SetAttribute("quantity", quantity.ToString());
}
```

And that's it, a simple inventory maintenance program. Granted, it's not a good idea to keep your inventory in a flat XML file; but if you think of the various ways you can construct an XmlDocument, you could actually be reading XML from a relational database, or some sort of web service, or almost anything you can imagine.

Example 5-3 shows the complete program.

Example 5-3. A program to update inventory

```
using System;
using System.Xml;

public class SellItems {

  private XmlDocument inventory;

  static void Main(string [] args) {
    new SellItems(args);
  }

  private SellItems(string [] files) {
    XmlDocument inventory = new XmlDocument( );
    inventory.Load("inventory.xml");

    foreach (string filename in files) {
      SellItemsFromPoFile(filename);
    }

    inventory.Save("inventory.xml ");
  }

  private void SellItemsFromPoFile(string filename) {
    XmlDocument po = new XmlDocument(inventory.NameTable);
    po.Load(filename);

    XmlNodeList elements = po.SelectNodes("//items/item");
    foreach (XmlElement element in elements) {
      SellItemsFromElement(element);
    }
  }

  private void SellItemsFromElement(XmlElement poItem) {
    string productCode = poItem.GetAttribute("productCode");
    int quantitySold = Int32.Parse(
      poItem.GetAttribute("quantity"));
    string xPathExpression =
      "//items/item[@productCode='" + productCode + "']";
    XmlElement inventoryItem =
      (XmlElement)inventory.SelectSingleNode(xPathExpression);

    int quantity = Int32.Parse(inventoryItem.GetAttribute("quantity"));
```

Example 5-3. A program to update inventory (continued)

```
        quantity -= quantitySold;
        inventoryItemElement.SetAttribute("quantity", quantity.ToString( ));
    }
}
```

Moving On

Now you've seen how to create a DOM document in memory, how to read one from disk, and how to manipulate one. You've looked at some different ways to manipulate a document once it's in memory, and you've used two XmlDocument instances simultaneously to manage an inventory system.

I also introduced XPath in this chapter. There's a lot more to say on that subject, so in Chapter 6 you'll learn about the System.Xml.XPath assembly.

Navigating XML with XPath

Once you have an XmlDocument in memory, you could choose to navigate through its nodes by using XmlNodeReader to read each node and do some action if it was of the desired type. Or, you could recursively iterate through its child nodes, interrogating each child node's node type and name, until you reach the one you're interested in. Or, you could use XPath.

In this chapter, I'll introduce the XPath specification, the syntax of XPath expressions, and some of its typical uses. Then I'll show you the System.Xml.XPath assembly, and how it allows you to use XPath in your .NET applications. Finally, I'll go through some examples using XPath.

What Is XPath?

XPath is a specification that allows you to address individual parts of an XML document, originally intended for use in the XSLT transformation language and the XPointer syntax for XML fragment identifiers. However, XPath is quite useful on its own, and is available for standalone use in .NET.

 Although XSLT is covered in Chapter 7, XPointer is not implemented in the .NET Framework. Thus, XPointer falls outside of the range of this book. For more information on XPath, XPointer, and their relationship, see John Simpson's *XPath & XPointer* (O'Reilly).

XPath 1.0 became a formal recommendation of the W3C in November, 1999, although XPath 2.0 is currently a working draft, still evolving as of this writing. The official XPath recommendation is located on the web at *http://www.w3.org/TR/xpath*.

The essence of XPath is that you can select certain nodes from within an XML document through a simple XPath expression. In addition, XPath allows you to do some simple string, numeric, and Boolean data transformation on selected nodes. XPath expressions take the form of strings with a certain well-known syntax. This syntax is not explicitly XML itself; it is similar to filesystem pathnames and URLs, and this is where XPath gets its name.

In addition to addressing nodes by name, XPath syntax enables pattern matching, so that you can select individual nodes by their attribute or content values.

In this section, I'll discuss the structure and syntax of XPath expressions, and some of the functions built in to the specification.

Introduction to the XPath Specification

Just like DOM, XPath operates on a tree-based view of an XML document. The XPath tree is built of the same node types used in DOM, except that CDATA sections, entity references, and document type declarations are not directly addressable. Their *content* is, however; the net result is that you can navigate to a text node's content, but you cannot tell whether that content contains plain text, CDATA, expanded entity references, or some combination thereof. You cannot access document type declarations at all with XPath.

For this discussion, I'll return to the inventory example from Chapter 5. That example included an inventory database that looked similar to the one in Example 6-1; here I've added some additional products.

Example 6-1. Angus Hardware inventory database

```
<?xml version="1.0" encoding="utf-8"?>
<!DOCTYPE inventory SYSTEM "inventory.dtd">
<inventory>
<!-- Warehouse inventory for Angus Hardware -->
<date year="2002" month="7" day="6" />
  <items>
    <item quantity="15" productCode="R-273" description="14.4 Volt Cordless Drill"
unitCost="189.95" />
    <item quantity="23" productCode="1632S" description="12 Piece Drill Bit Set"
unitCost="14.95" />
    <item quantity="10023" productCode="GN0250" description="1/4 inch Galvanized Steel
Nails, 1/2 pound box" unitCost="4.95" />
    <item quantity="9887" productCode="GN0375" description="3/8 inch Galvanized Steel
Nails, 1/2 pound box" unitCost="189.95" />
    <item quantity="8761" productCode="GN0500" description="1/2 inch Galvanized Steel
Nails, 1/2 pound box" unitCost="4.95" />
    <item quantity="3441" productCode="GN0625" description="5/8 inch Galvanized Steel
Nails, 1/2 pound box" unitCost="4.95" />
    <item quantity="9987" productCode="GN0750" description="3/4 inch Galvanized Steel
Nails, 1/2 pound box" unitCost="4.95" />
    <item quantity="10002" productCode="GN0875" description="7/8 inch Galvanized Steel
Nails, 1/2 pound box" unitCost="4.95" />
    <item quantity="596" productCode="GN1000" description="1 inch Galvanized Steel Nails,
1/2 pound box" unitCost="4.95" />
  </items>
</inventory>
```

Parts of an XPath expression

To introduce the proper terminology, each part of the XPath expression is called a *location step*. Each location step is made up of an *axis*, a *node test*, and zero or more *predicates*. Location steps are separated by the slash character (/).

The axis specifies the tree relationship between the nodes selected by the location step and the context node. Many axes have abbreviations which, while very convenient, are not always obvious to someone new to XPath. Table 6-1 shows the axes, their abbreviations, and brief descriptions of their meanings.

Table 6-1. Location step axes and their abbreviations

Axis	Abbreviation	Meaning
child		Contains the immediate children of the context node.
parent	..	Contains the immediate parent of the context node.
self	.	Contains the context node itself.
attribute	@	Contains the attributes of the context node, if it is an element.
ancestor		Contains the parent of the context node, its parent, and so on, all the way up to the root node.
ancestor-or-self		Contains the context node in addition to all the nodes contained in the ancestor axis.
descendant		Contains the children of the context node, their children, and so on, all the way down to the lowest level comment, element, processing instruction, and text node. It does not include attributes or namespaces.
descendant-or-self	//	Contains the context node in addition to all the nodes contained in the descendant axis. (Use sparingly for performance reasons.)
preceding-sibling		Contains all children of the context node's parent node which appear before the context node.
following-sibling		Contains all children of the context node's parent node which appear after the context node.
preceding		Contains all nodes which appear before the context node that are not ancestors.
following		Contains all nodes which appear after the context node that are not descendants.
namespace		Contains the context node's namespace node.

The node test specifies the type and name of the nodes selected by the location step. Node tests include text( ), which selects the text content of the context node; comment( ), which selects all the child nodes of the context node that are comments; processing-instruction( ), which selects all the child nodes of the context node that are processing instructions; and node( ), which is the default, and selects all children of the context node. The child axis is the default for any location step that does not have an explicit axis.

A predicate further refines the set of nodes selected by the location step. Predicates can include selecting a specific element by position, as well as functions like count( ). Predicates always appear in square brackets ([ ]).

 The double slash (//) represents the expression descendent-or-self:: node( ). The XPath query //foo would return all elements named foo anywhere in the document. While this is a very powerful expression, it is also very inefficient, as it requires the XPath processor to evaluate every node in the document to see if it contains an element named foo. It should be used sparingly, and preferably within controlled contexts.

I'll show you some of these terms in their proper context as we go along.

Selecting elements

If you have an XML document such as the inventory database in Example 6-1, you might wish to select certain nodes from it. For example, you might want to know the date the inventory numbers were recorded. The following XPath expression would return the date element:

```
/child::date
```

The double colon (::) separates the axis from the element being selected. Since child is the default axis, this can also be expressed in the abbreviated syntax:

```
/date
```

Every XPath expression has a *context node*. The context node is the node from which the search begins. In most cases, an XPath implementation allows you to select the node you wish to use as the context node. However, you can explicitly indicate that the search is to begin from the root element by beginning the expression with /. Following the slash, the string date indicates that the expression is to return all nodes that are descendants of the root node, and have the name date.

 The XPath recommendation does not require a standard way to set the XPath context node. In .NET, the XmlNode object's SelectNodes( ) method, which I introduced in Chapter 5, sets the context node to the XmlNode instance upon which you call the method.

For the inventory document example, this expression would return the element <date year="2002" month="7" day="6" />. If there are other nodes elsewhere in the tree with the name date, each of them would be returned as well. You can make your search more specific by including only those nodes with the name date that are children of any node named inventory, using this expression:

```
/child::inventory/child::date
```

And again, this can be expressed with the abbreviated syntax:

```
/inventory/date
```

In much the same vein, you could navigate to the items element with any of the following expressions; they can be considered equivalent if the context node is the root element:

```
//child::inventory/child::items
//inventory/items
/inventory/items
inventory/items
```

The single leading slash (/), as explained previously, is an axis that indicates that the context node is to be ignored and the search is to be done starting at the root. The double leading slash (//) has a slightly different meaning: at any point within the expression, it indicates that the search is to include the context node as well as all its descendants, although at the beginning of the expression the double slash is equivalent to a single slash. The expression with no leading slash indicates that the search is relative to the context node.

// is actually just an abbreviation for the descendant-or-self::node( )/ axis. So another equivalent to the expressions above would be:

```
descendant-or-self::node( )/inventory/child::items
```

This expansion and replacement of axes really could go on forever.

Once you have retrieved the items element, you can make it the context node for your next XPath expression. You can then return the list of item elements with this expression:

```
item
```

You can then iterate through each of these item nodes, doing as you wish with them.

If you have an item element and wish to gather information about the inventory date, you can use the double period axis (..), which is an abbreviation for parent::node( ). This axis selects the parent of the current node. So, to get the date element from an inventory element's context, you could use this expression:

```
../../date
```

The double period can be used anywhere in the expression. For example, you can combine some of the previous forms to return the date element in a fairly inefficient yet entirely legal way. This sort of construct really comes into its own when you start to build XPath expressions dynamically:

```
//item/../../date
```

It's interesting to note that although //item would select all the item elements within the document, //item/../../date returns only the one date element. This is because XPath removes duplicate nodes from the result set.

You can also select multiple elements at once, with the pipe character (|). The following expression selects both the date and item elements from the document:

```
//item|//date
```

Selecting attributes

XPath defines a special character to select an attribute node. The at sign (@) axis indicates that the node to select is an attribute. @ is an abbreviation for attribute::. Attributes can be intermingled with other nodes in the XPath expression. Thus, the following expression selects the year attribute of the date element:

```
//inventory/date/@year
```

And again, although it is an odd and somewhat inefficient way to do it, you could select the month attribute from any element that has a year attribute with this expression:

```
//@year/../@month
```

You can also use wildcards for element and attribute names. An asterisk (*) matches all element nodes, and @* matches all attribute nodes. This expression returns all attributes for all elements:

```
//*/@*
```

Finally, the node( ) function selects all nodes, of all types.

You may find it helpful to expand the axis abbreviations into their full axes as an aid to learning. For example, //inventory/date/@year is equivalent to descendant-or-self::node()/child::date/attribute::year, which, while specific, is not exactly terse.

Selecting text, comments, and processing instructions

XPath also defines several functions to select the other types of nodes. The first of these, text( ), selects any text node. The data returned will concatenate all text, whitespace, CDATA, and entity references into a continuous stream of characters, as long as there is no markup separating them:

```
//text( )
```

 Contrary to the XPath 1.0 recommendation, in .NET's XPath implementation, a CDATA section interrupts a text node. The CDATA itself and any text following the CDATA will not be returned by text( ).

The comment( ) function selects comments. Each comment is returned as a separate node, even if there is no text or markup between them:

```
//comment( )
```

As the name implies, the processing-instruction( ) function selects processing instructions:

```
//processing-instruction( )
```

With all the expressions you've seen so far, you can move up or down the node hierarchy at will, by inserting the appropriate axis. For example, you can select all the attributes of the parent nodes of any processing instructions with this expression:

```
//processing-instruction( )/../@*
```

Selecting nodes by value

However, there are times when selecting all the elements or attributes with a particular name is not enough. You may want to find all the elements with a particular attribute value. For this purposes, XPath defines *predicates*. The following expression selects any item elements that have a productCode attribute whose value is equal to GN0500:

```
//item[@productCode='GN0500']
```

You might also want to find all the items for which fewer than 10,000 units are in stock. The following XPath expression would discover that, and select their description attributes:

```
//item[@quantity<10000]/@description
```

XPath also supports the relational operators <, >, <=, >=, and !=, as well as and and or. Most values are converted automatically to an appropriate numeric or Boolean value, if the operator requires that type.

 Although there is a lot more included in the XPath recommendation, there is not room in this volume to list it all. If you're interested in learning more about XPath, I recommend *XML In a Nutshell* (O'Reilly). If you want to learn about XPath in an XSLT context, take a look at *XSLT* (O'Reilly).

When to Use XPath

You should use XPath when you have an XML node in memory and you wish to navigate directly to a particular child node. This presumes that you have either created or loaded an XmlDocument in memory. You can also load an XML document directly into an XPathDocument from a Stream, URL, TextReader, or XmlReader. This method obviates the need to create an XmlDocument at all, and is more efficient than the DOM, since the XPathDocument is a read-only representation of the XML document.

XPath is a good substitute for XmlReader when you have already read an entire document into memory, and the document is to be processed randomly. If you have an extremely large XML document, or you wish to access it strictly sequentially, however, there can be a performance advantage to writing an XmlReader client that handles parsing events. For example, if you are only interested in a certain node within the document, there is no need to load the entire document into memory; you should write an XmlReader client to handle the specific parsing event that indicates the node in question has been read, and skip the rest.

Using XPath

The System.Xml.XPath assembly is relatively small, containing only five classes, six enumerations, and one interface. There are two ways to select nodes from an XML document with XPath. The first, which was introduced in Chapter 5, uses the SelectNodes() and SelectSingleNode() methods of XmlNode. The second way uses the XPathNavigator class, obtained by calling XmlNode.GetNavigator() or XPathDocument.GetNavigator().

In this section, I'll discuss these methods of using XPath in .NET.

XmlNode

XmlNode defines two methods, with two overloads each, to allow navigation via XPath. SelectSingleNode() returns a single XmlNode that matches the given XPath, and SelectNodes() returns an XmlNodeList.

Selecting a single node

SelectSingleNode() returns a single XmlNode that matches the given XPath expression. If more than one node matches the expression, the first one is returned; the definition of "first" depends on the order of the axis used. The context node of the XPath query is set to the XmlNode instance on which the method is invoked.

One overload of SelectSingleNode() takes just the XPath expression. The other one takes the XPath expression and an XmlNamespaceManager. The XmlNamespaceManager is used to resolve any prefixes in the XPath expression.

Example 6-2 shows a simple program that selects a single node from an XML document and writes it to the console, with human-readable formatting.

Example 6-2. Program to execute an XPath query on a document

```
using System;
using System.Xml;
using System.Xml.XPath;

public class XPathQuery {

  public static void Main(string [] args) {

    string filename = args[0];
    string xpathExpression = args[1];
```

Example 6-2. Program to execute an XPath query on a document (continued)

```
    XmlDocument document = new XmlDocument( );
    document.Load(filename);

    XmlTextWriter writer = new XmlTextWriter(Console.Out);
    writer.Formatting = Formatting.Indented;

    XmlNode node = document.SelectSingleNode(xpathExpression);
    node.WriteTo(writer);

    writer.Close( );
  }
}
```

Because `SelectSingleNode( )` is called on the `XmlNode` instance that represents the entire document, the context node in this case *is* the document, and the XPath query will be executed relative to the entire document. However, the context node could be any other `XmlNode` in the document, depending on which `XmlNode` instance's `SelectSingleNode( )` method is invoked.

If you need to use a specific `XmlNode` subclass's methods or properties on the resulting `XmlNode` instance, it is up to the calling code to cast the `XmlNode` instance to the appropriate type. For example, if the XPath expression were to return an `XmlElement` instance, the code would explicitly have to cast the `XmlNode` to `XmlElement` in order to call, for example, `GetAttribute( )` on it. But then you could also construct your XPath expression to just go ahead and select the attribute in question directly.

 Casting an `XmlNode` to the incorrect type will cause an `InvalidCastException` to be thrown. You should be sure you know what type of XmlNode is returned by `SelectSingleNode( )` before casting. Two ways to determine an object instance's actual type are the `typeof` operator and the `GetType( )` method. You can also use the `as` operator to perform a typesafe cast. For more information on determining an instance's type at runtime, see *C# Essentials, 2nd Edition* (O'Reilly).

Selecting multiple nodes

`SelectNodes( )` is similar to `SelectSingleNode( )`, except that it returns an `XmlNodeList` rather than an `XmlNode`. `XmlNodeList` implements `IEnumerable`, so you can use any of the techniques commonly used to manage a collection. For example, you can interrogate the `XmlNodeList`'s `Count` property to discover how many elements it contains, access each element with its array indexer, or use a `foreach` statement to iterate through the elements in order.

I've modified the `SelectSingleNode( )` example to select a list of nodes. The changed lines are highlighted:

```
    XmlDocument document = new XmlDocument( );
    Document.Load(filename);
```

```
XmlTextWriter writer = new XmlTextWriter(Console.Out);
writer.Formatting = Formatting.Indented;

XmlNodeList nodeList = document.SelectNodes(xpathExpression);
Console.WriteLine("{0} nodes matched.", nodeList.Count);
foreach (XmlNode node in nodeList) {
  node.WriteTo(writer);
}

writer.Close();
```

As with SelectSingleNode( ), it is up to the calling code to ensure that any casts are correct; this includes the implicit cast in the foreach statement. In this example, however, the foreach will always succeed, because each element of an XmlNodeList is, by definition, an instance of XmlNode.

Also like SelectSingleNode( ), one overload of SelectNodes( ) takes an XmlNamespaceManager parameter.

Creating an XPathNavigator

In addition to the SelectSingleNode( ) and SelectNodes( ) methods, XmlNode implements the IXPathNavigable interface. The only method that IXPathNavigable requires is CreateNavigator( ). CreateNavigator( ) returns an XPathNavigator, which provides an efficient, read-only, random-access model of the XmlNode. Once you have an XPathNavigator, you can call its Select( ) method to navigate to a node or set of nodes using an XPath expression.

The following code produces the same output as the SelectNodes( ) example above:

```
XmlDocument document = new XmlDocument( );
document.Load(filename);

XmlTextWriter writer = new XmlTextWriter(Console.Out);
writer.Formatting = Formatting.Indented;

XPathNavigator navigator = document.CreateNavigator( );
XPathNodeIterator iterator = navigator.Select(xpathExpression);
Console.WriteLine("{0} nodes matched.", iterator.Count);
while (iterator.MoveNext( )) {
  XmlNode node = ((IHasXmlNode)iterator.Current).GetNode( );
  node.WriteTo(writer);
}
writer.Close( );
```

A couple of lines in this example bear closer investigation:

```
XPathNodeIterator iterator = navigator.Select(xpathExpression);
```

XPathNavigator has a Select( ) method that returns an XPathNodeIterator. Select( ) itself has two overloads, one that takes a string XPath expression, and one that takes a precompiled XPathExpression. A compiled XPathExpression can be obtained by passing a textual XPath expression to the XPathNavigator.Compile( ) method.

If you were going to select the same XPath expression multiple times or from differ-ent context nodes, it would be more efficient to use a compiled XPathExpression. In the previous example, I used the version of Select( ) that takes a string parameter. In the following example, I'm using a compiled XPathExpression:

```
XPathExpression expression = navigator.Compile(xpathExpression);
XPathNodeIterator iterator = navigator.Select(expression);
```

Other useful methods that XPathExpression provides include AddSort( ), whose two overloads allow you to sort the set of nodes resulting from the expression, and SetContext( ), which allows you to set the XmlNamespaceManager used to look up namespace prefixes.

In addition to the two Select( ) overloads, XPathNavigator provides a set of selector methods, including SelectAncestors( ), SelectChildren( ), and SelectDescendants( ), each of which returns an XPathNodeIterator ready for use in navigating the set of results.

 SelectChildren( ) selects only from among the direct child nodes of the context node, while SelectDescendants( ) selects from among the context node's direct children, plus their children, and so on.

Each of these methods has two overloads; one of which takes an XPathNodeType, while the other takes a string local name and namespace URI. In all these methods, the parameters determine which nodes will be selected, relative to the XPathNavigator's context node:

```
while (iterator.MoveNext( )) {
```

XPathNodeIterator represents a set of nodes returned from an XPath expression. Its interesting methods include Clone( ) and MoveNext( ). Clone( ), which implements the .NET Framework's ICloneable interface, returns a new XPathNodeIterator whose state is the same as the original one, but further changes to either the original or the clone will not affect the other. Thus, cloning an XPathNodeIterator allows you to work with XPath query results by allowing you to navigate through different branches of the XML tree. MoveNext( ) moves the XPathNodeIterator's position to the next node.

XPathNodeIterator's interesting properties include Count, Current, and CurrentPosition. Current returns a new XPathNavigator whose context node is the XPathNodeIterator's current node. Like cloning an XPathNodeIterator, this allows you to navigate through XML branches. Count and CurrentPosition return the num-ber of nodes selected and the XPathNodeIterator's current position, respectively:

```
XmlNode node = ((IHasXmlNode)iterator.Current).GetNode( );
```

Since the XPathNavigator in this example was obtained by calling XmlNode. GetNavigator( ), it implements the IHasXmlNode interface. IHasXmlNode's sole method,

GetNode( ), returns the XPathNodeIterator's context node. So this line of code gets an XPathNavigator whose context node is the same as the XPathIterator instance's current node and casts it to an IHasXmlNode in order to get its current XmlNode.

It's important to remember the distinction between the XPathNodeIterator.Current property, which returns a new XPathNavigator positioned at the context node, and the IHasXmlNode.GetNode( ) method, which returns the context node as an XmlNode. By casting an XPathNavigator to an IHasXmlNode, you can get access to the current XmlNode itself.

XPathDocument

You might not want to load a complete XmlDocument just to use XPath. An XmlDocument brings with it all the DOM overhead, allowing you to not only read but to write to the XML node tree. For read-only access, there is the XPathDocument class. Like XmlNode, it implements IXPathNavigable; but unlike XmlNode, it represents a read-only view of the XML document.

XPathDocument does not maintain node identity like XmlDocument, nor does it do any rule checking required by the DOM. It is optimized for XPath queries and XSLT processing.

 Starting to get the idea that this stuff is all intertwined? XSLT is covered in Chapter 7.

XPathDocument's sole purpose is to serve as an implementation of IXPathNavigable. It has constructors that take a Stream, a URL, a TextReader, and an XmlReader, respectively, and its only other method is CreateNavigator( ).

An XPathNodeIterator obtained from an XPathDocument does not implement IHasXmlNode. Each element of the XPathNodeIterator is actually an XPathDocumentNavigator, and does not have a GetNode( ) method. Remember that the XPathDocument is not an XmlDocument; that is, it does not implement the DOM specification, so it is not navigable as a tree of XmlNode instances. If it's important to you that you be able to access the nodes using DOM, use XmlDocument.CreateNavigator( ).

XPathDocumentNavigator does have some properties and methods with which you can access node-specific information. XPathDocumentNavigator implements the following abstract properties and methods of XPathNavigator: HasAttributes, HasChildren, IsEmptyElement, LocalName, Name, NamespaceURI, NodeType (which returns an XPathNodeType, *not* an XmlNodeType), Value, and GetAttribute( ).

With the following modifications to your XPath query code, the current node's name is written to the console:

```
XPathDocument document = new XPathDocument(filename);

XPathNavigator navigator = document.CreateNavigator();
XPathNodeIterator iterator = navigator.Select(xpathExpression);
Console.WriteLine("{0} nodes matched.", iterator.Count);
while (iterator.MoveNext()) {
  Console.WriteLine(iterator.Current.LocalName);
}
writer.Close();
```

 Again, be careful what you cast. An XPathNodeIterator obtained by calling XmlNode.GetNavigator() will implement IHasXmlNode, but one obtained by calling XPathDocument.GetNavigator() will not.

Navigating a Non-XML Document with XPath

One of the most interesting and unique aspects of .NET's XML implementation is the fact that you can read non-XML data as if it were XML by creating subclasses of its abstract types. You saw this already in XmlReader and XmlWriter.

Because you can read an XmlDocument from any XmlReader, it follows that you can call that XmlDocument's SelectSingleNode() and CreateNavigator() methods to navigate the document via XPath. You can also create an XPathDocument from any XmlReader, and use its CreateNavigator() method. In addition to that, however, you can also create a custom implementation of XPathNavigator to navigate any source document with XPath.

Using a custom XmlReader

You've already created and used XmlPyxReader in Chapter 4. Since XmlPyxReader is just like any other instance of XmlReader, you can pass it to XPathDocument's constructor and navigate it using XPath:

```
XmlReader reader = new XmlPyxReader(filename);
XPathDocument document = new XPathDocument(reader);

XPathNavigator navigator = document.CreateNavigator();
XPathNodeIterator iterator = navigator.Select(xpathExpression);
Console.WriteLine("{0} nodes matched.", iterator.Count);
while (iterator.MoveNext()) {
 Console.WriteLine(iterator.Current.LocalName);
}
writer.Close();
```

Using a custom XPathNavigator

The next possibility is to skip over the custom XmlReader and go directly to a custom XPathNavigator. Like custom XmlReaders, custom XPathNavigators have numerous methods and properties to implement.

You've already seen that Angus Hardware uses XML files to manage their purchase orders. But what about when they want to manage the purchase orders at a higher level? For example, POs may come in from any of several clients, and they should be managed by the date on which they arrive.

Angus Hardware's IT department maintains POs in a filesystem, with a structure as shown in Figure 6-1.

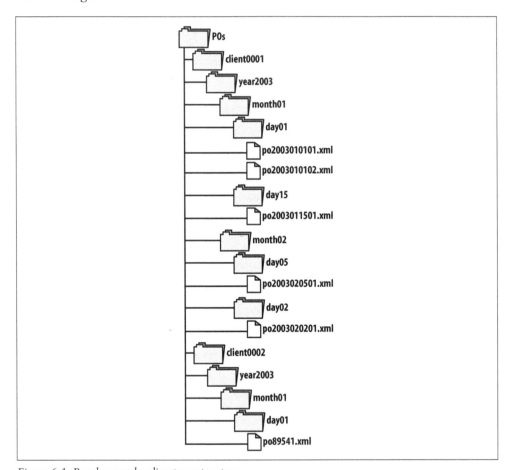

Figure 6-1. Purchase order directory structure

Obviously, they'd like to be able quickly to find particular invoices, either by client or by date. What they need is a custom `XPathNavigator`.

First, some design specifics. Each directory and PO file in the PO tree will be represented as an element. None of these elements have attributes. At the very lowest level, the PO XML file itself will be represented as an element with a name in the form *ponumber*.

I'm going to show you one way to write a custom XPathNavigator to navigate a file-system using XPath. I'll go through this code one section at a time, beginning with the constructors for the FileSystemNavigator class:

```
public FileSystemNavigator( ) {
    rootDir = new DirectoryInfo(Environment.CurrentDirectory);
    state.Push(new FileSystemState(rootDir));
}

public FileSystemNavigator(string path) {
    rootDir = new DirectoryInfo(path);
    state.Push(new FileSystemState(rootDir));
}

private FileSystemNavigator(FileSystemInfo d) {
    rootDir = (DirectoryInfo)d;
    state.Push(new FileSystemState(rootDir));
}
```

The three constructors should handle all the cases of interest: the default, which uses the current directory; one that takes a string, which is the path name; and one that takes a FileSystemInfo representing the root directory of the file structure. FileSystemInfo is the base type from which both FileInfo and DirectoryInfo are derived.

The three private instance variables hold the following: the root directory, for later reference; an XmlNameTable, which will be used externally for atomized name comparisons; and a Stack, holding the current node and its ancestors as the document is navigated:

```
private DirectoryInfo rootDir;
private XmlNameTable nameTable = new NameTable( );
private Stack state = new Stack( );
```

CurrentState is a property I've defined for convenience. It returns the current FileSystemState (an internal class which you'll see on the next page) by calling Peek( ) on the state instance variable:

```
private FileSystemState CurrentState {
    get {
        return (FileSystemState)state.Peek( );
    }
}
```

These two GetChildren( ) convenience methods, the instance version of which calls the static version, know how to return only the child nodes that you're interested in. For example, if the current node is the year2002 element, you're only interested in seeing its elements whose names begin with month, not any other files or directories that happen to be in the year2002 directory:

```
private FileSystemInfo [] GetChildren( ) {
    return GetChildren(CurrentState.Entry);
}
```

```
internal static FileSystemInfo [] GetChildren(FileSystemInfo entry) {
  if (entry is DirectoryInfo) {
    DirectoryInfo dir = (DirectoryInfo)entry;
    if (dir.Name == "POs") {
      return dir.GetDirectories("client*");
    } else if (dir.Name.StartsWith("client")) {
      return dir.GetDirectories("year*");
    } else if (dir.Name.StartsWith("year")) {
      return dir.GetDirectories("month*");
    } else if (dir.Name.StartsWith("month")) {
      return dir.GetDirectories("day*");
    } else if (dir.Name.StartsWith("day")) {
      return dir.GetFiles("po*.xml");
    } else {
      return dir.GetDirectories("POs");
    }
  }
  return new FileSystemInfo [0];
}
```

The Clone() method is required in order to implement the ICloneable interface, which is inherited from XPathNavigator:

```
public override XPathNavigator Clone() {
  FileSystemNavigator fsn = new FileSystemNavigator(CurrentState.Entry);
  fsn.nameTable = this.nameTable;
  return fsn;
}
```

The rest of the methods override XPathNavigator's abstract methods and properties. In the interest of saving space, I've not reproduced the ones that unconditionally return empty string instances (BaseURI, XmlLang, Value, GetAttribute(), GetNamespace(), Prefix NamespaceURI) or false (HasAttributes, MoveToAttribute(), MoveToFirstAttribute(), MoveToNextAttribute(), MoveToNamespace(), MoveToFirstNamespace(), MoveToNextNamespace(). MoveToId()). Since the filesystem model is not described with a URL, and isn't itself XML, the pseudo-elements have no value, and the model does not include attributes or namespaces, these methods and properties are irrelevant.

In this model, each node is either the root or an element. If the current directory is the root directory, the type must be XPathNodeType.Root. Otherwise, it is XPathNodeType.Element:

```
public override XPathNodeType NodeType {
  get {
    if (state.Count == 1)
      return XPathNodeType.Root;
    else
      return XPathNodeType.Element;
  }
}
```

Each element's `Name` is simply the name of the current `FileSystemInfo` entry. Since the filesystem has no namespace, the `Name` is the same as the `LocalName`. Within `LocalName`, the name is added to the `nameTable` instance variable so that atomized string comparisons use the `XmlNameTable` properly:

```
public override string LocalName {
  get {
string name = CurrentState.Entry.Name;
    nameTable.Add(name);
    return name;
  }
}

public override string Name {
  get {
    return LocalName;
  }
}
```

The `NameTable` property simply returns the `nameTable` instance variable.

```
public override XmlNameTable NameTable {
  get {
    return nameTable;
  }
}
```

Any node with no children is empty. The `HasChildren` property uses the `GetChildren( )` convenience method to get, and count, the child nodes:

```
public override bool IsEmptyElement {
  get {
    return !HasChildren;
  }
}

public override bool HasChildren {
  get {
    return (GetChildren( ).Length > 0);
  }
}
```

The `MoveTo*( )` methods make sure that the `FileSystemState` at the top of the stack always reflects the right information. To do this, it changes the `Entry` and `Position` variables, as necessary. Additionally, `MoveToParent( )` pops the `FileSystemState` off the top of the stack, and `MoveToFirstChild( )` pushes a new one on. `MoveToRoot( )` and `MoveToDocumentElement( )` clear the stack and push a new `FileSystemState` on, representing the top of the tree:

```
public override bool MoveToNext( ) {
  if (CurrentState.Position < CurrentState.Siblings.Length - 1) {
    CurrentState.Entry = CurrentState.Siblings[++CurrentState.Position];
    return true;
  } else {
```

```
        return false;
      }
    }

    public override bool MoveToPrevious() {
      if (CurrentState.Position > 0) {
        CurrentState.Entry = CurrentState.Siblings[--CurrentState.Position];
        return true;
      } else {
        return false;
      }
    }

    public override bool MoveToFirst() {
      CurrentState.Position = 0;
      CurrentState.Entry = CurrentState.Siblings[CurrentState.Position];
      return true;
    }

    public override bool MoveToFirstChild(){
      FileSystemInfo [] children = GetChildren();
      if (children.Length > 0) {
        state.Push(new FileSystemState(children[0]));
        return true;
      } else {
        return false;
      }
    }

    public override bool MoveToParent() {
      if (CurrentState.Entry == rootDir) {
        return false;
      } else {
        state.Pop();
        return true;
      }
    }

    public override void MoveToRoot() {
      state.Clear();
      state.Push(new FileSystemState(rootDir));
    }

    public bool MoveToDocumentElement() {
      MoveToRoot();
      return true;
    }

    public override bool MoveTo( XPathNavigator other ) {
      if (other is FileSystemNavigator) {
        FileSystemNavigator fsn = (FileSystemNavigator)other;
        state = fsn.state;
        return true;
      }
```

```
      return false;
   }
```

`IsSamePosition()` compares this `XPathNavigator` to another one, returning true if they share the same `XmlImplementation` and `XmlDocument`, and if they both share the same context node:

```
public override bool IsSamePosition( XPathNavigator other ) {
   if (other is FileSystemNavigator) {
      FileSystemNavigator fsn = (FileSystemNavigator)other;
      if (CurrentState == fsn.CurrentState) {
         return true;
      }
   }
   return false;
}
```

As I've already described, the `FileSystemState` class is used internally in the `FileSystemNavigator` to hold the data about a filesystem entry, which is represented as a node in the XML tree, and about its siblings:

```
internal class FileSystemState {
   public FileSystemInfo Entry;
   public int Position;
   public FileSystemInfo [] Siblings;

   public FileSystemState(FileSystemInfo dir) {
      Entry = dir;
      Position = 0;
      if (dir is DirectoryInfo) {
         Siblings = FileSystemNavigator.GetChildren(((DirectoryInfo)dir).Parent);
      } else {
         Siblings = FileSystemNavigator.GetChildren(((FileInfo)dir).Directory);
      }
   }

   public override bool Equals(object other) {
   FileSystemState state = other as FileSystemState;
   if (state != null && state.GetHashCode() == GetHashCode()) {
      return true;
   } else {
      return false;
   }
   }

   public override int GetHashCode() {
   return Entry.GetHashCode() | Position.GetHashCode();
   }
}
```

Example 6-3 shows the complete `FileSystemNavigator` program.

Example 6-3. FileSystemNavigator

```
using System;
using System.Collections;
using System.IO;
using System.Xml;
using System.Xml.XPath;

public class FileSystemNavigator : XPathNavigator {

  // Constructors

  public FileSystemNavigator( ) {
    rootDir = new DirectoryInfo(Environment.CurrentDirectory);
    state.Push(new FileSystemState(rootDir));
  }

  public FileSystemNavigator(string path) {
    rootDir = new DirectoryInfo(path);
    state.Push(new FileSystemState(rootDir));
  }

  private FileSystemNavigator(FileSystemInfo d) {
    rootDir = (DirectoryInfo)d;
    state.Push(new FileSystemState(rootDir));
  }

  // Private instance variables

  private DirectoryInfo rootDir;
  private XmlNameTable nameTable = new NameTable( );
  private Stack state = new Stack( );

  // private properties

  private FileSystemState CurrentState {
    get {
      return (FileSystemState)state.Peek( );
    }
  }

  // private methods

  private FileSystemInfo [] GetChildren( ) {
    return GetChildren(CurrentState.Entry);
  }

  internal static FileSystemInfo [] GetChildren(FileSystemInfo entry) {
    if (entry is DirectoryInfo) {
      DirectoryInfo dir = (DirectoryInfo)entry;
      if (dir.Name == "POs") {
        return dir.GetDirectories("client*");
      } else if (dir.Name.StartsWith("client")) {
        return dir.GetDirectories("year*");
```

Example 6-3. FileSystemNavigator (continued)

```
      } else if (dir.Name.StartsWith("year")) {
        return dir.GetDirectories("month*");
      } else if (dir.Name.StartsWith("month")) {
        return dir.GetDirectories("day*");
      } else if (dir.Name.StartsWith("day")) {
        return dir.GetFiles("po*.xml");
      } else {
        return dir.GetDirectories("POs");
      }
    }
  }
  return new FileSystemInfo [0];
}

// public methods, from ICloneable

public override XPathNavigator Clone() {
  FileSystemNavigator fsn = new FileSystemNavigator(CurrentState.Entry);
  fsn.nameTable = this.nameTable;
  return fsn;
}

// public methods, from XPathNavigator

public override string BaseURI {
  get {
    return String.Empty;
  }
}

public override string XmlLang {
  get {
    return String.Empty;
  }
}

public override XPathNodeType NodeType {
  get {
    if (state.Count == 1)
      return XPathNodeType.Root;
    else
      return XPathNodeType.Element;
  }
}

public override string LocalName {
  get {
    string name = CurrentState.Entry.Name;
    nameTable.Add(name);
    return name;
  }
}
```

Example 6-3. FileSystemNavigator (continued)

```
public override string NamespaceURI {
  get {
    return nameTable.Add(string.Empty);
  }
}

public override string Name {
  get {
    return LocalName;
  }
}

public override string Prefix {
  get {
    return nameTable.Add(string.Empty);
  }
}

public override string Value {
  get {
    return string.Empty;
  }
}

public override bool IsEmptyElement {
  get {
    return !HasChildren;
  }
}

public override XmlNameTable NameTable {
  get {
    return nameTable;
  }
}

public override bool HasAttributes {
  get {
    return false;
  }
}

public override string GetAttribute( string localName, string namespaceURI ) {
  return string.Empty;
}

public override bool MoveToAttribute( string localName, string namespaceURI ) {
  return false;
}

public override bool MoveToFirstAttribute( ) {
  return false;
```

Example 6-3. FileSystemNavigator (continued)

```csharp
  }

  public override bool MoveToNextAttribute( ) {
    return false;
  }

  public override string GetNamespace(string prefix) {
    return String.Empty;
  }

  public override bool MoveToNamespace(string prefix) {
    return false;
  }

  public override bool MoveToFirstNamespace(XPathNamespaceScope namespaceScope) {
    return false;
  }

  public override bool MoveToNextNamespace(XPathNamespaceScope namespaceScope) {
    return false;
  }

  public override bool HasChildren {
    get {
      return (GetChildren( ).Length > 0);
    }
  }

  public override bool MoveToNext( ) {
    if (CurrentState.Position < CurrentState.Siblings.Length - 1) {
      CurrentState.Entry = CurrentState.Siblings[++CurrentState.Position];
      return true;
    } else {
      return false;
    }
  }

  public override bool MoveToPrevious( ) {
    if (CurrentState.Position > 0) {
      CurrentState.Entry = CurrentState.Siblings[--CurrentState.Position];
      return true;
    } else {
      return false;
    }
  }

  public override bool MoveToFirst( ) {
    CurrentState.Position = 0;
    CurrentState.Entry = CurrentState.Siblings[CurrentState.Position];
    return true;
  }
```

Example 6-3. FileSystemNavigator (continued)

```
public override bool MoveToFirstChild( )  {
  FileSystemInfo [] children = GetChildren( );
  if (children.Length > 0) {
    state.Push(new FileSystemState(children[0]));
    return true;
  } else {
    return false;
  }
}

public override bool MoveToParent( ) {
  if (CurrentState.Entry == rootDir) {
    return false;
  } else {
    state.Pop( );
    return true;
  }
}

public override void MoveToRoot( ) {
  state.Clear( );
  state.Push(new FileSystemState(rootDir));
}

public bool MoveToDocumentElement( ) {
  MoveToRoot( );
  return true;
}

public override bool MoveTo( XPathNavigator other ) {
  if (other is FileSystemNavigator) {
    FileSystemNavigator fsn = (FileSystemNavigator)other;
    state = fsn.state;
    return true;
  }
  return false;
}

public override bool MoveToId( string id ) {
  return false;
}

public override bool IsSamePosition( XPathNavigator other ) {
  if (other is FileSystemNavigator) {
    FileSystemNavigator fsn = (FileSystemNavigator)other;
    if (fsn.CurrentState == CurrentState) {
      return true;
    }
  }
  return false;
}
}
```

Example 6-3. FileSystemNavigator (continued)

```
internal class FileSystemState {
  public FileSystemInfo Entry;
  public int Position;
  public FileSystemInfo [] Siblings;

  public FileSystemState(FileSystemInfo dir) {
    Entry = dir;
    Position = 0;
    if (dir is DirectoryInfo) {
      Siblings = FileSystemNavigator.GetChildren(((DirectoryInfo)dir).Parent);
    } else {
      Siblings = FileSystemNavigator.GetChildren(((FileInfo)dir).Directory);
    }
  }

  public override bool Equals(object other) {
    FileSystemState state = other as FileSystemState;
    if (state != null && state.GetHashCode() == GetHashCode()) {
      return true;
    } else {
      return false;
    }
  }

  public override int GetHashCode() {
    return Entry.GetHashCode() | Position.GetHashCode();
  }
}
```

Now you can navigate the PO directory structure using XPath with the previous code, with one small change to the program in Example 6-2:

```
XPathNavigator navigator = new FileSystemNavigator();
XPathNodeIterator iterator = navigator.Select(xpathExpression);
Console.WriteLine("{0} nodes matched.", iterator.Count);
while (iterator.MoveNext()) {
  Console.WriteLine(iterator.Current.LocalName);
}
writer.Close();
```

Moving On

Now that you've been introduced to the XPath specification, you're ready to learn about another standard that makes use of it. In the next chapter, I'll cover XSLT.

CHAPTER 7

Transforming XML with XSLT

You now know how to read XML from a variety of data sources and formats, write XML documents in different formats from arbitrary data structures, create and manipulate XML documents in memory using the DOM, and navigate through any XML tree using XPath. Each of these functions builds on those that came before to open up a new series of possibilities.

The next logical step is to transform the presentation of XML data from one format to another. Extensible Stylesheet Language Transformations (XSLT) is designed to do just that.

Extensible Stylesheet Language (XSL) is a language designed to provide presentation for the content of XML documents. It is composed of three parts: XSLT, XPath (which you're already familiar with from Chapter 6), and XSL Formatting Objects (XSL-FO).

In this chapter, I'll show you XSLT and the .NET assembly that deals with it, System. Xml.Xsl. But first, some background.

The Standards

The terms XSL and XSLT, while similar, do not refer to the same W3C specification. XSL, the Extensible Stylesheet Language itself, is simply a language for expressing stylesheets. A stylesheet is a document that controls the presentation of an XML document of a given type. XSL can be thought of as analogous to Cascading Style Sheets (CSS); in fact, XSL shares most of its properties with CSS2, although they have different syntaxes.

XSLT, the XSL Transformation language, is a subset of XSL that was originally designed to perform transformations of XML elements into complex styles, such as nested tables and indexes. XSLT is designed to be usable independent of XSL; however, its use is constrained by its design as a transformation language for the sorts of tasks required by XSL.

Despite the differences, you'll often see the acronyms XSL and XSLT used interchangeably. Unless the speaker is describing complete formatting systems, odds are good that XSL is probably actually a mis-cited reference to XSLT. To add to the confusion, Microsoft has chosen to call the .NET XSLT namespace System.Xml.Xsl.

XSL-FO, or XSL Formatting Objects, provides additional, more complex formatting for XML content. However, Microsoft does not implement any specific XSL-FO functionality in .NET, so it is outside the scope of this chapter. If you're interested in learning about XSL-FO, you should look into one of the available books about it, such as *XSL-FO* (O'Reilly) or *Definitive XSL-FO* (Prentice Hall).

Introducing XSLT

A document written in XSLT, referred to as a *stylesheet*, describes the transformation of a particular type of XML document into another format. These other formats can include not only XML languages, such as HTML and Scalable Vector Graphics (SVG), but languages using other syntaxes, such as plain text, Comma Separated Values (CSV), and any number of others—including your choice of proprietary formats. In fact, the range of output formats is limited only by the amount of work you want to do to create the appropriate stylesheet—or to locate an appropriate stylesheet created by a third party.

XSLT can be thought of as a *little language*, providing complete functionality for a limited set of tasks. A little language is defined as a specialized, concise notation, designed for a specific family of problems. Much simpler than a general-purpose programming language, a little program does a limited number of things very efficiently.

Although it was designed simply to provide for the transformation of XML documents, XSLT is often used to process XML documents in other ways. XSLT can be used to generate summary statistics about XML documents, store information from an XML file in a database, or communicate data from an XML file to a mobile device. Again, the applications are limited only by your imagination.

A Brief Introduction to the XSLT Specification

The XSLT specification was designed with several goals in mind. First, the XSLT stylesheet itself is an XML document. This allows you to manipulate the stylesheet like any other XML document, up to and including transforming the stylesheet itself into another format via XSLT.

Next, the XSLT language is based on pattern matching. In fact, much of the pattern matching power of XSLT comes from the XPath specification, which is discussed in Chapter 6.

Third, like any good functional programming language, each XSLT function is free of side effects. The benefit this design goal creates is that the same function will have the same effect on any source node on which it is invoked, no matter how many times it has already been invoked on that or any other node.

Finally, flow control in XSLT is managed through *iteration* and *recursion*. The concept of iteration will be familiar if you've used C#'s foreach statement. The idea is that, given a collection of nodes, the same set of functions will be applied to each one in order. Recursion should also be familiar to developers experienced with modern programming languages; a recursive function is one that calls itself during its execution.

XSLT processing consists of loading an XML source document into a source tree, applying a series of templates to the nodes in the source tree, and sending the resulting data to a result tree. Where the source document comes from, and where the result document is written to, are left up to the XSLT implementation.

As I've already mentioned, an XSLT stylesheet is an XML document. Any XML document can be considered an XSLT stylesheet if it contains the following namespace declaration, traditionally mapped to the xsl prefix:

```
xmlns:xsl="http://www.w3.org/1999/XSL/Transform"
```

The stylesheet's document element is one of xsl:stylesheet or xsl:transform, which are synonymous, according to the XSLT specification. The remainder of the stylesheet consists of a series of templates, in the form of xsl:template elements. The xsl:template element has a match attribute, the value of which is an XPath expression to be applied to the source tree. When a node in the source tree matches a template, further matching may be done. When all matching is complete, the matching node and other information from the template is written to the result tree. At the end of processing, the result tree is serialized to a document whose form is specified in the stylesheet's xsl:output element.

I'm going to construct a simple XSLT stylesheet, which transforms the *inventory.xml* document from Chapter 5 into an HTML representation of a catalog. Remember that, as with any programming language, there's more than one way to do it. This stylesheet represents just one way to transform the inventory document into HTML.

I'll call this file *catalog.xsl*. Let's examine it one element at a time. To begin with, since the XSLT stylesheet is an everyday XML document, it never hurts to have an XML declaration:

```
<?xml version="1.0" encoding="utf-8"?>
```

The root element of the stylesheet is xsl:stylesheet. Either xsl:stylesheet or xsl:transform *must* be present in an XSLT stylesheet, and the namespace URI and version must be included *exactly* as shown. Different XSLT processors may behave differently, but many will throw a warning or an error if the namespace or version is missing or different:

```
<xsl:stylesheet
  xmlns:xsl="http://www.w3.org/1999/XSL/Transform"
  version="1.0">
```

The xsl:output element indicates the output method for the transformation. The XSLT specification defines three: html, xml, and text. Specific XSLT processor implementations are free to define others. Some output methods allow method-specific attributes; for example, the html and xml output methods allow an indent attribute, to control whether the output is to be indented:

```
<xsl:output method="html"/>
```

The xsl:template element defines a template. The match attribute contains an XPath expression indicating which nodes in the document the template is to be executed for. In this case, the expression is /, which matches the document root. This template will be the first one executed when transforming an XML document:

```
<xsl:template match="/">
```

Anything within the xsl:template element that does not have the xsl prefix will be copied to output verbatim. In this case, upon reading the beginning of the source tree, this stylesheet will cause the HTML header information to be written to the result tree:

```
<html>
  <head>
    <title>Angus Hardware | Online Catalog</title>
  </head>
```

The xsl:apply-templates element indicates that any further templates are to be processed at this point. I'll define a number of other templates later in the stylesheet, and any one of them that match any elements in the source tree would now be executed:

```
<xsl:apply-templates/>
  </html>
```

The stylesheet is an XML document, remember? You have to close every element you open in order for the stylesheet to be valid:

```
</xsl:template>
```

This template matches the inventory element. Since this is the document element, the template's output is the HTML body element, followed by the output of any other matched templates:

```
<xsl:template match="inventory">
  <body bgcolor="#FFFFFF">
    <h1>Angus Hardware</h1>
    <h2>Online Catalog</h2>
    <xsl:apply-templates/>
  </body>
</xsl:template>
```

Upon matching the date element, this template will cause the element's attributes to be output, formatted as month/day/year. Here you can see again that anything within the xsl:template element that does not have the xsl prefix is sent to the output tree verbatim, including character data:

```
<xsl:template match="date">
  <p>Current as of
    <xsl:value-of select="@month" />/<xsl:value-of select="@day" />/<xsl:value-of
select="@year" />
  </p>
</xsl:template>
```

This template outputs a table element and the table header, and applies any other templates for nodes that are found within the items context:

```
<xsl:template match="items">
  <p>Currently available items:</p>
  <table border="1">
    <tr>
      <th>Product Code</th>
      <th>Description</th>
      <th>Unit Price</th>
      <th>Quantity in Stock</th>
    </tr>
    <xsl:apply-templates />
  </table>
</xsl:template>
```

This template is applied to each item element, sending a table row to the output context:

```
<xsl:template match="item">
  <tr>
    <td><xsl:value-of select="@productCode" /></td>
    <td><xsl:value-of select="@description" /></td>
    <td><xsl:value-of select="@unitCost" /></td>
    <td><xsl:value-of select="@quantity" /></td>
  </tr>
</xsl:template>
```

And finally, the stylesheet's document element must be closed:

```
</xsl:stylesheet>
```

Example 7-1 shows the complete stylesheet.

Example 7-1. An XSLT stylesheet for inventory.xml

```
<?xml version="1.0" encoding="utf-8"?>
<xsl:stylesheet
  xmlns:xsl="http://www.w3.org/1999/XSL/Transform"
  version="1.0">

  <xsl:output method="html"/>

  <xsl:template match="/">
    <html>
      <head>
```

Example 7-1. An XSLT stylesheet for inventory.xml (continued)

```
      <title>Angus Hardware | Online Catalog</title>
    </head>
    <xsl:apply-templates/>
  </html>
</xsl:template>

<xsl:template match="inventory">
  <body bgcolor="#FFFFFF">
    <h1>Angus Hardware</h1>
    <h2>Online Catalog</h2>
    <xsl:apply-templates/>
  </body>
</xsl:template>

<xsl:template match="date">
  <p>Current as of
    <xsl:value-of select="@month" />/<xsl:value-of select="@day" />/<xsl:value-of
select="@year" />
</p>
</xsl:template>

<xsl:template match="items">
  <p>Currently available items:</p>
  <table border="1">
    <tr>
      <th>Product Code</th>
      <th>Description</th>
      <th>Unit Price</th>
      <th>Quantity in Stock</th>
    </tr>
    <xsl:apply-templates />
  </table>
</xsl:template>

<xsl:template match="item">
  <tr>
    <td><xsl:value-of select="@productCode" /></td>
    <td><xsl:value-of select="@description" /></td>
    <td><xsl:value-of select="@unitCost" /></td>
    <td><xsl:value-of select="@quantity" /></td>
  </tr>
</xsl:template>

</xsl:stylesheet>
```

Example 7-2 shows the HTML output resulting from processing *inventory.xml* with *catalog.xsl*, and Figure 7-1 shows a screenshot of the HTML in a web browser.

Example 7-2. HTML output from the catalog.xsl stylesheet

```
<html>
  <head>
    <title>Angus Hardware | Online Catalog</title>
```

Example 7-2. HTML output from the catalog.xsl stylesheet (continued)

```
    </head>
    <body bgcolor="#FFFFFF">
      <h1>Angus Hardware</h1>
      <h2>Online Catalog</h2>
      <p>Current as of 6/22/2002</p>
      <p>Currently available items:</p>
      <table border="1">
        <tr>
          <th>Product Code</th>
          <th>Description</th>
          <th>Unit Price</th>
          <th>Number in Stock</th>
        </tr>
        <tr>
          <td>R-273</td>
          <td>14.4 Volt Cordless Drill</td>
          <td>189.95</td>
          <td>15</td>
        </tr>
        <tr>
          <td>1632S</td>
          <td>12 Piece Drill Bit Set</td>
          <td>14.95</td>
          <td>23</td>
        </tr>
      </table>
    </body>
</html>
```

Figure 7-1. Output of the catalog.xsl stylesheet

This sort of transformation is done with a *push model*, in which the source document controls the structure of the result document while the stylesheet controls the appearance of the result document. The other way to use XSLT is a *pull model*, wherein the stylesheet controls both the structure and appearance of the result document, pulling content out of the source document as needed.

I'll show you how to construct a pull model stylesheet to transform the same hardware catalog XML file into a summary text file below. First, the XML declaration and stylesheet element remain the same as with the push model stylesheet:

```
<?xml version="1.0" encoding="utf-8"?>
<xsl:stylesheet
  xmlns:xsl="http://www.w3.org/1999/XSL/Transform"
  version="1.0">
```

For this stylesheet, however, I want the output to go to a plain text file. The xsl:output element takes care of this:

```
<xsl:output method="text" />
```

Finally, the stylesheet has only one template. Because the output method is text, there's no need to put any HTML tags in the stylesheet. The text will be copied out to the result tree verbatim, except for the xsl:value-of element, which uses the sum( ) function to add up the total values of the quanity attributes of all the item elements:

```
<xsl:template match="/">
Angus Hardware
Inventory Summary
========= =======

There are <xsl:value-of select="sum(/inventory/items/item/@quantity)" /> units in
stock.
  </xsl:template>
```

Example 7-3 shows the complete stylesheet.

Example 7-3. Inventory summary stylesheet

```
<?xml version="1.0" encoding="utf-8"?>
<xsl:stylesheet
  xmlns:xsl="http://www.w3.org/1999/XSL/Transform"
  version="1.0">

  <xsl:output method="text" />

  <xsl:template match="/">
Angus Hardware
Inventory Summary
========= =======

There are <xsl:value-of select="sum(/inventory/items/item/@quantity)" /> units in stock.
  </xsl:template>
</xsl:stylesheet>
```

Example 7-4 shows the output resulting from this stylesheet.

Example 7-4. Inventory summary stylesheet output

```
Angus Hardware
Inventory Summary
========= =======

There are 38 units in stock.
```

Like XPath, XSLT itself has much more functionality than I can possibly describe here. Entire books have been written about it; if you are interested in learning more about XSLT, take a look at *XSLT* (O'Reilly) or *Learning XSLT* (O'Reilly).

When to Use XSLT

Using XSLT is entirely appropriate when you need to present XML data in a different format. For example, you may be providing a web site that needs to communicate with a variety of devices. Some devices may speak HTML, some may speak WAP, and some may understand some totally unrelated language, such as PDF, EDIFACT, or Minitel. XSLT can transform your XML source documents into the different formats required for diverse clients.

Another appropriate use for XSLT is when you need a common intermediate format for disparate XML data formats. If you can write XML, it can be transformed into any standard or proprietary XML schema for use in another computing environment. For example, you may wish to convert a proprietary XML format into another company's published XML format.

Pull templates make up another category of good use for XSLT. For example, you can use XSLT with a pull template to create summary documents.

In short, you should use XSLT whenever you need to place the content of an XML document into a different structure.

Using XSLT

`System.Xml.Xsl` is an extremely small namespace. Although it consists of just two exceptions, three types, and two interfaces, it still manages to provide full support for version 1.0 of the W3C XSLT specification, as well as providing additional support for embedded scripting in C#, Visual Basic .NET, and JScript.

Transforming an XML Document

Example 7-5 shows one of the simplest possible XSLT-related programs in C#. Given a source filename, a stylesheet filename, and a destination filename, it transforms the source into the destination using the stylesheet. It will work with any XML source file and any XSLT stylesheet.

Example 7-5. One of the simplest possible XSLT programs

```
using System.Xml.Xsl;

public class Transform {
  public static void Main(string [] args) {
    string source = args[0];
    string stylesheet = args[1];
    string destination = args[2];
    XslTransform transform = new XslTransform( );
    transform.Load(stylesheet);
    transform.Transform(source, destination);
  }
}
```

I won't explain in excruciating detail how this program works, but I will point out a few important facts about the XslTransform type. It only has one property, XmlResolver, and two methods, Load( ) and Transform( ), but it is still one of the most versatile pitchers in the .NET XML bullpen.

First, the Load( ) method has eight overloads. All of them load the specified XSLT stylesheet, but each of them takes the stylesheet in a different parameter type. The stylesheet may be specified as an IXPathNavigable (such as XmlDocument), URL, XmlReader, or XPathNavigator; together, these types cover every possible way to read an XML document. For each Load( ) method that takes one of these parameters, there is another one taking an XmlResolver as the second parameter. This XmlResolver is used to resolve any stylesheets referenced in xsl:import and xsl:include elements.

 xsl:import and xsl:include perform similar, but not identical, functions, Both allow you to place common templates in a separate stylesheet for easy reuse. However, xsl:import can only appear at the beginning of a stylesheet, and any imported templates have a lower priority than the template in the importing stylesheet. In contrast, xsl:include can appear anywhere in a stylesheet, and any included templates have the same priority as those in the including stylesheet.

If an overload of Load( ) with no resolver parameter is used, the default XmlResolver, XmlUrlResolver, is used; if a null instance is passed in, external namespaces are not resolved. The XmlResolver passed in is used only for purposes of loading the specified stylesheet, and is not cached for use in processing the XSL transform.

In version 1.1 of the .NET Framework, an additional parameter of type System.Security.Policy.Evidence is added to several overloads of the Load( ) method. The Evidence type provides information used to authorize assembly access and code generation for any scripts included in the stylesheet. I'll discuss scripting towards the end of this chapter.

Second, the Transform( ) method has a total of nine overloads. One takes two strings, an input URI and an output URI. The others take various combinations of IXPathNavigable or XPathNavigator as the first parameter, an XsltArgumentList as the second parameter, and nothing, a Stream, an XmlWriter, or a TextWriter as the third parameter. Two other overloads take only two parameters and return the result tree as an XmlReader, which can be navigated as you've already seen in Chapter 2.

Finally, in version 1.0 of the .NET Framework, the XmlResolver property contains the XmlResolver used when invoking the XSLT document( ) function. The document( ) function lets you process multiple source documents in a single stylesheet. This XmlResolver may be the same as the one passed in to the Load( ) method, but does not need to be. In version 1.1 of the .NET Framework, this XmlResolver instance is passed as a parameter to the Transform( ) method.

You may never need to do any more than this with XSLT but if you do, you should be aware that there is a lot more you can do with .NET and XSLT.

Associating a Stylesheet with an XML Document

Although it's not part of the actual XSLT specification, there is a way to associate a stylesheet with an XML document. The XML Stylesheet recommendation, Version 1.0, suggests that the xml-stylesheet processing instruction be used to link an XML document to its stylesheets:

```
<?xml-stylesheet href="stylesheet.xsl" type="text/xsl"?>
```

Although you're free to use the xml-stylesheet processing instruction in your source XML document, there is no guarantee that any given XSLT processor will do anything special with it; .NET's XslTransform, for example, does not.

You can make use of the xml-stylesheet processing instruction even though XslTransform does not use it automatically. Let's construct a program that examines the source document for an xml-stylesheet processing instruction, and transforms it according to the href contained within it. I'll just call it *Transform.cs*.

These familiar lines create an instance of XmlDocument and load it from the first command-line argument:

```
public class Transform {
  public static void Main(string [] args) {

    string source = args[0];
    string destination = args[1];

    XmlDocument document = new XmlDocument( );
    document.Load(source);
```

The next line will search the loaded XmlDocument for the XPath expression // processing-instruction('xml-stylesheet'). As you will recall, this expression will match any processing instruction with the target xml-stylesheet. If none is found, SelectSingleNode( ) will return a null instance:

```
XmlProcessingInstruction stylesheetPI =
  (XmlProcessingInstruction)document.SelectSingleNode(
    "//processing-instruction('xml-stylesheet')");
```

After determining that the `xml-stylesheet` processing instruction is present, these lines declare and initialize a couple of variables that will be used in a moment:

```
if (stylesheetPI != null) {
  char [] splitChars = new char [] { ' ', '=' };
  char [] quoteChars = new char [] { '"', '\'' };
  string stylesheet = null;
```

The `XmlProcessingInstruction` has a `Data` property, the contents of which are everything after the target. In this case, the data is `href="stylesheet.xsl" type="text/xsl"`. Here, the `string.Split()` method splits the string on every space and equals sign, returning an array containing four elements: `href`, `"stylesheet.xsl"`, `type`, and `"text/xsl"`:

```
String [] stylesheetParts = stylesheetPI.Data.Split(splitChars);
```

> The content of the `xml-stylesheet` processing instruction may look like two attributes, but it's not. It just happens to look that way for this particular processing instruction. In general, a processing instruction's data format is entirely dependent on the expectations of the processor that is consuming it. In .NET, you have to use `XmlProcessingInstruction.Data` to retrieve the pseudoattributes, and then do the work of parsing them into name/value pairs yourself.

Before proceeding, you need to ensure that the `xml-stylesheet` processing instruction you've located is one that links the document to an XSLT stylesheet. Since the `xml-stylesheet` processing instruction can also be used for CSS stylesheets, for example, this line checks the processing instruction's `Data` property to ensure that it contains the string `text/xsl`:

```
if (stylesheetPI.Data.IndexOf("text/xsl") != -1) {
```

Once you have verified that the processing instruction does specify an XSLT stylesheet, you then need to find the name of the stylesheet referenced. You know that the array should contain four items, and the item following `href` should be the name of the stylesheet. These lines of code pluck that item from the array, trimming off any quote characters at the start and end:

```
int indexOfHref = Array.IndexOf(stylesheetParts,"href");
if (indexOfHref != -1) {
  stylesheet = stylesheetParts[indexOfHref+1].Trim(quoteChar);
}
```

If, at the end of all this processing, the stylesheet is still not an empty `string`, you're ready to use it to transform the source document much as it was done in the first example:

```
if (stylesheet != null) {
  XslTransform transform = new XslTransform();
  transform.Load(stylesheet);
  transform.Transform(source, destination);
}
```

Example 7-6 shows the complete source code listing for *Transform.cs*.

Example 7-6. Using the xml-stylesheet processing instruction

```
using System.Xml;
using System.Xml.Xsl;

public class Transform {
  public static void Main(string [] args) {

    string source = args[0];
    string destination = args[1];

    XmlDocument document = new XmlDocument();
    document.Load(source);

    XmlProcessingInstruction stylesheetPI =
     (XmlProcessingInstruction)document.SelectSingleNode(
        "//processing-instruction('xml-stylesheet')");

      if (stylesheetPI != null) {
      char [] splitChars = new char [] { ' ', '=' };
      char [] quoteChars = new char [] { '"', '\'' };
      string stylesheet = null;

      string [] stylesheetParts = stylesheetPI.Data.Split(splitChars);

      if (stylesheetPI.Data.IndexOf("text/xsl") != -1) {
        int indexOfHref = Array.IndexOf(stylesheetParts,"href");

        if (indexOfHref != -1) {
          stylesheet = stylesheetParts[indexOfHref+1].Trim(quoteChar);
        }
      }

      if (stylesheet != null) {
        XslTransform transform = new XslTransform();
        transform.Load(stylesheet);
        transform.Transform(source, destination);
      }
    }
  }
}
```

The xml-stylesheet processing instruction can also specify the medium to which it applies with the media pseudoattribute; this allows you to transform the source document differently, depending on who's asking. Given what you've seen in Example 7-5, it should be fairly easy to figure out the additional steps to do that. Remember that more than one node may match the //processing-instruction('xml-stylesheet') XPath expression.

I've rewritten the Main( ) method in Example 7-7, with the changes highlighted. Simply put, it executes the transformation for every xsl-stylesheet processing instruction with media pseudoattribute equal to "printer" or no media pseudoattribute. Note that if there is more than one matching processing instruction, it will overwrite the destination file each time.

Example 7-7. Using the xml-stylesheet processing instruction with different media types

```
public static void Main(string [] args) {

  string source = args[0];
  string destination = args[1];

  XmlDocument document = new XmlDocument( );
  document.Load(source);

  XmlNodeList nodeList =
    document.SelectNodes("//processing-instruction('xml-stylesheet')");

  foreach (XmlProcessingInstruction stylesheetPI in nodeList) {
    char [] splitChars = new char [] { ' ', '=' };
    char [] quoteChars = new char [] { '"', '\'' };
    string stylesheet = null;

    string[] stylesheetParts = stylesheetPI.Data.Split(splitChars);

    if (stylesheetPI.Data.IndexOf("text/xsl") != -1) {
      int indexOfHref = Array.IndexOf(stylesheetParts,"href");
      if (indexOfHref != -1) {
        int indexOfMedia = Array.IndexOf(stylesheetParts,"media");
        string media = null;
        if (indexOfMedia != -1) {
          media = stylesheetParts[indexOfMedia+1].Trim(quoteChars);
        }
        if (media == null || media == "printer") {
          stylesheet = stylesheetParts[indexOfHref+1].Trim(quoteChars);
        }
      }
    }

    if (stylesheet != null) {
      XslTransform transform = new XslTransform( );
      transform.Load(stylesheet);
      transform.Transform(source, destination);
    }
  }
}
```

Working with a Stylesheet Programmatically

The real magic of XSLT in .NET comes from the fact that an XSLT stylesheet is just an XML document; therefore, you can create and manipulate the stylesheet just like any other XML document, using the tools you're already familiar with.

Creating a stylesheet

Example 7-8 shows a program that creates the stylesheet in Example 7-1 using XmlWriter. It's fairly straightforward, so I'll let the code speak for itself.

Example 7-8. Creating a stylesheet programmatically

```
using System;
using System.IO;
using System.Xml;
using System.Xml.Xsl;

public class CreateStylesheet {
  private const string ns = "http://www.w3.org/1999/XSL/Transform";

  public static void Main(string [] args) {
    XmlTextWriter writer = new XmlTextWriter(Console.Out);
    writer.Formatting = Formatting.Indented;

    writer.WriteStartDocument();

    writer.WriteStartElement("xsl","stylesheet",ns);
    writer.WriteAttributeString("version","1.0");

    writer.WriteStartElement("xsl:output");
    writer.WriteAttributeString("method","html");
    writer.WriteEndElement();

    CreateRootTemplate(writer);
    CreateInventoryTemplate(writer);
    CreateDateTemplate(writer);
    CreateItemsTemplate(writer);
    CreateItemTemplate(writer);

    writer.WriteEndElement(); // xsl:stylesheet
    writer.WriteEndDocument();
  }

  private static void CreateRootTemplate(XmlWriter writer) {

    writer.WriteStartElement("xsl:template");
    writer.WriteAttributeString("match","/");

    writer.WriteStartElement("html");

    writer.WriteStartElement("head");
```

Example 7-8. Creating a stylesheet programmatically (continued)

```
    writer.WriteStartElement("title");
    writer.WriteString("Angus Hardware | Online Catalog");
    writer.WriteEndElement( ); // title

    writer.WriteEndElement( ); // head

    writer.WriteStartElement("xsl:apply-templates");

    writer.WriteEndElement( ); // xsl:apply-templates
    writer.WriteEndElement( ); // html
    writer.WriteEndElement( ); // xsl:template
}

  private static void CreateInventoryTemplate(XmlWriter writer) {
    writer.WriteStartElement("xsl:template");
    writer.WriteAttributeString("match","inventory");

    writer.WriteStartElement("body");
    writer.WriteAttributeString("bgcolor","#FFFFFF");

    writer.WriteStartElement("h1");
    writer.WriteString("Angus Hardware");
    writer.WriteEndElement( ); // h1

    writer.WriteStartElement("h2");
    writer.WriteString("Online Catalog");
    writer.WriteEndElement( ); // h2

    writer.WriteStartElement("xsl:apply-templates");
    writer.WriteEndElement( );

    writer.WriteEndElement( ); // body
    writer.WriteEndElement( ); // xsl:template
}

  private static void CreateDateTemplate(XmlWriter writer) {
    writer.WriteStartElement("xsl:template");
    writer.WriteAttributeString("match","date");

    writer.WriteStartElement("p");

    writer.WriteString("Current as of ");

    writer.WriteStartElement("xsl:value-of");
    writer.WriteAttributeString("select", "@month");
    writer.WriteEndElement( ); // xsl:value-of

    writer.WriteString("/");

    writer.WriteStartElement("xsl:value-of");
    writer.WriteAttributeString("select", "@day");
    writer.WriteEndElement( ); // xsl:value-of
```

Example 7-8. Creating a stylesheet programmatically (continued)

```
    writer.WriteString("/");

    writer.WriteStartElement("xsl:value-of");
    writer.WriteAttributeString("select", "@year");
    writer.WriteEndElement( ); // xsl:value-of

    writer.WriteEndElement( ); // p
    writer.WriteEndElement( ); // xsl-template
  }

  private static void CreateItemsTemplate(XmlWriter writer) {
    writer.WriteStartElement("xsl:template");
    writer.WriteAttributeString("match","items");

    writer.WriteStartElement("p");
    writer.WriteString("Currently available items:");
    writer.WriteEndElement( ); // p

    writer.WriteStartElement("table");
    writer.WriteAttributeString("border","1");

    writer.WriteStartElement("tr");

    writer.WriteStartElement("th");
    writer.WriteString("Product Code");
    writer.WriteEndElement( ); // th

    writer.WriteStartElement("th");
    writer.WriteString("Description");
    writer.WriteEndElement( ); // th

    writer.WriteStartElement("th");
    writer.WriteString("Unit Price");
    writer.WriteEndElement( ); // th

    writer.WriteStartElement("th");
    writer.WriteString("Number in Stock");
    writer.WriteEndElement( ); // th

    writer.WriteStartElement("xsl:apply-templates");
    writer.WriteEndElement( ); // xsl:apply-templates

    writer.WriteEndElement( ); // tr
    writer.WriteEndElement( ); // table
    writer.WriteEndElement( ); // xsl:template
  }

  private static void CreateItemTemplate(XmlWriter writer) {
    writer.WriteStartElement("xsl:template");
    writer.WriteAttributeString("match","item");
```

Example 7-8. Creating a stylesheet programmatically (continued)

```
    writer.WriteStartElement("tr");

    writer.WriteStartElement("td");
    writer.WriteStartElement("xsl:value-of");
    writer.WriteAttributeString("select","@productCode");
    writer.WriteEndElement( ); // xsl:value-of
    writer.WriteEndElement( ); // td

    writer.WriteStartElement("td");
    writer.WriteStartElement("xsl:value-of");
    writer.WriteAttributeString("select","@description");
    writer.WriteEndElement( ); // xsl:value-of
    writer.WriteEndElement( ); // td

    writer.WriteStartElement("td");
    writer.WriteStartElement("xsl:value-of");
    writer.WriteAttributeString("select","@unitCost");
    writer.WriteEndElement( ); // xsl:value-of
    writer.WriteEndElement( ); // td

    writer.WriteStartElement("td");
    writer.WriteStartElement("xsl:value-of");
    writer.WriteAttributeString("select","@quantity");
    writer.WriteEndElement( ); // xsl:value-of
    writer.WriteEndElement( ); // td

    writer.WriteEndElement( ); // xsl:template

    writer.WriteEndElement( ); // xsl:
  }
}
```

This example is just one of many ways to create a stylesheet programmatically. In this case, I've used XmlTextWriter, which I introduced in Chapter 4, to create the document and write it to a file. I also could have created an XmlTextWriter from any other sort of Stream or TextWriter; for example, I could have written the XML to a MemoryStream, and then turned around and used that MemoryStream in the constructor of an XmlTextReader, which can be passed to XsltTransform's Load( ) method.

Assuming you had something like the code in Example 7-8 in a private method called WriteStylesheet( ), the following snippet would write the stylesheet to a memory buffer, then cause it to be loaded and used to transform an XML document from an input tree to an output tree:

```
MemoryStream stream = new MemoryStream( );
XmlTextWriter writer = new XmlTextWriter(stream, Encoding.UTF8);
this.WriteStylesheet(writer);

stream.Seek(SeekOrigin.begin, 0);

XslTransform transform = new XslTransform( );
```

```
transform.Load(new XmlTextReader(stream));

transform.Transform(input, output);
```

Manipulating an existing stylesheet

Just like any XML document, an XSLT stylesheet can be loaded into an XmlDocument and manipulated via the DOM, or navigated with XPath. For example, if you have a stylesheet on disk but wish to change the order of some nodes, you could load it into an XmlDocument, navigate to the desired node with SelectSingleNode( ), and then detach that node from its current location and place it into its new location.

Scripting with XslTransform

Creating and manipulating stylesheets is all well and good if all you need to do is use XSLT's built-in abilities. But .NET's XSLT tools can do a lot more. They allow you to execute arbitrary C#, Visual Basic, or JScript code embedded in the stylesheet, pass arguments to the XSLT processor, and call back to methods in your own C# code from expressions in the XSLT code.

Embedded scripts

.NET has the ability to interpret script code embedded within the XSLT stylesheet. Example 7-9 shows the same catalog.xsl stylesheet shown previously, but with a few minor changes. I'll explain the highlighted changes.

Example 7-9. Catalog stylesheet with embedded scripting

```
<?xml version="1.0" encoding="utf-8"?>
<xsl:stylesheet
  xmlns:xsl="http://www.w3.org/1999/XSL/Transform"
  xmlns:msxsl="urn:schemas-microsoft-com:xslt"
  xmlns:angus="http://angushardware.com/"
  version="1.0">

  <msxsl:script implements-prefix="angus" language="C#">
    <![CDATA[
      decimal CalculateInventoryValue(int number, decimal unitCost) {
          return number * unitCost;
      }
    ]]>
  </msxsl:script>

  <xsl:output method="html"/>

  <xsl:template match="/">
    <html>
      <head>
        <title>Angus Hardware | Online Catalog</title>
      </head>
```

Example 7-9. Catalog stylesheet with embedded scripting (continued)

```
      <xsl:apply-templates/>
    </html>
  </xsl:template>

  <xsl:template match="inventory">
    <body bgcolor="#FFFFFF">
      <h1>Angus Hardware</h1>
      <h2>Online Catalog</h2>
      <xsl:apply-templates/>
    </body>
  </xsl:template>

  <xsl:template match="date">
    <p>Current as of <xsl:value-of select="@month" />/<xsl:value-of select="@day" />/<xsl:
value-of select="@year" />
    </p>
  </xsl:template>

  <xsl:template match="items">
    <p>Currently available items:</p>
    <table border="1">
      <tr>
        <th>Product Code</th>
        <th>Description</th>
        <th>Unit Price</th>
        <th>Number in Stock</th>
        <th>Value of Inventory</th>
      </tr>
      <xsl:apply-templates />
    </table>
  </xsl:template>

  <xsl:template match="item">
    <tr>
      <td><xsl:value-of select="@productCode" /></td>
      <td><xsl:value-of select="@description" /></td>
      <td><xsl:value-of select="@unitCost" /></td>
      <td><xsl:value-of select="@quantity" /></td>
      <td><xsl:value-of select="angus:CalculateInventoryValue(@quantity,@unitCost)"/></td>
    </tr>
  </xsl:template>

</xsl:stylesheet>
```

Each new section of code is explained below:

```
xmlns:msxsl="urn:schemas-microsoft-com:xslt"
```

To use the scripting capabilities of XsltTransform, the stylesheet must include the namespace urn:schemas-microsoft-com:xslt. By convention, this namespace is mapped to the msxsl prefix:

```
xmlns:angus="http://angushardware.com/"
```

Each piece of script code in the stylesheet must belong to a namespace as well. This can be thought of as equivalent to a .NET assembly namespace. In this case, I've defined the namespace http://angushardware.com/ with the prefix angus:

```
<msxsl:script implements-prefix="angus" language="C#">
  <![CDATA[
    decimal CalculateInventoryValue(int number, decimal unitCost) {
        return number * unitCost;
    }
  ]]>
</msxsl:script>
```

Now the CalculateInventoryValue() method is defined, to return the total value of the stock on hand for each product type. The msxsl:script element indicates that this is a block of code. The implements-prefix attribute indicates that the code is associated with the angus prefix, and the language attribute indicates that this block of code is written in C#.

Although the permissible values of the msxsl:script element's language attribute are C#, CSharp, VisualBasic, VB, JScript, and JavaScript, all code with the same implements-prefix attribute value must use the same language. The default language is JScript. The language attribute is case insensitive, so VisualBasic and visualbasic are equivalent; and C# is an alias for CSharp, just as VisualBasic is for VB and JavaScript is for JScript.

The code within this msxsl:script element is enclosed within a CDATA section; while not strictly necessary, this is strongly recommended to avoid XML parsing problems.

The CalculateInventoryValue() method itself should require no further explanation:

```
<td><xsl:value-of select="angus:CalculateInventoryValue(@quantity,@unitCost)"/></td>
```

In this portion of the stylesheet, the CalculateInventoryValue() method defined previously is actually invoked. The xsl:value-of element converts the expression in the select attribute into a text node; in this case, the expression is the call to CalculateInventoryValue(), with the angus prefix. The parameters passed into the method are themselves XPath expressions, and they are coerced into the appropriate types (int and decimal, respectively) by XSLT.

The result of transforming the *inventory.xml* document with this stylesheet appears in Example 7-10, with changes highlighted.

Example 7-10. New HTML catalog output

```
<html xmlns:msxsl="urn:schemas-microsoft-com:xslt" xmlns:angus="http://angushardware.com/
">
  <head>
    <META http-equiv="Content-Type" content="text/html; charset=utf-8">
    <title>Angus Hardware | Online Catalog</title>
  </head>
```

Example 7-10. New HTML catalog output (continued)

```html
<body bgcolor="#FFFFFF">
  <h1>Angus Hardware</h1>
  <h2>Online Catalog</h2>
  <p>Current as of 6/22/2002</p>
  <p>Currently available items:</p>
  <table border="1">
    <tr>
      <th>Product Code</th>
      <th>Description</th>
      <th>Unit Price</th>
      <th>Number in Stock</th>
      <th>Value of Inventory</th>
    </tr>
    <tr>
      <td>R-273</td>
      <td>14.4 Volt Cordless Drill</td>
      <td>189.95</td>
      <td>15</td>
      <td>2849.25</td>
    </tr>
    <tr>
      <td>1632S</td>
      <td>12 Piece Drill Bit Set</td>
      <td>14.95</td>
      <td>23</td>
      <td>343.85</td>
    </tr>
  </table>
</body>
</html>
```

The obvious difference is the new fifth column on the HTML table in the output. In addition, the `msxsl` and `angus` namespaces are included in the `html` element, even though they are not used in the output document.

This technique of embedding code in the stylesheet can be quite convenient, because changes to the embedded code do not require you to recompile any C# code. However, embedded code is not portable to XSLT processors that do not support the languages in question or the `urn:schemas-microsoft-com:xslt` namespace. For that reason, passing additional arguments to the XSLT processor becomes an interesting solution.

Adding parameters with XsltArgumentList

`XsltArgumentList` is a type which may be passed as a parameter to most of the `XslTransform.Transform()` overloads. It allows additional parameters and extensions to be passed to the XSLT processor.

Compared to embedded scripting, `XsltArgumentList` provides for better encapsulation and code reuse, enables you to keep stylesheets smaller and thus more easily maintainable, supports use of classes in other namespaces besides those supported by XslTransform, and allows node fragments to be passed to the stylesheet using XPathNavigator.

There are two ways of using XsltArgumentList. The first allows you to pass a parameter into the stylesheet, to be replaced in the output tree whenever the xsl:value-of element with that name is evaluated.

The following code would set a parameter named greeting to a value of Hello!:

```
XslTransform transform = new XslTransform( );
transform.Load(stylesheet);

XsltArgumentList argList = new XsltArgumentList( );
argList.AddParam("greeting","","Hello!");

transform.Transform(new XPathDocument(source), argList, new
  StreamWriter(destination));
```

In the stylesheet, you would first need to declare the parameter with the following element:

```
<xsl:param name="greeting" />
```

The xsl:param element can appear either at the top-level element or within an xsl:template element. The parameter thus declared will then be scoped at the level of xsl:param's parent. The name attribute is required, and is used to map the name passed in to its value.

 xsl:param has an optional attribute, select, which can be used to define the parameter's value, although this defeats the purpose of XsltArgumentList.

To refer to the parameter within that scope, you can think of it as another XPath expression. The stylesheet uses the name of the parameter prefixed with a dollar sign ($) in the select attribute of an xsl:value-of element:

```
<xsl:value-of select="$greeting" />
```

Adding extensions with XsltArgumentList

In addition to direct parameter replacement, XsltArgumentList enables you to associate your own C# code with an xsl:value-of element. For example, you may wish to create a type that has a property to output today's date:

```
public class Utilities {
  public string Today {
    get {
      return DateTime.Now.ToString( );
    }
  }
}
```

The Utilities type simply has one property, Today, which returns a string representation of the current date and time. You could add other properties and methods, including methods that take parameters.

XSLT extensions only work with the *methods* of extension types, not their *properties*. However, if you know a simple trick, you can access properties just like methods. The trick to remember is that the C# compiler creates a method named get_XXX() for each property named XXX. So you can access a property named Today by using util:get_Today() in the select attribute of xsl:value-of.

Now, it's simply a matter of instantiating a Utilities object, and adding it to the XsltArgumentList. The changed lines of the source code are highlighted:

```
XslTransform transform = new XslTransform();
transform.Load(stylesheet);

XsltArgumentList argList = new XsltArgumentList();
argList.AddParam("greeting","","Hello!");
argList.AddExtensionObject("urn:Utilities", new Utilities());

transform.Transform(new XPathDocument(source), argList, new
  StreamWriter(destination));
```

The XsltArgumentList.AddExtensionObject() method allows you to associate a type with a qualified name in the stylesheet. In this example, urn:Utilities is the qualified name.

In order to use Utilities.Today(), you must make some small changes in *catalog.xsl*:

```
<xsl:stylesheet
  xmlns:xsl="http://www.w3.org/1999/XSL/Transform"
  xmlns:util="urn:Utilities"
version="1.0">
...
  <xsl:template match="inventory">
    <body bgcolor="#FFFFFF">
      <h1>Angus Hardware</h1>
      <h2>Online Catalog</h2>
      <p><xsl:value-of select="$greeting" /></p>
      <p><xsl:value-of select="util:get_Today()" /></p>
      <xsl:apply-templates/>
    </body>
</xsl:template>
```

In these lines, the util prefix is associated with the urn:Utilities namespace, and util:get_Today() is invoked in the select expression of an xsl:value-of element.

The relevant section of the HTML output is shown below:

```
<h1>Angus Hardware</h1>
<h2>Online Catalog</h2>
<p>Hello!</p>
<p>7/27/2002 7:14:57 PM</p>
<p>Current as of 6/22/2002</p>
```

An extension need not be a custom type. For example, to insert the XSLT process name and process ID into the output tree, you might add a System.Diagnostics. Process instance to the XsltArgumentList:

```
argList.AddExtensionObject("urn:Process",Process.GetCurrentProcess());
```

And then you could call the urn:Process extension from your XSLT stylesheet:

```
<xsl:stylesheet
  xmlns:xsl="http://www.w3.org/1999/XSL/Transform"
  xmlns:util="urn:Utilities"
  xmlns:proc="urn:Process"
  version="1.0">
...
<p>Generated by <xsl:value-of select="proc:get_ProcessName()" />,
  process ID <xsl:value-of select="proc:get_Id()" /></p>
```

Be careful when making a non-custom extension available to XSLT. Instead of proc:get_ProcessName( ), you could easily have called proc: Kill( ), which would terminate the XSLT processor—and any other threads in the same process, such as a web server—in mid-stream. When you make a type available as an extension, you make *all* its public methods available.

Moving On

In addition to all the simple XML reading, writing, manipulation, and navigation you started with, you have now seen how to create and use one particular type of XML document, the XSLT stylesheet. You should have learned a little bit about the XSLT language, and how to pass parameters and extension objects to it in order to customize your output.

Continuing along this theme, I'll show you another very specific type of XML document next, the W3C XML Schema definition document. Though you've already seen some use of XML Schema earlier in Chapter 2, in Chapter 8 I'll present a more in-depth look at W3C XML Schema and what it can do for you.

CHAPTER 8

Constraining XML with Schemas

Reading, writing, manipulating, navigating, and transforming an XML document is all well and good if you know what the document is supposed to look like. That's likely to be the case if you're developing tools in-house to deal with data formats that you control; but if you want to interchange XML data with other systems, you would probably find it convenient to define a more rigid structure for your documents.

You're not the only one to think of that, of course. Although the original XML specification included Document Type Definitions as an optional mechanism for defining a document's structure, developers quickly outgrew DTD's fairly limited capabilities. The World Wide Web Consortium developed W3C XML Schema to provide a mechanism for creating more formalized structure for XML documents. XML Schema was formally adopted as a W3C recommendation in 2001.

In this chapter, you'll learn about W3C XML Schema, and how .NET implements it. You'll see how to create XML Schemas using the .NET XML Schemas/DataTypes support utility. You'll work with schemas through both the standard XML types and the System.Xml.Schema assembly. And you'll look at some examples of data interchange, using XML Schema to constrain and validate XML data.

Introducing W3C XML Schema

W3C XML Schema is a standard that provides additional control over the structure of XML documents. A formalized structure allows for the following tasks:

validation
Ensuring that a document has all required elements and attributes, in the required order.

documentation
Informing users and developers what elements and attributes are required.

querying
If you know the document's structure, you can navigate it more efficiently.

data binding

When you know the document's structure, you can mirror it in other data structures and transfer data back and forth between them more efficiently.

editing

If you know the document structure, editing tools can provide guidance in creating and manipulating a document.

Simultaneously with the development of W3C XML Schema, other groups that saw the need for formalized XML document structure developed other schema languages. RELAX NG and Schematron are the results of some of these efforts; however, neither have the cachet of being an official W3C recommendation.

.NET supports W3C XML Schema version 1.0, Part 1 (XML Schemas for Structures) and Part 2 (XML Schemas for DataTypes). In addition, the XML Schema recommendation also includes Part 0, a primer. If you are interested in learning more about XML Schema than this book can provide, the Primer is a good place to start.

 The official W3C recommendations for Part 0, Part 1, and Part 2 are available at *http://www.w3.org/TR/xmlschema-0/*, *http://www.w3.org/TR/xmlschema-1/*, and *http://www.w3.org/TR/xmlschema-2/*, respectively.

Using W3C XML Schema

An XML Schema document (XSD), like an XSLT stylesheet, is itself an XML document. It may contain an XML declaration, and must contain a namespace declaration for the URI http://www.w3.org/2001/XMLSchema. This namespace is traditionally mapped to the prefix xs. The document element of an XSD is xs:schema; the simplest possible XSD, therefore, is the following:

```
<?xml version="1.0"?>
<xs:schema xmlns:xs="http://www.w3.org/2001/XMLSchema" />
```

Of course, this XSD defines no structure, so it is mostly useless. To be more useful, it should include at least one element, representing the document element of the XML document it describes:

```
<?xml version="1.0"?>
<xs:schema xmlns:xs="http://www.w3.org/2001/XMLSchema">
  <xs:element name="Customer" />
</xs:schema>
```

The xs:element element is called a *particle*. A particle can be thought of as representing a single unit of markup, or a grouping of such units. Other particles include xs:attribute, xs:choice, and xs:sequence, among others. xs:all, xs:sequence and xs:choice are also *compositors*, elements that define groups of particles.

A document using this schema would need to have the following content in order to be valid:

```
<Customer />
```

 You may have already noticed that I've deviated from the style used in earlier parts of this book by capitalizing the first letter of the Customer element. I'll be capitalizing the first letter of every element and attribute name in this XSD. Hold that thought! I'll explain the different style in a little while.

Still not very useful, is it? Let's add a little more to the XML Schema, *customer.xsd*:

```
<?xml version="1.0"?>
<xs:schema xmlns:xs="http://www.w3.org/2001/XMLSchema" version="1.0">
  <xs:element name="Customer">
    <xs:complexType>
      <xs:sequence>
        <xs:element name="Name" />
      </xs:sequence>
    </xs:complexType>
  </xs:element>
</xs:schema>
```

The xs:complexType schema element indicates that its enclosing element's content is more than just simple text; it actually has *structure*. This can be thought of as the real minimum requirement for using XML Schema, because a schema for a document with an empty document element is not very useful at all.

The xs:sequence element contains an ordered list of elements. Other compositors include xs:choice, which indicates that any one of the listed elements may appear, and xs:all, which indicates that the listed elements may appear in any order.

With xs:sequence, I've now defined a document structure that looks like this:

```
<Customer>
  <Name>Amalgamated Construction</name>
</Customer>
```

In order to constrain the number of times an element may appear in a sequence, you can add the minOccurs and maxOccurs attributes. Once you have done that, you might as well define the type of data that appears in the Name element as well. The new schema looks like this:

```
<?xml version="1.0"?>
<xs:schema xmlns:xs="http://www.w3.org/2001/XMLSchema" version="1.0">
  <xs:element name="Customer">
    <xs:complexType>
      <xs:sequence>
        <xs:element name="Name" minOccurs="1" maxOccurs="1" type="xs:token" />
      </xs:sequence>
    </xs:complexType>
  </xs:element>
</xs:schema>
```

Now you're constrained to exactly one `Name` element, and its content may consist of any valid XML token (a string with any whitespace collapsed). By virtue of its data type constraint, this relatively simple XSD is already more complex than anything that could have been defined with a DTD.

The values of `minOccurs` and `maxOccurs` both default to 1, so this change was not strictly necessary, and I'll omit them in the rest of the examples if they have the default values. The value of `minOccurs` must be a nonnegative integer, while `maxOccurs` may be any nonnegative integer greater than or equal to `minOccurs`, or the literal string "unbounded".

The type attribute can take on any of quite a number of values, for predefined types. It can also hold custom types, as you'll see in a moment.

This schema is acceptable, but customers have more information that could appear in the XML document. Customers should also have a customer ID and an address:

```
<?xml version="1.0"?>
<xs:schema xmlns:xs="http://www.w3.org/2001/XMLSchema" version="1.0">
  <xs:element name="Customer">
    <xs:complexType>
      <xs:sequence>
        <xs:element name="Name" type="xs:token" />
        <xs:element name="Address" maxOccurs="unbounded" type="xs:string" />
      </xs:sequence>
      <xs:attribute name="Id" type="xs:ID" />
    </xs:complexType>
  </xs:element>
</xs:schema>
```

The document can now have one or more `Address` elements, containing data of type `xs:string` (that is, character data with whitespace retained) to hold freeform address information. According to the schema, the `Address` elements must come after the `Name` element, because `xsd:sequence` constrains the order of elements. I've also added an `Id` attribute to the `Customer` element. `Id`'s value is of type `xs:ID` (it must contain only alphanumeric data or the punctuation marks _, -, ., and :; must begin with a non-numeric character; and must be unique amongst all attributes of type `xs:ID` in the document).

That `Address` element is not quite right, though. Although a freeform address may work well enough for many purposes, it really doesn't take proper advantage of XML's promise of structured data. Instead, a better document structure would look like this:

```
<Customer id="customer.8873">
  <Name>Amalgamated Construction</Name>
  <Address>
    <Street>81 San Leandro Blvd</Street>
    <Street>Suite 5D</Street>
    <City>Albequerque</City>
    <State>NM</State>
```

```
        <Zip>08765-9999</Zip>
      </Address>
    </Customer>
```

The XSD for this document could be the following:

```
<?xml version="1.0"?>
<xs:schema xmlns:xs="http://www.w3.org/2001/XMLSchema" version="1.0">
  <xs:element name="Customer">
    <xs:complexType>
      <xs:sequence>
        <xs:element name="Name" type="xs:token" />
        <xs:element name="Address" maxOccurs="unbounded">
          <xs:complexType>
            <xs:sequence>
              <xs:element name="Street" maxOccurs="3" type="xs:string" />
              <xs:element name="City" type="xs:string" />
              <xs:element name="State" type="xs:string" />
              <xs:element name="Zip" type="USZipCodeType" />
            </xs:sequence>
          </xs:complexType>
        </xs:element>
      </xs:sequence>
      <xs:attribute name="Id" type="xs:ID"/>
    </xs:complexType>
  </xs:element>

  <xs:simpleType name="USZipCodeType">
    <xs:restriction base="xs:token">
      <xs:pattern value="\d{5}(-\d{4})?" />
    </xs:restriction>
  </xs:simpleType>
</xs:schema>
```

With these changes, Address becomes an element which must have from one to three
Street elements, and exactly one each of City, State, and Zip elements. I also added
in a new twist by defining a simple type called USZipCodeType.

The xs:simpleType element defines USZipCodeType, a type that can be used in multiple places within the XSD. In this case, the type represents a United States zip code,
which must be composed of either five numerals, or five numerals followed by a
hyphen and four numerals; that is, nnnnn or nnnnn-nnnn. This pattern is expressed by
the regular expression \d{5}(-\d{4})?. The xs:restriction and xs:pattern elements
work together to restrict the value to a token that matches the regular expression in
the value attribute.

> XML Schema's regular expression syntax is based on Perl regular
> expressions, with some minor differences. To learn more about regular
> expressions, see *Mastering Regular Expressions, 2nd Edition* (O'Reilly).

Clearly you can keep going with this pattern of adding elements and attributes until the document is perfectly modeled. To sound a familiar refrain, XML Schema can do a lot more than this; see Eric van der Vlist's *XML Schema* (O'Reilly) to learn more.

When to Use W3C XML Schema

You should probably create XML Schema for your XML documents if any of the following apply:

- The order and number of nodes in your document must be constrained.
- The data within your document's nodes must be constrained more specifically than a DTD allows.
- You wish to generate code to read and write XML to and from .NET types or a relational database using `XmlSerializer` or `XmlDataDocument`.

Conversely, you should strongly consider sticking with validation by DTD only if all of the following apply:

- Nodes may appear in your XML document in any order and number.
- The data in your document's nodes may be free-form, and need not be constrained.
- You will be reading and writing data to and from XML documents only using `XmlReader`, `XmlWriter`, `XmlDocument`, `XPathDocument`, and the other built-in .NET XML types.

Other Ways to Constrain XML Structure

Although DTDs also provide a means of constraining XML, and validation using DTDs is supported by .NET, they do not provide as much control over XML content as XML Schema does. For example, a DTD cannot specify the required order of elements or attributes, nor can it enforce the data type of element or attribute content. XML Schema was actually designed to make up for DTD's lack of functionality, and does so quite well.

A common complaint about XML Schema, however, is that it is actually *too* complex. RELAX NG was developed concurrently with XML Schema, has been adopted as a standard by the Organization for the Advancement of Structured Information Standards (OASIS), and has been accepted as a draft international standard of the International Organization for Standardization (ISO). RELAX NG actually began its life as two competing validation languages, RELAX and TREX, which were merged in 2001. RELAX NG is as capable of describing XML Structures as XML Schema, and arguably simpler to use. However, .NET does not support validation with RELAX NG.

There is nothing to keep some enterprising developer from building a RELAX NG validator for .NET, of course. Also, James Clark's Trang processor (*http://www. thaiopensource.com/relaxng/trang.html*) lets you work in RELAX NG and convert your results to W3C XML Schema.

Using the XSD Tool

Microsoft provides a tool with the .NET Framework SDK called XSD, the XML Schemas/DataTypes support utility. With this tool, you can generate schemas from source code, compiled assemblies, and XML documents, as well as generating source code in various .NET languages from schemas.

The XSD command-line syntax shown here is explained in Table 8-1:

```
xsd.exe filename.ext [argument [...]]
```

Table 8-1. XSD tool command-line syntax

Argument	Description
`filename.ext`	This argument specifies the name of the file to use as input. This can be either a CLR DLL (`.dll`) or executable file (`.exe`); an XML (`.xml`) file; or an XML Schema Definition (`.xsd`) or XML-Data-Reduced (`.xdr`) file. The type of the input file determines what other arguments are allowed.
`/classes` `/c`	When an XSD file is specified, generates source code for classes as determined by the schema. This argument is mutually exclusive with `/dataset`.
`/dataset` `/d`	When an XSD file is specified, generates source code for classes that are subclasses of `System.Data.DataSet` as determined by the schema. This argument is mutually exclusive with `/classes`.
`/element:element` `/e:element`	When an XSD file is specified, this argument specifies which elements to generate types for. `/element` may be specified more than once. The default is to generate types for all elements.
`/language:language` `/l:language`	When an XSD file is specified, this argument specifies the language to generate types in. `language` may be one of `cs` (C#), `vb` (Visual Basic.NET), or `js` (JScript). You may also specify the fully qualified name of any class that implements `System.CodeDom.Compiler.CodeDomProvider`. The default is `cs`.
`/namespace:namespace` `/n:namespace`	When an XSD file is specified, this argument specifies the namespace to create types in. The default is `Schemas`.
`/outputdir:outputdir` `/o:outputdir`	Specifies the directory in which to put output files. The default is the current directory. Generated schema files are named `scheman.xsd`, where `n` is a sequential number starting with 0. Generated source files are named with the schema filename and the appropriate extension for the language.
`/uri:uri` `/u:uri`	When an XSD file is specified, this argument specifies the URI for the elements in the schema to generate code for.

Table 8-1. XSD tool command-line syntax (continued)

Argument	Description
/type:*type* /t:*type*	When a DLL or EXE file is specified, this argument specifies what types to generate a schema for. If *type* is a fully qualified type name, the schema for that type is generated. If *type* is a type name without a namespace, schemas for all types with that name are generated. If *type* ends with a *, schemas are generated for all types with names starting with the name up to the *. /type may be specified more than once. The default is to generate schemas for all types.
/h /?	Prints information on how to use XSD.
/nologo	Suppresses printing of the XSD copyright statement and version information banner.

As you can see from the command-line syntax, xsd can be used to generate either source code or an XML Schema, based on a variety of inputs. It's a very useful tool for generating an XSD based on a .NET type or XML document you have already written, as well as generating source code for a .NET type based on an existing XSD.

When an XML-Data-Reduced (XDR) document is specified on the command line, xsd generates an equivalent XSD document. XDR was introduced by Microsoft and the University of Edinburgh in 1998, based on the earlier XML-Data standard which formed the basis for much of XML Schema.

The most likely reason anyone would need to convert an XDR to an XSD is to support an application using Microsoft's BizTalk Server. Biz-Talk Server is an application server supporting workflow and process management.

Generating a Schema from an XML Document

xsd can be used to generate a best-guess schema from any XML document. It will make certain assumptions about the structure of your document, based on the data found in the example you provide. For example, it will always set minOccurs to 1 and maxOccurs to unbounded for each element. It will also always use the xs:sequence compositor for lists of elements, even if your example XML document has elements in various orders. This can present the odd situation of the sample document used to generate the XSD failing validation with the XSD generated from it. Finally, the type attribute of each xs:element and xs:attribute element defaults to xs:string.

For these reasons, you should never take the generated XSD for granted. Always edit it to make sure it will fit your real requirements.

Using the purchase order document from Chapter 2, you can generate an XSD with the following command line:

```
xsd po1456.xml
```

You can go ahead and use XSD to generate the source code. I've already done so, and tweaked the generated code to ensure that this XSD validates the PO correctly. These edits are highlighted in Example 8-1. I intentionally introduced a couple of mistakes in my edits. I've done this to point out how XmlSchema validates an XSD, and I'll explain that more in a moment.

Example 8-1. Generated XSD for purchase orders

```
<?xml version="1.0" encoding="utf-8"?>
<xs:schema id="NewDataSet" xmlns="" xmlns:xs="http://www.w3.org/2001/XMLSchema" xmlns:
msdata="urn:schemas-microsoft-com:xml-msdata">
  <xs:element name="po">
    <xs:complexType>
      <xs:attribute name="id" type="xs:ID" />
      <xs:sequence>
        <xs:element name="date">
          <xs:complexType>
            <xs:attribute name="year" type="xs:string" />
            <xs:attribute name="month" type="xs:string" />
            <xs:attribute name="day" type="xs:string" />
          </xs:complexType>
        </xs:element>
        <xs:element name="address" maxOccurs="unbounded">
          <xs:complexType>
            <xs:sequence>
              <xs:element name="name" type="xs:string" msdata:Ordinal="0" />
              <xs:element name="street" type="xs:string" maxOccurs="3" msdata:Ordinal="1" />
              <xs:element name="city" type="xs:string" msdata:Ordinal="2" />
              <xs:element name="state" type="xs:string" msdata:Ordinal="3" />
              <xs:element name="zip" type="xs:string" msdata:Ordinal="4" />
            </xs:sequence>
            <xs:attribute name="type" type="xs:string" />
          </xs:complexType>
        </xs:element>
        <xs:element name="items" minOccurs="2" maxOccurs="1">
          <xs:complexType>
            <xs:sequence>
              <xs:element name="item" minOccurs="0" maxOccurs="unbounded">
                <xs:complexType>
                  <xs:attribute name="quantity" type="xs:string" />
                  <xs:attribute name="productCode" type="xs:string" />
                  <xs:attribute name="description" type="xs:string" />
                  <xs:attribute name="unitCost" type="xs:string" />
                </xs:complexType>
              </xs:element>
            </xs:sequence>
          </xs:complexType>
        </xs:element>
      </xs:sequence>
    </xs:complexType>
  </xs:element>
  <xs:element name="NewDataSet" msdata:IsDataSet="true">
    <xs:complexType>
```

Example 8-1. Generated XSD for purchase orders (continued)

```
      <xs:choice maxOccurs="unbounded">
        <xs:element ref="po" />
      </xs:choice>
    </xs:complexType>
  </xs:element>
</xs:schema>
```

There are a few pieces of this generated XSD that you should note. First is the inclusion of the namespace prefix msdata in the attributes msdata:Ordinal and msdata:IsDataSet. The urn:schemas-microsoft-com:xml-msdata namespace provides hints to the DataSet class when serializing an XML instance to a database.

Second is the NewDataSet element itself. This is used when generating source code for the XSD with the /dataset flag; the resulting source code will provide the definition of a subclass of System.Data.DataSet.

I'll address both of these issues in depth in Chapters 9 and 11.

Given the generated XSD and the modifications to it, you can do two things. First, you can verify that it is a valid XML Schema after the changes. The program shown in Example 8-2 will do just that.

Example 8-2. Validation of an XML Schema

```
using System;
using System.IO;
using System.Xml.Schema;

public class ValidateSchema {
  public static void Main(string [] args) {
    ValidationEventHandler handler = new ValidationEventHandler(ValidateSchema.Handler);
    XmlSchema schema = XmlSchema.Read(File.OpenRead(args[0]),handler);
    schema.Compile(handler);
  }

  public static void Handler(object sender, ValidationEventArgs e) {
    Console.WriteLine(e.Message);
  }
}
```

A ValidationEventHandler can be called in two places. The first, checking the XML Schema itself, happens on the following line:

```
    XmlSchema schema = XmlSchema.Read(File.OpenRead(args[0]),handler);
```

XmlSchema.Read( ) reads the content of the XSD from a Stream, TextReader, or XmlReader, and takes a ValidationEventHandler delegate as its second parameter; the ValidationEventHandler is covered in Chapter 2. Any XML validation errors that arise while reading in the file will be reported to the ValidationEventHandler.

It's important to note that the `ValidationEventHandler` handles two different aspects of checking a schema's content; checking whether it contains valid XML, and verifying whether it constitutes an acceptable XSD. In Example 8-2, I'm using the same `ValidationEventHandler` for both checks, but they could be two separate delegates.

The second phase, validating the content of the XSD, happens here:

```
schema.Compile(handler);
```

In this phase, the content of the XSD is checked to make sure that it is really a valid instance of XML Schema. Its errors will also be reported to the `ValidationEventHandler`. With the XSD in Example 8-1, running this validator will produce the following output:

```
C:\Chapter 8>ValidateSchema po.xsd
The content model of a complex type must consist of 'annotation'(if present) followed
by zero or one of 'simpleContent' or 'complexContent' or 'group' or 'choice' or
'sequence' or 'all' followed by zero or more attributes or attributeGroups followed
by zero or one anyAttribute. An error occurred at (6, 8).
minOccurs value cannot be greater than maxOccurs value. An error occurred at (25,
10).
```

Looking back, I made two mistakes. First, the id attribute of the po element is in the wrong place; the `xsd:attribute` element must come *after* the `xsd:sequence` element when defining an element. You can move the attribute into its proper place to avoid this error. This validation error was caught by the `Read( )` method, because it is a case of the XML itself being invalid.

Granted, this error is a little contrived. xsd generated the elements in the correct order, but I moved the `xsd:attribute` element to make a point.

Second, the items element has `minOccurs` set to 3 and `maxOccurs` set to 1. In this case, the `Compile( )` method caught my error, because the XSD was a well-formed XML document, although it did not constitute a sane XML Schema instance.

At the end of the program, you'll notice that the entire XSD is loaded. Although it is not valid, it sits in memory, ready to be used. Rather than editing the schema on disk, you could have used the `XmlSchema` type's methods to work with it and make it valid, as you'll see later in this chapter.

You can now use the generated XSD, with the changes to correct my errors, to validate the document that was used to generate it. Example 8-3 shows a program that validates an XML document with an XSD, with a couple of interesting lines highlighted.

Example 8-3. Validation of an XML file with an XML Schema

```
using System;
using System.IO;
using System.Xml;
using System.Xml.Schema;

public class Validate {

private static bool valid = true;

  public static void Main(string [] args) {

    using (Stream stream = File.OpenRead(args[0])) {
      XmlValidatingReader reader = new XmlValidatingReader(new XmlTextReader(stream));
      reader.ValidationType = ValidationType.Schema;
      reader.Schemas.Add("", args[1]);
      reader.ValidationEventHandler += new ValidationEventHandler(Handler);

      while (reader.Read()) {
        // do nothing
      }
    }
    if (valid) {
      Console.WriteLine("Document is valid.");
    }
  }

public static void Handler(object sender, ValidationEventArgs e) {
    valid = false;
    Console.WriteLine(e.Message);
  }
}
```

Take a look at the lines that are highlighted in the example:

```
reader.ValidationType = ValidationType.Schema;
```

This line sets the XmlValidatingReader's ValidationType property to ValidationType.
Schema. As I mentioned in the discussion of validation by DTD in Chapter 2, this
alone is not enough to cause the document to be validated; the following line takes
care of that:

```
reader.Schemas.Add("", args[1]);
```

This line adds the XSD whose name is passed in on the command line to the
XmlSchemaCollection in XmlValidatingReader's Schemas property.
XmlSchemaCollection is just what it sounds like, a collection of schemas. Its Add( )
method has four overloads. The one used here takes two strings; the first is the
namespace URI to which the schema applies, and the second is the name of the XSD
file which will be read. Other overloads allow you to add an XmlSchema instance, an
XmlReader, or an entire XmlSchemaCollection to the list. The document will be validated with each schema in the XmlSchemaCollection:

```
while (reader.Read()) {
    // do nothing
}
```

These lines read and validate the XML document. Once XmlValidatingReader is told to validate the document, all you have to do is read it and it will be validated. The while loop need not do anything else.

It's worth noting that, had you not validated my faulty XSD before attempting to validate an XML document with it, the same errors would have been found. There are two differences, however. First, only the first error would have been reported via an XmlSchemaException, rather than being handled with the ValidationEventHandler. Since exceptions are not being caught in this program, the errors would have short-circuited the XmlReader's processing.

Second, the XSD is not explicitly being loaded into memory, so you would not have been given the opportunity to attempt to correct it (assuming your program had a way to do that, of course).

Generating a Schema from a DLL or Executable

The XSD tool also knows how to generate a an XSD from compiled types in a DLL or executable file. When generating a schema, xsd makes certain assumptions about the XSD types of instance variables. For any given CLR type, xsd chooses an XSD type for the schema. Table 8-2 lists each XSD type and its corresponding common language runtime type. In the cases where more than one XSD type maps to a single CLR type, the bold one will be used.

Table 8-2. XSD-to-CLR type mappings

XSD type	CLR type
xs:hexBinary	System.Byte[]
xs:base64Binary	
xs:Boolean	System.Boolean
xs:byte	System.SByte
xs:normalizedString	System.String
xs:ENTITY	
xs:ID	
xs:IDREF	
xs:language	
xs:Name	
xs:NCName	
xs:NMTOKEN	
xs:NOTATION	
xs:string	
xs:token	

Table 8-2. XSD-to-CLR type mappings (continued)

XSD type	CLR type
xs:date	System.DateTime
xs:gMonthDay	
xs:gDay	
xs:gYear	
xs:gYearMonth	
xs:month	
xs:time	
xs:timePeriod	
xs:decimal	System.Decimal
xs:integer	
xs:negativeInteger	
xs:nonNegativeInteger	
xs:nonPositiveInteger	
xs:positiveInteger	
xs:double	System.Double
xs:ENTITIES	System.String[]
xs:IDREFS	
xs:NMTOKENS	
xs:float	System.Single
xs:int	System.Int32
xs:long	System.Int64
xs:QName	System.Xml.XmlQualifiedName
xs:short	System.Int16
xs:unsignedByte	System.Byte
xs:unsignedInt	System.UInt32
xs:unsignedLong	System.UInt64
xs:unsignedShort	System.UInt16
xs:anyURI	System.Uri
xs:hexBinary	System.Byte[]
xs:base64Binary	
xs:Boolean	System.Boolean

Angus Hardware might have a class structure for product listings, such as is shown in Example 8-4. This code can be compiled into the library *Product.dll*.

Example 8-4. Product type in C#

```
using System;

public class Address {
  public string [] Street;
```

Example 8-4. Product type in C# (continued)

```
  public string City;
  public string State;
  public string Zip;
}

public class Manufacturer {
  public string Name;
  public Address [] Addresses;
}

public class Product {
  public string Name;
  public string ProductCode;
  public Manufacturer Manufacturer;
  public DateTime DateIntroduced;
  public decimal UnitCost;
}
```

When you run the command xsd Product.dll, you get the generated XSD shown in Example 8-5.

Example 8-5. Generated XML Schema for Product.dll

```
<?xml version="1.0" encoding="utf-8"?>
<xs:schema elementFormDefault="qualified" xmlns:xs="http://www.w3.org/2001/XMLSchema">
  <xs:element name="Address" nillable="true" type="Address" />
  <xs:complexType name="Address">
    <xs:sequence>
      <xs:element minOccurs="0" maxOccurs="1" name="Street" type="ArrayOfString" />
      <xs:element minOccurs="0" maxOccurs="1" name="City" type="xs:string" />
      <xs:element minOccurs="0" maxOccurs="1" name="State" type="xs:string" />
      <xs:element minOccurs="0" maxOccurs="1" name="Zip" type="xs:string" />
    </xs:sequence>
  </xs:complexType>
  <xs:complexType name="ArrayOfString">
    <xs:sequence>
      <xs:element minOccurs="0" maxOccurs="unbounded" name="string" nillable="true"
type="xs:string" />
    </xs:sequence>
  </xs:complexType>
  <xs:element name="Manufacturer" nillable="true" type="Manufacturer" />
  <xs:complexType name="Manufacturer">
    <xs:sequence>
      <xs:element minOccurs="0" maxOccurs="1" name="Name" type="xs:string" />
      <xs:element minOccurs="0" maxOccurs="1" name="Addresses" type="ArrayOfAddress" />
    </xs:sequence>
  </xs:complexType>
  <xs:complexType name="ArrayOfAddress">
    <xs:sequence>
      <xs:element minOccurs="0" maxOccurs="unbounded" name="Address" nillable="true"
type="Address" />
    </xs:sequence>
```

Example 8-5. Generated XML Schema for Product.dll (continued)

```
    </xs:complexType>
    <xs:element name="Product" nillable="true" type="Product" />
    <xs:complexType name="Product">
      <xs:sequence>
        <xs:element minOccurs="0" maxOccurs="1" name="Name" type="xs:string" />
        <xs:element minOccurs="0" maxOccurs="1" name="ProductCode" type="xs:string" />
        <xs:element minOccurs="0" maxOccurs="1" name="Manufacturer" type="Manufacturer" />
        <xs:element minOccurs="1" maxOccurs="1" name="DateIntroduced" type="xs:dateTime" />
        <xs:element minOccurs="1" maxOccurs="1" name="UnitCost" type="xs:decimal" />
      </xs:sequence>
    </xs:complexType>
</xs:schema>
```

Like the XSD generated for an XML instance, a few assumptions are made. For example, although you know from your previous usage that an Address element can only have up to three Street elements, the XSD does nothing to constrain the number; it's created a type called ArrayOfString, whose content is an unbounded number of String elements.

You can affect the generated XSD with the judicious use of C# attributes. There are a number of attributes that affect XSD generation, located in the System.Xml. Serialization namespace; a small subset is listed in Table 8-3. Refer to the .NET Framework SDK documentation section entitled "Attributes That Control XML Serialization" for the complete list.

Table 8-3. Attributes affecting XSD generation

Attribute name	Purpose	Properties
XmlRootAttribute	Identifies the class, structure, enumeration, or interface as the root element of an XML instance	DataType ElementName IsNullable Namespace
XmlElementAttribute	Identifies the class, structure, enumeration, or interface as an element in an XML instance	DataType ElementName Form IsNullable Namespace Type
XmlAttributeAttribute	Identifies the class, structure, enumeration, or interface as an attribute in an XML instance	DataType AttributeName Form Namespace Type

With this information, you can alter the original source code to force the generated code to appear in a form more to your liking. To take just the Product type from *Product.cs*, you can alter xsd's output significantly by marking some of its fields as attributes:

```
public class Product {
    [XmlAttributeAttribute(AttributeName="name")]
    public string Name;
    [XmlAttributeAttribute(AttributeName="productCode")]
    public string ProductCode;
    [XmlElementAttribute(IsNullable=false, ElementName="manufacturer")]
    public Manufacturer Manufacturer;
    [XmlAttributeAttribute(AttributeName="dateIntroduced")]
    public DateTime DateIntroduced;
    [XmlAttributeAttribute(AttributeName="unitCost")]
    public decimal UnitCost;
}
```

The corresponding element in the generated *schema0.xsd* now looks like this:

```
<xs:element name="product" type="Product" />
<xs:complexType name="Product">
  <xs:sequence>
    <xs:element minOccurs="0" maxOccurs="1" name="manufacturer" type="Manufacturer" /
>
  </xs:sequence>
  <xs:attribute name="name" type="xs:string" />
  <xs:attribute name="productCode" type="xs:string" />
  <xs:attribute name="dateIntroduced" type="xs:dateTime" />
  <xs:attribute name="unitCost" type="xs:decimal" />
</xs:complexType>
```

There's much more to learn about serialization, and I'll cover the topic in much more depth in Chapter 9.

Generating Types from a Schema

Once you have an XSD, whether generated by the XSD tool, produced from some other XML editor, or written by hand, the XSD tool can now generate source code to use an instance of the document it defines. Running the command xsd customer.xsd /classes generates the C# code shown in Example 8-6.

Example 8-6. Generated C# code for customer.xsd

```
//------------------------------------------------------------------------------
// <autogenerated>
//     This code was generated by a tool.
//     Runtime Version: 1.0.3705.209
//
//     Changes to this file may cause incorrect behavior and will be lost if
//     the code is regenerated.
// </autogenerated>
//------------------------------------------------------------------------------

//
// This source code was auto-generated by xsd, Version=1.0.3705.209.
//
using System.Xml.Serialization;
```

Example 8-6. Generated C# code for customer.xsd (continued)

```
/// <remarks/>
[System.Xml.Serialization.XmlRootAttribute(Namespace="", IsNullable=false)]
public class Customer {

    /// <remarks/>
    [System.Xml.Serialization.XmlElementAttribute(DataType="token")]
    public string Name;

    /// <remarks/>
    [System.Xml.Serialization.XmlElementAttribute("Address")]
    public CustomerAddress[] Address;

    /// <remarks/>
    [System.Xml.Serialization.XmlAttributeAttribute(DataType="ID")]
    public string Id;
}

/// <remarks/>
public class CustomerAddress {

    /// <remarks/>
    [System.Xml.Serialization.XmlElementAttribute("Street")]
    public string[] Street;

    /// <remarks/>
    public string City;

    /// <remarks/>
    public string State;

    /// <remarks/>
    [System.Xml.Serialization.XmlElementAttribute(DataType="token")]
    public string Zip;
}
```

Notice that although xsd has simply created the types necessary to read and write *customer.xml*, it has also inserted attributes that serve as hints to the XmlSerializer. These hints enable the XmlSerializer to properly read and write XML documents corresponding to the object instances in memory. They do not affect the storage of the object instance in memory, however. Even though Customer.Name is decorated with an XmlElementAttribute with DataType="token", there is no constraint on the data in memory; however, a document with non-token data in the Customer.Name element is invalid according to the XSD.

When I first started building customer.xsd, I pointed out the initial capital letters on element and attribute names. It should be clear now that the properties of the generated Customer and CustomerAddress types have exactly the same names as the types in the XSD. By capitalizing the first letters of the names, I've managed to comply with .NET naming convention, without having to change the generated code.

 Another way to handle the case issue is through the XmlElementAttribute's Name property. If the XML schema has lower-case names, you can conform to the .NET naming standards by setting this property. You would have to edit the generated source code, however, so it's important to consider carefully whether going to this length is worthwhile.

Generating a DataSet Subclass from a Schema

Much like generating classes, xsd can generate DataSet subclasses from an XSD. System.Data.DataSet is a type that represents a group of database tables cached in memory. The System.Data namespace constitutes the ADO.NET architecture, which we'll talk about in Chapter 11.

Working with Schemas

Because the XML Schema language is expressed as an XML vocabulary, it can be dealt with just as any other XML document. XmlReader, XmlWriter, XmlDocument, XPathNavigator, XsltTransform, and the rest of .NET's types can be used to read, write, manipulate, navigate, and transform an XSD document.

In addition to the standard ways of dealing with XML documents, however, the System.Xml.XmlSchema assembly includes a host of types that can be used to deal with schema documents in a very XSD-centric way.

Creating a Schema Programmatically

As you already know, xs:schema is the root element of an XSD document. XmlSchema is the type that represents the xs:schema element.

XmlSchema is a subclass of XmlSchemaObject, whose other subclasses are XmlSchemaAnnotated, XmlSchemaAnnotation, XmlSchemaAppInfo, XmlSchemaDocumentation, and XmlSchemaExternal. Each of these subclasses represents a specific type of XML Schema element, and some of them have their own subclasses. The .NET XmlSchema type hierarchy is shown in Figure 8-1.

Table 8-4 shows each XML Schema element name with its corresponding .NET type. In some cases, more than one .NET class is used for the same XML Schema element; typically, this is the case when the same element has different behavior in different contexts. There are many more types in the System.Xml.Schema assembly that do not correspond directly to an XML Schema element, and they are listed in the assembly reference in Chapter 17.

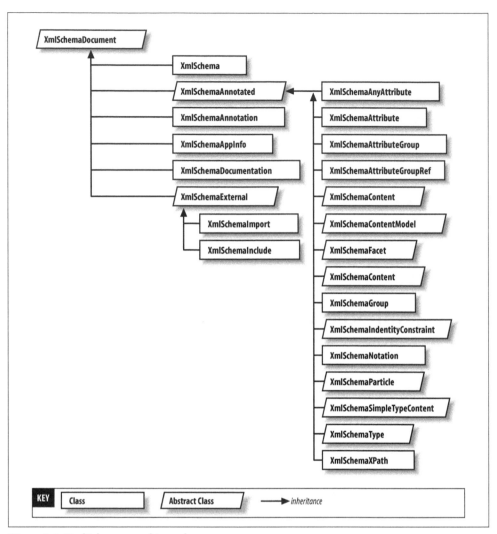

Figure 8-1. XmlSchema type hierarchy

Table 8-4. XML Schema element names and .NET types

XML Schema element name	.NET type
xs:all	XmlSchemaAll
xs:annotation	XmlSchemaAnnotation
xs:any	XmlSchemaAny
xs:anyAttribute	XmlSchemaAnyAttribute
xs:appinfo	XmlSchemaAppInfo
xs:attribute	XmlSchemaAttribute

Table 8-4. XML Schema element names and .NET types (continued)

XML Schema element name	.NET type
xs:attributeGroup	XmlSchemaAttributeGroup
	XmlSchemaAttributeGroupRef
xs:choice	XmlSchemaChoice
xs:complexContent	XmlSchemaComplexContent
xs:complexType	XmlSchemaComplexType
xs:documentation	XmlSchemaDocumentation
xs:element	XmlSchemaElement
xs:enumeration	XmlSchemaEnumerationFacet
xs:extension	XmlSchemaComplexContentExtension
	XmlSchemaSimpleContentExtension
xs:field	Collection of XmlSchemaXPath
xs:fractionDigits	XmlSchemaFractionDigitsFacet
xs:group	XmlSchemaGroup
	XmlSchemaGroupRef
xs:import	XmlSchemaImport
xs:include	XmlSchemaInclude
xs:key	XmlSchemaKey
xs:keyref	XmlSchemaKeyRef
xs:length	XmlSchemaLengthFacet
xs:list	XmlSchemaSimpleTypeList
xs:maxExclusive	XmlSchemaMaxExclusiveFacet
xs:maxInclusive	XmlSchemaMaxInclusiveFacet
xs:maxLength	XmlSchemaMaxLengthFacet
xs:minExclusive	XmlSchemaMinExclusiveFacet
xs:minInclusive	XmlSchemaMinInclusiveFacet
xs:minLength	XmlSchemaMinLengthFacet
xs:notation	XmlSchemaNotation
xs:pattern	XmlSchemaPatternFacet
xs:redefine	XmlSchemaRedefine
xs:restriction	XmlSchemaComplexContentRestriction
	XmlSchemaSimpleContentRestriction
	XmlSchemaSimpleTypeRestriction
xs:schema	XmlSchema
xs:selector	XmlSchemaXPath
xs:sequence	XmlSchemaSequence
xs:simpleContent	XmlSchemaSimpleContent

Table 8-4. XML Schema element names and .NET types (continued)

XML Schema element name	.NET type
xs:simpleType	XmlSchemaSimpleType
xs:totalDigits	XmlSchemaTotalDigitsFacet
xs:union	XmlSchemaSimpleTypeUnion
xs:unique	XmlSchemaUnique
xs:whiteSpace	XmlSchemaWhitespaceFacet

You can access all the attributes of each XSD element directly through the corresponding .NET type's properties; each property is named the same as the corresponding attribute, with an initial capital letter. In those cases where an attribute is not valid because a particular element can appear in different contexts, an exception is thrown if you try to access the corresponding property.

Creating an instance of an XSD programmatically, then, is a fairly simple process, illustrated in Example 8-7. The overall process should be reminiscent of creating a DOM instance with XmlDocument.

Example 8-7. Creating an XSD instance programmatically

```
using System;
using System.IO;
using System.Xml;
using System.Xml.Schema;

public class CreateSchema {
  public static void Main(string [] args) {
    string ns = "http://www.w3.org/2001/XMLSchema";
    XmlQualifiedName idType = new XmlQualifiedName("ID",ns);
    XmlQualifiedName stringType = new XmlQualifiedName("string",ns);
    XmlQualifiedName tokenType = new XmlQualifiedName("token",ns);

    XmlSchema schema = new XmlSchema( );
    schema.Version = "1.0";

    XmlSchemaElement customer = new XmlSchemaElement( );
    customer.Name = "Customer";
    schema.Items.Add(customer);

    XmlSchemaComplexType customerComplexType = new XmlSchemaComplexType( );
    customer.SchemaType = customerComplexType;

    XmlSchemaSequence customerSequence = new XmlSchemaSequence( );
    customerComplexType.Particle = customerSequence;

    XmlSchemaElement name = new XmlSchemaElement( );
    name.Name = "Name";
    name.MinOccurs = 1;
    name.MaxOccurs = 1;
```

Example 8-7. Creating an XSD instance programmatically (continued)

```
name.SchemaTypeName = tokenType;
customerSequence.Items.Add(name);

XmlSchemaElement address = new XmlSchemaElement( );
address.Name = "Address";
address.MinOccurs = 1;
address.MaxOccursString = "unbounded";
customerSequence.Items.Add(address);

XmlSchemaComplexType addressComplexType = new XmlSchemaComplexType( );
address.SchemaType = addressComplexType;

XmlSchemaSequence addressSequence = new XmlSchemaSequence( );
addressComplexType.Particle = addressSequence;

XmlSchemaElement street = new XmlSchemaElement( );
street.Name = "Street";
street.MinOccurs = 1;
street.MaxOccurs = 3;
street.SchemaTypeName = stringType;
addressSequence.Items.Add(street);

XmlSchemaElement city = new XmlSchemaElement( );
city.Name = "City";
city.MinOccurs = 1;
city.MaxOccurs = 1;
city.SchemaTypeName = stringType;
addressSequence.Items.Add(city);

XmlSchemaElement state = new XmlSchemaElement( );
state.Name = "State";
state.MinOccurs = 1;
state.MaxOccurs = 1;
state.SchemaTypeName = stringType;
addressSequence.Items.Add(state);

XmlSchemaElement zip = new XmlSchemaElement( );
zip.Name = "Zip";
zip.MinOccurs = 1;
zip.MaxOccurs = 1;
zip.SchemaTypeName = new XmlQualifiedName("USZipCodeType");
addressSequence.Items.Add(zip);

XmlSchemaAttribute customerId = new XmlSchemaAttribute( );
customerId.Name = "Id";
customerId.SchemaTypeName = idType;
customerComplexType.Attributes.Add(customerId);

XmlSchemaSimpleType usZipCodeType = new XmlSchemaSimpleType( );
usZipCodeType.Name = "USZipCodeType";
schema.Items.Add(usZipCodeType);
```

Example 8-7. Creating an XSD instance programmatically (continued)

```
    XmlSchemaSimpleTypeRestriction zipRestriction = new XmlSchemaSimpleTypeRestriction( );
    zipRestriction.BaseTypeName = tokenType;
    usZipCodeType.Content = zipRestriction;

    XmlSchemaPatternFacet zipPattern = new XmlSchemaPatternFacet( );
    zipPattern.Value = @"\d{5}(-\d{4})?";
    zipRestriction.Facets.Add(zipPattern);

    schema.Compile(new ValidationEventHandler(Handler));

    if (schema.IsCompiled) {
      Console.WriteLine("Schema compiled.");
      schema.Write(File.Create("Customer.xsd"));
    } else {
      Console.WriteLine("Schema compilation failed.");
    }
  }

  public static void Handler(object sender, ValidationEventArgs e) {
    Console.WriteLine(e.Message);
  }
}
```

Running this code produces an XSD equivalent to the *Customer.xsd* that started the chapter (there are minor differences, such as the order of attributes, but the canonical XML is the same). Most of this code should be self-explanatory. The general process takes the following steps:

1. Create an instance of an XmlSchemaObject subclass.

2. Set the object's properties.

3. Add the object to its parent's list of children.

A few particular sections of code do bear further explanation:

```
    XmlQualifiedName idType = new XmlQualifiedName("ID",ns);
    XmlQualifiedName stringType = new XmlQualifiedName("string",ns);
    XmlQualifiedName tokenType = new XmlQualifiedName("token",ns);
```

These lines create instances of the type XmlQualifiedName. XmlQualifedName represents a qualified name in XML, in the format namespace:localname. The document's XmlNameTable is used to resolved the namespace URI in the second parameter to the appropriate prefix; in this case, that's xs. You'll use these XmlQualifiedName instances later, when setting the type attributes of xs:element and xs:attribute elements:

```
    zip.SchemaTypeName = new XmlQualifiedName("USZipCodeType");
```

This line sets the Zip element's type attribute to USZipCodeType. This simple type hasn't actually been defined yet at this point, but that's ok. The document need not be valid until it is compiled; in fact, an invalid XSD may be written to disk without any error being raised. That's why the last few lines of the program are included:

```
if (schema.IsCompiled) {
  Console.WriteLine("Schema compiled.");
  schema.Write(File.Create("Customer.xsd"));
} else {
  Console.WriteLine("Schema compilation failed.");
}
```

These lines make sure that the XSD is valid before writing it to disk. Although the ValidationEventHandler would have written a message to the console if there were any problems, the IsCompiled property of the XmlSchema instance can be queried as a final check before writing the XSD to disk.

The entire process is fairly straightforward, and should need no further explanation.

Manipulating an Existing Schema

You already know how to load any XML document into memory. Once you have a document in memory, you can navigate through its elements using XmlDocument's standard methods, and read it into an XmlSchema for other purposes:

```
XmlDocument document = new XmlDocument();
document.Load(args[0]);

XmlNodeReader reader = new XmlNodeReader(document);

ValidationEventHandler handler = new ValidationEventHandler(Handler);
XmlSchema schema = XmlSchema.Read(reader, handler);

schema.Compile(handler);
```

In much the same way, you can use XmlDocument's GetNavigator( ), SelectNodes( ), and SelectSingleNode( ) methods to navigate an XSD. You can also transform it into any other format, given an appropriate XSLT stylesheet. For example, you might wish to transform an XSD into a DTD; you could write an XSLT transform to do so.

Moving On

XML Schema is one of the most complicated W3C specifications. Learning it is the work of more than one chapter, but .NET makes a fairly short job of actually using it.

In the next chapter, you'll learn how to serialize objects in memory to XML, in a variety of formats. Chapter 9 will build on the work you've done here, as well as adding some SOAP into the mix.

SOAP and XML Serialization

Chapter 8 laid the groundwork for more discussion about serializing data to XML. In this chapter, I'll talk more about using an XML Schema to control the serialization of objects to XML, and introduce you to SOAP (formerly known as the *Simple Object Access Protocol*, but now an acronym with no expansion), the heart of .NET's distributed processing abilities.

First, I'll tell you about serialization in general, and the .NET Framework's two modes of serialization: runtime serialization and XML serialization.

Defining Serialization

Serialization refers to the process of transforming data from an object instance in memory into a structured representation of that data in a stream. Serialization allows you to preserve the state of an application's objects, whether to simply save the data you're working with or to transmit the data to another application. By using the framework to serialize an object to a stream, you can avoid much of the tedium of hand-coding the logic of reading each field from the object and writing its data to the stream. Instead, the serialization class knows how to do this translation with minimal intervention from the programmer.

The process of reading a stream of data into a new object instance in memory is *deserialization*, which is the opposite of serialization. Although you would hope that no data would ever be lost in the serialization-deserialization process, the reality is that different formats support different datatypes, and they do not always map well to each other. .NET takes two different approaches to serialization, runtime serialization and XML serialization. Each has its advantages, and I'll compare them later.

 Object serialization should not be confused with *transaction serialization*, in which database transactions are performed in sequence so that each transaction happens in complete isolation from all others.

In *runtime serialization*, the .NET framework uses a formatter class to create a serialized version of an object, using information available about the object from *reflection*. Reflection is the mechanism by which objects in memory can be interrogated at runtime for information about their fields, properties, methods, and attributes. Different formatters do the actual work of serialization, based on hints the object provides through reflection.

In *XML serialization*, the structured representation is defined via XML syntax. I introduced you to a simple form of serialization in Chapter 8, wherein the XmlSerializer class was used to control the transformation specified by an XML Schema document.

XML Schema is one way to specify the serialization format, and I'll talk about .NET's XML serialization functionality in a moment. But first, I'll introduce SOAP.

Introducing the SOAP Specification

SOAP is one of the underlying technologies behind Web Services. I'll talk more about Web Services in Chapter 10.

The development of SOAP began in 1998. The World Wide Web Consortium released a note on SOAP in 2000. .NET explicitly supports section 5 of the SOAP note, which is available on the Web at *http://www.w3.org/TR/SOAP/*.

What SOAP actually provides is a standard mechanism for packaging data for transmission between interoperating computer systems. While other remote procedure call (RPC) protocols exist, most of them were designed before the era of distributed, object-oriented programming. SOAP's design goals include several features not normally found in RPC protocols:

Distributed garbage collection
Distributed garbage collection allows for objects to be removed from memory automatically when all remote references to them go out of scope.

Message batching
Also known as *boxcarring* or *pipelining*, message batching allows several messages to be grouped together for sequential transactional processing.

Objects-by-reference
In the programming concept of pass-by-reference, an instance of an object is passed to methods in such a way that changes to the instance are visible after the method exits. This concept is pretty much a requirement for distributed programming, when you're invoking an object located at a remote machine.

Activation
To instantiate a local object, you use the C# new operator. However, to instantiate an object on a remote machine, there must be something on the other end to receive your request to instantiate the object. Activation refers to the ability to instantiate a remote object.

The SOAP specification is made up of three parts:

SOAP envelope
> Because SOAP is a general-purpose messaging framework, one part of the message has to describe the message. The envelope includes such information as what is included in the data, who the message is intended for, and whether the actions described are required or optional. The envelope also provides information on how to deal with errors.

Encoding rules
> The encoding rules provide standard data types and structures that disparate systems can use to marshal the data in a SOAP message to their own native data types. These rules are largely based on XML Schema's data types.

RPC representation
> The RPC representation rules are used to allow methods on one system to be invoked by code running on another system, including both one-way and two-way messaging.

Although the SOAP specification provides for what is fundamentally a one-way transmission, two-way messaging is possible by sending a SOAP message in response to a SOAP message.

Although SOAP is designed to provide messaging regardless of the underlying network protocols, it is typically implemented atop HTTP. A message follows a message path, along which it may reach a number of different applications. Each application that receives the message must take the following steps:

1. Examine the message to find all the actions intended for the current application.
2. If the current application can support all the mandatory actions specified in the message, take those actions. Otherwise, return a fault message.
3. After removing any parts of the envelope that were intended only for the current application, pass the message along to the next recipient.

Example 9-1 shows a hypothetical SOAP message that might be used to communicate an order between Angus Hardware and a supplier. I'll use this example throughout the discussion of the SOAP specification.

Example 9-1. A SOAP message for a wholesale product order

```
<?xml version ="1.0" encoding="UTF-8" ?>
<SOAP-ENV:Envelope
  xmlns:SOAP-ENV="http://schemas.xmlsoap.org/soap/envelope/"
  xmlns:xsi="http://www.w3.org/2001/XMLSchema-instance"
  xmlns:xsd="http://www.w3.org/2001/XMLSchema">

  <SOAP-ENV:Header>
    <ns1:terms xmlns:ns1="urn:angushardware"
      SOAP-ENV:MustUnderstand="1">Net 30</ns1:terms>
  </SOAP-ENV:Header>
```

Example 9-1. A SOAP message for a wholesale product order (continued)

```
<SOAP-ENV:Body>
  <ns1:placeOrder
    SOAP-ENV:encodingStyle="http://schemas.xmlsoap.org/soap/encoding/">
    <productCode xsi:type="xsd:string">99HGTY</productCode>
    <quantity xsi:type="xsd:int">300</quantity>
  </ns1:placeOrder>
</SOAP-ENV:Body>

</SOAP-ENV:Envelope>
```

 A SOAP message may not contain a document type declaration or processing instructions. If you're creating and responding to SOAP messages automatically through the .NET Framework, this is not an issue. However, you should be aware of this restriction when dealing with SOAP messages produced or consumed by clients and servers written in other frameworks and languages.

The SOAP envelope

There are four namespaces included in the SOAP message. The first one, with the prefix SOAP-ENV, refers to the SOAP envelope:

```
xmlns:SOAP-ENV="http://schemas.xmlsoap.org/soap/envelope/"
```

The SOAP-ENV:Envelope element has two sub-elements, SOAP-ENV:Header and SOAP-ENV:Body. The SOAP-ENV:Header element is optional, and it provides information to the application that processes the message.

The element within the SOAP-ENV:Header element can be any element from any namespace other than SOAP-ENV, and it can have any attributes without restriction. Although it is open-ended to allow for maximum flexibility, the SOAP-ENV:Header's sub-elements do have two specific optional attributes, MustUnderstand and Actor.

The MustUnderstand attribute has a Boolean value, indicating to the application that if it does not know how to process the message, it must discard the entire message. The Actor attribute, whose value is a URI, can be used when a SOAP message is sent to several applications on a message path, and indicates which application the message is intended for:

```
<SOAP-ENV:Header>
  <ns1:terms xmlns:ns1="urn:angushardware"
    SOAP-ENV:MustUnderstand="1">Net 30</ns1:terms>
</SOAP-ENV:Header>
```

In Example 9-1, the ns1:terms element indicates the terms Angus Hardware is willing to give their vendor in purchasing more inventory. The terms are Net 30, and the application processing the order must understand the ns1:terms element in order to continue processing.

Like `SOAP-ENV:Header`, the `SOAP-ENV:Body` element can have any sub-elements. However, unlike `SOAP-ENV:Header`, `SOAP-ENV:Body` cannot have any attributes. The content of the `SOAP-ENV:Body` element is a sequence of actions to be processed; in Example 9-1, the action is a call to the `placeOrder` method:

```
<SOAP-ENV:Body>
  <ns1:placeOrder
    SOAP-ENV:encodingStyle="http://schemas.xmlsoap.org/soap/encoding/">
    <productCode xsi:type="xsd:string">99HGTY</productCode>
    <quantity xsi:type="xsd:int">300</quantity>
  </ns1:getInventory>
</SOAP-ENV:Body>
```

The `ns1:placeOrder` element has one attribute, `SOAP-ENV:encodingStyle`. This attribute indicates the encoding rules for the message, which I'll talk about shortly.

A SOAP envelope can also contain a response, as shown in Example 9-2.

Example 9-2. A SOAP response message for a wholesale product order

```
<?xml version ="1.0" encoding="UTF-8" ?>
<SOAP-ENV:Envelope
  xmlns:SOAP-ENV="http://schemas.xmlsoap.org/soap/envelope/"
  xmlns:xsi="http://www.w3.org/2001/XMLSchema-instance"
  xmlns:xsd="http://www.w3.org/2001/XMLSchema">

  <SOAP-ENV:Body>
    <ns1:placeOrderResponse xmlns:ns1="urn:angushardware"
      SOAP-ENV:encodingStyle="http://schemas.xmlsoap.org/soap/encoding/">
      <ns1:deliveryDate xsi:type="xsd:date">2002-09-04</deliveryDate>
    </ns1:placeOrderResponse>
  </SOAP-ENV:Body>

</SOAP-ENV:Envelope>
```

Example 9-2 shows a possible response to the message in Example 9-1. In this case, the server responds with a `ns1:placeOrderResponse` element, containing an `ns1:deliveryDate` element, which indicates an expected delivery date of September 4, 2002. However, a SOAP response can also include a `SOAP-ENV:Fault` element, indicating an error. Example 9-3 shows a SOAP fault message.

Example 9-3. A SOAP fault message for a wholesale product order

```
<?xml version ="1.0" encoding="UTF-8" ?>
<SOAP-ENV:Envelope
  xmlns:SOAP-ENV="http://schemas.xmlsoap.org/soap/envelope/"
  xmlns:xsi="http://www.w3.org/2001/XMLSchema-instance"
  xmlns:xsd="http://www.w3.org/2001/XMLSchema">

  <SOAP-ENV:Body>
    <SOAP-ENV:Fault>
      <SOAP-ENV:faultCode xsi:type="xsd:string">
        SOAP-ENV:MustUnderstand
```

```
      </SOAP-ENV:faultCode>
      <SOAP-ENV:faultString xsi:type="xsd:string">
        The server did not understand the header element ns1:terms
      </SOAP-ENV:faultString>
      <SOAP-ENV:faultActor xsi:type="xsd:string">
        Smith's Sprocket Company
      </SOAP-ENV:faultActor>
    </SOAP-ENV:Fault>
  </SOAP-ENV:Body>

</SOAP-ENV:Envelope>
```

As you can see, this SOAP message is very similar in overall structure to both the previous examples, except that it includes a SOAP-ENV:Fault element.

The SOAP-ENV:faultCode element contains a fault code, which indicates the type of error that occurred. SOAP-ENV:faultString provides a human-readable explanation of the fault; there's also an optional SOAP-ENV:detail element, which could provide more information about the error. Finally, the SOAP-ENV:faultActor indicates which actor had the fault. In this case, the SOAP server at Smith's Sprocket Company has indicated that it does not understand the ns1:terms element in the request header.

A few standard SOAP-ENV:faultCode values are defined in the SOAP specification, and they are listed in Table 9-1.

Table 9-1. Standard SOAP fault codes

Fault code	Fault description
SOAP-ENV:VersionMismatch	The namespace URI for the SOAP envelope does not match the content.
SOAP-ENV:MustUnderstand	The actor designated to process an element in the SOAP header with a SOAP-ENV:mustUnderstand value of 1 could not process the element.
SOAP-ENV:Client	The message was not properly formed or was missing some information, and should not be resent without correcting the errors.
SOAP-ENV:Server	The message could not be processed for some reason other than its content or structure. For example, some external process required to process the message may have failed.

The SOAP-ENV:Header and SOAP-ENV:Fault elements are optional in any SOAP message. The two SOAP messages, request and response, actually have identical structure; the only difference is in which of the two optional elements are included, and in the specific syntax of the body elements.

The overall structure of the SOAP message is extremely flexible, which makes it important for the client and server to have well-established rules for the syntax of their communications.

The XML Schema Definition for the SOAP envelope is located at *http://schemas.xmlsoap.org/soap/envelope/*, and it makes a fine reference to the contents of the envelope since you learned about the XML Schema language in Chapter 8.

There are places where the XSD differs from the prose of the specification. However, the XSD documents these differences in xs:documentation elements.

Encoding rules

Several of the elements in the SOAP messages I just discussed include the SOAP-ENV:encodingStyle attribute:

```
SOAP-ENV:encodingStyle="http://schemas.xmlsoap.org/soap/encoding/"
```

The SOAP-ENV:encodingStyle attribute specifies the encoding system to be used. The encoding system is a mutually agreed-upon way of representing data in a SOAP message. Although the examples use the SOAP 1.1 encoding rules, you may actually use any encoding you wish, or none at all, in your SOAP envelope. To use the SOAP 1.2 encoding system, for example, you would specify http://www.w3.org/2003/05/soap-encoding. The URI, like namespace URIs, is used as a unique name rather than an actual Internet resource.

The encoding style applies to the entire scope of the element on which the attribute appears. In Examples 9-1 and 9-2, the SOAP-ENV:encodingStyle attributes appear on the ns1:placeOrder and ns1:placeOrderResponse elements, respectively.

RPC representation

Although the SOAP envelope provides information about the remote method to be called and the encoding of the data being passed to the remote object, it does not inherently contain any information about the remote program or system. SOAP depends on the transport protocol to provide this. While HTTP works very well as a transport, and SOAP has specific bindings for HTTP, there is nothing in the specification that limits your choice of transport protocols.

There's not enough room in this book to cover everything about SOAP. For more information, see *Programming Web Services with SOAP* (O'Reilly).

When to Use Serialization

In general, you should consider using XML serialization when your application requires data to be exchanged between possibly disparate systems, whose only commonality might be the ability to read and write XML. Although this case covers XML serialization in general, it's also important to determine which form of serialization to use.

Simple XML serialization is appropriate when you have an existing XML schema (whether a formal W3C XML Schema or simply an agreed-upon format) and wish to read the data into an object; or when you have existing objects and wish to produce a representation of their data in an XML format. These cases usually involve non-interactive data exchange; that is, data is being exchanged, but not in a Web Services context.

On the other hand, you should use SOAP serialization when you know that your data exchange partner supports it, or when you are designing a new distributed application that requires interactive data exchange.

Finally, you should consider runtime serialization when the communication is happening between two .NET applications.

SOAP Versus XML-RPC

Remote procedure calling (RPC) refers to the ability to invoke a method of an object that resides outside of the caller's address space, as if it were local. Although RPC is an old term, dating back to the early days of networked computers, the concept of using XML as an RPC mechanism dates back to the early days of Web Services.

SOAP is not the only XML RPC mechanism; in fact, another mechanism, called XML-RPC, is arguably simpler and easier to use. However, this simplicity comes at the expense of flexibility. Although XML-RPC evolved from an early version of SOAP, Microsoft has chosen not to support XML-RPC directly in .NET. However, there is nothing to stop some enterprising developer from producing an XML-RPC framework for .NET.

 In fact, Charles Cook has developed just such a beast. Cook Computing offers XML-RPC.NET, currently at Version 0.8.1 as of this writing. XML-RPC.NET is available for download at *http://www.xml-rpc.net/*, licensed under the Lesser GNU Public License.

As I said earlier, .NET supports two general methods of serialization. Which one you should choose depends on your needs.

Runtime Serialization

Runtime serialization is used to serialize objects to binary or user-defined formats. In mapping CLR types to serialization format, the CLR type is favored; that is, it is assumed that both ends of the serialization channel understand how to map any given CLR type to a serialization format. With runtime serialization, you're guaranteed full fidelity between the objects you started with and the new objects you end up with. You can use one of the concrete formatter classes (`BinaryFormatter` or `SoapFormatter`) to serialize your data, or you can write your own class that implements `IFormatter` or extends `Formatter` to do the work.

In runtime serialization, serializable objects may be marked as such with the `Serializable` attribute, in which case the `IFormatter` class does all the work of serialization. Alternatively, a serializable object may implement `ISerializable`, in which case you are responsible for implementing the `GetObjectData( )` method to provide the necessary information to the `IFormatter`.

Because the built-in formatters favor CLR datatypes, .NET remoting uses them to serialize objects. This also means that the `SoapFormatter` assumes that the remote end of the serialization stream knows about the CLR, and how to convert objects from their SOAP representation to CLR types. This is fine for homogeneous systems, but the point of XML is to enable disparate systems to communicate. SOAP is useful for such communication between disparate systems, because it provides an XML schema that can contain all the information necessary to recreate an object remotely.

Example 9-4 shows the code that defines Angus Hardware's personnel records. I'll use this code throughout the examples in this chapter.

Example 9-4. Angus Hardware personnel records

```
public enum AddressType {
  Home,
  Office,
  Billing,
  Shipping,
  Mailing,
  Day,
  Evening,
  FAX
}

public enum State {
  AK, AL, AR, AZ, CA, CO,
  CT, DC, DE, FL, GA, HI,
  IA, ID, IL, IN, KS, KY,
  LA, MA, MD, ME, MI, MN,
  MO, MS, MT, NC, ND, NE,
  NH, NJ, NM, NV, NY, OH,
  OK, OR, PA, PR, RI, SC,
  SD, TN, TX, UT, VA, WA,
  WI, WV, WY
}

public class Address {
  public AddressType AddressType;
  public string[] Street;
  public string City;
  public State State;
```

Example 9-4. Angus Hardware personnel records (continued)

```
  public string Zip;
}

public class TelephoneNumber {
  public string AreaCode;
  public string Exchange;
  public string Number;
}

public class Employee {
  public string FirstName;
  public string MiddleInitial;
  public string LastName;
  public Address [] Addresses;
  public TelephoneNumber [] TelephoneNumbers;
  public DateTime HireDate;
}

public class Personnel {
  public Employee [] Employees;
}
```

To use these objects, of course, you would use a method something like this:

```
    private static Personnel CreatePersonnel( ) {
      Personnel personnel = new Personnel( );
      personnel.Employees = new Employee [] {new Employee( )};
      personnel.Employees[0].FirstName = "Niel";
      personnel.Employees[0].MiddleInitial = "M";
      personnel.Employees[0].LastName = "Bornstein";

      personnel.Employees[0].Addresses = new Address [] {new Address( )};
      personnel.Employees[0].Addresses[0].AddressType = AddressType.Home;
      personnel.Employees[0].Addresses[0].Street = new string [] {"999 Wilford Trace"};
      personnel.Employees[0].Addresses[0].City = "Atlanta";
      personnel.Employees[0].Addresses[0].State = State.GA;
      personnel.Employees[0].Addresses[0].Zip = "30037";
      personnel.Employees[0].HireDate = new DateTime(2001,1,1);
    }
```

To serialize these objects to SOAP, you need to use the SoapFormatter. Here's the Main( ) method of a program that uses the personnel objects and the CreatePersonnel( ) method defined above to serialize a personnel record to SOAP:

```
    public static void Main(string [] args) {
      Personnel personnel = CreatePersonnel( );
      IFormatter soapFormatter = new SoapFormatter( );
      using (FileStream stream = File.OpenWrite("PersonnelSoap.xml")) {
        soapFormatter.Serialize(stream,personnel);
      }
    }
```

If you run it as is, you'll get the following exception:

```
Unhandled Exception: System.Runtime.Serialization.SerializationException: The type
Personnel in Assembly personnelSoap, Version=0.0.0.0, Culture=neutral,
PublicKeyToken=null is not marked as serializable.
...
```

What went wrong? The SoapFormatter does not know how to serialize the type Personnel because it is not marked as serializable with the Serializable attribute. If you go back and apply that attribute to Personnel, you'll get the same exception for each of the Personnel object's fields.

In order to serialize an object using runtime serialization, it, and each object it contains, must either be marked as serializable or implement the ISerializible interface. Example 9-5 shows the complete program with Serializable attributes.

Example 9-5. Program to serialize personnel records to SOAP

```
using System;
using System.IO;
using System.Runtime.Serialization;
using System.Runtime.Serialization.Formatters.Soap;

[Serializable]
public enum AddressType {
  Home,
  Office,
  Billing,
  Shipping,
  Mailing,
  Day,
  Evening,
  FAX
}

[Serializable]
public enum State {
  AK, AL, AR, AZ, CA, CO,
  CT, DC, DE, FL, GA, HI,
  IA, ID, IL, IN, KS, KY,
  LA, MA, MD, ME, MI, MN,
  MO, MS, MT, NC, ND, NE,
  NH, NJ, NM, NV, NY, OH,
  OK, OR, PA, PR, RI, SC,
  SD, TN, TX, UT, VA, WA,
  WI, WV, WY
}

[Serializable]
public class Address {
  public AddressType AddressType;
  public string[] Street;
  public string City;
```

Example 9-5. Program to serialize personnel records to SOAP (continued)

```
  public State State;
  public string Zip;
}

[Serializable]
public class TelephoneNumber {
  public AddressType AddressType;
  public string AreaCode;
  public string Exchange;
  public string Number;
}

[Serializable]
public class Employee {
  public string FirstName;
  public string MiddleInitial;
  public string LastName;

  public Address [] Addresses;
public TelephoneNumber [] TelephoneNumbers;

  public DateTime HireDate;
}

[Serializable]
public class Personnel {
  public Employee [] Employees;
}

public class Serializer {
  public static void Main(string [] args) {
    IFormatter formatter = new SoapFormatter();
    Personnel personnel = CreatePersonnel();
    formatter.Serialize(File.OpenWrite("PersonnelSoap.xml"),personnel);
  }

  private static Personnel CreatePersonnel() {
    Personnel personnel = new Personnel();
    personnel.Employees = new Employee [] {new Employee()};
    personnel.Employees[0].FirstName = "Niel";
    personnel.Employees[0].MiddleInitial = "M";
    personnel.Employees[0].LastName = "Bornstein";

    personnel.Employees[0].Addresses = new Address [] {new Address()};
    personnel.Employees[0].Addresses[0].AddressType = AddressType.Home;
    personnel.Employees[0].Addresses[0].Street =
      new string [] {"999 Wilford Trace"};
    personnel.Employees[0].Addresses[0].City = "Atlanta";
    personnel.Employees[0].Addresses[0].State = State.GA;
    personnel.Employees[0].Addresses[0].Zip = "30037";
    personnel.Employees[0].HireDate = new DateTime(2001,1,1);
```

Example 9-5. Program to serialize personnel records to SOAP (continued)

```
    return personnel;
  }
}
```

The SOAP instance that this code produces looks pretty much like the ones you saw before, except that there's a lot more information included. These SOAP messages include everything the .NET Framework needs to completely reconstruct all the objects in the Personnel instance I serialized. I'll walk you through the generated SOAP data to explain what's been done:

```
<SOAP-ENV:Envelope
    xmlns:xsi="http://www.w3.org/2001/XMLSchema-instance"
    xmlns:xsd="http://www.w3.org/2001/XMLSchema"
    xmlns:SOAP-ENC="http://schemas.xmlsoap.org/soap/encoding/"
    xmlns:SOAP-ENV="http://schemas.xmlsoap.org/soap/envelope/"
    xmlns:clr="http://schemas.microsoft.com/soap/encoding/clr/1.0"
    SOAP-ENV:encodingStyle="http://schemas.xmlsoap.org/soap/encoding/">
```

The SOAP-ENV:Envelope element seems to have all the standard namespaces you'd expect for any SOAP message. One, however, is a little different. The clr prefix, assigned to the URI *http://schemas.microsoft.com/soap/encoding/clr/1.0*, represents the encoding for types in the .NET CLR. There is no actual web page at that URI; it's just used as a convention to indicate CLR encoding, which each instance of the .NET Framework inherently knows how to do:

```
<SOAP-ENV:Body>
    <a1:Personnel id="ref-1" xmlns:a1="http://schemas.microsoft.com/clr/assem/
personnelSoap%2C%20Version%3D0.0.
0%2C%20Culture%3Dneutral%2C%20PublicKeyToken%3Dnull">
```

The a1:Personnel element represents an instance of the Personnel type. The a1 namespace prefix, assigned to the URI *http://schemas.microsoft.com/clr/assem/ personnelSoap%2C%20Version%3D0.0.0.0%2C%20Culture%3Dneutral%2C%20 PublicKeyToken%3Dnull*, is used to mark types defined in the personnelSoap assembly; that is, the assembly generated from the source in Example 9-5.

Likewise, there is no web page at the URI *http://schemas.microsoft.com/clr/assem/ personnelSoap%2C%20Version%3D0.0.0.0%2C%20Culture%3Dneutral%2C%20 PublicKeyToken%3Dnull*. How would Microsoft know anything about the personnelSoap assembly you just generated? Like the clr prefix, the namespace URI is used as a convention to indicate what assembly the types come from, so that the object can be recreated correctly when reading it in from the serialization stream.

 If you decode the URI in the previous paragraph, you'll see that it actually consists of two parts: http://schemas.microsoft.com/clr/assem/, which indicates that the elements represent types defined in a CLR assembly; and personnelSoap, Version=0.0.0.0, Culture=neutral, PublicKeyToken=null, which indicates the particular assembly that defines the types. The assembly is identified by the return value of its ToString() method.

This instance of a1:Personnel is given the id attribute with the value ref-1, in case it's needed for future reference:

```
    <Employees href="#ref-3"/>
  </a1:Personnel>
```

The Employees element here indicates that the instance of a1:Personnel contains the instance of SOAP-ENC:Array with the id value of ref-3. That instance will be defined later in the SOAP document:

```
  <SOAP-ENC:Array id="ref-3" SOAP-ENC:arrayType="a1:Employee[1]" xmlns:a1="http://
  schemas.microsoft.com/clr/assem/personnelSoap%2C%20Version%3D0.0.0.
  0%2C%20Culture%3Dneutral%2C%20PublicKeyToken%3Dnull">
    <item href="#ref-4"/>
  </SOAP-ENC:Array>
```

The SOAP-ENC:Array element defines the encoding for an array. In this case, it's an array of one Employee (SOAP-ENC:arrayType="a1:Employee[1]"). The array's id value is ref-3, which was referenced above by the a1:Personnel element. The actual array elements are contained in item elements; the one element of this array refers to the object with id value ref-4:

```
  <a1:Employee id="ref-4" xmlns:a1="http://schemas.microsoft.com/clr/assem/
  personnelSoap%2C%20Version%3D0.0.0.
  0%2C%20Culture%3Dneutral%2C%20PublicKeyToken%3Dnull">
    <FirstName id="ref-5">Niel</FirstName>
    <MiddleInitial id="ref-6">M</MiddleInitial>
    <LastName id="ref-7">Bornstein</LastName>
    <Addresses href="#ref-8"/>
    <TelephoneNumbers xsi:null="1"/>
    <HireDate>2001-01-01T00:00:00.0000000-05:00</HireDate>
  </a1:Employee>
```

This a1:Employee element represents an actual instance of the Employee object with the id value of ref-4, which represents an item in the array. The first three of its child elements are simple string types, and their values are included inline. The Addresses and TelephoneNumbers elements, however, are arrays, and as such are referenced by their id attribute values:

```
  <SOAP-ENC:Array id="ref-8" SOAP-ENC:arrayType="a1:Address[1]" xmlns:a1="http://
  schemas.microsoft.com/clr/assem/personnelSoap%2C%20Version%3D0.0.0.
  0%2C%20Culture%3Dneutral%2C%20PublicKeyToken%3Dnull">
    <item href="#ref-9"/>
  </SOAP-ENC:Array>
```

This SOAP-ENC:Array element represents an array of a1:Address elements:

```
  <a1:Address id="ref-9" xmlns:a1="http://schemas.microsoft.com/clr/assem/
  personnelSoap%2C%20Version%3D0.0.0.
  0%2C%20Culture%3Dneutral%2C%20PublicKeyToken%3Dnull">
    <AddressType>Home</AddressType>
    <Street href="#ref-10"/>
    <City id="ref-11">Atlanta</City>
    <State>GA</State>
    <Zip id="ref-12">30037</Zip>
  </a1:Address>
```

This a1:Address element represents an array element, and itself contains another array of a1:Street elements:

```
<SOAP-ENC:Array id="ref-10" SOAP-ENC:arrayType="xsd:string[1]">
  <item id="ref-13">999 Wilford Trace</item>
</SOAP-ENC:Array>
    </SOAP-ENV:Body>
  </SOAP-ENV:Envelope>
```

Finally, there's the a1:Street element, and that's the end. Example 9-6 shows the complete serialized *PersonnelSoap.xml* file (with indentation added to make it easier to read).

Example 9-6. Personnel records serialized as SOAP

```
<SOAP-ENV:Envelope
  xmlns:xsi="http://www.w3.org/2001/XMLSchema-instance"
  xmlns:xsd="http://www.w3.org/2001/XMLSchema"
  xmlns:SOAP-ENC="http://schemas.xmlsoap.org/soap/encoding/"
  xmlns:SOAP-ENV="http://schemas.xmlsoap.org/soap/envelope/"
  xmlns:clr="http://schemas.microsoft.com/soap/encoding/clr/1.0"
  SOAP-ENV:encodingStyle="http://schemas.xmlsoap.org/soap/encoding/">

  <SOAP-ENV:Body>
    <a1:Personnel id="ref-1" xmlns:a1="http://schemas.microsoft.com/clr/assem/
personnelSoap%2C%20Version%3D0.0.0.0%2C%20Culture%3Dneutral%2C%20PublicKeyToken%3Dnull">
      <Employees href="#ref-3"/>
    </a1:Personnel>
    <SOAP-ENC:Array id="ref-3" SOAP-ENC:arrayType="a1:Employee[1]" xmlns:a1="http://
schemas.microsoft.com/clr/assem/personnelSoap%2C%20Version%3D0.0.0.
0%2C%20Culture%3Dneutral%2C%20PublicKeyToken%3Dnull">
      <item href="#ref-4"/>
    </SOAP-ENC:Array>
    <a1:Employee id="ref-4" xmlns:a1="http://schemas.microsoft.com/clr/assem/
personnelSoap%2C%20Version%3D0.0.0.0%2C%20Culture%3Dneutral%2C%20PublicKeyToken%3Dnull">
      <FirstName id="ref-5">Niel</FirstName>
      <MiddleInitial id="ref-6">M</MiddleInitial>
      <LastName id="ref-7">Bornstein</LastName>
      <Addresses href="#ref-8"/>
      <TelephoneNumbers xsi:null="1"/>
      <HireDate>2001-01-01T00:00:00.0000000-05:00</HireDate>
    </a1:Employee>
    <SOAP-ENC:Array id="ref-8" SOAP-ENC:arrayType="a1:Address[1]" xmlns:a1="http://
schemas.microsoft.com/clr/assem/personnelSoap%2C%20Version%3D0.0.0.
0%2C%20Culture%3Dneutral%2C%20PublicKeyToken%3Dnull">
      <item href="#ref-9"/>
    </SOAP-ENC:Array>
    <a1:Address id="ref-9" xmlns:a1="http://schemas.microsoft.com/clr/assem/
personnelSoap%2C%20Version%3D0.0.0.0%2C%20Culture%3Dneutral%2C%20PublicKeyToken%3Dnull">
      <AddressType>Home</AddressType>
      <Street href="#ref-10"/>
      <City id="ref-11">Atlanta</City>
      <State>GA</State>
      <Zip id="ref-12">30037</Zip>
```

Example 9-6. Personnel records serialized as SOAP (continued)

```
    </a1:Address>
    <SOAP-ENC:Array id="ref-10" SOAP-ENC:arrayType="xsd:string[1]">
      <item id="ref-13">999 Wilford Trace</item>
    </SOAP-ENC:Array>
  </SOAP-ENV:Body>
</SOAP-ENV:Envelope>
```

This serialized object can be read in by any assembly that has access to the PersonnelSoap assembly because of the namespace URI referencing personnelSoap, Version=0.0.0.0, Culture=neutral, PublicKeyToken=null. The code to deserialize a SOAP-serialized object is simple:

```
IFormatter formatter = new SoapFormatter();
Personnel personnel = (Personnel)formatter.Deserialize(
  File.OpenRead("PersonnelSoap.xml"));
```

 I haven't really touched on it, but the same process works equally well for binary serialization. Just use an instance of System.Runtime. Serialization.Formatter.Binary.BinaryFormatter instead of System. Runtime.Serialization.Formatter.Soap.SoapFormatter. The difference is that you can't write binary serialized objects to a text stream, as they contain binary data that won't be preserved in an 8-bit text stream environment.

Another way to control runtime serialization is to implement the ISerializable interface. When you use Serializable, all the work is on the SoapFormatter or BinaryFormatter, but the ISerializable interface requires you to implement the method GetObjectData().

GetObjectData() takes two parameters. The first is an instance of SerializationInfo to be populated by the method, and the second is an instance of StreamContext giving information about the actual bits being serialized or deserialized. This information is obtained at runtime, which gives runtime serialization its name.

Clearly, SOAP and binary serialization require that both the reader and the writer of the serialized data have full knowledge of the CLR and its types. Since one of the major goals of XML is to make disparate systems work together, runtime serialization places some extra requirements on the program doing the deserializing.

XML Serialization

XML serialization addresses the requirements mentioned in the previous section. In XML serialization, no assumptions are made about the program that produces the XML or the one that reads it. You may lose some precise CLR type detail, but interoperation with disparate applications is better than with runtime serialization. In order to completely divorce the XML from the CLR, the serialization uses XML

Schema datatypes. I mentioned in Table 8-2 that not every XSD datatype has a corresponding CLR datatype. Although each XSD datatype mapped to exactly one CLR datatype, many CLR datatypes could, potentially, each be represented by a number of different XSD datatypes.

The essential point to remember when differentiating runtime serialization from XML serialization is that, in the runtime serialization, the object being serialized actively controls the format of the serialization, whereas in the XML serialization, the object is passively serialized.

The XmlSerializer type contains the methods Serialize() and Deserialize(). Any object can be serialized to XML and, by default, all fields in an object are serialized as elements. Certain attributes can also be used to decorate existing classes and methods. Table 9-2 shows a complete listing of attributes that affect XML serialization.

Table 9-2. Attributes that affect XML serialization

Attribute name	Description
XmlAnyAttributeAttribute	Place this attribute on a member whose type or return type is an array of XmlAttribute or XmlNode. Any attributes deserialized from XML that do not have a corresponding member in the class are placed in the array.
XmlAnyElementAttribute	Place this attribute on a member whose type or return type is an array of XmlElement or XmlNode. Any elements deserialized from XML that do not have a corresponding member in the class are placed in the array.
XmlArrayAttribute	Place this attribute on a member that returns an array of objects to produce nested XML elements.
XmlArrayItemAttribute	Place this attribute on a member that returns an array of objects to indicate the type of each of the nested XML elements.
XmlAttributeAttribute	Place this attribute on a member to indicate that it is to be serialized as an XML attribute.
XmlChoiceIdentifierAttribute	Place this attribute on a member to indicate that the type of the data to be serialized is indicated by another member, returning an enumeration.
XmlElementAttribute	Place this attribute on a member to indicate that it is to be serialized as an XML element.
XmlEnumAttribute	Place this attribute on a member of an enumeration to set the name that XmlSerializer uses for the member.
XmlIgnoreAttribute	Place this attribute on a member to indicate that it should be ignored for purposes of serialization.
XmlIncludeAttribute	Place this attribute on a member to have XmlSerializer recognize base and derived classes.
XmlRootAttribute	Place this attribute on a class to indicate that the class should be serialized as the document element.
XmlTextAttribute	Place this attribute on a member to indicate that it should be serialized as XML text.

Table 9-2. Attributes that affect XML serialization (continued)

Attribute name	Description
XmlTypeAttribute	Place this attribute on a class to indicate the name of the type and namespace of the XML element.
System.ComponentModel. DefaultValueAttribute	Place this attribute on a member to indicate the default value for a member if no value is assigned.

With these attributes, you can take an arbitrary C# type and tell XmlSerializer exactly how you would like to serialize it to XML.

Example 9-7 shows a new XML format for an instance of the personnel records from Example 9-4.

Example 9-7. Angus Hardware personnel records in XML

```xml
<?xml version="1.0"?>
<personnel>
<employee firstname="Niel" middleinitial="M" lastname="Bornstein"
    hiredate="2001-01-01T00:00:00.0000000-05:00">
    <addresses>
      <address type="Home">
        <street>999 Wilford Trace</street>
        <city>Atlanta</city>
        <state>Georgia</state>
        <zip>30037</zip>
      </address>
    </addresses>
  </employee>
</personnel>
```

If you were to just serialize a Personnel object to XML, all the data would appear in elements as shown in Example 9-8.

Example 9-8. XML serialized without attributes

```xml
<?xml version="1.0"?>
<Personnel xmlns:xsd="http://www.w3.org/2001/XMLSchema" xmlns:xsi="http://www.w3.org/2001/
XMLSchema-instance">
  <Employees>
    <Employee>
      <FirstName>Niel</FirstName>
      <MiddleInitial>M</MiddleInitial>
      <LastName>Bornstein</LastName>
      <Addresses>
        <Address>
          <AddressType>Home</AddressType>
          <Street>
            <string>999 Wilford Trace</string>
          </Street>
          <City>Atlanta</City>
```

Example 9-8. XML serialized without attributes (continued)

```
        <State>GA</State>
        <Zip>30037</Zip>
      </Address>
    </Addresses>
    <HireDate>2001-01-01T00:00:00.0000000-05:00</HireDate>
  </Employee>
 </Employees>
</Personnel>
```

That's fine, if you want all your data in elements, but some people prefer a healthy mix of elements and attributes; this element-centric output does not match the format in Example 9-7. In addition, the element names don't match the format you want.

To generate the XML you want, repeat the code from Example 9-4, with the addition of attributes to control the serialization. Let me step through the changes in each class. First, AddressType doesn't need to change at all:

```
public enum AddressType {
    Home,
    Office,
    Billing,
    Shipping,
    Mailing,
    Day,
    Evening,
    FAX
}
```

If you'll look again at Example 9-7, you'll see that each state is actually listed by its full name, not the abbreviation as listed in the State enumeration. Here I've added an XmlEnumAttribute for each state name. Note that I've skipped some in the interest of space:

```
public enum State {
    [XmlEnum(Name="Alaska")]
    AK,
    [XmlEnum(Name="Alabama")]
    AL,
    [XmlEnum(Name="Arkansas")]
    AR,
    [XmlEnum(Name="Arizona")]
    AZ,
// ...
    [XmlEnum(Name="Washington")]
    WA,
    [XmlEnum(Name="Wisconsin")]
    WI,
    [XmlEnum(Name="West Virginia")]
    WV,
    [XmlEnum(Name="Wyoming")]
    WY
}
```

The Address class has one attribute, type, and four elements. Here I've added XmlAttributeAttribute and XmlElementAttribute, as appropriate. The AttributeName and ElementName fields of each attribute are used to set the names of the XML attributes and elements, respectively:

```
public class Address {
    [XmlAttribute(AttributeName="type")]
    public AddressType AddressType;
    [XmlElement(ElementName="street")]
    public string[] Street;
    [XmlElement(ElementName="city")]
    public string City;
    [XmlElement(ElementName="state")]
    public State State;
    [XmlElement(ElementName="zip")]
    public string Zip;
}
```

Similar to Address, the TelephoneNumber class has one attribute and three elements. Again, I've decorated each member with the appropriate attribute. Note also that here, as in Address, I've set the names of the attributes and elements to match the ones in the XML; that is, they all start with lowercase letters:

```
public class TelephoneNumber {
    [XmlAttribute(AttributeName="type")]
    public AddressType AddressType;
    [XmlElement(ElementName="areacode")]
    public string AreaCode;
    [XmlElement(ElementName="exchange")]
    public string Exchange;
    [XmlElement(ElementName="number")]
    public string Number;
}
```

Now we come to the meat of the personnel record, the Employee. This class has three attributes: firstname, middleinitial, and lastname, which I've treated with the appropriate attribute. However, the Employee class also has two additional elements, addresses and telephones. These two elements actually contain nested arrays of elements, so I've used the XmlArray and XmlArrayItem attributes to help the serializer figure out what to do with the XML elements it reads:

```
public class Employee {
    [XmlAttribute(AttributeName="firstname")]
    public string FirstName;
    [XmlAttribute(AttributeName="middleinitial")]
    public string MiddleInitial;
    [XmlAttribute(AttributeName="lastname")]
    public string LastName;

    [XmlArray(ElementName="addresses")]
    [XmlArrayItem(ElementName="address")]
    public Address [] Addresses;
    [XmlArray(ElementName="telephones")]
```

```
[XmlArrayItem(ElementName="telephone")]
public TelephoneNumber [] TelephoneNumbers;

[XmlAttribute(AttributeName="hiredate")]
public DateTime HireDate;
}
```

Here's the document element, personnel, which is decorated with XmlRootAttribute. Although the Employees member is an array of Employee objects, it is not a nested array, like addresses and telephones. By adding the XmlElement attribute directly to the member, the XmlSerializer knows that this member is to be serialized as an array of employee elements, without a separate top-level element:

```
[XmlRoot(ElementName="personnel")]
public class Personnel {
   [XmlElement(ElementName="employee")]
   public Employee [] Employees;
}
```

Finally, I've made some changes to the Serializer class, which I introduced in Example 9-5. Serializer's Main( ) method still uses the CreatePersonnel( ) to create some personnel records, but it then instantiates an XmlSerializer to deserialize the objects it created back out to a file:

```
public class Serializer {
   public static void Main(string [] args) {
      Personnel personnel = CreatePersonnel( );
      XmlSerializer serializer = new XmlSerializer(typeof(Personnel));
      using (FileStream stream = File.OpenWrite("Personnel.xml")) {
        serializer.Serialize(stream,personnel);
      }
   }
}
```

Unlike the SoapFormatter and BinaryFormatter, the XmlSerializer constructor takes the Type of the object being serialized as a parameter. This is because, unlike the formatters, the serializer is actually created specifically to handle one particular type of object.

 The XmlSerializer actually generates and compiles the source code of a class to serialize the object to XML at runtime. Because of this, you may notice a slight performance difference the first time you instantiate an XmlSerializer for a particular type during each run of your program.

Deserializing an object from XML is as simple as calling the XmlSerializer's Deserialize( ) method:

```
XmlSerializer serializer = new XmlSerializer(typeof(Personnel));
using (FileStream stream = File.OpenRead("Personnel.xml")) {
   personnel = (Personnel)serializer.Deserialize(stream);
}
```

This data is being serialized to and deserialized from files, but it could be any Stream. When deserializing from an XmlReader, you can ensure that the data stream is valid for the XmlSerializer instance you're using. The CanDeserialize( ) method takes an XmlReader parameter, and returns a Boolean value indicating whether the XmlReader contains data that can be deserialized by the XmlSerializer.

This is convenient, because when you're deserializing data from a source outside of your control, you don't always know what the file contains. The CanDeserialize( ) method can be used to control processing when you're unsure of the XML stream's contents.

At runtime, you can override the attributes that affect serialization with the XmlAttributeOverrides class. This class serves as the container for a collection of XmlAttributes instances, each one of which holds the overridden attributes for a particular type. XmlAttributes has a property for each type of XML attribute; for example, the XmlAttributeAttribute can be set with the XmlAttribute property. For those attributes that can exist in multiples, such as XmlElementAttribute, the property returns a collection of those attributes. For example, the XmlElements property returns a XmlElementAttributes collection, to which you can add XmlElementAttribute instances.

XmlAttributeOverrides is convenient if you want to serialize an object for which you don't have or can't alter the source code. You can customize the serialization in exactly the same ways as you could by applying the attributes in the source.

I've altered the same program we've been using to change the name of the root element from personnel to employees. The new lines are highlighted:

```
Personnel personnel = CreatePersonnel( );

XmlAttributeOverrides overrides = new XmlAttributeOverrides( );
XmlAttributes attributes = new XmlAttributes( );
attributes.XmlRoot = new XmlRootAttribute("employees");
overrides.Add(typeof(Personnel), attributes);

XmlSerializer serializer =
  new XmlSerializer(typeof(Personnel), overrides);
using (FileStream stream = File.OpenWrite("Personnel.xml")) {
  serializer.Serialize(stream,personnel);
}
```

SOAP Serialization

There's another form of XML serialization, which may seem redundant at first. You'll recall that runtime serialization was able to encode an object using SOAP. The SoapFormatter produced a SOAP stream that was optimized for recreating the original object in another .NET application; specifically, the object and all its members were encoded using CLR types. A non-.NET application reading that SOAP stream would most likely have no idea what to do with the data.

However, the `XmlSerializer` can also serialize an object to SOAP, with an emphasis on the standard SOAP encodings. With SOAP serialization, you get all the interoperability of XML, with additional CLR awareness. The key to standards-compliant SOAP serialization is the `SoapReflectionImporter` class.

The .NET Framework SDK Documentation will tell you that `SoapReflectionImporter` is reserved for internal use, and should not be used by your application. However, it does have one constructor and one method that you can use to serialize objects to SOAP.

The code in Example 9-9 demonstrates how to serialize the personnel records from earlier examples to SOAP, using the same `Personnel` class and the `CreatePersonnel()` method from before.

Example 9-9. Serializing personnel records to SOAP

```
public static void Main(string [] args) {

  Personnel personnel = CreatePersonnel();

  SoapReflectionImporter importer = new SoapReflectionImporter();
  XmlTypeMapping mapping = importer.ImportTypeMapping(typeof(Personnel));
  XmlSerializer serializer = new XmlSerializer(mapping);

  using (StreamWriter stream = File.CreateText("PersonnelSoap2.xml")) {
    XmlTextWriter writer = new XmlTextWriter(stream);
    writer.Formatting = Formatting.Indented;
    writer.WriteStartElement("AngusHardware");
    serializer.Serialize(writer,personnel);
    writer.WriteEndElement();
  }
}
```

The object will be serialized to the XML shown below:

```
<AngusHardware>
  <Personnel xmlns:xsd="http://www.w3.org/2001/XMLSchema" xmlns:xsi="http://www.w3.
org/2001/XMLSchema-instance" id="id1">
    <Employees href="#id2" />
  </Personnel>
  <q1:Array id="id2" q1:arrayType="Employee[1]" xmlns:q1="http://schemas.xmlsoap.org/
soap/encoding/">
    <Item href="#id3" />
  </q1:Array>
  <Employee id="id3" d2p1:type="Employee" xmlns:d2p1="http://www.w3.org/2001/
XMLSchema-instance">
    <FirstName xmlns:q2="http://www.w3.org/2001/XMLSchema" d2p1:type="q2:string">
Niel</FirstName>
    <MiddleInitial xmlns:q3="http://www.w3.org/2001/XMLSchema" d2p1:type="q3:string">
M</MiddleInitial>
    <LastName xmlns:q4="http://www.w3.org/2001/XMLSchema" d2p1:type="q4:string">
Bornstein</LastName>
```

```
    <Addresses href="#id4" />
    <HireDate xmlns:q5="http://www.w3.org/2001/XMLSchema" d2p1:type="q5:dateTime">
2001-01-01T00:00:00.0000000-05:00</HireDate>
  </Employee>
  <q6:Array id="id4" q6:arrayType="Address[1]" xmlns:q6="http://schemas.xmlsoap.org/
soap/encoding/">
    <Item href="#id5" />
  </q6:Array>
  <Address id="id5" d2p1:type="Address" xmlns:d2p1="http://www.w3.org/2001/XMLSchema-
instance">
    <AddressType d2p1:type="AddressType">Home</AddressType>
    <Street href="#id6" />
    <City xmlns:q7="http://www.w3.org/2001/XMLSchema" d2p1:type="q7:string">Atlanta</
City>
    <State d2p1:type="State">GA</State>
    <Zip xmlns:q8="http://www.w3.org/2001/XMLSchema" d2p1:type="q8:string">30037</
Zip>
  </Address>
  <q9:Array id="id6" xmlns:q10="http://www.w3.org/2001/XMLSchema" q9:arrayType="q10:
string[1]" xmlns:q9="http://schemas.xmlsoap.org/soap/encoding/">
    <Item>999 Wilford Trace</Item>
  </q9:Array>
</AngusHardware>
```

That's not very pretty. Fortunately, just as there are attributes that affect the serialization of an object to XML, there are attributes that affect the serialization of an object to SOAP. Table 9-3 lists them, with their descriptions.

Table 9-3. Attributes that affect SOAP serialization

Attribute name	Description
SoapAttributeAttribute	Place this attribute on a member to indicate that it is to be serialized as a SOAP attribute.
SoapElementAttribute	Place this attribute on a member to indicate that it is to be serialized as a SOAP element.
SoapEnumAttribute	Place this attribute on a member that returns an enumeration type to indicate how it is to be serialized to SOAP.
SoapIgnoreAttribute	Place this attribute on a member to indicate that it is not to be serialized to SOAP.
SoapIncludeAttribute	Place this attribute on a member to have XmlSerializer recognize base and derived classes.
SoapTypeAttribute	Place this attribute on a class to indicate that the class is to be included in the generated XML Schema definition.

Just as with XML attributes, you can override the SOAP attributes that affect serialization at runtime. To make the Personnel object serialize a little more sensibly, you can either add the attributes to the Personnel type's source code, or you can add them using the SoapAttributeOverrides class.

The use of SoapAttributeOverrides is similar to XmlAttributeOverrides. Rather than go into extreme detail, I'll just show you the code, again with the changes highlighted:

```
Personnel personnel = CreatePersonnel();

SoapAttributeOverrides overrides = new SoapAttributeOverrides();
SoapAttributes attributes = new SoapAttributes();
attributes.SoapElement = new SoapElementAttribute("employees");
overrides.Add(typeof(Personnel), "Employees", attributes);

SoapReflectionImporter importer = new SoapReflectionImporter(overrides);
XmlTypeMapping mapping = importer.ImportTypeMapping(typeof(Personnel));
XmlSerializer serializer = new XmlSerializer(mapping);

using (StreamWriter stream = File.CreateText("PersonnelSoap2.xml")) {
  XmlTextWriter writer = new XmlTextWriter(stream);
  writer.Formatting = Formatting.Indented;
  writer.WriteStartElement("AngusHardware");
  serializer.Serialize(writer,personnel);
  writer.WriteEndElement();
}
```

The only changes effected by the SoapAttributeOverrides in this example is to change the name of the Employees element to employees, as shown here:

```
<AngusHardware>
  <Personnel xmlns:xsd="http://www.w3.org/2001/XMLSchema" xmlns:xsi="http://www.w3.
org/2001/XMLSchema-instance" id="id1">
    <employees href="#id2" />
  </Personnel>
  ...
</AngusHardware>
```

Moving On

All of the serialization methods I discussed in this chapter provide a robust environment for distributed computing. As you'll see in Chapter 10, SOAP is the basis for the .NET Framework's advanced web services and remoting capabilities.

XML and Web Services

Web Services is the buzz word that's making the rounds these days, and, in a way, it's probably the main reason you're reading this book at all. As you've seen, there are tons of XML support built into .NET, and it's all usable in any number of ways. But one of the ultimate goals of .NET's XML support is to enable Web Services.

Web Services is a framework for building distributed applications. That means that Web Services, by itself, is not a distributed application, but it provides a mechanism by which you can implement a distributed application.

> I sometimes have trouble deciding whether the term *Web Services* is singular or plural. I'll generally use the plural "Web Services," capitalized, as if it were singular, when I'm referring to the concept or mechanism, and the singular "web service," in lower case, when I'm talking about a particular application.

I don't have room here to give a thorough explanation of building a distributed application using Web Services. However, what I can do is provide an overview of the concept, show you the XML schemas behind it, and demonstrate how you can use the .NET Framework to deal with those schemas.

Defining Web Services

In its working draft, "Web Services Architecture Requirements" (*http://www.w3.org/TR/2002/WD-wsa-reqs-20020819*), the W3C Web Services Working Group lists the following definition:

> A Web service is a software application identified by a URI, whose interfaces and bindings are capable of being defined, described, and discovered as XML artifacts. A Web service supports direct interactions with other software agents using XML based messages exchanged via Internet-based protocols.

From this, you can isolate several key features of the Web Services architecture.

1. A web service is a distributed software application.
2. A web service is identifiable by a URI.
3. A web service's interfaces and bindings are *definable* via XML.
4. A web service's interfaces and bindings are *describable* via XML.
5. A web service's interfaces and bindings are *discoverable* via XML.
6. A web service communicates via XML messages.
7. A web service communicates over Internet-based protocols.

As you'll see later in this chapter, although all of these features are present in .NET, some of them are optional. In particular, the terms definable, describable, and discoverable are significant. As you'll see in a moment, three specific Web Services standards are responsible for the realization of these three features; they are W3C XML Schema, WSDL, and UDDI, respectively.

Web Services is built on a variety of standards, some of which actually serve multiple purposes. You've already seen some of them in other parts of this book, and others will be introduced for the first time here.

HTTP

Most web services, although by no means all, use the Hypertext Transfer Protocol, or *HTTP*, as their transport mechanism. The reason for this goes back to the roots of Web Services.

Web Services was conceived as a way to use the Internet, and specifically the World Wide Web, to perform more sophisticated tasks than it was originally intended for. The Web did support some rudimentary abilities to perform distributed processing via its *Common Gateway Interface (CGI)* protocol, but CGI was really intended to act as a gateway to other applications running on a web server or externally. Granted, these applications could do some interesting things, but their input was limited to HTTP POST or GET variables, and their output was limited to HTML or other formats that a web browser could interpret.

Web Services grew out of the idea that input and output could both be specified in XML, and the processing could be done by an application other than a web server. To get around the firewalls that some corporations use to block other types of traffic, many web services use the Internet port reserved for HTTP traffic; in fact, Web Services communication *is* HTTP traffic.

Although, as the W3C's definition makes explicit, a web service is uniquely addressable via a URI, a single web service may provide multiple functions. The actual function being invoked is determined at a higher-level protocol.

XML

XML is the basis for all the Web Services standards and protocols. Web Services uses XML as its language of choice because XML's strengths provide some very important Web Services features.

- XML provides a flexible, customizable format for structured data, meaning that many sorts of functions can be invoked, consuming and producing many sorts of data.

- XML can easily be transformed into an unlimited number of other formats, meaning that upstream processors need not be altered in order to use them in a Web Services environment.

- XML is license-free and platform independent, meaning that anyone can implement Web Services applications on any hardware platform without paying royalties.

XML Schema

XML Schema, which I introduced in Chapter 8, is used to define Web Services messages. The SOAP envelope, as you saw in Chapter 9, uses XML Schema types as the basis for its data encoding mechanism. XML Schema is also ideally suited for use in distributed applications because it guarantees that an XML request generated by a client will meet all the constraints required by the server that processes the request.

SOAP

SOAP, which I introduced in Chapter 9, is the serialization and messaging format used in .NET Web Services. As I also mentioned in Chapter 9, there are others, such as XML-RPC, but .NET does not support any other serialization formats natively.

WSDL

The *Web Services Description Language*, or *WSDL*, serves as a standard language for describing a particular web service. WSDL describes the public interface to a web service. Users of CORBA, another distributed application framework, may be familiar with *Interface Definition Language (IDL)*; WSDL serves a similar function. In addition to describing the interface, WSDL also describes the binding of services to lower level protocols.

The WSDL note is located at *http://www.w3.org/TR/2002/WD-wsa-reqs-20020819*.

UDDI

Universal Description, Discovery, and Integration, or *UDDI*, is the mechanism that provides for the discovery of available web services. The UDDI schema is fairly complex, and I'll describe it in detail—along with all the other relevant XML schemas—in the following section. In addition to the XML schema, UDDI includes the infrastructure necessary for web service discovery. Access to this infrastructure is itself implemented in the form of web services.

The various UDDI specifications are located at *http://www.uddi.org/specification. html*. And the major players each have UDDI documentation available on their own web sites; for example, IBM has *http://uddi.ibm.com/*, and Microsoft has *http://uddi. microsoft.com/*.

Where to Learn More About Web Services

There are many new books about Web Services, some of them good. For a good introduction to Web Services, although a bit Java-centric, check out *Web Services Essentials* (O'Reilly), by Ethan Cerami. For a more .NET-oriented book, look at *NET Web Services: Architecture and Implementation* by Keith Ballinger (Addison Wesley). If you are developing your projects with Visual Studio .NET, you may want to read some of the later chapters of *Building Web Services and .NET Applications*, by Lonnie Wall and Andrew Lader (McGraw-Hill).

Using Web Services

Using Web Services can be broken down into five distinct steps: choosing and implementing the Web Services provider, describing the web service, handling web service requests, creating web service clients, and publishing the web service.

Choosing a Web Services Provider

Before you begin developing your web service, you need to decide how you're going host it. You have several choices: ASP.NET and .NET Remoting are the easiest ones to choose, and I'll be focusing on ASP.NET in these examples, because it's the option that gives you the most flexibility.

If you choose to serve your web services with ASP.NET, you need to be sure you have a web server capable of serving ASP.NET pages. IIS, the web server that ships with all Windows NT and Windows Server installations, will do just fine. However, if you're running on Windows XP personal workstation, you don't have a web server.Describing Web Services

---

A web service is described with a WSDL file. The following elements are involved in a WSDL document:

definitions
> This is the root element of a WSDL document.

types
> This optional element can be used to define the data types which are used to describe the messages exchanged by this service.

message
> This element is used to describe the messages exchanged by this service. The message element may have any number of part sub-elements, each of which can represent an individual parameter to the message. In general, there will be two message elements for each combination of method and transport; one for the request and one for the response.

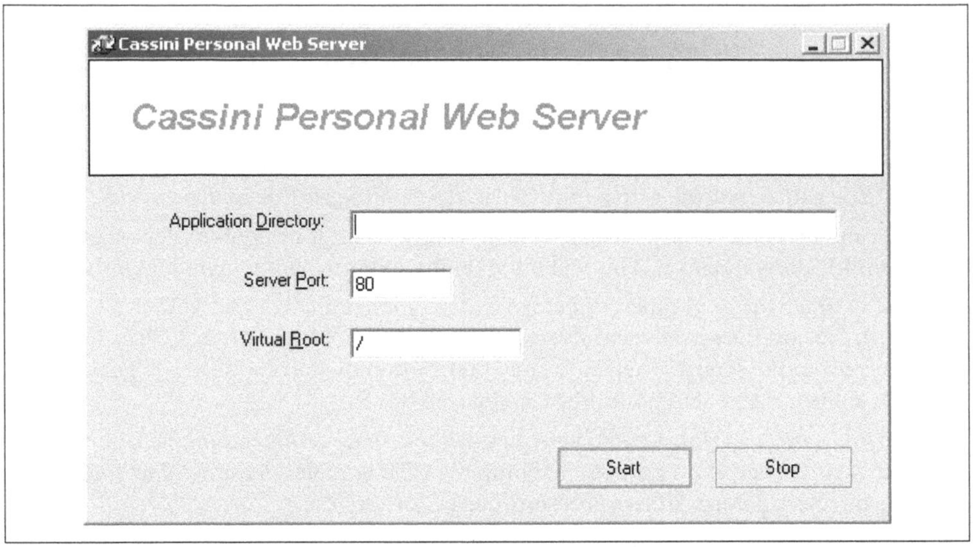

Figure 10-1. Cassini start screen

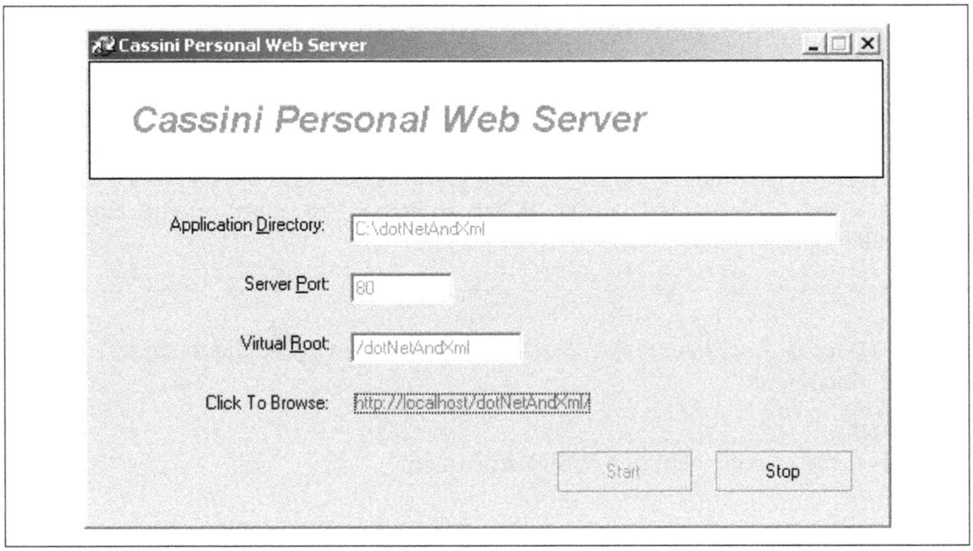

Figure 10-2. Cassini Web Server settings

portType

> This element is used to define a set of abstract operations. An abstract operation represents a single round-trip query and response, and gives it a name which will be used in the binding element. In general, there will be one portType element for each transport.

binding

> This element is used to connect an abstract operation to its message and transport. Transports can include SOAP, HTTP GET, and HTTP POST. In general, there will be one binding element for each transport.

service

> This element is used to map each portType to its binding, including a URL used to access the service.

documentation

> This element is used to contain additional, human-readable information about the service. It may appear anywhere in the WSDL document, has a mixed content model, and may contain any number of any other element (xs:any in XML Schema).

import

This element is used to allow a WSDL document to include the contents of another.

Now I'll build a relatively simple WSDL document, which describes an inventory query service which I'll introduce a little later. The XML prolog and document element are fairly uneventful, except for the large number of namespaces. The namespaces will be used for various purposes later in the document:

```
<?xml version="1.0" encoding="utf-8"?>
<definitions xmlns:soap="http://schemas.xmlsoap.org/wsdl/soap/"
  xmlns:s="http://www.w3.org/2001/XMLSchema"
  xmlns:s0="http://angushardware.com"
  xmlns:soapenc="http://schemas.xmlsoap.org/soap/encoding/"
  xmlns:tm="http://microsoft.com/wsdl/mime/textMatching/"
  xmlns:mime="http://schemas.xmlsoap.org/wsdl/mime/"
  targetNamespace="http://angushardware.com"
  xmlns="http://schemas.xmlsoap.org/wsdl/">
```

The types element defines three elements using XML Schema: GetNumberInStock, GetNumberInStockResponse, and int. These elements will all be scoped in the target namespace, http://angushardware.com. The first two are complex types which define the parameters and return values of the messages, and the last one is equivalent to the predefined xs:int type:

```
<types>
  <s:schema elementFormDefault="qualified"
    targetNamespace="http://angushardware.com">
    <s:element name="GetNumberInStock">
      <s:complexType>
        <s:sequence>
          <s:element minOccurs="0" maxOccurs="1" name="productCode" type="s:string" />
        </s:sequence>
      </s:complexType>
    </s:element>
    <s:element name="GetNumberInStockResponse">
      <s:complexType>
```

```
      <s:sequence>
        <s:element minOccurs="1" maxOccurs="1" name="GetNumberInStockResult"
type="s:int" />
      </s:sequence>
    </s:complexType>
  </s:element>
  <s:element name="int" type="s:int" />
 </s:schema>
</types>
```

The two messages are defined here. GetNumberInStockSoapIn is a SOAP version of the GetNumberinStock request message, and GetNumberInStockSoapOut is a SOAP version of the GetNumberInStockResponse response message:

```
<message name="GetNumberInStockSoapIn">
  <part name="parameters" element="s0:GetNumberInStock" />
</message>
<message name="GetNumberInStockSoapOut">
  <part name="parameters" element="s0:GetNumberInStockResponse" />
</message>
```

This web service only supports a single operation, GetNumberInStock, so there is only one portType element. This element maps the GetNumberInStock operation to its SOAP input and output messages:

```
<portType name="InventoryQuerySoap">
  <operation name="GetNumberInStock">
    <input message="s0:GetNumberInStockSoapIn" />
    <output message="s0:GetNumberInStockSoapOut" />
  </operation>
</portType>
```

The binding element associates the InventoryQuerySoap portType with the SOAP transport, and defines the GetNumberInStock operation as a SOAP message:

```
<binding name="InventoryQuerySoap" type="s0:InventoryQuerySoap">
  <soap:binding transport="http://schemas.xmlsoap.org/soap/http" style="document" />
  <operation name="GetNumberInStock">
    <soap:operation soapAction="http://angushardware.com/GetNumberInStock"
style="document" />
    <input>
      <soap:body use="literal" />
    </input>
    <output>
      <soap:body use="literal" />
    </output>
  </operation>
</binding>
```

The service element describes the InventoryQuery service as being located at the URL *http://127.0.0.1/dotNetAndXml/InventoryQuery.asmx*, using the InventoryQuerySoap binding:

```
<service name="InventoryQuery">
  <port name="InventoryQuerySoap" binding="s0:InventoryQuerySoap">
    <soap:address location="http://127.0.0.1/dotNetAndXml/InventoryQuery.asmx" />
```

```
        </port>
    </service>
```

Finally, as in all XML documents, the root element has to be closed:

```
    </definitions>
```

That's it, the InventoryQuery web service is now fully described.

Example 10-1 shows the complete WSDL document I built. It's not a very compli-cated schema, but its contents can be confusing. Don't worry, though; you'll very rarely have to create it by hand. You'll see in a moment how the .NET Framework creates one for you on demand.

Example 10-1. WSDL document for InventoryQuery service

```xml
<?xml version="1.0" encoding="utf-8"?>
<definitions xmlns:soap="http://schemas.xmlsoap.org/wsdl/soap/"
xmlns:s="http://www.w3.org/2001/XMLSchema"
xmlns:s0="http://angushardware.com"
xmlns:soapenc="http://schemas.xmlsoap.org/soap/encoding/"
xmlns:tm="http://microsoft.com/wsdl/mime/textMatching/"
xmlns:mime="http://schemas.xmlsoap.org/wsdl/mime/"
targetNamespace="http://angushardware.com"
  xmlns="http://schemas.xmlsoap.org/wsdl/">
  <types>
    <s:schema elementFormDefault="qualified" targetNamespace="http://angushardware.com">
      <s:element name="GetNumberInStock">
        <s:complexType>
          <s:sequence>
            <s:element minOccurs="0" maxOccurs="1" name="productCode" type="s:string" />
          </s:sequence>
        </s:complexType>
      </s:element>
      <s:element name="GetNumberInStockResponse">
        <s:complexType>
          <s:sequence>
            <s:element minOccurs="1" maxOccurs="1" name="GetNumberInStockResult"
             type="s:int" />
          </s:sequence>
        </s:complexType>
      </s:element>
      <s:element name="int" type="s:int" />
    </s:schema>
  </types>
  <message name="GetNumberInStockSoapIn">
    <part name="parameters" element="s0:GetNumberInStock" />
  </message>
  <message name="GetNumberInStockSoapOut">
    <part name="parameters" element="s0:GetNumberInStockResponse" />
  </message>
  <portType name="InventoryQuerySoap">
    <operation name="GetNumberInStock">
      <input message="s0:GetNumberInStockSoapIn" />
```

Example 10-1. WSDL document for InventoryQuery service (continued)

```
        <output message="s0:GetNumberInStockSoapOut" />
      </operation>
  </portType>
  <binding name="InventoryQuerySoap" type="s0:InventoryQuerySoap">
    <soap:binding transport="http://schemas.xmlsoap.org/soap/http" style="document" />
    <operation name="GetNumberInStock">
      <soap:operation soapAction="http://angushardware.com/GetNumberInStock"
style="document" />
      <input>
        <soap:body use="literal" />
      </input>
      <output>
        <soap:body use="literal" />
      </output>
    </operation>
  </binding>
  <service name="InventoryQuery">
    <port name="InventoryQuerySoap" binding="s0:InventoryQuerySoap">
      <soap:address location="http://127.0.0.1/dotNetAndXml/InventoryQuery.asmx" />
    </port>
  </service>
</definitions>
```

The WSDL specification supported by .NET, currently at Version 1.1, is available at *http://www.w3.org/TR/wsdl*. It is technically a W3C Note, which means that it is only a submission to the W3C, and not an official recommendation or standard.

Creating a Web Service

At its simplest, creating a web service in .NET can be almost trivially easy. I'm going to start with a simple inventory query service. Example 10-2 shows the basic ASP.NET skeleton for such a service.

Example 10-2. InventoryQuery.asmx source code

```
<%@ WebService Language="C#" Class="InventoryQuery" %>

using System.Web.Services;

[WebService(Namespace="http://angushardware.com/InventoryQuery")]
public class InventoryQuery : WebService {
  [WebMethod]
  public int GetNumberInStock(string productCode) {
    return 0;
  }
}
```

Let's break this skeleton down into its basic components.

The presence of the @ WebService directive in a file with the .asmx extension tells the ASP.NET provider that the web service is located at InventoryQuery.asmx, that the web service's source code is written in C#, and that the implementation is in the class named InventoryQuery. The code could also be written in JScript .NET (JS) or Visual Basic .NET (VB). Additionally, the code could actually reside in a separate file, compiled into an assembly located in the .\Bin directory relative to the .asmx file:

```
<%@ WebService Language="C#" Class="InventoryQuery" %>
```

There is no restriction on the name of the assembly containing the class that implements a web service, and multiple web services may exist in the same directory. However, if multiple assemblies in the .\Bin directory each contain a class with the name listed in an .asmx file, there is no guarantee which one will be used when that web service is invoked.

The WebService attribute comes from the System.Web.Services namespace, and indicates that the class in question represents the implementation of a web service. The Namespace property sets the default namespace for the web service. The WebService attribute also has Name and Description properties, which allow you to set the public name of the web service, and give it a short textual description. The Name property defaults to the name of the class. A class that implements a web service does not actually need to have the WebService attribute; any class can implement a web service:

```
using System.Web.Services;

[WebService(Namespace="http://angushardware.com/")]
```

Although the Namespace property is optional, if you leave it off the ASP .NET provider will use *http://tempuri.org/* as the default, and it will generate many strong hints that you should change the namespace.

Web service implementations can extend the WebService type. The WebService type provides access to state information through its Application, Context, Server, Session, and User properties. Although extending WebService is not required for a web service implementation, I have chosen to do so in this example:

```
public class InventoryQuery : WebService {
```

Although the names are the same, the WebService attribute and the WebService type are completely different beasts. If it helps you to keep the distinction clear, remember that while attribute names always end with Attribute, they also have an alias to the name without Attribute on the end. So the WebService attribute type is actually formally called WebServiceAttribute, whereas the WebService type is just called WebService.

Finally, the GetNumberInStock method represents the InventoryQuery web service's GetNumberInStock message itself. Right now it will always return 0, since I've only created a stub method.

The WebMethod attribute indicates that the method it is attached to implements a particular web service message. By default, the name of the message is the name of the method itself, although the WebMethod attribute has a MessageName property that allows you to override the name. WebMethod also has an optional Description property:

```
[WebMethod]
public int GetNumberInStock(string productCode) {
  return 0;
}
```

 The WebMethod attribute is the only attribute that is absolutely required to implement a web service using ASP.NET. If no method within a class has the WebMethod attribute, the ASP.NET provider has no way of knowing what messages the web service supports.

To see the InventoryQuery web service in action, make sure the InventoryQuery.asmx file is in *C:\dotNetAndXml* (or whatever directory you set as the application directory in your web server), and navigate your web browser to *http://localhost/dotNetAndXml/InventoryQuery.asmx*. You should see the page in Figure 10-3.

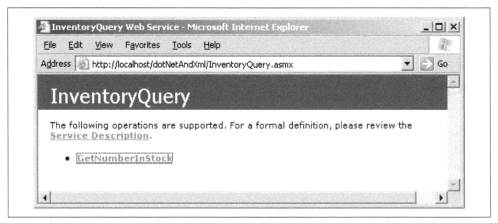

Figure 10-3. Main screen of the InventoryQuery web service

This HTML page is generated by the ASP.NET provider, based on the metadata included in the .asmx file and the class that implements the web service. If either the WebService attribute or the WebMethod attribute included a Description property, the descriptive text would be displayed here as well. If any more methods were exposed by attaching the WebMethod attribute to them, they would all be listed on this page as well.

Clicking on the "Service Description" link opens a new window containing the WSDL file that the ASP.NET provider has automatically generated. Example 10-3 shows the generated WSDL for the InventoryQuery web service. Note the similarities to Example 10-1.

Example 10-3. Generated WSDL for the InventoryQuery web service

```
<?xml version="1.0" encoding="utf-8"?>
<definitions xmlns:http="http://schemas.xmlsoap.org/wsdl/http/"
xmlns:soap="http://schemas.xmlsoap.org/wsdl/soap/"
xmlns:s="http://www.w3.org/2001/XMLSchema"
  xmlns:s0="http://angushardware.com"
xmlns:soapenc="http://schemas.xmlsoap.org/soap/encoding/"
xmlns:tm="http://microsoft.com/wsdl/mime/textMatching/"
  xmlns:mime="http://schemas.xmlsoap.org/wsdl/mime/"
targetNamespace="http://angushardware.com"
  xmlns="http://schemas.xmlsoap.org/wsdl/">
  <types>
    <s:schema elementFormDefault="qualified" targetNamespace="http://angushardware.com">
      <s:element name="GetNumberInStock">
        <s:complexType>
          <s:sequence>
            <s:element minOccurs="0" maxOccurs="1" name="productCode" type="s:string" />
          </s:sequence>
        </s:complexType>
      </s:element>
      <s:element name="GetNumberInStockResponse">
        <s:complexType>
          <s:sequence>
            <s:element minOccurs="1" maxOccurs="1" name="GetNumberInStockResult"
              type="s:int" />
          </s:sequence>
        </s:complexType>
      </s:element>
      <s:element name="int" type="s:int" />
    </s:schema>
  </types>
  <message name="GetNumberInStockSoapIn">
    <part name="parameters" element="s0:GetNumberInStock" />
  </message>
  <message name="GetNumberInStockSoapOut">
    <part name="parameters" element="s0:GetNumberInStockResponse" />
  </message>
  <message name="GetNumberInStockHttpGetIn">
    <part name="productCode" type="s:string" />
  </message>
  <message name="GetNumberInStockHttpGetOut">
    <part name="Body" element="s0:int" />
  </message>
  <message name="GetNumberInStockHttpPostIn">
    <part name="productCode" type="s:string" />
  </message>
  <message name="GetNumberInStockHttpPostOut">
```

```
    <part name="Body" element="s0:int" />
  </message>
  <portType name="InventoryQuerySoap">
    <operation name="GetNumberInStock">
      <input message="s0:GetNumberInStockSoapIn" />
      <output message="s0:GetNumberInStockSoapOut" />
    </operation>
  </portType>
  <portType name="InventoryQueryHttpGet">
    <operation name="GetNumberInStock">
      <input message="s0:GetNumberInStockHttpGetIn" />
      <output message="s0:GetNumberInStockHttpGetOut" />
    </operation>
  </portType>
  <portType name="InventoryQueryHttpPost">
    <operation name="GetNumberInStock">
      <input message="s0:GetNumberInStockHttpPostIn" />
      <output message="s0:GetNumberInStockHttpPostOut" />
    </operation>
  </portType>
  <binding name="InventoryQuerySoap" type="s0:InventoryQuerySoap">
    <soap:binding transport="http://schemas.xmlsoap.org/soap/http" style="document" />
    <operation name="GetNumberInStock">
      <soap:operation soapAction="http://angushardware.com/GetNumberInStock"
style="document" />
      <input>
        <soap:body use="literal" />
      </input>
      <output>
        <soap:body use="literal" />
      </output>
    </operation>
  </binding>
  <binding name="InventoryQueryHttpGet" type="s0:InventoryQueryHttpGet">
    <http:binding verb="GET" />
    <operation name="GetNumberInStock">
      <http:operation location="/GetNumberInStock" />
      <input>
        <http:urlEncoded />
      </input>
      <output>
        <mime:mimeXml part="Body" />
      </output>
    </operation>
  </binding>
  <binding name="InventoryQueryHttpPost" type="s0:InventoryQueryHttpPost">
    <http:binding verb="POST" />
    <operation name="GetNumberInStock">
      <http:operation location="/GetNumberInStock" />
      <input>
        <mime:content type="application/x-www-form-urlencoded" />
      </input>
```

```
    <output>
      <mime:mimeXml part="Body" />
    </output>
  </operation>
</binding>
<service name="InventoryQuery">
  <port name="InventoryQuerySoap" binding="s0:InventoryQuerySoap">
    <soap:address location="http://127.0.0.1/dotNetAndXml/InventoryQuery.asmx" />
  </port>
  <port name="InventoryQueryHttpGet" binding="s0:InventoryQueryHttpGet">
    <http:address location="http://127.0.0.1/dotNetAndXml/InventoryQuery.asmx" />
  </port>
  <port name="InventoryQueryHttpPost" binding="s0:InventoryQueryHttpPost">
    <http:address location="http://127.0.0.1/dotNetAndXml/InventoryQuery.asmx" />
  </port>
</service>
</definitions>
```

As you'll recall from the earlier discussion, the WSDL document provides a complete description of the web service, including all the supported messages, types, port types, bindings, and services. In this case, the ASP.NET provider automatically supports REST-style HTTP POST and GET methods as well as SOAP over HTTP POST.

> There is an alternative style for web services known as *Representational State Transfer*, or REST. The basic premise of REST is that the HTTP methods GET, POST, PUT, and DELETE provide all the functionality needed to interact with any resources addressable by its URI. WSDL supports REST-based web services as well as SOAP and XML-RPC.

The generated WSDL file in Example 10-3 contains more information than the one in Example 10-1. However, you can see that the only real difference is the inclusion of additional transports for HTTP GET and HTTP POST. The .NET Web Services provider creates these bindings, in addition to SOAP, automatically.

Clicking on the "GetNumberInStock" link in Figure 10-3 will bring you to the page shown in Figure 10-4. This HTML page is also generated automatically by the ASP.NET Web Services provider.

From this page, you can issue a request to the GetNumberInStock method of the InventoryQuery web service. Entering in a value—say, "803B"—and clicking the Invoke button causes the method to be invoked with the given parameter.

This example uses the HTTP GET version of the web service, so the request that was actually sent to the web service provider used the following URL: *http://127.0.0.1/ dotNetAndXml/InventoryQuery.asmx/GetNumberInStock?productCode=803B.*

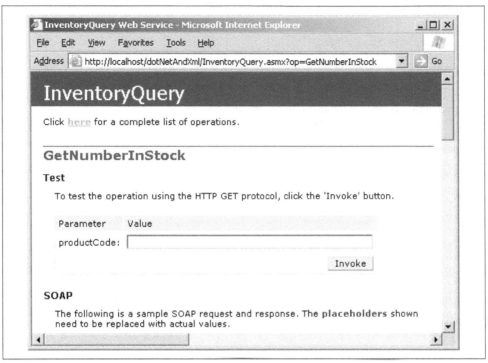

Figure 10-4. GetNumberInStock test page

Because right now the C# code always returns 0, the following response is always returned:

```
<?xml version="1.0" encoding="utf-8" ?>
<int xmlns="http://angushardware.com">0</int>
```

This would also be returned from the HTTP POST version. The SOAP request, however, would look quite a bit different. It would be sent with the following HTTP header and SOAP request envelope:

```
POST /dotNetAndXml/InventoryQuery.asmx HTTP/1.1
Host: 127.0.0.1
Content-Type: text/xml; charset=utf-8
Content-Length: 365
SOAPAction: "http://angushardware.com/GetNumberInStock"

<?xml version="1.0" encoding="utf-8"?>
<soap:Envelope xmlns:xsi="http://www.w3.org/2001/XMLSchema-instance" xmlns:xsd="http:
//www.w3.org/2001/XMLSchema" xmlns:soap="http://schemas.xmlsoap.org/soap/envelope/">
  <soap:Body>
    <GetNumberInStock xmlns="http://angushardware.com">
      <productCode>803B</productCode>
    </GetNumberInStock>
  </soap:Body>
</soap:Envelope>
```

The HTTP response header and SOAP response envelope would be the following:

```
HTTP/1.1 200 OK
Content-Type: text/xml; charset=utf-8
Content-Length: 400

<?xml version="1.0" encoding="utf-8"?>
<soap:Envelope xmlns:xsi="http://www.w3.org/2001/XMLSchema-instance" xmlns:xsd="http:
//www.w3.org/2001/XMLSchema" xmlns:soap="http://schemas.xmlsoap.org/soap/envelope/">
  <soap:Body>
    <GetNumberInStockResponse xmlns="http://angushardware.com">
      <GetNumberInStockResult>0</GetNumberInStockResult>
    </GetNumberInStockResponse>
  </soap:Body>
</soap:Envelope>
```

If you scroll a little further down the page in Figure 10-4, you'll see examples of requests and responses in all three versions of the web service.

Issuing a Web Service Request

You can use the .NET Framework's networking and XML classes to write code to issue web service requests and handle the responses quite easily. First, I'll show you how to write the code yourself; then I'll show you how to use the .NET Framework to generate the code for you.

Issuing an HTTP GET request

Once you have the InventoryQuery web service, it is possible to write a simple client that invokes the GetNumberInStock method over HTTP GET. Example 10-4 shows one possible implementation.

Example 10-4. Program to access GetNumberInStock via HTTP GET

```
using System;
using System.IO;
using System.Net;
using System.Xml.XPath;

public class GetNumberInStockHttpGet {

  public static void Main(string [] args) {
    WebRequest request = WebRequest.Create("http://127.0.0.1/dotNetAndXml
    /InventoryQuery.asmx/GetNumberInStock?productCode=803B");
    request.Method = "GET";

WebResponse response = request.GetResponse( );
    Stream stream = response.GetResponseStream( );

    XPathDocument document = new XPathDocument(stream);
    XPathNavigator nav = document.CreateNavigator( );
```

Example 10-4. Program to access GetNumberInStock via HTTP GET (continued)

```
    XPathNodeIterator nodes = nav.Select("//int");
    Console.WriteLine(nodes.Current);
  }
}
```

This example uses several classes you've seen before, including WebRequest, Stream, and XPathNavigator, to send a web service request to a URI and parse the response. If it doesn't look fairly intuitive at this point, I'd suggest reviewing Chapter 2 for a refresher on basic I/O, Chapter 4 for HTTP requests, and Chapter 6 for XPath.

The response is formatted as XML, as you saw the web service tester generated:

```
    <?xml version="1.0" encoding="utf-8" ?>
    <int xmlns="http://angushardware.com">0</int>
```

Parsing this response is a simple matter with XPath.

Issuing an HTTP POST request

The HTTP POST request is almost identical to the HTTP GET request, except that rather than including parameter values in the URL, they are sent to the server in the content of the HTTP request. Example 10-5 shows a program which uses HTTP POST to invoke the GetNumberInStock method.

Example 10-5. Program to access GetNumberInStock via HTTP POST

```
using System;
using System.IO;
using System.Net;

public class GetNumberInStockHttpPost {

  public static void Main(string [] args) {
    string content = "productCode=803B";

    HttpWebRequest request = (HttpWebRequest)WebRequest.Create(
      "http://127.0.0.1:80/dotNetAndXml/InventoryQuery.asmx/GetNumberInStock");
    request.Method = "POST";
    request.ContentType = "application/x-www-form-urlencoded";
    request.ContentLength = content.Length;

    StreamWriter streamWriter =
      new StreamWriter(request.GetRequestStream());
    streamWriter.Write(content);
    streamWriter.Flush();

    WebResponse response = request.GetResponse();
    Stream stream = response.GetResponseStream();

    XPathDocument document = new XPathDocument(stream);
    XPathNavigator nav = document.CreateNavigator();
```

```
    XPathNodeIterator nodes = nav.Select("//int");
    Console.WriteLine(nodes.Current);
  }
}
```

In Example 10-5, the content variable holds the content of the POST request, and the response to the request is the same as for Example 10-4. Note that the Content-Type header of the HTTP POST request must be set to application/x-www-form-urlencoded, which is the same encoding used for submitting forms in a web browser.

The content of the POST request takes the form of name/value pairs, with the name of the variable, followed by a = character and its value. The name/value pairs are separated from each other with the & character. Each name and value is further encoded as follows:

- Any space characters are replaced with the + character.
- The reserved characters /, ?, :, @, = and & are escaped by replacing them with %HH, a percent sign and two hexadecimal digits representing the ASCII code of the character.

Issuing a SOAP request

Like the HTTP GET request, you can write a simple program to issue the SOAP request and handle the SOAP response. Example 10-6 shows one possible program to do this.

Example 10-6. Program to generate GetNumberInStock request via SOAP

```
using System;
using System.IO;
using System.Net;
using System.Xml;

public class GetNumberInStockSoap {

  private const string soapNS =
    "http://schemas.xmlsoap.org/soap/envelope/";
  private static readonly encoding = Encoding.UTF8;

  public static void Main(string [] args) {
    MemoryStream stream = new MemoryStream( );
    XmlTextWriter writer = new XmlTextWriter(stream,encoding);

    writer.WriteStartDocument( );
    writer.WriteStartElement("soap","Envelope",soapNS);
    writer.WriteStartElement("Body",soapNS);
    writer.WriteStartElement("GetNumberInStock",angusNS);
    writer.WriteElementString("productCode","803B");
    writer.WriteEndElement( ); // GetNumberInStock
    writer.WriteEndElement( ); // soap:Body
```

```
    writer.WriteEndElement( ); // soap:Envelope
    writer.WriteEndDocument( );
    writer.Flush( );
    stream.Seek(0,SeekOrigin.Begin);
    StreamReader reader = new StreamReader(stream);
    string soap = reader.ReadToEnd( );

    HttpWebRequest request = (HttpWebRequest)WebRequest.Create(
      "http://127.0.0.1/dotNetAndXml/InventoryQuery.asmx");

    request.Method = "POST";
    request.ContentType = "text/xml; charset=" + encoding.HeaderName;
    request.ContentLength = soap.Length;
    request.Headers["SOAPAction"] = "http://angushardware.com/InventoryQuery/
GetNumberInStock";

    StreamWriter streamWriter =
      new StreamWriter(request.GetRequestStream( ));
    streamWriter.Write(soap);
    streamWriter.Flush( );

    WebResponse response = request.GetResponse( );
    Stream responseStream = response.GetResponseStream( );
    XPathDocument document = new XPathDocument(responseStream);
    XPathNavigator nav = document.CreateNavigator( );
    XPathNodeIterator nodes =
      nav.Select("//Envelope/Body/GetNumberInStockResponse/GetNumberInStockResult");
    Console.WriteLine(nodes.Current);
  }
}
```

Example 10-6 bears a closer look. It consists of three major parts. The first part, shown here, creates the SOAP envelope using an XmlTextWriter instance wrapped around a MemoryStream, and stores it in a string variable named soap:

```
    MemoryStream stream = new MemoryStream( );
    XmlTextWriter writer = new XmlTextWriter(stream,encoding);

    writer.WriteStartDocument( );
    writer.WriteStartElement("soap","Envelope",soapNS);
    ...
    writer.WriteEndElement( ); // soap:Envelope
    writer.WriteEndDocument( );
    writer.Flush( );
    stream.Seek(0,SeekOrigin.Begin);
    StreamReader reader = new StreamReader(stream);
    string soap = reader.ReadToEnd( );
```

The MemoryStream is necessary because the web services provider will only accept requests with UTF-8 encoding, and you can only set the encoding of an XmlTextWriter when passing a base Stream in the XmlTextWriter's constructor.

The second part creates the HTTP request. I'll step through it in smaller chunks, below:

```
HttpWebRequest request = (HttpWebRequest)WebRequest.Create(
    "http://127.0.0.1/dotNetAndXml/InventoryQuery.asmx");
```

This line uses the WebRequest.Create( ) method to create an HTTP request for the URI *http://127.0.0.1/dotNetAndXml/InventoryQuery.asmx*, which is the URI to which the InventoryQuery web service is bound:

```
request.Method = "POST";
```

A SOAP request can be sent over a variety of transports. However, an HTTP request must use the POST or PUT method in order to have content:

```
request.ContentType = "text/xml; charset=" + encoding.HeaderName;
```

A SOAP request must have XML content, and the character encoding rules must match that of the XML document. Since I created the XmlTextWriter by passing a Stream into the constructor, here I set the Content-Type header to text/xml and the same encoding I passed into the XmlTextWriter's constructor:

```
request.ContentLength = soap.Length;
```

When the HTTP request has content, the Content-Length header must be set to the length of the request's content:

```
request.Headers["SOAPAction"] = "http://angushardware.com/InventoryQuery/
GetNumberInStock";
```

To complete the HTTP headers, I set the SOAPAction header so that the web service provider knows which method is being called. Note that some SOAP implementations may require quotes around the URI, although they are optional in .NET.

The third part, shown below, extracts the returned value from the SOAP response, using a familiar XPathNavigator with the XPath query //Envelope/Body/GetNumberInStockResponse/GetNumberInStockResult, and writes the result to the console:

```
XPathDocument document = new XPathDocument(responseStream);
XPathNavigator nav = document.CreateNavigator( );
XPathNodeIterator nodes = nav.Select("//Envelope/Body/GetNumberInStockResponse/
GetNumberInStockResult");
Console.WriteLine(nodes.Current);
```

Generating Client Code

Of course, you shouldn't have to build HTTP or SOAP requests by hand. And indeed, you don't; the .NET Framework SDK includes a tool, wsdl.exe, which can generate web service client code from any WSDL file.

Run the command line wsdl /language:vb http://127.0.0.1/dotNetAndXml/ InventoryQuery.asmx?WSDL to produce the Visual Basic .NET source code listed in Example 10-7 for the InventoryQuery service.

Example 10-7. VB .NET client code for the InventoryQuery web service, using SOAP

```
'------------------------------------------------------------------------------
' <autogenerated>
'     This code was generated by a tool.
'     Runtime Version: 1.0.3705.288
'
'     Changes to this file may cause incorrect behavior and will be lost if
'     the code is regenerated.
' </autogenerated>
'------------------------------------------------------------------------------

Option Strict Off
Option Explicit On

Imports System
Imports System.ComponentModel
Imports System.Diagnostics
Imports System.Web.Services
Imports System.Web.Services.Protocols
Imports System.Xml.Serialization


'
'This source code was auto-generated by wsdl, Version=1.0.3705.288.
'

'<remarks/>
<System.Diagnostics.DebuggerStepThroughAttribute( ), _
 System.ComponentModel.DesignerCategoryAttribute("code"), _
 System.Web.Services.WebServiceBindingAttribute(Name:="InventoryQuerySoap", [Namespace]:
="http://angushardware.com/InventoryQuery")> _
Public Class InventoryQuery
    Inherits System.Web.Services.Protocols.SoapHttpClientProtocol

    '<remarks/>
    Public Sub New( )
        MyBase.New
        Me.Url = "http://127.0.0.1/dotNetAndXml/InventoryQuery.asmx"
    End Sub

    '<remarks/>
```

Example 10-7. VB .NET client code for the InventoryQuery web service, using SOAP (continued)

```
    <System.Web.Services.Protocols.SoapDocumentMethodAttribute("http://angushardware.com/
InventoryQuery/GetNumberInStock", RequestNamespace:="http://angushardware.com/
InventoryQuery", ResponseNamespace:="http://angushardware.com/InventoryQuery", Use:
=System.Web.Services.Description.SoapBindingUse.Literal, ParameterStyle:=System.Web.
Services.Protocols.SoapParameterStyle.Wrapped)> _
    Public Function GetNumberInStock(ByVal productCode As String) As Integer
        Dim results() As Object = Me.Invoke("GetNumberInStock", New Object()
{productCode})
        Return CType(results(0),Integer)
    End Function

    '<remarks/>
    Public Function BeginGetNumberInStock(ByVal productCode As String, ByVal callback As
System.AsyncCallback, ByVal asyncState As Object) As System.IAsyncResult
        Return Me.BeginInvoke("GetNumberInStock", New Object() {productCode}, callback,
asyncState)
    End Function

    '<remarks/>
    Public Function EndGetNumberInStock(ByVal asyncResult As System.IAsyncResult) As
Integer
        Dim results() As Object = Me.EndInvoke(asyncResult)
        Return CType(results(0),Integer)
    End Function
End Class
```

 Although SOAP is the default, wsdl.exe can also generate client code for HTTP GET and POST services. Use the command-line argument /protocol:HttpGet to generate the HTTP GET version, and /protocol:HttpPost to generate the HTTP POST version.

I've used Visual Basic .NET for this example in part to emphasize the fact that a Web Services need not be written in the same language as the server. In reality, the client need not even be a Windows-based computer.

Now that you've got the generated InventoryQuery proxy class, you can write a console application to use the proxy to call the web service. Example 10-8 shows one possible implementation in Visual Basic .NET.

Example 10-8. Visual Basic .NET program to call the InventoryQuery proxy class

```
Class InventoryQueryClient
  Shared Sub Main(byVal args as String())
    Dim query As InventoryQuery = New InventoryQuery()
    System.Console.WriteLine(query.GetNumberInStock(args(0)))
  End Sub
End Class
```

To compile this code outside of Visual Studio .NET, you'll need to use the following command line:

```
vbc.exe /reference:Microsoft.VisualBasic.dll /reference:System.dll /reference:System.
Web.Services.dll /reference:System.Xml.dll InventoryQueryClient.vb InventoryQuery.vb
```

This method of creating Web Services client code hides all the details of the XML and HTTP from you, although it still requires you to implement the web service code on the server side (unless you're creating a client for some third party's web service). Obviously, this is a much easier way to create Web Services client code.

Although the parameter list and behavior are identical, the InventoryQuery proxy class generated by wsdl.exe is not the same class I wrote in Example 10-2. To clarify the difference, you can specify the namespace for the generated proxy class by including the /namespace argument on the wsdl.exe command line. Also remember that the .asmx file looks in its .\Bin subdirectory for the assembly containing the InventoryQuery class that it uses to serve requests.

Building Requests with Remoting

Even the automatically generated code requires you to write code specifically to serve web service requests. There is one more way to use Web Services to invoke methods across a distributed application. *.NET Remoting* puts together everything you've seen up to this point to form the very heart of .NET's distributed application framework.

> *Remoting* refers to a specific form of Web Services that is tuned to work only between .NET applications. You should think of it as a form of Web Services, but not as fitting the purest definition of Web Services, because it depends on specific knowledge of the .NET typing system and assemblies.

There are three major differences between .NET Remoting and the previous Web Services examples. First, although Web Services uses the ASP.NET provider as the web service host, Remoting can run within any .NET application. Second, Remoting does not provide a WSDL file for the service, instead relying on the fact that server and client code are written specifically to work with each other. Finally, Remoting uses the runtime form of SOAP serialization I introduced in Chapter 9 rather than the SOAP serialization that Web Services uses.

The first step in implementing a Remoting server is to alter the InventoryQuery class from Example 10-2 as follows. As you'll see, the only difference is that I've removed the WebService and WebMethod attributes, and made InventoryQuery derive from MarshalbyRefObject:

```
using System;

public class InventoryQuery : MarshalByRefObject {
  public int GetNumberInStock(string productCode) {
```

```
      return 0;
    }
  }
```

The next step is to create a server to listen for requests to the InventoryQuery object. I'll call it InventoryQueryServer, and here's the code:

```
using System;
using System.Runtime.Remoting;
using System.Runtime.Remoting.Channels;
using System.Runtime.Remoting.Channels.Tcp;

public class InventoryQueryServer {
  public static void Main(string [] args) {
    TcpChannel chan = new TcpChannel(8085);
    ChannelServices.RegisterChannel(chan);

    RemotingConfiguration.RegisterWellKnownServiceType(
      Type.GetType("InventoryQuery"),
      "GetNumberInStock", WellKnownObjectMode.Singleton);

    System.Console.WriteLine("Hit return to exit...");
    System.Console.ReadLine();
  }
}
```

This program simply registers the service and waits for client requests. All that's left now is to write the client code:

```
using System;
using System.Runtime.Remoting;
using System.Runtime.Remoting.Channels;
using System.Runtime.Remoting.Channels.Tcp;

public class InventoryQueryRemotingClient {
  public static void Main(string [] args) {
    TcpChannel chan = new TcpChannel();
    ChannelServices.RegisterChannel(chan);

    InventoryQuery query = (InventoryQuery)Activator.GetObject(
      Type.GetType("InventoryQuery"),
      "tcp://localhost:8085/GetNumberInStock");

    Console.WriteLine(query.GetNumberInStock("803B"));
  }
}
```

That's a fairly sketchy overview of the Remoting process, but that topic moves beyond this book's realm. *Programming .NET Components* by Juval Löwy (O'Reilly) covers the topic more thoroughly than I can here.

Publishing a Web Service

Once you have set up your server to host a web service, you need to inform potential clients of its existence. Additionally, you might want to access a web service published by someone else. These are both jobs for UDDI.

 The UDDI specifications are maintained by OASIS, and as of this writing version 3.0 is available. However, I'll be referring to UDDI Version 2.04 in this chapter because Microsoft is currently only supporting the 1.x and 2.x releases of the specification.

The UDDI data model

The UDDI data model, described in an XML Schema, consists of five basic information elements. The following lists the elements of the UDDI document:

businessEntity

> The businessEntity element represents information about an entity that has published information about its services; it need not be a business *per se*. A businessEntity is uniquely identified by a businessKey, which is a *universally unique identifier* (UUID). The businessEntity contains additional information, including the name, description, contacts, alternate discovery URLs, identifiers such as Dun & Bradstreet D-U-N-S® Number, and categorys such as ISO 3166 Geographic Taxonomy. The businessEntity element also contains the businessService elements. All name and description elements in the UDDI document may have an optional language specified by the xml:lang element.

businessService

> The businessService element represents information about the web service published by a businessEntity. It has a serviceKey (UUID), and may be related back to its businessEntity by the businessKey. In addition to name, description, and category elements, each businessService element also contains bindingTemplate elements.

bindingTemplate

> The bindingTemplate element indicates the address and access method for the web service. It is uniquely identified by its bindingKey. This element contains description and tModelInstanceDetails elements, as well as either an accessPoint or hostingRedirector element. Possible accessPoint bindings include mailto, http, https, ftp, fax, phone, and other.

tModel

> The tModel, or *technical model*, element, indicates where the web service is documented. It is uniquely identified by its tModelKey. Possible documentation can include formal specifications such as a WSDL file, or a simple web page describing the service implementation.

publisherAssertion

The publisherAssertion element is used to indicate that two different businessEntities are in related in some way. Both businessEntities must make the same assertion, but with fromKey and toKey reversed. This element has no unique key; however, it can be uniquely identified by the concatenation of its elements: fromKey, toKey, and keyedReference.

 The XML Schema for UDDI Version 2 is available online at *http:// www.uddi.org/schema/uddi_v2.xsd.*

The UDDI APIs

Since UDDI is itself accessible as a web service, you can use .NET's tools to generate client code to access a UDDI registry. There are two SOAP APIs to access the UDDI registry: inquiry and publishing. I'll discuss inquiry first, and publishing in a moment.

Inquiry involves searching the UDDI registry for a given business, service, or binding. After you find the information you're interested in, you need to get specific instances of UDDI registry objects. The Inquire API provides four methods to find entities and four to retrieve detailed information about a known entity. The following lists the find and get methods:

find_binding

Finds a particular binding within a particular business in the UDDI registry. Returns a bindingDetail.

find_business

Finds businesses in the UDDI registry. Returns a businessList.

find_service

Finds services within a particular business in the UDDI registry. Returns a serviceList.

find_tModel

Finds tModel structures in the UDDI registry. Returns a tModelList.

get_bindingDetail

Returns a bindingDetail message for a given bindingKey.

get_businessDetail

Returns a businessDetail message for a given businessKey.

get_serviceDetail

Returns a serviceDetail message for a given serviceKey.

get_tModelDetail

Returns a tModelDetail message for a given tModelKey.

The UDDI Inquire API is described using WSDL at *http://uddi.microsoft.com/inquire. asmx?WSDL*, and the Publish API is at *http://uddi.microsoft.com/publish. asmx?WSDL*. You can use the wsdl tool to generate client code to access either of these services, and use the generated classes to find a business in the UDDI registry. The program in Example 10-9 finds any information for businesses whose names contain the string "bornstein".

Example 10-9. Program to search the UDDI registry for business named "bornstein"

```
using System;

public class FindBornstein {
  public static void Main(string[] args) {
    InquireSoap inquireSoap = new InquireSoap( );
    inquireSoap.Url = "http://test.uddi.microsoft.com/inquire";

    name businessName = new name( );
    businessName.Value = "bornstein";

    find_business find = new find_business( );
    find.name = new name [] { businessName };
    find.generic = "2.0";

    businessList businesses = inquireSoap.find_business(find);
    for (int i = 0; i < businesses.businessInfos.Length; i++) {
      businessInfo info = businesses.businessInfos[i];
      Console.WriteLine("Business name: {0} ({2})",
        info.name[0].Value, info.name[0].lang);
      Console.WriteLine("Business key: {0}", info.businessKey);
    }
  }
}
```

The classes generated by wsdl.exe may seem a bit convoluted, but it only generates the classes as needed by the UDDI Inquire API. The fact that there are a find_ business( ) method and a find_business class reflect the fact that the SOAP message is itself an object. You instantiate a find_business object and then send it to the UDDI server with the find_business( ) method.

Publishing a web service involves registering a service with the UDDI registry service. Again, there is an API whose methods you can call. The UDDI Publishing API can be broken down into three general areas: assertion, authorization, and others. The following describes the assertion methods of the UDDI Publishing API, which deal with the relationships between business entities:

add_publisherAssertions
    Adds an assertion describing the relationship between two business entities.

delete_publisherAssertions
    Removes an assertion describing the relationship between two business entities.

get_publisherAssertions
> Gets the set of assertions made by a particular publisher.

set_publisherAssertions
> Replaces the entire set of assertions made by a particular publisher.

get_assertionStatusReport
> Gets a report on the status of all assertions made by a particular publisher.

The authorization methods deal with *authorization tokens*. An authorization token represents a session between the UDDI registry operator and the client that is publishing information. get_registeredInfo is also included in this group:

discard_authToken
> Makes an authorization token invalid. This method is used as a logout method.

get_authToken
> Gets an authorization token from the UDDI registry site. This method is used as a login method.

get_registeredInfo
> Gets all information managed by a given client.

The remainder of the methods deal with creating and deleting the UDDI registry objects. For each object type (bindingTemplate, businessEntity, businessService, and tModel), there are corresponding save and delete methods:

delete_binding
> Deletes a bindingTemplate for a businessService.

save_binding
> Creates or updates a bindingTemplate for a businessService.

delete_business
> Deletes a businessEntity from the registry.

save_business
> Creates or updates a businessEntity.

delete_service
> Deletes a businessService for a businessEntity.

save_service
> Creates or updates a businessService for a businessEntity.

delete_tModel
> Logically deletes a tModel. The tModel is still available for use, but is simply hidden from searches using the find_tModel method.

save_tModel
> Creates or updates a tModel.

These web service methods can be accessed just as any web service method, by generating a proxy class using the wsdl tool, or by adding a web reference to your project in Visual Studio .NET.

The Microsoft UDDI registry is also available for interactive searching and publishing via an HTML front end. You can access the registry at *http://uddi.microsoft.com*.

 It is important to note that you can only publish a web service on the Microsoft UDDI servers if you have registered at *http://uddi.microsoft.com*. Microsoft also operates a test UDDI server at *http://test.uddi.microsoft.com*.

You can also set up your own UDDI server with Windows Server 2003.

Moving On

One of the promises of Web Services is to provide access to vast stores of information in meaningful ways. Web sites have been building interfaces to database for years, but with XML and Web Services, that data can be marked up in machine-readable formats. In the next chapter, I'll talk about some of the other ways the .NET Framework uses XML to work with data in relational databases.

CHAPTER 11

XML and Databases

XML is good for many things. It makes an excellent data interchange format for sharing data between disparate systems, whether through files on disk or through web services on a network. It can be used to share data among homogeneous systems, as in .NET remoting. It can even be used to present data to a person using a text editor for review and modification. In the end, though, the uses of XML are limited by the underlying data storage associated with the XML data; whether it's in a file or accessed across a network, it usually comes down to some sort of I/O stream.

Relational databases are optimized to store large amounts of data, provide non-sequential access to it, and search and sort the data, all things which XML is not great at. Ultimately, this comes down to the structural difference between a piece of software that is built for the specific purpose of providing this sort of data storage versus XML, a data format which is not optimized for anything in particular.

In addition to the structural differences, relational databases provide several properties that XML by itself cannot. The main properties of a relational database are usually referred to by their acronym ACID:

Atomicity

Any group of actions (called a *transaction*) taken on the database are done as a group and can only be undone as a group. Any failure of a part of a transaction causes the entire transaction to fail, and roll back the previous actions.

Consistency

Any transaction must cause the database to move from one consistent state to another. If a transaction causes the database to enter an inconsistent state, the whole transaction must fail atomically.

Isolation

Each transaction takes place in its own transaction space, and changes that are made within one transaction are invisible to other transactions until the transaction is complete. This ensures that other transactions always see the rest of the database in a consistent state.

Durability

> The completed results of each transaction are permanent and will survive any sort of system failure.

Obviously, XML is only a data format and cannot by itself ensure that any of the ACID properties will be implemented. In conjunction with ACID, relational databases provide fast, direct access to data in a way that XML cannot.

It's important to note that XML could be used as the underlying storage format for a relational database, if the database designer wanted to implement the layers of logic to enforce ACID. XML can also be stored within a database to take advantage of ACID. XML, as a technology, does not provide a reliable data store for the sorts of mission-critical application that relational databases are designed for.

The .NET Framework contains support for relational database access, and, as you might suspect, this support includes a rich set of XML-related features. I can't hope to tell you everything about using XML in databases with .NET, but I hope to give you a good introduction and tell you where to look for more information.

In addition to ADO.NET, SQL Server and Microsoft Access both have their own native methods of accessing their data as XML. For basic information on SQL Server, the Microsoft SQL Server home page at *http://www.microsoft.com/sql/* contains links to a wealth of information. SQL Server Magazine, at *http://www.sqlmag.com/*, is an excellent resource for SQL Server database administrators. The Microsoft Access home page is at *http://www.microsoft.com/office/access/*.

 I assume some knowledge of relational databases and the Structured Query Language (SQL) in this chapter. If you don't already know what SQL is, I suggest picking up *SQL in a Nutshell*, by Kevin Kline with Daniel Kline, Ph.D. (O'Reilly). For specific information on the flavor of SQL used in Microsoft SQL Server, look at *Transact-SQL Programming*, by Kevin Kline, Lee Gould, and Andrew Zanevsky (O'Reilly).

Introduction to ADO.NET

The .NET data access layer is called ADO.NET and consists of two major ways of dealing with data. The first way, and the easiest for developers familiar with SQL, is implemented in terms of the `IDataReader` interface. The second way is the `DataSet`.

Out of the box, .NET Framework Version 1.0 provides implementations of `IDataReader` in `System.Data.SqlClient.SqlDataReader` (for SQL Server data sources) and `System.Data.OleDb.OleDbDataReader` (for OLE data sources). .NET 1.1 adds the `System.Data.Odbc` and `System.Data.OracleClient` namespaces for access to ODBC and Oracle databases, respectively.

In fact, most of the classes in the System.Data.OleDb and System.Data. SqlClient namespaces simply provide implementations of interfaces in the System.Data namespace, so I'll just refer to the interfaces by their interface names, such as IDataReader, until we get down to examples. If you want to learn more about ADO.NET, I suggest *ADO.NET in a Nutshell*, by Bill Hamilton and Matthew MacDonald (O'Reilly).

Before you can actually use the IDataReader to read data, you need to set up a connection to the database using the IDbConnection interface. Exactly how you do that depends on whether you're using the SqlConnection or the OleDbConnection, but each one has a ConnectionString property that you can use to specify the database you're connecting to.

Creating an IDbConnection does not actually create the physical connection to the database. In fact, you can wait until the very last minute to open the connection, which you do by calling IDbConnection.Open( ).

Once you've created the connection, you must specify what data you want to read. The IDbCommand interface represents a SQL command, and you can create an instance of it by calling IDbConnection.CreateCommand( ) or its constructor. You can create an IDbCommand before you call IDbConnection.Open( ).

Executing the IDbCommand is as simple as calling one of its execute methods. There are three:

- IDbCommand.ExecuteNonQuery( ) is used to execute a SQL command that does not return any data, such as an insert, update, or delete statement.

- IDbCommand.ExecuteScalar( ) is used to execute a SQL command that returns a single value, such as select count(*).

- IDbCommand.ExecuteReader( ) is used to execute a SQL select command that returns a DataReader, which you can use to iterate over a number of rows and columns of resulting data.

The usage of the first two methods should be fairly obvious, but ExecuteReader( ) bears a little further explanation.

Reading Data

Angus Hardware, like most retail stores, occasionally offers its customers discounts in the form of coupons. They like to track which customers take advantage of which coupons, both as a marketing tool, and to aid in fraud detection. They've decided that the best way to manage this coupon usage data is with a relational database.

Figure 11-1 shows the portion of the coupon database schema I use in this chapter.

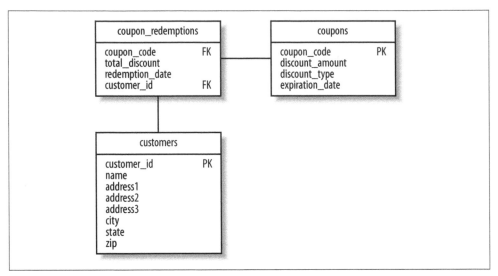

Figure 11-1. Coupon database schema

The results of any SQL select statement come in the form of a table of data. Although it may not represent any actual table in the database, it still consists of rows and columns. Take, for example, the following query:

```
select coupon_code, total_discount, redemption_date
from coupon_redemptions
where redemption_date >= '11/7/2002' order by customer_id;
```

This query returns a table of data that looks like Table 11-1.

Table 11-1. Results of SQL select statement

coupon_code	total_discount	redemption_date
117GG	10.00	11/7/2002
167YH	10.00	11/8/2002
987UI	20.00	11/8/2002
...		

The coupon_redemption table actually contains other columns, but because I only selected three, the result set only includes those three. In fact, you can see that these results are actually returned in order of a column that is not included in the result set, the customer_id. The result set also does not include all the rows, only the ones redeemed on or after November 7, 2002.

The IDataReader returned from ExecuteReader() provides a forward-only, unbuffered view of the data result set. Its Read() method is used to iterate through the result records in whatever order they were returned, and returns false when there are no more records to read.

The IDataReader interface also implements IDataRecord, which represents an individual data record. It provides a set of methods to read individual columns from the record. Although the IDataRecord is smart enough to do some conversions, it's up to you to know the type of each database column and what CLR types they can safely be converted to.

The SQL script used to create the database used for the examples in this chapter are on the web site for this book, along with all the sample code. If you don't have access to a SQL Server database, you can also use any OLE-compliant database by changing the classes from the ones in the System.Data.SqlClient namespace to those in the System.Data.OleDb namespace (or System.Data.Odbc or System.Data.OracleClient for an ODBC or Oracle database server if you're using Version 1.1 of the .NET Framework).

You can also use MSDE, the Microsoft Data Engine, which is a freely redistributable desktop version of SQL Server with some minor restrictions. See *http://www.microsoft.com/sql/techinfo/development/2000/MSDE2000.asp* for more information on MSDE 2000.

Let's build a program that reads redeemed coupons from a SQL Server database and prints them to the console.

The database connect string is different for every sort of database. You should consult your database administrator for the exact parameters for your database connection.

First, create the database connection. This is a SQL Server database named "AngusHardware", and you can connect as the system administrator without a password:

```
SqlConnection connection = new SqlConnection(
    "Initial Catalog=AngusHardware; User ID=sa");
```

Of course, in the interest of system security, a real database server would always require a password for the sa user, and you would never want to connect your application to a database as the sa user in any case.

Once the connection has been created (but not actually opened), you're free to use that connection to create SQL commands. This command will perform the query I introduced earlier, returning some coupons from the database:

```
SqlCommand command = new SqlCommand(
    "select coupon_code, total_discount, redemption_date " +
    "from coupon_redemptions where redemption_date >= '11/7/2002' " +
    "order by customer_id",
    connection);
```

Now that everything is set up, it's time to actually open the database connection:

```
connection.Open( );
```

Note that this method call can fail if the database connect string was not specified correctly, even though the SqlConnection constructor has come and gone without incident. This can make it difficult to trace connection problems, so be sure your connect string is correct before getting too involved in other program logic.

With an open connection, the SqlCommand can be executed. It's a select statement, so you can call ExecuteQuery( ) to return a SqlDataReader:

```
SqlDataReader reader = command.ExecuteReader( );
```

The SqlDataReader.Read( ) method returns a bool indicating whether a record was read from the database, so the while loop exits after the last record has been read. The code within the loop writes a line of text to the console containing the three columns selected from the database:

```
while (reader.Read( )) {
  Console.WriteLine("{0} {1} {2}", reader.GetString(0),
    reader.GetDouble(1), reader.GetDateTime(2));
}
```

IDataRecord has methods to get nearly every type of data from a data record, as well as indexers by column number or column name. With the indexer, the statement above could have been written as the following:

```
Console.WriteLine("{0} {1} {2}",
reader["coupon_code"],
reader["discount_amount"],
reader["date_redeemed"]);
```

If you use the indexer, however, you do have to cast the object to whatever type you are expecting.

Finally, it's always good to free up any resources you might have allocated:

```
reader.Close( );
connection.Close( );
```

Although it's not strictly necessary to close the SqlDataReader, because it will be closed when the underlying DbConnection is closed, it is considered good form to go ahead and close it.

Example 11-1 shows the complete program.

Example 11-1. Program to print redeemed coupons

```
using System;
using System.Data.SqlClient;

public class CouponPrinter {

  public static void Main(string [] args) {
    SqlConnection connection = new SqlConnection(
      "Initial Catalog=AngusHardware; Integrated Security=SSPI; User ID=sa");

    SqlCommand command = new SqlCommand(
      "select coupon_code, total_discount, redemption_date " +
      "from coupon_redemptions where redemption_date >= '11/7/2002' " +
      "order by customer_id",
      connection);

    connection.Open();

    SqlDataReader reader = command.ExecuteReader();

    while (reader.Read()) {
      Console.WriteLine("{0} {1} {2}", reader.GetString(0),
        reader.GetDouble(1), reader.GetDateTime(2));
    }

    reader.Close();
    connection.Close();
  }
}
```

Updating Data

Like TextReader and XmlReader, DataReader provides a read-only, forward-only view of the underlying data stream. This means that updating a database requires a new IDbCommand and the ExecuteNonQuery() method, which I mentioned earlier.

Example 11-2 shows a program to insert a new coupon into the database.

Example 11-2. Program to insert a new coupon into a database

```
using System;
using System.Data.SqlClient;

public enum DiscountType {
  Percentage,
  Fixed
}

public class AddCoupon {
  public static void Main(string [] args) {
    SqlConnection connection = new SqlConnection(
      "Initial Catalog=AngusHardware; User ID=sa");
```

Example 11-2. Program to insert a new coupon into a database (continued)

```
    SqlCommand command = new SqlCommand(
      "insert into coupons ( coupon_code, discount_amount, discount_type, expiration_date
) " +
      "values ( '077GH', 15, " + (int)DiscountType.Percentage +
      ", '11/30/2002' )", connection);

    connection.Open( );

    command.ExecuteNonQuery( );

    connection.Close( );
  }
}
```

The SqlCommand.ExecuteNonQuery( ) method simply executes the SQL command without expecting any values to be returned. If you're familiar with SQL, this insert statement should need no explanation.

Building a SQL Command

In the examples so far, I've built the SQL commands as simple text. There is another way that's more flexible. Of course, more flexibility usually involves more code.

The basic concept is that an IDbCommand.Parameters property returns an IDataParameterCollection, which is a collection of IDataParameter instances. The IDataParameter interface's properties include the name of a parameter coded into the IDbCommand, and the value you wish to bind to that name. Look at the following code snippet for an example:

```
    SqlCommand command = new SqlCommand(
      "insert into coupons ( coupon_code, discount_amount, " +
      "discount_type, expiration_date ) " +
      "values ( @coupon_code, @discount_amount, @discount_type, " +
      "@expiration_date )", connection);

    command.Parameters.Add(new SqlParameter("@coupon_code", "665RQ"));
    command.Parameters.Add(new SqlParameter("@discount_amount", 15));
    command.Parameters.Add(new SqlParameter("@discount_type",
      DiscountType.Percentage));
    command.Parameters.Add(new SqlParameter("@expiration_date ",
      new DateTime(2002,11,30)));
```

As you can see, the names of the parameters are embedded into the SQL command itself. Each parameter is then added to the IDataParameterCollection as a SqlParameter, with its name and value. The names I've used in this snippet match the names of the respective columns, with an @ prefixed; while the naming of the parameters is entirely up to you, the @ prefix is required.

You can use the Parameters property on any IDbCommand, for any select, insert, update, or delete statement. There are other properties to the IDbParameter sub-classes that pertain to the specific types of databases they know about.

The major benefit of building an IDbCommand this way is that every parameter can be assigned dynamically, instead of having to hard-code the command by repeatedly appending strings. Another benefit is that type conversion is automatic, so you don't have to use the ToString( ) method or any sort of string formatting to get a value that the database will accept. Finally, most database servers actually run more efficiently when a query is built this way; the query does not need to be parsed again every time it is run again with different data values.

Example 11-3 shows how both these benefits can be exploited in a rewritten version of the AddCoupon program from Example 11-2.

Example 11-3. Program to insert a new coupon using parameters

```
using System;
using System.Data;
using System.Data.SqlClient;

public class AddCoupon {
  public static void Main(string [] args) {
    SqlConnection connection = new SqlConnection(
      "Initial Catalog=AngusHardware; User ID=sa");

    SqlCommand command = new SqlCommand(
      "insert into coupons ( coupon_code, discount_amount, " +
      "discount_type, expiration_date ) " +
      "values ( @coupon_code, @discount_amount, " +
      "@discount_type, @expiration_date )", connection);

    SqlParameter couponCode = command.Parameters.Add(
      new SqlParameter("@coupon_code", SqlDbType.Char));
    SqlParameter discountAmount = command.Parameters.Add(
      new SqlParameter("@discount_amount", SqlDbType.Decimal));
    SqlParameter discountType = command.Parameters.Add(
      new SqlParameter("@discount_type", SqlDbType.TinyInt));
    SqlParameter expirationDate = command.Parameters.Add(
      new SqlParameter("@expiration_date", SqlDbType.DateTime));

    connection.Open( );

    couponCode.Value = "99GGY";
    discountAmount.Value = 5d;
    discountType.Value = DiscountType.Percentage;
    expirationDate.Value = new DateTime(2002,12,31);
    command.ExecuteNonQuery( );

    command.Parameters["@coupon_code"].Value = "81BIN";
    command.Parameters["@discount_amount"].Value = 10d;
    command.Parameters["@discount_type"].Value = DiscountType.Fixed;
```

Example 11-3. Program to insert a new coupon using parameters (continued)

```
    command.Parameters["@expiration_date"].Value =
      new DateTime(2003,1,31);
    command.ExecuteNonQuery( );

    connection.Close( );
  }
}
```

This example shows two ways to deal with the SqlParameter objects. Each of the SqlParameter objects is created and added to the SqlCommand's Parameters property, which is a SqlParameterCollection. The Add( ) method returns the newly created SqlParameter, which is then assigned to a local variable.

For the first execution of the SqlCommand, the SqlParameter instances are accessed by the local variables, and their values are assigned using the Value parameter. The SqlCommand.ExecuteNonQuery( ) method causes the SQL statement to be executed with those values.

In the second SqlCommand execution, the SqlParameter instances are accessed by name using the SqlParameterCollection's indexer (the other indexer accesses a SqlParameter by its integer index). Then, like before, its Value is set and the SqlCommand is executed with those values.

Manipulating Data Offline

Despite all these classes, there are times when you won't want to write SQL for every database operation, and you'll want to be able to manipulate entire sets of data as a whole without maintaining an open database connection. The mechanism for such operations is the DataSet.

A DataSet is an in-memory representation of a database. Just as a database contains tables, a DataSet contains a DataTableCollection (a collection of DataTable objects). Just as tables are related to one another, a DataSet contains a DataRelationCollection (a collection of DataRelation objects). Each DataTable contains a DataColumnCollection, which represents the table's columns, and a DataRowCollection, which represents the table's rows. The DataTable also contains references to various DataRelation and Constraint objects, which reflect the underlying table's relations and constraints. You can create a DataSet from scratch and fill it with data, or you can use an IDbDataAdapter to map a DataSet to a database.

Figure 11-2 shows the structure of the DataSet class and its related classes.

Here's where the talk about the databases meets the subject of this book, XML. You can serialize the data and structure of a DataSet to XML. You can generate a DataSet subclass from an XML Schema. You can read data from a DataSet as if it were an XML document. And finally, you can use the DataSet to track changes to a database using the DiffGram, which is, you guessed it, an XML document.

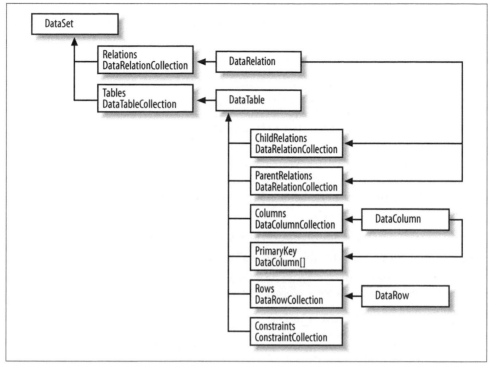

Figure 11-2. The DataSet object model

Creating a DataSet

The most obvious way to create a DataSet is to construct each of its objects and add them to the appropriate collections. First, create a new instance of DataSet named "AngusHardware." The DataSet represents the entire database schema:

```
DataSet dataSet = new DataSet("AngusHardware");
```

Next, add a table named "customers" to the DataSet. The DataTableCollection.Add( ) method has several overloads; by passing a string parameter, you're creating a new DataTable with the given name, and adding it to the DataSet's Tables property. Add( ) returns the newly created DataTable, which you'll use to create columns:

```
DataTable customers = dataSet.Tables.Add("customers");
```

Next, add a column to the "customers" table. The DataColumnCollection.Add( ) method returns the newly created DataColumn, which you'll use in a minute to assign the primary key. This Add( ) method, like the one on DataTableCollection, has several overloads. The one used here simply takes the name of the database column and the Type of the data it contains:

```
DataColumn customersCustomerId = customers.Columns.Add("customer_id",
    typeof(long));
```

The process is similar for each column. Note that some columns are nullable in the database and others are not; the AllowDBNull property indicates whether the column is nullable:

```
customers.Columns.Add("name",typeof(string)).AllowDBNull = false;
customers.Columns.Add("address1",typeof(string)).AllowDBNull = false;
customers.Columns.Add("address2",typeof(string));
customers.Columns.Add("address3",typeof(string));
customers.Columns.Add("city",typeof(string)).AllowDBNull = false;
customers.Columns.Add("state",typeof(string)).AllowDBNull = false;
customers.Columns.Add("zip",typeof(string)).AllowDBNull = false;
```

The last step for the "customers" table is to set the primary key, using the customersCustomerId DataColumn created a minute ago. Although this table has a simple, one-column primary key, the DataSet allows for concatenated primary keys via an array of DataColumn objects:

```
customers.PrimaryKey = new DataColumn [] {customersCustomerId};
```

A very similar process creates the "coupons" table:

```
DataTable coupons = dataSet.Tables.Add("coupons");
DataColumn couponCouponCode = coupons.Columns.Add("coupon_code",
  typeof(string));
coupons.Columns.Add("discount_amount",
  typeof(Double)).AllowDBNull = false;
coupons.Columns.Add("discount_type", typeof(int)).AllowDBNull = false;
coupons.Columns.Add("expiration_date",
  typeof(DateTime)).AllowDBNull = false;
coupons.PrimaryKey = new DataColumn [] {couponCouponCode};
```

And again for the "coupon_redemptions" table:

```
DataTable couponRedemptions =
  dataSet.Tables.Add("coupon_redemptions");
DataColumn couponRedemptionsCouponCode =
  couponRedemptions.Columns.Add("coupon_code", typeof(string));
couponRedemptions.Columns.Add("total_discount", typeof(Double)).AllowDBNull = false;
couponRedemptions.Columns.Add("redemption_date", typeof(DateTime)).AllowDBNull =
false;
DataColumn couponRedemptionsCustomerId =
  couponRedemptions.Columns.Add("customer_id", typeof(long));
```

Now that all the tables are created, it's time to assign the relations between them. The DataSet has a DataRelationCollection, whose Add( ) method has several overloads. The one used here takes the parent DataColumn and the child DataColumn. There are two relations in this example; one between coupons.coupon_code and coupon_redemptions.coupon_code, and one between customers.customer_id and coupon_redemptions.customer_id:

```
dataSet.Relations.Add(couponCouponCode, couponRedemptionsCouponCode);
dataSet.Relations.Add(customersCustomerId,
  couponRedemptionsCustomerId);
```

Finally, this line writes an XML Schema document that describes the DataSet to a file:

```
dataSet.WriteXmlSchema("Coupons.xsd");
```

The XML Schema that this program saved in *Coupons.xsd* is a normal XML Schema, and it can be used to recreate the DataSet in memory. The code to read in a DataSet's structure from a schema is very simple. In fact, it can be expressed succinctly in two statements:

```
DataSet dataSet = new DataSet();
dataSet.ReadXmlSchema("Coupons.xsd");
```

Example 11-4 shows the complete program that creates the DataSet for the coupon database, and saves an XML Schema for it.

Example 11-4. Creating a DataSet for the coupon database

```
using System;
using System.Data;

public class CreateDataSet {
  public static void Main(string [] args) {

    DataSet dataSet = new DataSet("AngusHardware");

    DataTable customers = dataSet.Tables.Add("customers");
    DataColumn customersCustomerId = customers.Columns.Add("customer_id",
      typeof(long));
    customers.Columns.Add("name",typeof(string)).AllowDBNull = false;
    customers.Columns.Add("address1",typeof(string)).AllowDBNull = false;
    customers.Columns.Add("address2",typeof(string));
    customers.Columns.Add("address3",typeof(string));
    customers.Columns.Add("city",typeof(string)).AllowDBNull = false;
    customers.Columns.Add("state",typeof(string)).AllowDBNull = false;
    customers.Columns.Add("zip",typeof(string)).AllowDBNull = false;
    customers.PrimaryKey = new DataColumn [] {customersCustomerId};

    DataTable coupons = dataSet.Tables.Add("coupons");
    DataColumn couponCouponCode = coupons.Columns.Add("coupon_code",
      typeof(string));
    coupons.Columns.Add("discount_amount",
      typeof(Double)).AllowDBNull = false;
    coupons.Columns.Add("discount_type", typeof(int)).AllowDBNull = false;
    coupons.Columns.Add("expiration_date",
      typeof(DateTime)).AllowDBNull = false;
    coupons.PrimaryKey = new DataColumn [] {couponCouponCode};

    DataTable couponRedemptions =
      dataSet.Tables.Add("coupon_redemptions");
    DataColumn couponRedemptionsCouponCode =
      couponRedemptions.Columns.Add("coupon_code", typeof(string));
    couponRedemptions.Columns.Add("total_discount",
      typeof(Double)).AllowDBNull = false;
```

Example 11-4. Creating a DataSet for the coupon database (continued)

```
    couponRedemptions.Columns.Add("redemption_date",
      typeof(DateTime)).AllowDBNull = false;
    DataColumn couponRedemptionsCustomerId =
      couponRedemptions.Columns.Add("customer_id", typeof(long));

    dataSet.Relations.Add(couponCouponCode, couponRedemptionsCouponCode);
    dataSet.Relations.Add(customersCustomerId,
      couponRedemptionsCustomerId);

    dataSet.WriteXmlSchema("Coupons.xsd");
  }
}
```

Populating a DataSet

The DataSet is now ready to use just as if you had created it procedurally. You can create new rows in each of its tables, using the DataTable.NewRow( ) and DataTable. Rows.Add( ) methods, as shown in Example 11-5.

Example 11-5. Populating the DataSet

```
using System;
using System.Data;

public class CreateData {
  public static void Main(string [] args) {

    DataSet dataSet = new DataSet( );
    dataSet.ReadXmlSchema("Coupons.xsd");

    DataTable couponsTable = dataSet.Tables["coupons"];

    DataRow couponRow = couponsTable.NewRow( );
    couponRow["coupon_code"] = "763FF";
    couponRow["discount_amount"] = 0.5;
    couponRow["discount_type"] = DiscountType.Fixed;
    couponRow["expiration_date"] = new DateTime(2002,12,31);
    couponsTable.Rows.Add(couponRow);

    dataSet.WriteXml("Coupons.xml");
  }
}
```

Some important highlights of this program are listed below. First, a new DataSet instance is created, and its structure is populated with the saved *Coupons.xsd* schema:

```
    DataSet dataSet = new DataSet( );
    dataSet.ReadXmlSchema("Coupons.xsd");
```

Next, the "coupons" table is retrieved using the DataTableCollection's string indexer:

```
DataTable couponsTable = dataSet.Tables["coupons"];
```

You can only create a new row using the DataTable's NewRow( ) factory method. This is because the columns must be populated according to the database schema stored in the DataTable. Note that the NewRow( ) method does not actually add the new DataRow to the DataTable; that happens later:

```
DataRow couponRow = couponsTable.NewRow( );
```

Now you can access each column from the new DataRow and set its value:

```
couponRow["coupon_code"] = "763FF";
couponRow["discount_amount"] = 0.5;
couponRow["discount_type"] = DiscountType.Fixed;
couponRow["expiration_date"] = new DateTime(2002,12,31);
```

Now that the DataRow is fully populated with data, it's time to add it to the DataTable's DataRowCollection. If some constraint or relation was not satisfied at this point, a specific DataException is thrown, giving details as to what constraint or relation was violated:

```
couponsTable.Rows.Add(couponRow);
```

Finally, the last line writes the entire DataSet to an XML file:

```
dataSet.WriteXml("Coupons.xml");
```

The *Coupons.xml* file generated by the last line is shown in Example 11-6. You can see that it's a normal XML file, and it is valid according to the schema in *Coupons.xsd*.

Example 11-6. Coupons.xml file

```
<?xml version="1.0" standalone="yes"?>
<AngusHardware>
  <coupons>
    <coupon_code>763FF</coupon_code>
    <discount_amount>0.5</discount_amount>
    <discount_type>1</discount_type>
    <expiration_date>2002-12-31T00:00:00.0000000-05:00</expiration_date>
  </coupons>
</AngusHardware>
```

Remember, you can always verify that any XML file is valid according to a DTD or XML Schema with the XmlValidatingReader:

```
XmlSchema schema  = XmlSchema.Read(
  new FileStream("Coupons.xsd", FileMode.Open), null);

XmlValidatingReader reader = new XmlValidatingReader(
  new XmlTextReader("Coupons.xml"));
reader.Schemas.Add(schema);
```

```
reader.ValidationType = ValidationType.Schema;

while (reader.Read()) {
  // this will throw an exception if invalid
}
```

You can also create an XML file that contains both the schema to define the DataSet structure and the data to populate it. The DataSet.WriteXml( ) method takes an additional optional parameter, an XmlWriteMode enumeration instance. The following list shows its values and what effect they have:

DiffGram

> The output file contains a DiffGram, which is an XML format that specifies the differences between a DataSet in memory and the underlying database. I'll talk more about the DiffGram later:

```
<?xml version="1.0" standalone="yes"?>
<diffgr:diffgram xmlns:msdata="urn:schemas-microsoft-com:xml-msdata" xmlns:
diffgr="urn:schemas-microsoft-com:xml-diffgram-v1">
  <AngusHardware>
    <coupons diffgr:id="coupons1" msdata:rowOrder="0" diffgr:
hasChanges="inserted">
      ...
    </coupons>
  </AngusHardware>
</diffgr:diffgram>
```

IgnoreSchema

> Only the data are written to the output file. This is the default:

```
<?xml version="1.0" standalone="yes"?>
<AngusHardware>
  <coupons>
    ...
  </coupons>
</AngusHardware>
```

WriteSchema

> The data and the schema are both written to the file:

```
<?xml version="1.0" standalone="yes"?>
<AngusHardware>
  <xs:schema id="AngusHardware" xmlns="" xmlns:xs="http://www.w3.org/2001/
XMLSchema" xmlns:msdata="urn:schemas-microsoft-com:xml-msdata">
    <xs:element name="AngusHardware" msdata:IsDataSet="true">
      ...
    </xs:element>
  </xs:schema>
  <coupons>
    ...
  </coupons>
</AngusHardware>
```

Reading a DataSet's structure and contents is done in a similar fashion. The DataSet. ReadXml() method takes an optional XmlReadMode enumeration parameter. The following lists its possible values and their effects:

Auto

If the data is a DiffGram, this is equivalent to XmlReadMode.DiffGram. If the DataSet already has a schema, or if the data has an inline schema (that is, it was written with XmlWriteMode.WriteSchema), this is equivalent to XmlReadMode. ReadSchema. Otherwise, it is equivalent to XmlReadMode.InferSchema.

DiffGram

The DiffGram is read and the changes are made to the DataSet in memory.

Fragment

The data is assumed to have come directly from a SQL Server FOR XML query.

IgnoreSchema

Any inline schema in the XML file is ignored, and the data are read into the DataSet's existing schema. Any data that do not fit the schema are discarded.

InferSchema

Any inline schema in the XML file is ignored. If the DataSet in memory already has a schema, the data are loaded and any necessary tables and columns are added to the schema. In case of a namespace clash between the DataSet's schema and the inferred schema, an exception is thrown.

ReadSchema

The inline schema in the XML file is read. If the DataSet in memory already has a schema, and new tables from the XML file are added, but an exception is thrown if any tables in the inline schema already exist in the DataSet.

Generating a DataSet

I said the generated schema is a normal XML Schema document, and it is. It does, however, contain a few extra attributes with the msdata prefix. These attributes help the XSD tool to generate a subclass of DataSet with convenience methods to access tables and columns in a more type-safe manner. After running the CreateDataSet program, execute this command:

```
xsd /dataset Coupons.xsd
```

 This is the same XSD tool that I introduced in Chapter 8.

The resulting file, *Coupons.cs*, contains the class AngusHardware, which extends DataSet, as well as a number of support classes. It's a much more complex structure than the one we generated in Chapters 8 and 9, and with good reason; it is used to create a DataSet, not just to load XML data with XmlSerializer.

You can see the benefit of the generated DataSet if you compare the code in Example 11-5 with that in Example 11-7.

Example 11-7. Populating a DataSet generated by xsd

```
using System;

public class CreateData {
  public static void Main(string [] args) {

    AngusHardware dataSet = new AngusHardware( );

    dataSet.coupons.AddcouponsRow(
      "763FF", 0.5, (int)DiscountType.Fixed, new DateTime(2002,12,31));

    dataSet.WriteXml("Coupons.xml");
  }
}
```

The generated DataSet class contains members named after the tables and columns in the schema. To start with, the name of the main class, AngusHardware, reflects the name of the DataSet. Each DataTable of the DataSet is represented by a generated private class within the DataSet; the "coupons" table, for example, is represented by the generated class AngusHardware.couponsDataTable. The AngusHardware.coupons property provides direct access to the "coupons" DataTable instance. The AngusHardware.couponsDataTable class has a method called AddcouponsRow( ), whose parameters match the columns of the table in the order in which they were added.

The object model for the generated AngusHardware Dataset is represented by Figure 11-3.

Connecting a DataSet to the Database

I haven't yet shown you how to actually connect the DataSet to an actual database. This is achieved using the IDataAdapter interface, which serves as an intermediate layer between the database table and the DataSet. You specify the SQL commands to select, insert, update, and delete from each table, and then use the Fill( ) method to fill the DataSet with data from the database, or the Update( ) method to update the database with data from the DataSet.

The first step is create a database connection, a SqlDataAdapter, and an AngusHardware DataSet:

```
SqlConnection connection = new SqlConnection(
  "Initial Catalog=AngusHardware; User ID=sa");
SqlDataAdapter adapter = new SqlDataAdapter( );
AngusHardware dataSet = new AngusHardware( );
```

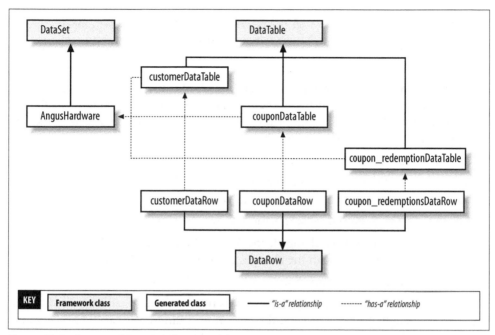

Figure 11-3. Generated DataSet object model

After that, you can create the select command for the SqlDataAdapter. This is the SqlCommand that will be used to populate the DataSet with data from the database:

```
adapter.SelectCommand = new SqlCommand("SELECT coupon_code, " +
  "discount_amount, discount_type, expiration_date FROM coupons",
  connection);
```

Because you'll be updating some of the data in this example and you would like those changes to be reflected in the database, the next step is to set the SqlDataAdapter's UpdateCommand property. Again, this is a normal SqlCommand, but unlike the SelectCommand it is necessary to add SqlParameters so that any updates get mapped to the correct columns:

```
adapter.UpdateCommand = new SqlCommand(
  "UPDATE coupons SET coupon_code = @couponCode, discount_amount = " +
  "@discountAmount, discount_type = @discountType, expiration_date = " +
  "@expirationDate WHERE coupon_code = @couponCode", connection);
adapter.UpdateCommand.Parameters.Add("@couponCode",
  SqlDbType.Char,10,"coupon_code");
adapter.UpdateCommand.Parameters.Add("@discountAmount",
  SqlDbType.Float,8,"discount_amount");
adapter.UpdateCommand.Parameters.Add("@discountType",
  SqlDbType.TinyInt,1,"discount_type");
adapter.UpdateCommand.Parameters.Add("@expirationDate",
  SqlDbType.DateTime,8,"expiration_date");
```

It's also possible to set the InsertCommand and DeleteCommand properties, but since you're only selecting and updating rows in this example, it's not necessary.

With the SqlDataAdapter all set up, the Fill( ) method is used to fill the DataSet with data from the database using the SelectCommand. The second parameter to Fill( ) tells the SqlDataAdapter the name of the DataTable to fill with data; this name can differ from the name of the database table:

```
adapter.Fill(dataSet, "coupons");
```

Updating a row of data is a simple matter of locating the row of interest and setting its properties. Here we set the expiration date to the current date and time:

```
dataSet.coupons[0].expiration_date = DateTime.Now;
```

Since some of the data were changed, the SqlDataAdapter.Update( ) method causes the database to be updated with the changes currently in the DataSet:

```
adapter.Update(dataSet, "coupons");
```

Note that although in this case the DataSet was filled, modified, and updated within the span of a single database session, the operation could just as easily have spanned a larger time. The DataSet is a disconnected view of the database, which means that a connection need not be maintained while the data are modified.

Example 11-8 shows the complete program.

Example 11-8. Creating a DataSet with IDataAdapter

```
using System;
using System.Data;
using System.Data.SqlClient;
using System.Data.SqlTypes;

public class FillDataSet {

  public static void Main(string [] args) {

    SqlConnection connection = new SqlConnection(
      "Initial Catalog=AngusHardware; User ID=sa");
    SqlDataAdapter adapter = new SqlDataAdapter( );
    AngusHardware dataSet = new AngusHardware( );

    adapter.SelectCommand = new SqlCommand("SELECT coupon_code, " +
      "discount_amount, discount_type, expiration_date FROM coupons",
      connection);

    adapter.UpdateCommand = new SqlCommand(
      "UPDATE coupons SET coupon_code = @couponCode, discount_amount = " +
      "@discountAmount, discount_type = @discountType, expiration_date = " +
      "@expirationDate WHERE coupon_code = @couponCode", connection);
```

Example 11-8. Creating a DataSet with IDataAdapter (continued)

```
    adapter.UpdateCommand.Parameters.Add("@couponCode",
      SqlDbType.Char,10,"coupon_code");
    adapter.UpdateCommand.Parameters.Add("@discountAmount",
      SqlDbType.Float,8,"discount_amount");
    adapter.UpdateCommand.Parameters.Add("@discountType",
      SqlDbType.TinyInt,1,"discount_type");
    adapter.UpdateCommand.Parameters.Add("@expirationDate",
      SqlDbType.DateTime,8,"expiration_date");

    adapter.Fill(dataSet, "coupons");

    dataSet.coupons[0].expiration_date = DateTime.Now;

    adapter.Update(dataSet, "coupons");
  }
}
```

Tracking Changes to a DataSet

When making changes to a DataSet, it is often useful to keep a record of the changes. That way you can make a set of related changes on the client machine, then transmit just the changes back to the server. This technique saves network time, because the changes are all transmitted at once, and it saves bandwidth, because only the changes are transmitted.

You could add another line of code to Example 11-8 to see that the DataSet maintains a "before" and "after" view of the data. Add this line before the Update( ) statement:

```
    dataSet.WriteXml(Console.Out, XmlWriteMode.DiffGram);
```

And you'll see the following output when you run the program:

```
<diffgr:diffgram xmlns:msdata="urn:schemas-microsoft-com:xml-msdata" xmlns:
diffgr="urn:schemas-microsoft-com:xml-diffgram-v1">
  <AngusHardware>
    <coupons diffgr:id="coupons1" msdata:rowOrder="0" diffgr:hasChanges="modified">
      <coupon_code>077GH       </coupon_code>
      <discount_amount>15</discount_amount>
      <discount_type>0</discount_type>
      <expiration_date>2002-11-09T14:17:41.6372544-05:00</expiration_date>
    </coupons>
    <coupons diffgr:id="coupons2" msdata:rowOrder="1">
      <coupon_code>665RQ       </coupon_code>
      <discount_amount>15</discount_amount>
      <discount_type>0</discount_type>
      <expiration_date>2002-11-30T00:00:00.0000000-05:00</expiration_date>
    </coupons>
    <coupons diffgr:id="coupons3" msdata:rowOrder="2">
      <coupon_code>81BIN       </coupon_code>
      <discount_amount>10</discount_amount>
      <discount_type>1</discount_type>
      <expiration_date>2003-01-31T00:00:00.0000000-05:00</expiration_date>
    </coupons>
```

```
    <coupons diffgr:id="coupons4" msdata:rowOrder="3">
      <coupon_code>99GGY     </coupon_code>
      <discount_amount>5</discount_amount>
      <discount_type>0</discount_type>
      <expiration_date>2002-12-31T00:00:00.0000000-05:00</expiration_date>
    </coupons>
  </AngusHardware>
  <diffgr:before>
    <coupons diffgr:id="coupons1" msdata:rowOrder="0">
      <coupon_code>077GH     </coupon_code>
      <discount_amount>15</discount_amount>
      <discount_type>0</discount_type>
      <expiration_date>2002-11-09T14:01:24.1830000-05:00</expiration_date>
    </coupons>
  </diffgr:before>
</diffgr:diffgram>
```

This is the DiffGram, and it shows the current state ("after") of the data in the DataSet, as well as a "before" state in the diffgr:before element.

The DiffGram is an XML document that has three sections. The first, the current data instance, is represented by an XML element whose name matches the DataSet name; in this case, that's the AngusHardware element. Under the data instance element, the current state of each row in each of the DataSet's DataTables is serialized as a simple XML element.

The second section, diffgr:before, lists the values of any rows that have changed before the change. And the third section, diffgr:errors, shows any errors that occurred during the generation of the DiffGram.

Example 11-9 shows the general format of the DiffGram.

Example 11-9. The DiffGram format

```
<diffgr:diffgram xmlns:msdata="urn:schemas-microsoft-com:xml-msdata" xmlns:diffgr="urn:
schemas-microsoft-com:xml-diffgram-v1">
  <DataSetName>
    <DataTableName diffgr:id="DataTableName1" msdata:rowOrder="0" diffgr:
hasChanges="modified">
      <DataColumnName>DataColumnValue</DataColumnName>
      <DataColumnName>DataColumnValue</DataColumnName>
      ...
    </DataTableName>
    <DataTableName diffgr:id="DataTableName2" msdata:rowOrder="1">
      <DataColumnName>DataColumnValue</DataColumnName>
      <DataColumnName>DataColumnValue</DataColumnName>
      ...
    </DataTableName>
  </DataSetName>
  <diffgr:before>
    <DataTableName diffgr:id="DataTableNamen" msdata:rowOrder="DataRown">
      <DataColumnName>DataColumnValue</DataColumnName>
      <DataColumnName>DataColumnValue</DataColumnName>
      ...
```

Example 11-9. The DiffGram format (continued)

```
      </DataTableName>
      ...
  </diffgr:before>
  <diffgr:errors>
    <DataTableName diffgr:id="DataTableNamen" diffgr:Error="ErrorText"/>
    ...
  </diffgr:errors>
</diffgr:diffgram>
```

The following details the `DiffGram` elements, attributes, and content:

`diffgr:diffgram`

This is the root element of the `DiffGram`. It uses two namespaces, prefixed with `msdata` and `diffgr`, respectively.

DataSetName

This element's name is the name of the `DataSet`. All the current values of each `DataTable`'s `DataRows` are included within this element.

DataTableName

This element's name is the name of the `DataTable`, and the element represents an individual `DataRow`.

DataColumnName

This element represents a `DataColumn` within a single `DataRow`. Its content is the current value of the column for that row.

`diffgr:before`

This is the element that contains the previous values of any changed `DataRows`. Its content represents the previous value of a `DataRow` instance with the matching value of the *DataTableName*'s `diffgr:id` attribute.

`diffgr:errors`

This is the element that contains any error messages. Its `diffgr:Error` attribute contains the error message for the `DataRow` instance with the matching value of the *DataTableName*'s `diffgr:id` attribute.

`diffgr:id`

This attribute represents a unique identifier for a `DataRow`. Its content is made up of the `DataTable` name and a sequential number. It is used to map the current value of a `DataRow` to the previous value in the `diffgr:before` section or to any errors in the `diffgr:errors` section.

`msdata:rowOrder`

This attribute indicates the order of the `DataRow` within the `DataTable`.

`diffgr:hasChanges`

This attribute is used to indicate whether the current value of a `DataRow` represents any changes, in which case the previous values will be listed in the `diffgr:`

before section. `diffgr:hasChanges` can have the value inserted, modified, or descent:

inserted
> The value `inserted` identifies an element which has been added

modified
> The value `modified` identifies an element that has been modified

descent
> The value `descent` identifies an element where one or more children from a parent-child relationship have been modified

`diffgr:Error`
> This attribute's content is a textual error message describing an error that arose while attempting to change the data in a `DataSet`.

Although the `DiffGram` is used internally by .NET for remoting and web services, it can also be used by any external system that needs to communicate database changes to a .NET `DataSet`.

Reading XML from a Database

In addition to writing the contents of a `DataSet` to an XML file, there are other ways to deal with a database's contents as XML. There are two general ways to do this: you can read the XML data directly, or you can read the data into a DOM tree.

Reading XML Data Directly

The `SqlCommand` class has another method that executes SQL queries, namely `ExecuteXmlReader()`. `ExecuteXmlReader()` returns an instance of `XmlReader` that can be used to read the data.

`ExecuteXmlReader()` is a method of `SqlCommand` and not `OleDbCommand` (or the `IDbCommand` interface) because it uses the SQL Server for xml clause. The result of such a query is XML, which can then be read using the `XmlReader` instance. Example 11-10 shows a program to read data using `ExecuteXmlReader()`.

> The `XmlReader` returned from `ExecuteXmlReader()` is actually of the type `XmlTextReader`, because the data returned from the query is a text stream.

Example 11-10. Reading data using ExecuteXmlReader()

```
using System;
using System.Data.SqlClient;
using System.Xml;

public class ReadDataAsXml {
```

Example 11-10. Reading data using ExecuteXmlReader() (continued)

```
public static void Main(string [] args) {
  string command = "SELECT name, expiration_date, total_discount " +
    "FROM coupons, coupon_redemptions, customers " +
    "WHERE coupons.coupon_code = coupon_redemptions.coupon_code " +
    "AND coupon_redemptions.customer_id = customers.customer_id " +
    "FOR XML AUTO";

  SqlCommand xmlCommand = new SqlCommand(command, connection);

  connection.Open( );
  XmlReader reader = xmlCommand.ExecuteXmlReader( );

  XmlDocument doc = new XmlDocument( );
  doc.Load(reader);
  doc.Save(Console.Out);

  connection.Close( );
  }
}
```

> Like all XmlReader subclasses, the XmlReader returned from SqlCommand.
> ExecuteXmlReader( ) keeps the underlying data source open, which
> means that the SqlConnection remains open as long as the XmlReader is.

The resulting XML document output to the console is shown here:

```
<?xml version="1.0" encoding="IBM437"?>
<customers name="Mark's Roofing">
  <coupons expiration_date="2002-11-30T00:00:00">
    <coupon_redemptions total_discount="2.150000000000000e+001" />
    <coupon_redemptions total_discount="1.525000000000000e+001" />
  </coupons>
</customers>
```

It already looks different from the DiffGram. First, all the column values are represented as XML attributes rather than elements. Second, the numeric data values are shown with full precision.

> SQL Server has a lot of built-in XML functionality, including the for
> xml clause, but it's outside of the scope of this book. For more infor-
> mation on selecting XML data directly from a SQL Server database,
> see chapter 8 of *Applied XML Programming for Microsoft .NET* by
> Dino Esposito (Microsoft Press).

Reading Data Into a DOM Tree

There's another way to read XML directly from a database. The XmlDataDocument, which extends XmlDocument, presents the contents of a DataSet as an XML document. At that point, the data can be treated just like any other XmlDocument, including navigating to specific nodes with XPath, writing it to any sort of Stream, transforming it with XSLT, and in fact any of the other techniques I've shown you in this book. Example 11-11 shows a program that executes the same query from example 11-10 and writes the resulting XML to the console.

Example 11-11. Reading data as XML using XmlDataDocument

```
using System;
using System.Data;
using System.Data.SqlClient;
using System.Xml;

public class ReadDataAsXml {
  public static void Main(string [] args) {

    DataSet dataSet = new DataSet("AngusHardware");

    SqlConnection connection = new SqlConnection(
      "Initial Catalog=AngusHardware; User ID=sa");

    string command = "SELECT name, redemption_date, total_discount " +
      "FROM coupon_redemptions a, customers b " +
      "WHERE a.customer_id = b.customer_id";
    SqlDataAdapter adapter = new SqlDataAdapter(command, connection);

    adapter.Fill(dataSet, "CouponsRedeemed");

    XmlDataDocument doc = new XmlDataDocument(dataSet);

    XmlTextWriter writer = new XmlTextWriter(Console.Out);
    writer.Formatting = Formatting.Indented;
    doc.WriteTo(writer);
  }
}
```

You've seen most of this before, but here's a quick look at some of the more important steps. First, you create the DataSet, the SqlConnection, a SQL select command, and the SqlDataAdapter:

```
DataSet dataSet = new DataSet("AngusHardware");
SqlConnection connection = new SqlConnection(
  "Initial Catalog=AngusHardware; User ID=sa");
string command = "SELECT name, redemption_date, total_discount " +
  "FROM coupon_redemptions a, customers b " +
  "WHERE a.customer_id = b.customer_id";
SqlDataAdapter adapter = new SqlDataAdapter(command, connection);
```

Next, you fill the adapter with data, naming the DataTable "CouponsRedeemed":

```
adapter.Fill(dataSet, "CouponsRedeemed");
```

Now, create an XmlDataDocument to wrap the DataSet. After this, doc is now ready to use, including all the base XmlDocument members:

```
XmlDataDocument doc = new XmlDataDocument(dataSet);
```

In this case, you can just use an XmlWriter to output the XmlDataDocument to the console:

```
XmlTextWriter writer = new XmlTextWriter(Console.Out);
writer.Formatting = Formatting.Indented;
doc.WriteTo(writer);
```

Other options include doing some sort of XPath query:

```
XmlNodeList nodes = doc.SelectNodes("//total_discount");
foreach (XmlElement element in nodes) {
  Console.WriteLine("Total discount is {0}", element.InnerText);
}
```

Unlike the XmlReader, the DataSet is a disconnected view of the data in the database. Once the DataSet is populated, you won't use up a database connection, so you can do as much with the DataSet as you want. The flip side of that is that all the data are stored locally, so large databases can use a lot of local storage.

 Another downside of the XmlDataDocument is that XPath queries are less efficient than SQL Server's built-in search capabilities. Use it wisely.

Hierarchical XML

XML that comes from a database, whether generated directly from a DataSet or through an XmlDataDocument, is inherently *relational*. That is, each table is represented by a single element, and its columns are represented by elements within it. Relations between tables are indicated by foreign key constraints and row identifiers. This makes perfect sense for relational data, but sometimes you might want to use a more hierarchical format.

XML is ideal for representing *hierarchical* data, because it is itself a tree-oriented format. The data from the coupon database could easily be represented in a combination of relational hierarchical XML structures, as shown in Example 11-12.

Example 11-12. Hierarchical representation of coupon database

```
<AngusHardware>
  <customers>
    <customer_id>1</customer_id>
    <name>Mark's Roofing</name>
    <address1>99 Beltline Pkwy</address1>
    <address2>Suite 100</address2>
    <city>Wannaque</city>
    <state>NH</state>
    <zip>05461    </zip>
  </customers>
  <coupons>
```

Example 11-12. Hierarchical representation of coupon database (continued)

```
    <coupon_code>077GH      </coupon_code>
    <discount_amount>15</discount_amount>
    <discount_type>0</discount_type>
    <expiration_date>2002-11-09T14:17:41.6370000-05:00</expiration_date>
  </coupons>
  <coupons>
    <coupon_code>665RQ      </coupon_code>
    <discount_amount>15</discount_amount>
    <discount_type>0</discount_type>
    <expiration_date>2002-11-30T00:00:00.0000000-05:00</expiration_date>
    <coupon_redemptions>
      <coupon_code>665RQ      </coupon_code>
      <total_discount>21.5</total_discount>
      <redemption_date>2002-11-10T00:00:00.0000000-05:00</redemption_date>
      <customer_id>1</customer_id>
    </coupon_redemptions>
  </coupons>
  <coupons>
    <coupon_code>81BIN      </coupon_code>
    <discount_amount>10</discount_amount>
    <discount_type>1</discount_type>
    <expiration_date>2003-01-31T00:00:00.0000000-05:00</expiration_date>
  </coupons>
  <coupons>
    <coupon_code>99GGY      </coupon_code>
    <discount_amount>5</discount_amount>
    <discount_type>0</discount_type>
    <expiration_date>2002-12-31T00:00:00.0000000-05:00</expiration_date>
  </coupons>
</AngusHardware>
```

This differs from the straight relational output from the DataSet, shown in
Example 11-13.

Example 11-13. Relational representation of coupon database

```
<AngusHardware>
  <customers>
    <customer_id>1</customer_id>
    <name>Mark's Roofing</name>
    <address1>99 Beltline Pkwy</address1>
    <address2>Suite 100</address2>
    <city>Wannaque</city>
    <state>NH</state>
    <zip>05461      </zip>
  </customers>
  <coupons>
    <coupon_code>077GH      </coupon_code>
    <discount_amount>15</discount_amount>
    <discount_type>0</discount_type>
    <expiration_date>2002-11-09T14:17:41.6370000-05:00</expiration_date>
  </coupons>
```

Example 11-13. Relational representation of coupon database (continued)

```
<coupons>
  <coupon_code>665RQ      </coupon_code>
  <discount_amount>15</discount_amount>
  <discount_type>0</discount_type>
  <expiration_date>2002-11-30T00:00:00.0000000-05:00</expiration_date>
</coupons>
<coupons>
  <coupon_code>81BIN      </coupon_code>
  <discount_amount>10</discount_amount>
  <discount_type>1</discount_type>
  <expiration_date>2003-01-31T00:00:00.0000000-05:00</expiration_date>
</coupons>
<coupons>
  <coupon_code>99GGY      </coupon_code>
  <discount_amount>5</discount_amount>
  <discount_type>0</discount_type>
  <expiration_date>2002-12-31T00:00:00.0000000-05:00</expiration_date>
</coupons>
<coupon_redemptions>
  <coupon_code>665RQ      </coupon_code>
  <total_discount>21.5</total_discount>
  <redemption_date>2002-11-10T00:00:00.0000000-05:00</redemption_date>
  <customer_id>1</customer_id>
</coupon_redemptions>
</AngusHardware>
```

There is one major difference between the relational and hierarchical views. In the relational view, each row's elements are direct children of the root element. In the hierarchical view, however, the coupon_redemptions element is a child of the coupons element; because any coupon_redemptions row can only be related to exactly one coupons row, it makes sense to present them in this hierarchical fashion.

How can you have the DataSet present this hierarchical XML view of the data? There are a couple of ways: transformation and synchronizing data.

Transformation

Because both the relational and hierarchical views are XML, one can be transformed into the other with an XSLT transformation. A program to transform the DataSet from one format to another is shown in Example 11-14.

Example 11-14. Program to transform a DataSet to another XML format

```
using System;
using System.Data;
using System.Data.SqlClient;
using System.Xml;
using System.Xml.Xsl;

public class TransformData {
```

Example 11-14. Program to transform a DataSet to another XML format (continued)

```
public static void Main(string [] args) {

    DataSet dataSet = new DataSet("AngusHardware");

    SqlConnection connection = new SqlConnection(
      "Initial Catalog=AngusHardware; Integrated Security=SSPI; User ID=sa");

    SqlDataAdapter customersAdapter = new SqlDataAdapter(
      "SELECT * FROM customers", connection);
    SqlDataAdapter couponsAdapter = new SqlDataAdapter(
      "SELECT * FROM coupons", connection);
    SqlDataAdapter couponRedemptionsAdapter = new SqlDataAdapter(
      "SELECT * FROM coupon_redemptions", connection);

    customersAdapter.Fill(dataSet, "customers");
    couponsAdapter.Fill(dataSet, "coupons");
    couponRedemptionsAdapter.Fill(dataSet, "coupon_redemptions");

    XmlDataDocument doc = new XmlDataDocument(dataSet);

    XmlTextWriter writer = new XmlTextWriter(Console.Out);
    writer.Formatting = Formatting.Indented;

    XslTransform transform = new XslTransform( );
    transform.Load("Coupons.xsl");
    transform.Transform(doc, null, writer);
  }
}
```

You've seen most of this already at one point or another. The main variation that you have not seen yet is the inclusion of several SqlDataAdapter instances in the same DataSet. Once the DataSet is populated using each SqlDataAdapter's Fill( ) method, it's a simple matter to create an XmlDataDocument and an XslTransform. The XslTransform is loaded from the stylesheet *Coupons.xsl*, and the output goes to the console.

The beauty of this approach is that it does any transformation that can be specified via an XSLT stylesheet. Example 11-15 shows an example of a stylesheet that does the transformation from relational XML to hierarchical XML. You could just as easily write one to produce an HTML or plain text view of the DataSet.

Example 11-15. XSLT stylesheet to transform relational XML to hierarchical XML

```
<xsl:stylesheet xmlns:xsl="http://www.w3.org/1999/XSL/Transform" version="1.0">
  <xsl:output method="xml" />

  <xsl:template match="/">
    <xsl:apply-templates select="AngusHardware" />
  </xsl:template>

  <xsl:template match="AngusHardware">
```

```
    <AngusHardware>
      <xsl:apply-templates select="customers" />
      <xsl:apply-templates select="coupons" />
    </AngusHardware>
  </xsl:template>

  <xsl:template match="customers">
    <xsl:copy-of select="." />
  </xsl:template>

  <xsl:template match="coupons">
    <coupons>
      <xsl:copy-of select="./coupon_code" />
      <xsl:copy-of select="./discount_amount" />
      <xsl:copy-of select="./discount_type" />
      <xsl:copy-of select="./expiration_date" />
      <xsl:variable name="coupon_code" select="./coupon_code" />
      <xsl:if test="count(//coupon_redemptions[coupon_code=$coupon_code]) > 0">
        <xsl:for-each select="//coupon_redemptions[coupon_code=$coupon_code]">
          <xsl:copy-of select="." />
        </xsl:for-each>
      </xsl:if>
    </coupons>
  </xsl:template>

</xsl:stylesheet>
```

Synchronizing Data

Take a look at the following code snippet:

```
AngusHardware dataSet = new AngusHardware();

XmlDataDocument doc = new XmlDataDocument(dataSet);
doc.Load("HierarchicalCoupons.xml");

XmlTextWriter writer = new XmlTextWriter(Console.Out);
writer.Formatting = Formatting.Indented;

dataSet.WriteXml(writer);
```

You've already seen code that uses this pattern It creates an instance of a DataSet, specifically the one we generated for the Angus Hardware coupon database. Then it loads the DataSet with data from an XML file by creating an XmlDataDocument for it. When the data is written to the console, it appears in a relational XML format.

But if you change the last line, as shown below, you get hierarchical XML output that matches the format and content of the document you loaded into the XmlDataDocument:

```
doc.WriteTo(writer);
```

The XmlDataDocument knows how to map between the relational form of the DataSet and the hierarchical form of the document it's been loaded with, as long as the element names are the same. In fact, it handily ignores any elements it's not familiar with from the schema in the DataSet when it writes the relational XML.

This is handy because you can read in XML from the hierarchical format and edit it using the DataSet, then output it back into the hierarchical XML. In other words, you can accomplish all the work this lengthy bit of DOM code does:

```
dataSet.EnforceConstraints = false;
XmlElement coupons = doc.CreateElement("coupons");
doc.DocumentElement.AppendChild(coupons);

XmlElement coupon_code = doc.CreateElement("coupon_code");
coupon_code.AppendChild(doc.CreateTextNode("542HH"));
coupons.AppendChild(coupon_code);

XmlElement discount_amount = doc.CreateElement("discount_amount");
discount_amount.AppendChild(doc.CreateTextNode("10"));
coupons.AppendChild(discount_amount);

XmlElement discount_type = doc.CreateElement("discount_type");
discount_type.AppendChild(doc.CreateTextNode(
    ((int)DiscountType.Percentage).ToString()));
coupons.AppendChild(discount_type);

XmlElement expiration_date = doc.CreateElement("expiration_date");
expiration_date.AppendChild(doc.CreateTextNode(
    new DateTime(2003, 1, 31).ToString(
    "yyyy-MM-ddT00:00:00.0000000-05:00")));
coupons.AppendChild(expiration_date);
dataSet.EnforceConstraints = true;
```

with this single line of DataSet code:

```
dataSet.coupons.AddcouponsRow("542HH", 10, 0, new DateTime(2003,1,31));
```

I think you'd have to agree that that's worthwhile.

PART II

.NET XML Namespace Reference

CHAPTER 12

How to Use These Quick Reference Chapters

The quick reference section that follows packs a lot of information into a small space. This introduction explains how to get the most out of that information. It describes how the quick reference is organized and how to read the individual quick-ref entries.

Finding a Quick-Reference Entry

The quick reference is organized into chapters, one per namespace. Each chapter begins with an overview of the namespace and includes a hierarchy diagram for the types (classes, interfaces, enumerations, delegates, and structs) in the namespace. Following the overview are quick-reference entries for all of the types in the namespace.

Figure 12-1 is a sample diagram showing the notation used in this book. This notation is similar to that used in *Java in a Nutshell* (O'Reilly), but borrows some features from UML. Abstract classes are shown as a slanted rectangle, and sealed classes as an octagonal rectangle. Inheritance is shown as a solid line from the subtype, ending with a hollow triangle that points to the supertype. There are two notations that indicate interface implementation. The lollipop notation is used most of the time, since it is easier to read. In some cases, especially where many types implement a given interface, the shaded box notation with the dashed line is used.

Important relationships between types (associations) are shown with a dashed line ending with an arrow. The figures don't show every possible association. Some types have strong containing relationships with one another. For example, a System.Net. WebException includes a System.Net.WebResponse that represents the HTTP response containing the error details (HTTP status code and error message). To show this relationship, a filled diamond is attached to the containing type with a solid line that points to the contained type.

Entries are organized alphabetically by type *and* namespace, so that related types are grouped near each other. Thus, in order to look up a quick reference entry for a particular type, you must also know the name of the namespace that contains that type.

Usually, the namespace is obvious from the context, and you should have no trouble looking up the quick-reference entry you want. Use the tabs on the outside edge of the book and the dictionary-style headers on the upper outside corner of each page to help you find the namespace and type you are looking for.

Occasionally, you may need to look up a type for which you do not already know the namespace. In this case, refer to *Type, Method, Property, and Field Index*. This index allows you to look up a type by its name and find out what namespace it is part of.

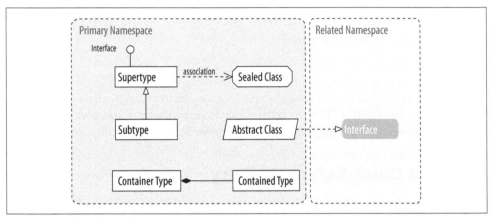

Figure 12-1. Class hierarchy notation

Reading a Quick-Reference Entry

Each quick-reference entry contains quite a bit of information. The sections that follow describe the structure of a quick-reference entry, explaining what information is available, where it is found, and what it means. While reading the descriptions that follow, you will find it helpful to flip through the reference section itself to find examples of the features being described.

Type Name, Namespace, Assembly, Type Category, and Flags

Each quick-reference entry begins with a four-part title that specifies the name, namespace (followed by the assembly in parentheses), and type category of the type, and may also specify various additional flags that describe the type. The type name appears in bold at the upper left of the title. The namespace and assembly appear, in smaller print, in the lower left, below the type name.

The upper-right portion of the title indicates the type category of the type (class, delegate, enum, interface, or struct). The class category may include modifiers such as sealed or abstract.

In the lower-right corner of the title you may find a list of flags that describe the type. The possible flags and their meanings are as follows:

ECMA
> The type is part of the ECMA CLI specification

Serializable
> The type, or a supertype, implements System.Runtime.Serialization.ISerializable or has been flagged with the System.Serializable attribute

Marshal by reference
> This class, or a superclass, derives from System.MarshalByRefObject

Context bound
> This class, or a superclass, derives from System.ContextBoundObject

Disposable
> The type implements the System.IDisposable interface

Flag
> The enumeration is marked with the System.FlagsAttribute

Description

The title of each quick-reference entry is followed by a short description of the most important features of the type. This description may be anywhere from a couple of sentences to several paragraphs long.

Synopsis

The most important part of every quick-reference entry is the synopsis, which follows the title and description. The synopsis for a type looks a lot like its source code, except that the member bodies are omitted and some additional annotations are added. If you know C# syntax, you know how to read the type synopsis.

The first line of the synopsis contains information about the type itself. It begins with a list of type modifiers, such as **abstract** and **sealed**. These modifiers are followed by the **class, delegate, enum, interface,** or **struct** keyword and then by the name of the type. The type name may be followed by a colon (:) and a supertype or interfaces that the type implements.

The type definition line is followed by a list of the members that the type defines. This list includes only those members that are explicitly declared in the type, are overridden from a base class, or are implementations of an interface member. Members that are simply inherited from a base class are not shown; you will need to look up the base class definition to find those members. Once again, if you understand basic C# syntax, you should have no trouble making sense of these lines. The listing for each member includes the modifiers, type, and name of the member. For methods, the synopsis also includes the type and name of each method parameter.

The member names are in boldface, so it is easy to scan the list of members looking for the one you want. The names of method parameters are in italics to indicate that they are not to be used literally. The member listings are printed on alternating gray and white backgrounds to keep them visually separate.

Member availability and flags

Each member listing is a single line that defines the API for that member. These listings use C# syntax, so their meaning is immediately clear to any C# programmer. There is some auxiliary information associated with each member synopsis, however, that requires explanation.

The area to the right of the member synopsis is used to display a variety of flags that provide additional information about the member. Some of these flags indicate additional specification details that do not appear in the member API itself.

The following flags may be displayed to the right of a member synopsis:

Overrides
> Indicates that a method overrides a method in one of its supertypes. The flag is followed by the name of the supertype that the method overrides.

Implements
> Indicates that a method implements a method in an interface. The flag is followed by the name of the interface that is implemented.

=

> For enumeration fields and constant fields, this flag is followed by the constant value of the field. Only constants of primitive and String types and constants with the value null are displayed. Some constant values are specification details, while others are implementation details. Some constants are platform dependent, such as System.BitConverter.IsLittleEndian. Platform-dependent values shown in this book conform to the System.PlatformID.Win32NT platform (32-bit Windows NT, 2000, or XP). The reason that symbolic constants are defined, however, is so you can write code that does not rely directly upon the constant value. Use this flag to help you understand the type, but do not rely upon the constant values in your own programs.

Functional grouping of members

Within a type synopsis, the members are not listed in strict alphabetical order. Instead, they are broken down into functional groups and listed alphabetically within each group. Constructors, events, fields, methods, and properties are all listed separately. Instance methods are kept separate from static (class) methods. Public members are listed separately from protected members. Grouping members by category breaks a type down into smaller, more comprehensible segments, making the type easier to understand. This grouping also makes it easier for you to find a desired member.

Functional groups are separated from each other in a type synopsis with C# comments, such as // Public Constructors, // Protected Instance Properties, and // Events. The various functional categories are as follows (in the order in which they appear in a type synopsis):

Constructors
> Displays the constructors for the type. Public constructors and protected constructors are displayed separately in subgroupings. If a type defines no constructor at all, the C# compiler adds a default no-argument constructor that is displayed here. If a type defines only private constructors, it cannot be instantiated, so no constructor appears. Constructors are listed first because the first thing you do with most types is instantiate them by calling a constructor.

Fields
> Displays all of the fields defined by the type, including constants. Public and protected fields are displayed in separate subgroups. Fields are listed here, near the top of the synopsis, because constant values are often used throughout the type as legal values for method parameters and return values.

Properties
> Lists all the properties of the type, breaking them down into subgroups for public and protected static properties and public and protected instance properties. After the property name, its accessors (get or set) are shown.

Static Methods
> Lists the static methods (class methods) of the type, broken down into subgroups for public static methods and protected static methods.

Public Instance Methods
> Contains all of the public instance methods.

Protected Instance Methods
> Contains all of the protected instance methods.

Class Hierarchy

For any type that has a non-trivial inheritance hierarchy, the synopsis is followed by a "Hierarchy" section. This section lists all of the supertype of the type, as well as any interfaces implemented by those supertypes. It will also list any interfaces implemented by an interface. In the hierarchy listing, arrows indicate supertype to subtype relationships, while the interfaces implemented by a type follow the type name in parentheses. For example, the following hierarchy indicates that System.IO.Stream implements IDisposable and extends MarshalByRefObject, which itself extends Object:

> System.Object → System.MarshalByRefObject → System.IO.Stream(System.IDisposable)

If a type has subtypes, the "Hierarchy" section is followed by a "Subtypes" section that lists those subtypes. If an interface has implementations, the "Hierarchy" section is followed by an "Implementations" section that lists those implementations.

While the "Hierarchy" section shows ancestors of the type, the "Subtypes" or "Implementations" section shows descendants.

Cross References

The hierarchy section of a quick-reference entry is followed by a number of optional cross reference sections that indicate other, related types and methods that may be of interest. These sections are the following:

Passed To

> This section lists all of the members (from other types) that are passed an object of this type as an argument, including properties whose values can be set to this type. This is useful when you have an object of a given type and want to know where it can be used.

Returned By

> This section lists all of the members that return an object of this type, including properties whose values can take on this type. This is useful when you know that you want to work with an object of this type, but don't know how to obtain one.

Valid On

> For attributes, this lists the attribute targets that the attribute can be applied to.

Associated Events

> For delegates, lists the events it can handle.

A Note About Type Names

Throughout the quick reference, you'll notice that types are sometimes referred to by type name alone and at other times referred to by type name and namespace. If namespaces were always used, the type synopses would become long and hard to read. On the other hand, if namespaces were never used, it would sometimes be difficult to know what type was being referred to. The rules for including or omitting the namespace name are complex. They can be summarized approximately as follows, however:

- If the type name alone is ambiguous, the namespace name is always used.
- If the type is part of the System namespace or is a very commonly used type like System.Collection.ICollection, the namespace is omitted.
- If the type being referred to is part of the current namespace (and has a quick-reference entry in the current chapter), the namespace is omitted. The namespace is also omitted if the type being referred to is part of a namespace that contains the current namespace.

CHAPTER 13

The Microsoft.XmlDiffPatch Namespace

When dealing with XML files from different sources, you may find it necessary to compare two revisions of the same document. You may also want to update one XML document to match another. For this purpose, Microsoft has released the XmlDiffPatch namespace. XmlDiffPatch may be downloaded from *http://apps.gotdotnet.com/ xmltools/xmldiff/*.

Using the XmlDiffPatch Namespace

Since XmlDiffPatch is a .NET assembly, it can be included in any .NET project by adding it as a reference in Visual Studio .NET, or by specifying the /r:xmldiffpatch.dll command-line switch to the C# compiler. If you plan to use XmlDiffPatch in multiple projects, you may find it useful to add it to your Global Assembly Cache using the *installutil* executable or the Microsoft .NET Framework Configuration tool.

Once you've added the XmlDiffPatch reference to your project or Makefile, you can include it in your own source code with the using statement:

```
using Microsoft.XmlDiffPatch;
```

Example 13-1 shows a program which constructs two XmlDocument instances in memory, then compares them using XmlDiff.

Example 13-1. Program to construct and compare two XmlDocument instances

```
using System;
using System.Text;
using System.Xml;

using Microsoft.XmlDiffPatch;

public class DoDiff {
  public static void Main(string [] args) {
    XmlDocument doc1 = new XmlDocument();
```

```
    doc1.AppendChild(doc1.CreateXmlDeclaration("1.0", null, null));
    doc1.AppendChild(doc1.CreateElement("foo"));

    XmlDocument doc2 = new XmlDocument( );
    doc2.AppendChild(doc2.CreateXmlDeclaration("1.0", null, null));
    doc2.AppendChild(doc2.CreateElement("bar"));
    doc2.DocumentElement.AppendChild(doc2.CreateElement("baz"));

    XmlTextWriter diffgram = new XmlTextWriter(Console.Out);
    diffgram.Formatting = Formatting.Indented;

    XmlDiff diff = new XmlDiff(XmlDiffOptions.None);
    diff.Compare(doc1, doc2, diffgram);

    diffgram.Flush( );
  }
}
```

This program simply creates two **XmlDocument** instances, with one element each. The original document's root element is named **foo**, and the modified document's root element is named **bar**. The modified document's **bar** element is then given a child element named **baz**. The program then creates an instance of the **XmlDiff** class and calls its **Compare( )** method, which sends the following output to the console. Note that I've formatted it for readability:

```
    <?xml version="1.0" encoding="IBM437"?>
    <xd:xmldiff
      version="1.0" srcDocHash="12600313001788880892"
      options="None" fragments="no"
        xmlns:xd="http://schemas.microsoft.com/xmltools/2002/xmldiff">
    <xd:node match="1" />
    <xd:remove match="2" subtree="no" />
    <xd:add type="1" name="bar">
      <xd:add type="1" name="baz" />
    </xd:add>
    </xd:xmldiff>
```

The **XmlDiff** constructor has an **XmlDiffOptions** parameter which can be used to specify that certain information should be ignored while computing the difference. Things to be ignored can include the order of child nodes, comments, DTDs, XML declarations, processing instructions, XML namespaces and namespace prefixes, and whitespace.

Compare( ) has six overloads to deal with the various types of inputs, including URI, **XmlNode**, and **XmlReader**. It is also capable of dealing with non-well-formed XML fragments and partial documents. The overload of **Compare( )** which I've used here takes two **XmlNode** instances as input and sends the output to an **XmlWriter**. The output is an XML Diff Language (XDL) Diffgram, about which I'll talk more in a minute.

Once you've run **Compare( )** and written the XDL Diffgram to an **XmlWriter**, you can use **XmlPatch** to apply the Diffgram to the original XML document, and duplicate the changes necessary to produce the modified document.

Example 13-2 shows modifications to the original program to patch the original XML document. The changes are highlighted.

Example 13-2. Program to patch an XML document

```
using System;
using System.IO;
using System.Text;
using System.Xml;

using Microsoft.XmlDiffPatch;

public class DoDiff {
  public static void Main(string [] args) {
    XmlDocument doc1 = new XmlDocument( );
    doc1.AppendChild(doc1.CreateXmlDeclaration("1.0", null, null));
    doc1.AppendChild(doc1.CreateElement("foo"));

    XmlDocument doc2 = new XmlDocument( );
    doc2.AppendChild(doc2.CreateXmlDeclaration("1.0", null, null));
    doc2.AppendChild(doc2.CreateElement("bar"));
    doc2.DocumentElement.AppendChild(doc2.CreateElement("baz"));

    Stream stream = new MemoryStream( );
    XmlTextWriter diffgram = new XmlTextWriter(new StreamWriter(stream));
    diffgram.Formatting = Formatting.Indented;

    XmlDiff diff = new XmlDiff(XmlDiffOptions.None);
    diff.Compare(doc1, doc2, diffgram);

    stream.Seek(0, SeekOrigin.Begin);

    XmlPatch patch = new XmlPatch( );
    patch.Patch(doc1, new XmlTextReader(stream));

    XmlTextWriter writer = new XmlTextWriter(Console.Out);
    writer.Formatting = Formatting.Indented;
    doc1.WriteTo(writer);
  }
}
```

In the first group of highlighted lines, the Diffgram is written to an **XmlTextWriter** which wraps a **MemoryStream** instead of to the console. Then the **MemoryStream** is reset back to the beginning, and a new **XmlPatch** instance is created. The **XmlPatch.Patch( )** method is called to patch the **doc1 XmlDocument** according to the Diffgram. Finally, the patched **doc1** is written to the console with an **XmlTextWriter**.

The output from the modified program is below. It should look just the same as doc2 would have looked if it were serialized to the console:

```
<?xml version="1.0"?>
<bar>
  <baz />
</bar>
```

The XDL Diffgram format

Despite its similar name and appearance, this XML format is not directly related to the Diffgram format used in ADO.NET. The XDL Diffgram contains a list of the changes made to the original document. The root element of the XDL Diffgram, xd: xmldiff, has a namespace of *http://schemas.microsoft.com/xmltools/2002/xmldiff*. Its attributes are listed below:

version
> Indicates the version of the XDL Diffgram format being used.

srcDocHash
> Provides a hashed value which is used to verify that the XML document the Diffgram is being used to patch is the same as the original XML document used to generate the Diffgram.

options
> Contains the names of the XmlDiffOptions passed into the XmlDiff constructor, if any. The names are separated by spaces.

fragments
> If the value is yes, the Diffgram contains differences between XML nodes. If the value is no, the Diffgram contains differences between XML documents.

xmlns:xd
> Indicates the XML namespace URI for the xd: prefix.

The xd:diffgram element may have any number of xd:node child nodes. Each xd:node element represents a node in the original document that has changed in the changed document, or the position of a new or deleted node in the changed document. The xd:node element's match attribute contains a path descriptor for the node.

Although they look similar, the XDL path syntax is not XPath. XDL paths are based on the original XML document after it has been loaded into a DOM tree. An XDL path consists of a combination of numerals, the characters /, −, and |, and attribute names preceded with the character @. Table 13-1 lists the meanings of the XDL path values.

Table 13-1. XDL path values

Value	Description
n	nth child node of the current node
n1-n2	n1st through n2nd child node of the current node

Table 13-1. XDL path values (continued)

Value	Description
n1|*n2*	*n*1st and *n*2nd child node of the current node
/*n*	*n*th child node of the root node
n1/*n2*	*n*2nd child node of the *n*1st child node of the current node
@*name*	attribute named *name* of the current node

The various XDL path values may be combined to produce a path describing each node in the original XML document.

The child elements of xd:node may be any combination of xd:add, which indicates a node that was added in the new XML document; xd:change, which indicates that the node was changed in the new XML document; and xd:remove, which indicates that the node was removed in the new XML document. The list below describes the attributes of the xd:add element:

type
    The node type, matching the XmlNodeType enumeration values (see Table 2-1).

name
    Name of the new node. If the new node is an element or attribute, this is the local name.

ns
    Namespace URI of the new node.

prefix
    Namespace prefix of the new node.

systemId
    System ID of the new node if it is a document type declaration.

publicId
    Public ID of the new node if it is a document type declaration.

opId
    The operation ID of the addition. The opId value is used to tie changes in different parts of the Diffgram together.

The xd:add element's content may be a text value if the new node is an attribute or XML declaration, a CDATA section if the new node is a document type declaration, or any number xd:add elements if the new node is an element. If the xd:add has no attributes, its content may also be any complete XML fragment matching the new content.

The opId attribute is used to tie together changes that appear in a Diffgram. For example, a node that is moved from one location in the original XML document to another in the changed document will appear in an xd:remove element and an xd:add element in the Diffgram. The xd:remove and xd:add elements will have the same opId attribute value to indicate that they represent two parts of the same operation.

The following list describes the attributes of the xd:change element:

match
> The relative path from the current node to the child node which has changed.

name
> New name of the node. If the changed node is an element or attribute, this is the local name.

ns
> New namespace URI of the node.

prefix
> New namespace prefix of the node.

systemId
> New system ID of the node if it is a document type declaration.

publicId
> New public ID of the node if it is a document type declaration.

opId
> The operation ID of the change. The opId value is used to tie changes in different parts of the Diffgram together.

The content of an xd:change element may be text if the changed node is a text node or attribute value, a CDATA section if the changed node is a CDATA section or document type declaration, a processing instruction if the changed node is a processing instruction, or a comment if the changed node is a comment. If the changed node is an element, the xd:change may have any number of xd:node, xd:add, xd:change, or xd:remove child elements representing differences for the changed node's child nodes.

The following list describes the attributes of the xd:remove element:

match
> The relative path from the current node to the list of nodes which have been removed.

subtree
> If the entire subtree of each of the matching nodes has been removed, the attribute's value is yes. Otherwise, the attribute's value is no and the match attribute must evaluate to a single node.

opId
> The operation ID of the removal. The opId value is used to tie changes in different parts of the Diffgram together.

If the subtree attribute is set to no, the xd:remove element's content may be any number of xd:node, xd:add, xd:change, or xd:remove, indicating differences to the removed node's child nodes. The child nodes become child nodes of the removed node's parent.

Using the XmlDiff and XmlPatch Executables

The *XmlDiff.exe* executable is a thin wrapper around the XmlDiff class. It allows you to compute the differences between two XML files on disk and optionally place the resulting XDL Diffgram in a third file. The following list shows the command-line options to *XmlDiff.exe*:

/o

Ignore child order (XmlDiffOptions.IgnoreChildOrder)

/c

Ignore comments (XmlDiffOptions.IgnoreComments)

/p

Ignore processing instructions (XmlDiffOptions.IgnorePI)

/w

Ignore whitespace (XmlDiffOptions.IgnoreWhitespace)

/n

Ignore namespaces (XmlDiffOptions.IgnoreNamespaces)

/r

Ignore prefixes (XmlDiffOptions.IgnorePrefixes)

/x

Ignore XML declaration (XmlDiffOptions.IgnoreDecl)

/d

Ignore DTD (XmlDiffOptions.IgnoreDtd)

/f

The files contain XML fragments (XmlDiffOptions.IgnoreComments)

/t

Use fast algorithm (XmlDiffAlgorithm.Fast)

/z

Use precise algorithm (XmlDiffAlgorithm.Precise)

If no command-line options are given, the XmlDiffOptions.None and XmlDiffAlgorithm.Auto are assumed, and it is assumed that the files do not contain XML fragments.

Like *XmlDiff.exe*, *XmlPatch.exe* is a thin wrapper around the XmlPatch class. *XmlPatch.exe* allows you to patch an XML file with a given XDL Diffgram, and optionally place the resulting patched XML document in a new file on disk. Since any options used in the creation of the Diffgram are written to the xd:diffgram element's options and fragments attributes, there are no other command-line options to *XmlPatch.exe*.

Microsoft.XmlDiffPatch Namespace Reference

The Microsoft.XmlDiffPatch namespace contains classes which allow you to compare two XML documents. You can use the XmlDiff class to produce a third XML document, called an XML Difference Language (XDL) Diffgram, which lists the differences between the source documents, and you can use the XmlPatch class to recreate the changed document. You can specify details of how the differences are computed using the XmlDiffOptions and XmlDiffAlgorithm enumerations.

XmlDiff

Microsoft.XmlDiffPatch (xmldiffpatch.dll)   class

```
public class XmlDiff {
// Public Constructors
  public XmlDiff( );
  public XmlDiff( XmlDiffOptions options);
// Public Static Fields
  public const string NamespaceUri;                           // =http://schemas.microsoft.com/xmltools/2002/xmldiff
// Public Instance Fields
  public XmlDiffPerf _xmlDiffPerf;
// Public Instance Properties
  public XmlDiffAlgorithm Algorithm{set; get; }
  public bool IgnoreChildOrder{set; get; }
  public bool IgnoreComments{set; get; }
  public bool IgnoreDtd{set; get; }
  public bool IgnoreNamespaces{set; get; }
  public bool IgnorePI{set; get; }
  public bool IgnorePrefixes{set; get; }
  public bool IgnoreWhitespace{set; get; }
  public bool IgnoreXmlDecl{set; get; }
  public XmlDiffOptions Options{set; }
// Public Static Methods
  public static XmlDiffOptions ParseOptions( string options);
  public static bool VerifySource( System.Xml.XmlNode node, ulong hashValue, XmlDiffOptions options);
// Public Instance Methods
  public bool Compare( string sourceFile, string changedFile, bool bFragments);
  public bool Compare( string sourceFile, string changedFile, bool bFragments, System.Xml.XmlWriter diffgramWriter);
  public bool Compare( System.Xml.XmlNode sourceNode, System.Xml.XmlNode changedNode);
  public bool Compare( System.Xml.XmlNode sourceNode, System.Xml.XmlNode changedNode, System.Xml.XmlWriter diffgramWriter);
  public bool Compare( System.Xml.XmlReader sourceReader, System.Xml.XmlReader changedReader);
  public bool Compare( System.Xml.XmlReader sourceReader, System.Xml.XmlReader changedReader,
    System.Xml.XmlWriter diffgramWriter);
}
```

This type is used to generate an XML Difference Language Diffgram which describes the differences between two XML documents. The constructor takes an optional XmlDiffOptions argument, which specifies which XML node types may be ignored. Each XmlDiffOptions value may also be specified by one of the properties IgnoreChildOrder, IgnoreComments, IgnoreDtd, Ignore-Namespaces, IgnorePI, IgnorePrefixes, IgnoreWhitespace, and IgnoreXmlDecl, as well as through the Options property. The algorithm used to compute the Diffgram may be specified by setting the Algorithm property.

The Compare() method is used to actually compute the Diffgram and write it to a System.Xml.XmlWriter. The input XML documents may be specified as URIs, System.Xml.XmlNodes, or System.Xml.XmlReaders. You can specify a System.Xml.XmlWriter to output the Diffgram to. Compare() returns true if the input documents are equal.

XmlDiffAlgorithm
serializable

Microsoft.XmlDiffPatch (xmldiffpatch.dll) enum

```
public enum XmlDiffAlgorithm {
  Auto = 0,
  Fast = 1,
  Precise = 2
}
```

This enumeration is used to specify the comparison algorithm for the XmlDiff class. For a quick but imprecise comparison, use Fast. For a more precise but slower comparison using the Zhang-Shasha algorithm, use Precise. To have XmlDiff make a best guess as to the best algorithm, based on document size, use Auto. Auto is the default value.

Hierarchy System.Object → System.ValueType → System.Enum(System.IComparable, System.IFormattable, System.IConvertible) → XmlDiffAlgorithm

Returned By XmlDiff.Algorithm

Passed To XmlDiff.Algorithm

XmlDiffOptions
serializable

Microsoft.XmlDiffPatch (xmldiffpatch.dll) enum

```
public enum XmlDiffOptions {
  None = 0,
  IgnoreChildOrder = 1,
  IgnoreComments = 2,
  IgnorePI = 4,
  IgnoreWhitespace = 8,
  IgnoreNamespaces = 16,
  IgnorePrefixes = 32,
  IgnoreXmlDecl = 64,
  IgnoreDtd = 128
}
```

This enumeration is used to specify whether the XmlDiff class should ignore certain types of nodes when computing differences.

Hierarchy System.Object → System.ValueType → System.Enum(System.IComparable, System.IFormattable, System.IConvertible) → XmlDiffOptions

Returned By XmlDiff.ParseOptions( )

Passed To XmlDiff.{Options, VerifySource( ), XmlDiff( )}

XmlPatch

Microsoft.XmlDiffPatch (xmldiffpatch.dll)   class

```
public class XmlPatch {
// Public Constructors
  public XmlPatch( );
// Public Instance Methods
  public void Patch( string sourceFile, System.IO.Stream outputStream, System.Xml.XmlReader diffgram);
  public void Patch( System.Xml.XmlDocument sourceDoc, System.Xml.XmlReader diffgram);
  public void Patch( ref System.Xml.XmlNode sourceNode, System.Xml.XmlReader diffgram);
  public void Patch( System.Xml.XmlReader sourceReader, System.IO.Stream outputStream, System.Xml.XmlReader diffgram);
}
```

This type is used to recreate a changed XML document by applying the XML Difference Language Diffgram generated by XmlDiff to the original document.

CHAPTER 14

The Microsoft.XsdInference Namespace

Although the XML Schema Definition tool, *xsd.exe*, that ships with the .NET Framework is capable of inferring an XML Schema from an instance of an XML document, Microsoft has provided an additional assembly which contains a more advanced XSD inference model.

Available for download from *http://www.gotdotnet.com/team/xmltools/xsdinference/ XSDInference.exe*, the XSD Inference Tool is comprised of an additional .NET assembly that provides extended ability to infer an XML Schema definition from an XML document instance, and a .NET executable that uses that assembly to allow XML Schema inference from the command line.

The installer creates a directory named *C:\Program Files\XSDInference*, which contains the XSDInfer.dll assembly, the Infer.exe executable, documentation, and source code for both the assembly and the executable.

Using the XsdInference Namespace

Like XmlDiffPatch, XsdInference can be added to your Global Assembly Cache for your convenience, and you can add it as a reference in your Visual Studio .NET project or Makefile.

The XsdInference namespace contains one class, Infer. Infer has a single overloaded method, InferSchema( ), which returns an XmlSchemaCollection. One overload takes just an XmlReader, and the other one takes an XmlReader and an XmlSchemaCollection.

Given an XmlReader for a particular XML document, you can create an XML Schema definition and write it to the console using the code in Example 14-1.

Example 14-1. Using the XsdInference assembly

```
using System;
using System.Xml;
using System.Xml.Schema;
```

Example 14-1. Using the XsdInference assembly (continued)

```
using Microsoft.XsdInference;

public class XsdInfer {
  public static void Main(string [] args) {
    try {
      XmlSchemaCollection schemas = null;
      Infer infer = new Infer( );
      XmlTextReader reader = new XmlTextReader(args[0]);
      schemas = infer.InferSchema(reader);
      foreach (XmlSchema schema in schemas) {
        schema.Write(Console.Out);
      }
    } catch (Exception e) {
      Console.Error.WriteLine(e);
    }
  }
}
```

The usage of the Infer class is fairly straightforward. In Example 14-1, you can see that an instance of Infer is created, and its Infer( ) method is called. Infer( ) returns an XmlSchemaCollection.

Example 14-2 shows another pattern of usage for the Infer class, in which several XML documents are used to progressively refine an XML Schema. The changed lines are highlighted.

Example 14-2. Using Infer to progressively infer a schema

```
using System;
using System.Xml;
using System.Xml.Schema;

using Microsoft.XsdInference;

public class XsdInfer {
  public static void Main(string [] args) {
    try {
      XmlSchemaCollection schemas = new XmlSchemaCollection( );
      Infer infer = new Infer( );
      foreach (string filename in args) {
        XmlTextReader reader = new XmlTextReader(filename);
        schemas = infer.InferSchema(reader, schemas);
      }
      foreach (XmlSchema schema in schemas) {
        schema.Write(Console.Out);
      }
    } catch (Exception e) {
      Console.Error.WriteLine(e);
    }
  }
}
```

The first change is to create an XmlSchemaCollection to pass into the InferSchema() method call. The first time in, this collection will be empty, and InferSchema() will infer a schema and place it into the collection.

The second change is to repeatedly call InferSchema() for each filename on the command line, each time passing in the XmlSchemaCollection returned from the previous call. The schema will be refined by each call, and the final inferred schema will be able to validate any of the XML documents that were used to infer it.

Note that this mechanism will work for any number of XML documents. One unique XML schema will be inferred for each different XML namespace in the XML documents.

Using the Infer Executable

Infer.exe is a thin wrapper around the Infer class. It only handles inferring an XML Schema from a single XML document instance. Its parameters are simply the name of the XML file to infer a schema for and, optionally, the name of the file to write the XML Schema to.

Microsoft.XsdInference Namespace Reference

The Microsoft.XsdInference namespace contains one class, Infer, which can be used to infer an XML Schema Definition from an XML document instance.

Infer

Microsoft.XsdInference (xsdinfer.dll)   class

```
public class Infer {
// Public Constructors
  public Infer( );
// Public Instance Methods
  public XmlSchemaCollection InferSchema( System.Xml.XmlReader xmlTR);
  public XmlSchemaCollection InferSchema( System.Xml.XmlReader xmlTR, System.Xml.Schema.XmlSchemaCollection xsc);
}
```

Infer has a single overloaded method, InferSchema(), which returns a System.Xml.Schema. XmlSchemaCollection. One overload takes just a System.Xml.XmlReader, and the other one takes a System.Xml.XmlReader and a System.Xml.Schema.XmlSchemaCollection. If the XML document in the System.Xml.XmlReader matches one of the System.Xml.Schema.XmlSchema instances in the System.Xml. Schema.XmlSchemaCollection, the inferred schema is used to refine the matched schema. Repeated calls to InferSchema() with different XML documents can thus be used to infer and progressively refine an XML schema.

CHAPTER 15

The System.Configuration Namespace

Applications and services in the .NET Framework can be configured with XML files in several locations. You can use these files to customize the behavior of the entire .NET Framework using certain well-known settings, and to customize the operation of your own application using several different methods.

The Configuration Files

Each of the .NET configuration files shares a common XML format, although their scopes differ depending on which location the file is in. Some of the files are installed and configured automatically when the framework is installed.

Although the contents of the files differ, they share a common schema. The root element of each file is the **configuration** element, although different elements will appear as child nodes in the different files. Because the configuration files are all XML, you can deal with them as you would any XML document, including editing them with a text editor, or using the classes in the **System.Xml** namespace to manipulate them.

 Although you can edit the configuration file as much as you want, be sure to note that you're just editing the file on disk. No changes you make on disk will affect the configuration settings once they've been read into the configuration system by a running application.

The Security Configuration Files

There are several different security policy configuration files: the enterprise security policy configuration file in *%windir%\Microsoft.NET\Framework\v%version%\ CONFIG\enterprisesec.config*, the machine security policy configuration file in *%windir%\Microsoft.NET\Framework\v%version%\CONFIG\security.config*, and the user security policy configuration file in *%userprofile%\Application data\Microsoft*

CLR security config\v%version%\security.config (for Windows 2000 and Windows NT) or *%windir%\username\CLR security config\v%version%\security.config* (for Windows 98 and Windows Me). There may also be *web_hightrust.config, web_lowtrust.config*, and *web_notrust.config* files in the *%windir%\Microsoft.NET\Framework\v%version%\CONFIG* directory.

The security policy files contain configuration settings that pertain to security for particular assemblies. It is strongly recommended that you do not edit these files directly, instead using the .NET Framework Configuration tool (**mscorcfg.msc**) or Code Access Security Policy tool (**caspol.exe**) to edit security policies. For more information on configuring .NET security policies, see *.NET Framework Security* by Brian A. LaMacchia, Sebastian Lange, Matthew Lyons, Rudi Martin, and Kevin T. Price (Addison Wesley).

The Machine Configuration File

The machine configuration file, located in *%windir%\Microsoft.NET\Framework\v%version%\CONFIG\machine.config*, contains configuration settings specific to the machine it is installed on. While most of these settings pertain to functionality internal to the .NET Framework, it may also be used to store configuration settings common to more than one application. If you do use it store shared application configuration settings, you should be careful to name your settings in a unique way. You should also take care not to disrupt any existing machine configuration settings when adding your own configuration settings to the machine configuration file.

Some of the settings in this file include debugging and error message configuration; network configuration, such as authentication details and web proxy location; a large number of ASP.NET configuration settings, including settings that let you specify how different web browser platforms and versions should be recognized; and remoting configuration. Many of the settings in the machine configuration file may also be configured at runtime for a particular application instance. However, changes to these settings at runtime do not persist in the machine configuration file, nor are they shared across different application instances.

The Application Configuration File

The application configuration file is the one configuration file that you have complete control over, and it is where you should put your application configuration settings. The application configuration file is automatically read when necessary, and it must be located in the same directory as the application, and named with the same name as the application executable plus the extension *.config*. If your application executable is named *C:\MyApp.exe*, for example, the application configuration file must be named *C:\MyApp.exe.config*.

In the next section, I'll describe how you can add your own settings to the machine or application configuration files.

Adding Your Own Configuration Settings

There are two ways to add your own configuration settings to the configuration files. You can use the **appSettings** configuration section, which the .NET Framework knows how to interpret automatically, or you can add your own configuration section and write the code for the framework to access it.

Using the appSettings Element

The easiest way to add configuration settings to a configuration file is to use the **appSettings** element. Configuration settings added this way take the form of key-value pairs. These key-value pairs may be added anywhere in the hierarchy of configuration files. Once added, key-value pairs can be removed individually in a configuration file lower in the hierarchy, or the entire set can be cleared.

Example 15-1 shows an excerpt from a machine configuration file, with an **appSettings** element added.

Example 15-1. Excerpt from the machine configuration file

```xml
<?xml version="1.0" encoding="UTF-8" ?>

<configuration>
  ...
  <appSettings>
    <add key="some key" value="some value" />
  </appSettings>
  ...
</configuration>
```

This configuration file simply adds a configuration setting whose key is "some key" and whose value is "some value". The added key will be available to all .NET applications running on this machine.

Example 15-2 shows an application configuration file that uses the **appSettings** element to remove the key added in the machine configuration file and add another key.

Example 15-2. The application configuration file

```xml
<?xml version="1.0" encoding="UTF-8" ?>

<configuration>
    <appSettings>
        <remove key="some key" />
        <add key="some other key" value="some other value" />
```

Example 15-2. The application configuration file (continued)

```
    </appSettings>
</configuration>
```

The application that loads this application configuration file will no longer have the key-value pair with key "some key", but it will have a key-value pair with key "some other key". The application configuration file can also use the clear element to remove all the **appSettings** key-value pairs.

The key-value pairs are accessed using the **System.Configuration.ConfigurationSettings** class. Example 15-3 shows how you can access the key-value pairs defined in Examples 15-1 and 15-2.

Example 15-3. Program to read and display app settings

```
using System;
using System.Configuration;

public class AppSettingsTest {
  public static void Main(string [] args) {
    string someKey = "some key";
    string someOtherKey = "some other key";
    Console.WriteLine("\"{0}\"=\"{1}\"", someKey,
                      ConfigurationSettings.AppSettings[someKey]);
    Console.WriteLine("\"{0}\"=\"{1}\"", someOtherKey,
                      ConfigurationSettings.AppSettings[someOtherKey]);
  }
}
```

Running the **AppSettingsTest** executable, you can expect to see the following output:

```
"some key"=""
"some other key"="some other value"
```

That's fine, if you're only interested in string values. If you need to retrieve a different type of data, however, you can use the **AppSettingsReader** class. **AppSettingsReader** has only one method, **GetValue()**, which takes as parameters the key name and the **Type** of data you wish to have returned. For example, take the following **appSettings** element:

```
<appSettings>
    <add key="some numeric key" value="5.00987" />
</appSettings>
```

To return that value as a **decimal**, you would use the following code:

```
AppSettingsReader reader = new AppSettingsReader();
decimal value = (decimal)reader.GetValue("some numeric key",typeof(decimal));
```

 Unlike **ConfigurationSettings**, **AppSettingsReader** has no static members. You must create an instance of **AppSettingsReader** before calling its **GetValue()** method.

Custom Elements

The appSettings element is actually a special case of the general mechanism for adding custom configuration elements, called the *configuration section*. A configuration section is simply an element in a configuration file. The ConfigSettings class knows how to read an arbitrary configuration section because you add a configSection element to the configuration file to tell it how. The appSettings configuration section is defined in the machine configuration file, as shown below:

```
<section name="appSettings" type="System.Configuration.NameValueFileSectionHandler,
System, Version=1.0.3300.0, Culture=neutral, PublicKeyToken=b77a5c561934e089" />
```

I'll explain more about the section element in a moment. You can see, though, that the section element shows us that the appSettings section is handled by the System.Configuration. NameValueFileSectionHandler type. This type's Create() method reads the XML that is passed to it as an XmlNode, and creates the System.Collections.Specialized.NameValueCollection that is eventually returned by the ConfigSettings.AppSettings property.

The steps to create your own custom configuration sections are as follows:

1. Select a configuration section handler to handle the configuration section. If none of the built-in configuration section handlers are appropriate, write your own class that implements IConfigurationSectionHandler.

2. Add a section element to the configSections element of the machine or application configuration file, which links the section name to the type of the class you created in step 1.

3. Add the configuration section defined in step 2 to the machine or application configuration file.

4. Write the code to access the configuration settings using the ConfigSettings.GetConfig() method.

Choosing a configuration section handler

The IConfigurationSectionHandler interface requires only one method, Create(), which returns an object containing the configuration section's settings in a useful form. This object will be returned by ConfigurationSettings.GetConfig(). The .NET Framework includes five built-in configuration section handlers, which are listed below:

DictionarySectionHandler

Create() will return a Hashtable containing the key-value pairs of the configuration section element's child add elements. The configuration section may also contain remove and clear child elements. Because the Hashtable is more efficient for large numbers of key-value pairs, this handler should be reserved for use with a large number of configuration settings.

IgnoreSectionHandler

Used to indicate that the configuration system class should ignore this configuration section. The IgnoreSectionHandler.Create() method always returns null. This handler is typically used internally by the .NET Framework, although you can use it if you wish.

NameValueSectionHandler

Behaves similarly to DictionarySectionHandler, except that Create() returns a NameValueCollection rather than a Hashtable. This handler is better suited for configuration sections with fewer than ten settings.

NameValueFileSectionHandler

Behaves similarly to NameValueSectionHandler, except that it also allows the element to have a file attribute, which specifies an additional XML file to read for configuration settings. The external file's root element name must be the same as the current element. This is the handler used for appSettings configuration sections, as shown in Examples 15-1 and 15-2.

SingleTagSectionHandler

Create() will return a Hashtable containing key-value pairs of the element's attribute names and values. The element may not have any child nodes. You should use this handler if you configuration section will consist of a single element with one or more attributes.

For some purposes, none of the built-in configuration section handlers may be appropriate. In that case, you can write your own handler by implementing IConfigurationSectionHandler. This interface has only method to implement, Create(). One of Create()'s parameters is the XmlNode containing the configuration section element itself.

Perhaps the simplest custom section handler would just return the XML used to construct the configuration section. Example 15-4 shows an implementation of XmlSectionHandler that does that.

Example 15-4. A simple implementation of XmlSectionHandler

```
using System;
using System.Configuration;
using System.Xml;

public class XmlSectionHandler : IConfigurationSectionHandler {
  public object Create(object parent, object configContext, XmlNode section) {
    return section;
  }
}
```

If you use this XmlSectionHandler, you'll see that the Create() returns an instance of System.Configuration.XmlConfigElement, which is an undocumented subclass of XmlElement. You shouldn't care what concrete type it is, as long as you treat it as an XmlElement.

Defining the configuration section

Once you've selected or written a configuration section handler, you need to define the configuration section and tell the configuration system of how to deal with it. To do this, you add a **section** element to the configuration file's **configSections** element.

The **section** elements define how a configuration section is to be handled. The **section** element has two attributes, **name** and **type**. The **name** attribute matches the name of a configuration section element that appears in a configuration file, and the **type** attribute specifies the name of the **IConfigurationSectionHandler** instance that will handle the configuration section.

section elements may be organized into a hierarchy using section groups. The element that defines section groups is called, appropriately, **sectionGroup**, and its only attribute is **name**. You can nest as many **sectionGroup** elements as you want, and a **sectionGroup** may contain both **section** elements and other **sectionGroup** elements.

Example 15-5 shows the **configSections** element of an application configuration file using the **XmlSectionHandler** in a configuration section group.

Example 15-5. Application configuration using an XmlSectionHandler in a configuration section group

```
<configSections>
    <sectionGroup name="Group">
        <section name="Custom" type="XmlSectionHandler, AppSettingsTest" />
    </sectionGroup>
</configSections>
```

 The **type** attribute contains the full class name of the configuration section handler in standard .NET style: class name, assembly name, version, culture, and public token key. You can omit the version, culture, and public key token if the assembly is not in the global assembly cache. In this case, **XmlSectionHandler** is contained in the same assembly as the **AppSettingsTest** executable.

Adding the configuration section

The next step is to add the configuration section itself to the configuration file. Because of the way I wrote the **XmlSectionHandler**, it will accept any XML content. The only restriction on how it's used in the configuration file is that it must appear in the section group as defined in Example 15-5. Example 15-6 shows the complete application configuration file containing the **configSections** element, the **Custom** element I defined in the **configSections** element, and the **appSettings** element from Example 15-2.

Example 15-6. Complete application configuration file

```
<?xml version="1.0" encoding="UTF-8" ?>

<configuration>
```

Example 15-6. Complete application configuration file (continued)

```
    <configSections>
        <sectionGroup name="Group">
            <section name="Custom" type="XmlSectionHandler, AppSettingsTest" />
        </sectionGroup>
    </configSections>

    <appSettings>
        <remove key="some key" />
        <add key="some other key" value="some other value" />
        <add key="some numeric key" value="5.00987" />
    </appSettings>

    <Group>
        <Custom>
            <someElement attribute="attribute1">some
content &amp; stuff
<![CDATA[Some <text> that the parser won't even try to parse
]]>
            </someElement>
        </Custom>
    </Group>

</configuration>
```

> Remember that you don't need to add a **section** element for the **appSettings** configuration section in your application configuration file because it's already included in the machine configuration file. Also, be sure to note that, although I've put it in the application configuration file, all of this configuration could also go in the machine configuration file.

Reading the custom configuration programmatically

Now you're ready to actually use the configuration data in the application configuration file. You already know how to access configuration settings in the **appSettings** section using **ConfigurationSetting.AppSettings** property. You can also access them using the **ConfigurationSettings.GetConfig( )** method. The only parameter to **GetConfig( )** is a **string** containing the path to the configuration section you want to get.

> In fact, the **AppSettings** property is simply a proxy that calls the **GetConfig( )** method, passing the string "appSettings".

Example 15-7 shows a program that gets configuration settings from the **appSettings** and **Custom** configuration sections.

Example 15-7. Reading various configuration information programmatically

```
using System;
using System.Configuration;
using System.Xml;

public class AppSettingsTest {
  public static void Main(string [] args) {
    try {
      string someKey = "some key";
      Console.WriteLine("{0}={1}", someKey,
                        ConfigurationSettings.AppSettings[someKey]);
      string someOtherKey = "some other key";
      Console.WriteLine("{0}={1}", someOtherKey,
                        ConfigurationSettings.AppSettings[someOtherKey]);

      string someNumericKey = "some numeric key";
      AppSettingsReader reader = new AppSettingsReader( );
      Console.WriteLine("{0}={1}", someNumericKey,
                        reader.GetValue(someNumericKey,typeof(decimal)));

      Console.WriteLine( );

      string custom = "Group/Custom";
      XmlNode customConfig = (XmlNode)ConfigurationSettings.GetConfig(custom);
      Console.WriteLine("{0}={1}", custom, customConfig);
      Console.WriteLine("{0}={1}", customConfig.Name, customConfig.InnerXml);

    } catch (Exception e) {
      Console.Error.WriteLine(e);
    }
  }
}

public class XmlSectionHandler : IConfigurationSectionHandler {
  public object Create(object parent, object configContext, XmlNode section) {
    return section;
  }
}
```

Running this program, you'll see the following output:

```
some key=
some other key=some other value
some numeric key=5.00987

Group/Custom=System.Configuration.ConfigXmlElement
Custom=<someElement attribute="attribute1">some
content &amp; stuff
<![CDATA[Some <text> that the parser won't even try to parse
]]></someElement>
```

When calling **ConfigurationSettings.GetConfig( )**, you are responsible for knowing what type of object is being returned by the configuration section handler. If you cast the returned object to an incompatible type, an **InvalidCastException** will be thrown.

It's particularly important to be aware of return types if you try to use NameValueSectionHandler and DictionarySectionHandler interchangeably. Although both handlers will happily read the same XML from the configuration file, NameValueSectionHandler returns a NameValueCollection, while DictionarySectionHandler returns a Hashtable.

System.Configuration Namespace Reference

The System.Configuration namespace contains classes that are used to read the contents of the hierarchy of .NET Framework configuration files. The main workhorse of the System.Configuration namespace is the ConfigurationSettings class, whose staticAppSettings property provides access to a collection of key-value pairs in the appSettings section of the configuration files, and whose GetConfig() method provides access to other, custom configuration sections. Another class, AppSettingsReader, enables typesafe access to configuration settings.

The appSettings configuration section may contain add, remove, and clear elements. add causes a key-value pair to be added to the configuration system. remove causes a key-value pair to be removed from the configuration system. clear causes any key-value pairs already in the configuration system to be removed. The configuration files themselves are not affected, only the key-value pairs in memory for an application instance.

Custom configuration sections may be added using the section element. Each section element specifies the name of the configuration section and the name of a type that implements IConfigurationSectionHandler to handle the configuration section.

This namespace contains several classes which, although public, are reserved for internal use by the .NET Framework. No documentation is included in this quick reference for those classes. Figure 15-1 shows the types in this namespace.

AppSettingsReader

System.Configuration (system.dll)   class

```
public class AppSettingsReader {
// Public Constructors
  public AppSettingsReader( );
// Public Instance Methods
  public object GetValue( string key, Type type);
}
```

The AppSettingsReader provides a single method, GetValue(), which allows you to read a value from the configuration file while specifying the type of object to return.

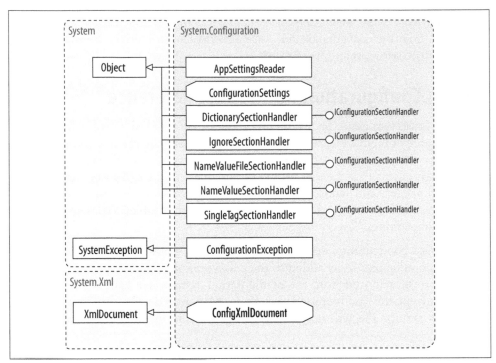

Figure 15-1. The System.Configuration namespace

ConfigurationException

serializable

System.Configuration (system.dll)

class

```
public class ConfigurationException : SystemException {
// Public Constructors
  public ConfigurationException( );
  public ConfigurationException( string message);
  public ConfigurationException( string message, Exception inner);
  public ConfigurationException( string message, Exception inner, string filename, int line);
  public ConfigurationException( string message, Exception inner, System.Xml.XmlNode node);
  public ConfigurationException( string message, string filename, int line);
  public ConfigurationException( string message, System.Xml.XmlNode node);
// Protected Constructors
  protected ConfigurationException( System.Runtime.Serialization.SerializationInfo info,
     System.Runtime.Serialization.StreamingContext context);
// Public Instance Properties
  public string BareMessage{get; }
  public string Filename{get; }
  public int Line{get; }
  public override string Message{get; }                                       // overrides Exception
```

```
// Public Static Methods
   public static string GetXmlNodeFilename( System.Xml.XmlNode node);
   public static int GetXmlNodeLineNumber( System.Xml.XmlNode node);
// Public Instance Methods
   public override void GetObjectData( System.Runtime.Serialization.SerializationInfo info,
      System.Runtime.Serialization.StreamingContext context);                          // overrides Exception
}
```

This exception indicates that a problem was encountered in the Configuration system.

Hierarchy System.Object → System.Exception(System.Runtime.Serialization.ISerializable) → System.SystemException → ConfigurationException

ConfigurationSettings

System.Configuration (system.dll)   sealed class

```
public sealed class ConfigurationSettings {
// Public Static Properties
   public static NameValueCollection AppSettings{get; }
// Public Static Methods
   public static object GetConfig( string sectionName);
}
```

This class includes a static method and property that provide access to the configuration settings in the .NET Framework configuration files. GetConfig( ) returns an object that represents a specific configuration section; the type of object returned is determined by the configuration section handler associated with the configuration section by the section element in the configuration file. The AppSettings property is a proxy for the GetConfig( ) method that returns a NameValueCollection of key-value pairs for the appSettings configuration section.

DictionarySectionHandler

System.Configuration (system.dll)   class

```
public class DictionarySectionHandler : IConfigurationSectionHandler {
// Public Constructors
   public DictionarySectionHandler( );
// Protected Instance Properties
   protected virtual string KeyAttributeName{get; }
   protected virtual string ValueAttributeName{get; }
// Public Instance Methods
   public virtual object Create( object parent, object context, System.Xml.XmlNode section);   // implements IConfigurationSectionHandler
}
```

This type implements IConfigurationSectionHandler. Its Create( ) method returns a System.Collections. Hashtable containing all the key-value pairs read from a configuration section.

IConfigurationSectionHandler

System.Configuration (system.dll)   interface

```
public interface IConfigurationSectionHandler {
// Public Instance Methods
  public object Create( object parent, object configContext, System.Xml.XmlNode section);
}
```

This is the interface that all configuration section handlers must implement. Its **Create**( ) method reads the **System.Xml.XmlNode** passed in and returns a **System.Object** containing the configuration settings for the configuration section.

IgnoreSectionHandler

System.Configuration (system.dll)   class

```
public class IgnoreSectionHandler : IConfigurationSectionHandler {
// Public Constructors
  public IgnoreSectionHandler( );
// Public Instance Methods
  public virtual object Create( object parent, object configContext,
    System.Xml.XmlNode section);                                 // implements IConfigurationSectionHandler
}
```

IgnoreSectionHandler is used to instruct the configuration system to ignore the configuration section. Its **Create**( ) methods always returns **null**. A configuration section with this type of configuration section handler will usually read the XML data from the configuration file using some method other than the .NET Framework's configuration system.

NameValueFileSectionHandler

System.Configuration (system.dll)   class

```
public class NameValueFileSectionHandler : IConfigurationSectionHandler {
// Public Constructors
  public NameValueFileSectionHandler( );
// Public Instance Methods
  public object Create( object parent, object configContext, System.Xml.XmlNode section);   // implements IConfigurationSectionHandler
}
```

This type's **Create**( ) method returns a **System.Collections.Specialized.NameValueCollection** containing all the key-value pairs read from a configuration section. It also allows the configuration section element to have an attribute named **file**, which contains the name of an external file containing additional configuration settings. The root element of the external file must have the same name as the configuration section. **NameValueFileSectionHandler** is the configuration section handler used for the **appSettings** configuration section.

NameValueSectionHandler

System.Configuration (system.dll)   class

```
public class NameValueSectionHandler : IConfigurationSectionHandler {
// Public Constructors
   public NameValueSectionHandler( );
// Protected Instance Properties
   protected virtual string KeyAttributeName{get; }
   protected virtual string ValueAttributeName{get; }
// Public Instance Methods
   public object Create( object parent, object context, System.Xml.XmlNode section);    // implements IConfigurationSectionHandler
}
```

This type's Create( ) method returns a System.Collections.Specialized.NameValueCollection containing all the key-value pairs read from a configuration section. NameValueSectionHandler behaves identically to NameValueFileSectionHandler except that it does not allow the file attribute.

SIngleTagSectionHandler

System.Configuration (system.dll)   class

```
public class SingleTagSectionHandler : IConfigurationSectionHandler {
// Public Constructors
   public SingleTagSectionHandler( );
// Public Instance Methods
   public virtual object Create( object parent, object context, System.Xml.XmlNode section);    // implements IConfigurationSectionHandler
}
```

SingleTagSectionHandler is the configuration section handler that should be used when the configuration section consists of a single element with one or more attributes and without child nodes. Its Create( ) methods returns a System.Collections.Hashtable whose keys are the attributes' names and whose values are the attributes' values.

CHAPTER 16

The System.Xml Namespace

The System.Xml namespace provides support for managing XML documents according to a set of standards defined by the World Wide Web Consortium (W3C). The classes implement objects that comply with the XML 1.0 specification and the DOM Core Level 1 and Core Level 2. Additional support is provided for XML Schemas (the System.Xml.Schema namespace), XSLT (System.Xml.Xsl), and XPath (System.Xml.XPath), covered in Chapter 17.

Figure 16-1 and Figure 16-2 show the types in this namespace.

EntityHandling   CF 1.0, serializable

System.Xml (system.xml.dll)   enum

```
public enum EntityHandling {
  ExpandEntities = 1,
  ExpandCharEntities = 2
}
```

This enumeration defines how entities are expanded. ExpandCharEntities expands only character entities, returning the entity text, while general entities are returned as nodes. ExpandEntities expands all entities; this is the default.

Hierarchy	System.Object → System.ValueType → System.Enum(System.IComparable, System.IFormattable, System.IConvertible) → EntityHandling
Returned By	XmlValidatingReader.EntityHandling
Passed To	XmlValidatingReader.EntityHandling

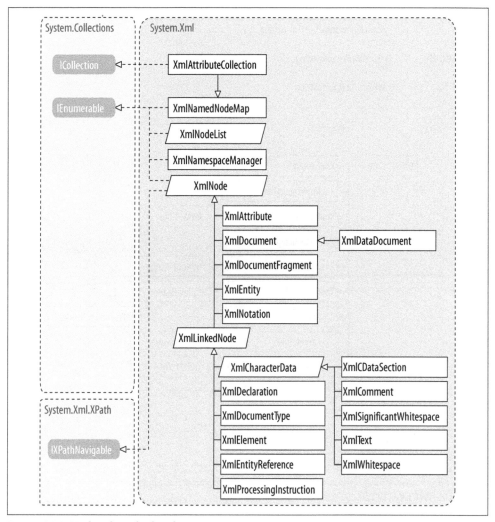

Figure 16-1. XmlNode and related types

Formatting
CF 1.0, ECMA 1.0, serializable

System.Xml (system.xml.dll)   enum

```
public enum Formatting {
  None = 0,
  Indented = 1
}
```

This enumeration specifies whether element content that is output from XmlTextWriter is indented. This is only of interest to human consumers of XML; if the destination of the XML document is another machine or software process, the additional whitespace adds only to the file size.

Hierarchy   System.Object → System.ValueType → System.Enum(System.IComparable, System.IFormattable, System.IConvertible) → Formatting

Returned By   XmlTextWriter.Formatting

Passed To   XmlTextWriter.Formatting

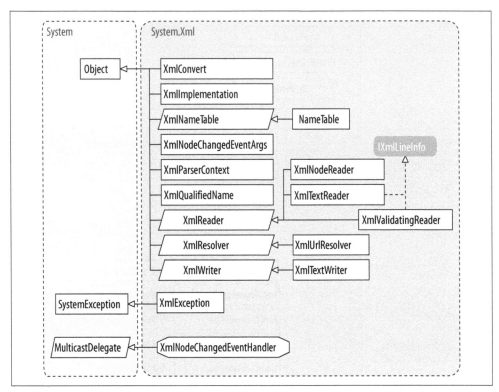

Figure 16-2. More types from System.Xml

IHasXmlNode

System.Xml (system.xml.dll)   interface

```
public interface IHasXmlNode {
// Public Instance Methods
  public XmlNode GetNode( );
}
```

This interface is used to get the current or context node from an implementing class, such as XmlDocument or System.Xml.XPath.XPathNavigator. The GetNode( ) method returns the XmlNode that the navigator is currently positioned on.

IXmlLineInfo

System.Xml (system.xml.dll)   interface

```
public interface IXmlLineInfo {
// Public Instance Properties
  public int LineNumber{get; }
  public int LinePosition{get; }
// Public Instance Methods
  public bool HasLineInfo( );
}
```

This interface allows XML reader classes (XmlTextReader and XmlValidatingReader) to return line and position information currently being read. If the class is reading data from a stream or other form of input, the HasLineInfo( ) method returns a boolean indicating if line information is provided.

Implemented By   XmlTextReader, XmlValidatingReader

NameTable

System.Xml (system.xml.dll)   class

```
public class NameTable : XmlNameTable {
// Public Constructors
  public NameTable( );
// Public Instance Methods
  public override string Add( char[ ] key, int start, int len);        // overrides XmlNameTable
  public override string Add( string key);                             // overrides XmlNameTable
  public override string Get( char[ ] key, int start, int len);        // overrides XmlNameTable
  public override string Get( string value);                           // overrides XmlNameTable
}
```

This class is a concrete implementation of the XmlNameTable type (described later in this chapter). It is entirely an optimization within the .NET XML stack; it provides a table of string objects for element and attribute names used in an XML document. The XML parser uses these string objects for efficient manipulation of repeated element and attribute names. See XmlNameTable for more discussion of its behavior and usage.

Normally .NET applications have no need to use this class directly. At most, a new instance is passed in blindly when constructing various XML-related types, such as XmlNamespaceManager.

Hierarchy   System.Object → XmlNameTable → NameTable

Passed To   System.Xml.Xsl.XsltContext.XsltContext( )

ReadState

CF 1.0, ECMA 1.0, serializable

System.Xml (system.xml.dll)   enum

```
public enum ReadState {
  Initial = 0,
  Interactive = 1,
  Error = 2,
  EndOfFile = 3,
  Closed = 4
}
```

This enumeration identifies the current state of an XmlReader instance: closed (Closed); not yet started (Initial); an error is preventing further reading within the document (Error); the read is in process (Interactive); or the end of file (or stream, or wherever the XML is coming from) has been reached (EndOfFile).

Hierarchy   System.Object → System.ValueType → System.Enum(System.IComparable, System.IFormattable, System.IConvertible) → ReadState

Returned By   XmlReader.ReadState

ValidationType

serializable

System.Xml (system.xml.dll)   enum

```
public enum ValidationType {
  None = 0,
  Auto = 1,
  DTD = 2,
  XDR = 3,
  Schema = 4
}
```

This enumeration is used by XmlValidatingReader to determine the type of validation requested: DTD, schema, XDR, or no validation. If the type is set to Auto, the validation type is determined from the document; if there is a reference to a DTD, then DTD-style validation is performed. This is also true if the document contains references to XML Schema types, and so on. (See XmlValidatingReader for details.)

Hierarchy   System.Object → System.ValueType → System.Enum(System.IComparable, System.IFormattable, System.IConvertible) → ValidationType

Returned By   XmlValidatingReader.ValidationType

Passed To   XmlValidatingReader.ValidationType

308 | Chapter 16: The System.Xml Namespace

WhitespaceHandling

CF 1.0, ECMA 1.0, serializable

System.Xml (system.xml.dll)   enum

```
public enum WhitespaceHandling {
  All = 0,
  Significant = 1,
  None = 2
}
```

This enumeration contains settings that determine if whitespace is preserved in text sections of XML documents. This is important if the XML document contains whitespace-sensitive text nodes; for example, HTML is a whitespace-insensitive language.

Hierarchy   System.Object → System.ValueType → System.Enum(System.IComparable, System.IFormattable, System.IConvertible) → WhitespaceHandling

Returned By   XmlTextReader.WhitespaceHandling

Passed To   XmlTextReader.WhitespaceHandling

WriteState

CF 1.0, ECMA 1.0, serializable

System.Xml (system.xml.dll)   enum

```
public enum WriteState {
  Start = 0,
  Prolog = 1,
  Element = 2,
  Attribute = 3,
  Content = 4,
  Closed = 5
}
```

As its name implies, this enumeration specifies the state of an XmlWriter instance: closed (Closed), not yet started (Start), or in the process of writing some portion of the XML document (Attribute, Content, Element, or Prolog).

Hierarchy   System.Object → System.ValueType → System.Enum(System.IComparable, System.IFormattable, System.IConvertible) → WriteState

Returned By   XmlWriter.WriteState

XmlAttribute

CF 1.0

System.Xml (system.xml.dll)   class

```
public class XmlAttribute : XmlNode {
// Protected Constructors
  protected internal XmlAttribute( string prefix, string localName, string namespaceURI, XmlDocument doc);
// Public Instance Properties
```

```
public override string BaseURI{get; }                                    // overrides XmlNode
public override string InnerText{set; get; }                             // overrides XmlNode
public override string InnerXml{set; get; }                              // overrides XmlNode
public override string LocalName{get; }                                  // overrides XmlNode
public override string Name{get; }                                       // overrides XmlNode
public override string NamespaceURI{get; }                               // overrides XmlNode
public override XmlNodeType NodeType{get; }                              // overrides XmlNode
public override XmlDocument OwnerDocument{get; }                         // overrides XmlNode
public virtual XmlElement OwnerElement{get; }
public override XmlNode ParentNode{get; }                                // overrides XmlNode
public override string Prefix{set; get; }                                // overrides XmlNode
public virtual bool Specified{get; }
public override string Value{set; get; }                                 // overrides XmlNode
// Public Instance Methods
public override XmlNode CloneNode( bool deep);                           // overrides XmlNode
public override void WriteContentTo( XmlWriter w);                       // overrides XmlNode
public override void WriteTo( XmlWriter w);                              // overrides XmlNode
}
```

This class represents a single attribute of an element. The OwnerElement property returns the element node that contains this attribute. The Specified property indicates if the value was explicitly set or if a default value was used.

Hierarchy	System.Object → XmlNode(System.ICloneable, System.Collections.IEnumerable, System.Xml.XPath. IXPathNavigable) → XmlAttribute
Returned By	XmlAttributeCollection.{Append( ), InsertAfter( ), InsertBefore( ), Prepend( ), Remove( ), RemoveAt( ), this}, XmlDocument.CreateAttribute( ), XmlElement.{GetAttributeNode( ), RemoveAttributeNode( ), SetAttributeNode( )}
Passed To	XmlAttributeCollection.{Append( ), CopyTo( ), InsertAfter( ), InsertBefore( ), Prepend( ), Remove( )}, XmlElement.{RemoveAttributeNode( ), SetAttributeNode( )}

XmlAttributeCollection   CF 1.0

System.Xml (system.xml.dll)   class

```
public class XmlAttributeCollection : XmlNamedNodeMap, ICollection {
// Public Instance Properties
  public virtual XmlAttribute this[ string localName, string namespaceURI ]{get; }
  public virtual XmlAttribute this[ string name ]{get; }
  public virtual XmlAttribute this[ int i ]{get; }
// Public Instance Methods
  public virtual XmlAttribute Append( XmlAttribute node);
  public void CopyTo( XmlAttribute[ ] array, int index);
  public virtual XmlAttribute InsertAfter( XmlAttribute newNode, XmlAttribute refNode);
  public virtual XmlAttribute InsertBefore( XmlAttribute newNode, XmlAttribute refNode);
  public virtual XmlAttribute Prepend( XmlAttribute node);
  public virtual XmlAttribute Remove( XmlAttribute node);
  public virtual void RemoveAll( );
```

```
public virtual XmlAttribute RemoveAt( int i );
public override XmlNode SetNamedItem( XmlNode node );                                    // overrides XmlNamedNodeMap
}
```

This class defines a collection of attributes for an XmlElement node. An XmlAttributeCollection is returned by the XmlElement.Attributes property. The collection contains XmlAttribute objects that can be specified by either an object name or a zero-based index. Attribute nodes can be added and removed from the collection with methods, such as InsertBefore( ), InsertAfter( ), Prepend( ), and RemoveAt( ).

Hierarchy   System.Object → XmlNamedNodeMap(System.Collections.IEnumerable) → XmlAttributeCollection(System.Collections.ICollection)

Returned By   XmlNode.Attributes

XmlCDataSection   CF 1.0

System.Xml (system.xml.dll)   class

```
public class XmlCDataSection : XmlCharacterData {
// Protected Constructors
   protected internal XmlCDataSection( string data, XmlDocument doc );
// Public Instance Properties
   public override string LocalName{get; }                                               // overrides XmlNode
   public override string Name{get; }                                                    // overrides XmlNode
   public override XmlNodeType NodeType{get; }                                            // overrides XmlNode
// Public Instance Methods
   public override XmlNode CloneNode( bool deep );                                        // overrides XmlNode
   public override void WriteContentTo( XmlWriter w );                                    // overrides XmlNode
   public override void WriteTo( XmlWriter w );                                           // overrides XmlNode
}
```

This class represents a CDATA (character data) section node of a document. A CDATA section is element content that is unparsed, i.e., entities and markup are ignored.

Hierarchy   System.Object → XmlNode(System.ICloneable, System.Collections.IEnumerable, System.Xml.XPath.IXPathNavigable) → XmlLinkedNode → XmlCharacterData → XmlCDataSection

Returned By   XmlDocument.CreateCDataSection( )

XmlCharacterData   CF 1.0

System.Xml (system.xml.dll)   abstract class

```
public abstract class XmlCharacterData : XmlLinkedNode {
// Protected Constructors
   protected internal XmlCharacterData( string data, XmlDocument doc );
// Public Instance Properties
   public virtual string Data{set; get; }
```

```
    public override string InnerText{set; get; }                                    // overrides XmlNode
    public virtual int Length{get; }
    public override string Value{set; get; }                                        // overrides XmlNode
// Public Instance Methods
    public virtual void AppendData( string strData);
    public virtual void DeleteData( int offset, int count);
    public virtual void InsertData( int offset, string strData);
    public virtual void ReplaceData( int offset, int count, string strData);
    public virtual string Substring( int offset, int count);
}
```

This class is an abstract parent class for the character data node types: XmlCDataSection, XmlComment, XmlSignificantWhitespace, XmlText, and XmlWhitespace. It defines methods for manipulating the text-based data of these nodes.

Hierarchy	System.Object → XmlNode(System.ICloneable, System.Collections.IEnumerable, System.Xml.XPath. IXPathNavigable) → XmlLinkedNode → XmlCharacterData
Subclasses	XmlCDataSection, XmlComment, XmlSignificantWhitespace, XmlText, XmlWhitespace

XmlComment   CF 1.0

System.Xml (system.xml.dll)   class

```
public class XmlComment : XmlCharacterData {
// Protected Constructors
    protected internal XmlComment( string comment, XmlDocument doc);
// Public Instance Properties
    public override string LocalName{get; }                                        // overrides XmlNode
    public override string Name{get; }                                             // overrides XmlNode
    public override XmlNodeType NodeType{get; }                                     // overrides XmlNode
// Public Instance Methods
    public override XmlNode CloneNode( bool deep);                                  // overrides XmlNode
    public override void WriteContentTo( XmlWriter w);                             // overrides XmlNode
    public override void WriteTo( XmlWriter w);                                     // overrides XmlNode
}
```

This class represents an XmlComment node. An XML comment is contained within <!-- and --> markup symbols and is not represented in the resulting XML Infoset tree.

Hierarchy	System.Object → XmlNode(System.ICloneable, System.Collections.IEnumerable, System.Xml.XPath. IXPathNavigable) → XmlLinkedNode → XmlCharacterData → XmlComment
Returned By	XmlDocument.CreateComment( )

```
public class XmlConvert {
// Public Constructors
   public XmlConvert( );
// Public Static Methods
   public static string DecodeName( string name);
   public static string EncodeLocalName( string name);
   public static string EncodeName( string name);
   public static string EncodeNmToken( string name);
   public static bool ToBoolean( string s);
   public static byte ToByte( string s);
   public static char ToChar( string s);
   public static DateTime ToDateTime( string s);
   public static DateTime ToDateTime( string s, string format);
   public static DateTime ToDateTime( string s, string[ ] formats);
   public static decimal ToDecimal( string s);
   public static double ToDouble( string s);
   public static Guid ToGuid( string s);
   public static short ToInt16( string s);
   public static int ToInt32( string s);
   public static long ToInt64( string s);
   public static sbyte ToSByte( string s);
   public static float ToSingle( string s);
   public static string ToString( bool value);
   public static string ToString( byte value);
   public static string ToString( char value);
   public static string ToString( DateTime value);
   public static string ToString( DateTime value, string format);
   public static string ToString( decimal value);
   public static string ToString( double value);
   public static string ToString( Guid value);
   public static string ToString( short value);
   public static string ToString( int value);
   public static string ToString( long value);
   public static string ToString( sbyte value);
   public static string ToString( float value);
   public static string ToString( TimeSpan value);
   public static string ToString( ushort value);
   public static string ToString( uint value);
   public static string ToString( ulong value);
   public static TimeSpan ToTimeSpan( string s);
   public static ushort ToUInt16( string s);
   public static uint ToUInt32( string s);
   public static ulong ToUInt64( string s);
   public static string VerifyName( string name);
   public static string VerifyNCName( string name);
}
```

This type is used to convert XML elements into other, non-XML types, such as CLR objects. In particular, it is used to convert XSD types into CLR types, for easy transformation of schema-valid XML documents into .NET objects and back again. It is also used within a variety of other areas, including ADO.NET (for automatic conversion of XML documents into relational tables and rows).

For the most part, .NET programmers use this type indirectly as part of the .NET Web Services stack or else directly in order to convert between XML documents and CLR objects (as part of a home-grown XML-to-RDBMS system, for example).

Note that although a constructor is provided, all methods of any interest are declared static and therefore require no instance to use. In essence, this type is a collection of C-style functions.

XmlDataDocument

System.Xml (system.data.dll)   class

```
public class XmlDataDocument : XmlDocument {
// Public Constructors
  public XmlDataDocument( );
  public XmlDataDocument( System.Data.DataSet dataset);
// Public Instance Properties
  public DataSet DataSet{get; }
// Public Instance Methods
  public override XmlNode CloneNode( bool deep);                                          // overrides XmlDocument
  public override XmlElement CreateElement( string prefix, string localName, string namespaceURI);   // overrides XmlDocument
  public override XmlEntityReference CreateEntityReference( string name);                 // overrides XmlDocument
  public override XmlElement GetElementById( string elemId);                              // overrides XmlDocument
  public XmlElement GetElementFromRow( System.Data.DataRow r);
  public DataRow GetRowFromElement( XmlElement e);
  public override void Load( System.IO.Stream inStream);                                  // overrides XmlDocument
  public override void Load( string filename);                                            // overrides XmlDocument
  public override void Load( System.IO.TextReader txtReader);                             // overrides XmlDocument
  public override void Load( XmlReader reader);                                           // overrides XmlDocument
// Protected Instance Methods
  protected override XPathNavigator CreateNavigator( XmlNode node);                       // overrides XmlDocument
}
```

The XmlDataDocument is a marriage of XML and RDBMS technology; it is an XmlDocument-inheriting class that particularly understands ADO.NET DataSet objects. This offers a variety of opportunities to the .NET programmer—for example, a DataSet can be loaded into the XmlDataDocument, and then navigated using traditional DOM-style navigation using the XmlNode API. In fact, because XmlDataDocument also inherits the System.Xml.XPath.IXPathNavigable interface, XPath queries can be issued against the DataSet data, as well.

In order to build this relationship, construct the XmlDataDocument with the DataSet holding the data as its constructor parameter. Alternatively, use the Load( ) method to read in the data via an XmlReader. The resulting XML can also then be written out to another medium with the WriteTo( ) method.

XmlDeclaration

CF 1.0

System.Xml (system.xml.dll)

class

```
public class XmlDeclaration : XmlLinkedNode {
// Protected Constructors
  protected internal XmlDeclaration( string version, string encoding, string standalone, XmlDocument doc);
// Public Instance Properties
  public string Encoding{set; get; }
  public override string InnerText{set; get; }                               // overrides XmlNode
  public override string LocalName{get; }                                    // overrides XmlNode
  public override string Name{get; }                                         // overrides XmlNode
  public override XmlNodeType NodeType{get; }                                // overrides XmlNode
  public string Standalone{set; get; }
  public override string Value{set; get; }                                   // overrides XmlNode
  public string Version{get; }
// Public Instance Methods
  public override XmlNode CloneNode( bool deep);                             // overrides XmlNode
  public override void WriteContentTo( XmlWriter w);                         // overrides XmlNode
  public override void WriteTo( XmlWriter w);                                // overrides XmlNode
}
```

This class contains the XML declaration of a document, which is the first element of an XML document containing the XML version number, encoding, and other optional information about the file.

Hierarchy   System.Object → XmlNode(System.ICloneable, System.Collections.IEnumerable, System.Xml.XPath. IXPathNavigable) → XmlLinkedNode → XmlDeclaration

Returned By   XmlDocument.CreateXmlDeclaration( )

XmlDocument

CF 1.0

System.Xml (system.xml.dll)

class

```
public class XmlDocument : XmlNode {
// Public Constructors
  public XmlDocument( );
  public XmlDocument( XmlNameTable nt);
// Protected Constructors
  protected internal XmlDocument( XmlImplementation imp);
// Public Instance Properties
  public override string BaseURI{get; }                                      // overrides XmlNode
  public XmlElement DocumentElement{get; }
  public virtual XmlDocumentType DocumentType{get; }
  public XmlImplementation Implementation{get; }
  public override string InnerXml{set; get; }                                // overrides XmlNode
```

```
public override bool IsReadOnly{get; }                                                                          // overrides XmlNode
public override string LocalName{get; }                                                                         // overrides XmlNode
public override string Name{get; }                                                                              // overrides XmlNode
public XmlNameTable NameTable{get; }
public override XmlNodeType NodeType{get; }                                                                      // overrides XmlNode
public override XmlDocument OwnerDocument{get; }                                                                 // overrides XmlNode
public bool PreserveWhitespace{set; get; }
public virtual XmlResolver XmlResolver{set; }
// Public Instance Methods
public override XmlNode CloneNode( bool deep);                                                                   // overrides XmlNode
public XmlAttribute CreateAttribute( string name);
public XmlAttribute CreateAttribute( string qualifiedName, string namespaceURI);
public virtual XmlAttribute CreateAttribute( string prefix, string localName, string namespaceURI);
public virtual XmlCDataSection CreateCDataSection( string data);
public virtual XmlComment CreateComment( string data);
public virtual XmlDocumentFragment CreateDocumentFragment( );
public virtual XmlDocumentType CreateDocumentType( string name, string publicId, string systemId, string internalSubset);
public XmlElement CreateElement( string name);
public XmlElement CreateElement( string qualifiedName, string namespaceURI);
public virtual XmlElement CreateElement( string prefix, string localName, string namespaceURI);
public virtual XmlEntityReference CreateEntityReference( string name);
public virtual XmlNode CreateNode( string nodeTypeString, string name, string namespaceURI);
public virtual XmlNode CreateNode( XmlNodeType type, string name, string namespaceURI);
public virtual XmlNode CreateNode( XmlNodeType type, string prefix, string name, string namespaceURI);
public virtual XmlProcessingInstruction CreateProcessingInstruction( string target, string data);
public virtual XmlSignificantWhitespace CreateSignificantWhitespace( string text);
public virtual XmlText CreateTextNode( string text);
public virtual XmlWhitespace CreateWhitespace( string text);
public virtual XmlDeclaration CreateXmlDeclaration( string version, string encoding, string standalone);
public virtual XmlElement GetElementById( string elementId);
public virtual XmlNodeList GetElementsByTagName( string name);
public virtual XmlNodeList GetElementsByTagName( string localName, string namespaceURI);
public virtual XmlNode ImportNode( XmlNode node, bool deep);
public virtual void Load( System.IO.Stream inStream);
public virtual void Load( string filename);
public virtual void Load( System.IO.TextReader txtReader);
public virtual void Load( XmlReader reader);
public virtual void LoadXml( string xml);
public virtual XmlNode ReadNode( XmlReader reader);
public virtual void Save( System.IO.Stream outStream);
public virtual void Save( string filename);
public virtual void Save( System.IO.TextWriter writer);
public virtual void Save( XmlWriter w);
public override void WriteContentTo( XmlWriter xw);                                                              // overrides XmlNode
public override void WriteTo( XmlWriter w);                                                                      // overrides XmlNode
// Protected Instance Methods
protected internal virtual XmlAttribute CreateDefaultAttribute( string prefix, string localName, string namespaceURI);
protected internal virtual XPathNavigator CreateNavigator( XmlNode node);
// Events
public event XmlNodeChangedEventHandler NodeChanged;
public event XmlNodeChangedEventHandler NodeChanging;
public event XmlNodeChangedEventHandler NodeInserted;
```

```
public event XmlNodeChangedEventHandler NodeInserting;
public event XmlNodeChangedEventHandler NodeRemoved;
public event XmlNodeChangedEventHandler NodeRemoving;
}
```

This class represents an XML document according to the W3C DOM specification. The document is represented as a node tree, in which elements and attributes (and their values) are stored as nodes that contain relational information (e.g., parent, child, siblings). XmlDocument derives from the generic XmlNode class and therefore has a node-type of Document.

The set of Create* methods create new objects of any type of node. These objects are created within the context of the XmlDocument; they share the document properties and name table of the parent document. However, they are not inserted into the document. To do this, you need to use the methods for node insertion from XmlNode. A new XmlNode is created from the root node of the XmlDocument, then methods for walking the node tree and appending or inserting nodes can be used to alter the source document.

Events are noted when any nodes (even created node objects that have not been inserted into the document) from this object change. Register an instance of the XmlNodeChangedEventHandler delegate with any of the following event types on XmlDocument to receive the corresponding notification: NodeChanged or NodeChanging for notification when a node has or is in the middle of changing (the element name is being modified, an attribute is being modified, added, or removed, and so on); NodeInserted or NodeInserting for notifications of new nodes having been or in the process of being added to the document; and NodeRemoved or NodeRemoving for nodes removed or in the process of being removed. The XmlNodeChangedEventHandler takes two arguments: the object sending the notification (this object), and an XmlNodeChangedEventArgs instance containing information about the change.

Hierarchy	System.Object → XmlNode(System.ICloneable, System.Collections.IEnumerable, System.Xml.XPath. IXPathNavigable) → XmlDocument
Subclasses	XmlDataDocument
Returned By	XmlImplementation.CreateDocument( ), XmlNode.OwnerDocument

XmlDocumentFragment   CF 1.0

System.Xml (system.xml.dll)   class

```
public class XmlDocumentFragment : XmlNode {
// Protected Constructors
  protected internal XmlDocumentFragment( XmlDocument ownerDocument);
// Public Instance Properties
  public override string InnerXml{set; get; }                              // overrides XmlNode
  public override string LocalName{get; }                                  // overrides XmlNode
  public override string Name{get; }                                       // overrides XmlNode
  public override XmlNodeType NodeType{get; }                              // overrides XmlNode
  public override XmlDocument OwnerDocument{get; }                         // overrides XmlNode
  public override XmlNode ParentNode{get; }                               // overrides XmlNode
// Public Instance Methods
```

```
public override XmlNode CloneNode( bool deep);                              // overrides XmlNode
public override void WriteContentTo( XmlWriter w);                          // overrides XmlNode
public override void WriteTo( XmlWriter w);                                 // overrides XmlNode
}
```

This class represents a lightweight piece or tree section of an XML document. A document fragment has a null parent node. This object is useful for tree insert operations that use the ImportNode( ) method of the XmlDocument class. To create an XmlDocumentFragment, use the XmlDocument.CreateDocumentFragment( ) method of an XmlDocument instance.

Hierarchy	System.Object → XmlNode(System.ICloneable, System.Collections.IEnumerable, System.Xml.XPath.IXPathNavigable) → XmlDocumentFragment
Returned By	XmlDocument.CreateDocumentFragment( )

XmlDocumentType

System.Xml (system.xml.dll)   class

```
public class XmlDocumentType : XmlLinkedNode {
// Protected Constructors
   protected internal XmlDocumentType( string name, string publicId, string systemId, string internalSubset, XmlDocument doc);
// Public Instance Properties
   public XmlNamedNodeMap Entities{get; }
   public string InternalSubset{get; }
   public override bool IsReadOnly{get; }                                   // overrides XmlNode
   public override string LocalName{get; }                                 // overrides XmlNode
   public override string Name{get; }                                      // overrides XmlNode
   public override XmlNodeType NodeType{get; }                             // overrides XmlNode
   public XmlNamedNodeMap Notations{get; }
   public string PublicId{get; }
   public string SystemId{get; }
// Public Instance Methods
   public override XmlNode CloneNode( bool deep);                          // overrides XmlNode
   public override void WriteContentTo( XmlWriter w);                      // overrides XmlNode
   public override void WriteTo( XmlWriter w);                             // overrides XmlNode
}
```

This class represents the DOCTYPE declaration of an XML document and its contents.

Hierarchy	System.Object → XmlNode(System.ICloneable, System.Collections.IEnumerable, System.Xml.XPath.IXPathNavigable) → XmlLinkedNode → XmlDocumentType
Returned By	XmlDocument.{CreateDocumentType( ), DocumentType}

XmlElement   CF 1.0

System.Xml (system.xml.dll)   class

```
public class XmlElement : XmlLinkedNode {
// Protected Constructors
```

```
    protected internal XmlElement( string prefix, string localName, string namespaceURI, XmlDocument doc);
// Public Instance Properties
    public override XmlAttributeCollection Attributes{get; }                                              // overrides XmlNode
    public virtual bool HasAttributes{get; }
    public override string InnerText{set; get; }                                                          // overrides XmlNode
    public override string InnerXml{set; get; }                                                           // overrides XmlNode
    public bool IsEmpty{set; get; }
    public override string LocalName{get; }                                                               // overrides XmlNode
    public override string Name{get; }                                                                    // overrides XmlNode
    public override string NamespaceURI{get; }                                                            // overrides XmlNode
    public override XmlNode NextSibling{get; }                                                       // overrides XmlLinkedNode
    public override XmlNodeType NodeType{get; }                                                           // overrides XmlNode
    public override XmlDocument OwnerDocument{get; }                                                      // overrides XmlNode
    public override string Prefix{set; get; }                                                             // overrides XmlNode
// Public Instance Methods
    public override XmlNode CloneNode( bool deep);                                                        // overrides XmlNode
    public virtual string GetAttribute( string name);
    public virtual string GetAttribute( string localName, string namespaceURI);
    public virtual XmlAttribute GetAttributeNode( string name);
    public virtual XmlAttribute GetAttributeNode( string localName, string namespaceURI);
    public virtual XmlNodeList GetElementsByTagName( string name);
    public virtual XmlNodeList GetElementsByTagName( string localName, string namespaceURI);
    public virtual bool HasAttribute( string name);
    public virtual bool HasAttribute( string localName, string namespaceURI);
    public override void RemoveAll( );                                                                    // overrides XmlNode
    public virtual void RemoveAllAttributes( );
    public virtual void RemoveAttribute( string name);
    public virtual void RemoveAttribute( string localName, string namespaceURI);
    public virtual XmlNode RemoveAttributeAt( int i);
    public virtual XmlAttribute RemoveAttributeNode( string localName, string namespaceURI);
    public virtual XmlAttribute RemoveAttributeNode( XmlAttribute oldAttr);
    public virtual string SetAttribute( string localName, string namespaceURI, string value);
    public virtual void SetAttribute( string name, string value);
    public virtual XmlAttribute SetAttributeNode( string localName, string namespaceURI);
    public virtual XmlAttribute SetAttributeNode( XmlAttribute newAttr);
    public override void WriteContentTo( XmlWriter w);                                                    // overrides XmlNode
    public override void WriteTo( XmlWriter w);                                                           // overrides XmlNode
}
```

This class represents an element in an XML document.

Hierarchy	System.Object → XmlNode(System.ICloneable, System.Collections.IEnumerable, System.Xml.XPath. IXPathNavigable) → XmlLinkedNode → XmlElement
Returned By	XmlAttribute.OwnerElement, XmlDataDocument.GetElementFromRow( ), XmlDocument. {CreateElement( ), DocumentElement, GetElementById( )}, XmlNode.this
Passed To	XmlDataDocument.GetRowFromElement( )

XmlEntity

System.Xml (system.xml.dll)   class

```
public class XmlEntity : XmlNode {
// Public Instance Properties
  public override string BaseURI{get; }                                       // overrides XmlNode
  public override string InnerText{set; get; }                                // overrides XmlNode
  public override string InnerXml{set; get; }                                 // overrides XmlNode
  public override bool IsReadOnly{get; }                                      // overrides XmlNode
  public override string LocalName{get; }                                     // overrides XmlNode
  public override string Name{get; }                                          // overrides XmlNode
  public override XmlNodeType NodeType{get; }                                 // overrides XmlNode
  public string NotationName{get; }
  public override string OuterXml{get; }                                      // overrides XmlNode
  public string PublicId{get; }
  public string SystemId{get; }
// Public Instance Methods
  public override XmlNode CloneNode( bool deep);                              // overrides XmlNode
  public override void WriteContentTo( XmlWriter w);                         // overrides XmlNode
  public override void WriteTo( XmlWriter w);                                // overrides XmlNode
}
```

This class represents an entity in an XML document.

Hierarchy   System.Object → XmlNode(System.ICloneable, System.Collections.IEnumerable, System.Xml.XPath.IXPathNavigable) → XmlEntity

XmlEntityReference   CF 1.0

System.Xml (system.xml.dll)   class

```
public class XmlEntityReference : XmlLinkedNode {
// Protected Constructors
  protected internal XmlEntityReference( string name, XmlDocument doc);
// Public Instance Properties
  public override string BaseURI{get; }                                       // overrides XmlNode
  public override bool IsReadOnly{get; }                                      // overrides XmlNode
  public override string LocalName{get; }                                     // overrides XmlNode
  public override string Name{get; }                                          // overrides XmlNode
  public override XmlNodeType NodeType{get; }                                 // overrides XmlNode
  public override string Value{set; get; }                                    // overrides XmlNode
// Public Instance Methods
  public override XmlNode CloneNode( bool deep);                              // overrides XmlNode
  public override void WriteContentTo( XmlWriter w);                         // overrides XmlNode
  public override void WriteTo( XmlWriter w);                                // overrides XmlNode
}
```

This class represents an entity reference in an XML document.

System.Object → XmlNode(System.ICloneable, System.Collections.IEnumerable, System.Xml.XPath. IXPathNavigable) → XmlLinkedNode → XmlEntityReference

Returned By   XmlDocument.CreateEntityReference( )

XmlException   CF 1.0, ECMA 1.0, serializable

System.Xml (system.xml.dll)   class

```
public class XmlException : SystemException {
// Public Constructors
   public XmlException( );
   public XmlException( string message);
   public XmlException( string message, Exception innerException);
   public XmlException( string message, Exception innerException, int lineNumber, int linePosition);
// Protected Constructors
   protected XmlException( System.Runtime.Serialization.SerializationInfo info, System.Runtime.Serialization.StreamingContext context);
// Public Instance Properties
   public int LineNumber{get; }
   public int LinePosition{get; }
   public override string Message{get; }                                              // overrides Exception
// Public Instance Methods
   public override void GetObjectData( System.Runtime.Serialization.SerializationInfo info, System.Runtime.Serialization.
StreamingContext context);                                                           // overrides Exception
}
```

This class contains errors thrown by XML-parsing operations. The LineNumber and LinePosition properties store the location of the error in the source document, and Message describes the reason for the error.

Hierarchy   System.Object → System.Exception(System.Runtime.Serialization.ISerializable) → System.SystemException → XmlException

XmlImplementation   CF 1.0

System.Xml (system.xml.dll)   class

```
public class XmlImplementation {
// Public Constructors
   public XmlImplementation( );
// Public Instance Methods
   public virtual XmlDocument CreateDocument( );
   public bool HasFeature( string strFeature, string strVersion);
}
```

This class instantiates a new XmlDocument object using the same XmlNameTable of an existing XmlDocument.

Returned By   XmlDocument.Implementation

XmlLinkedNode

System.Xml (system.xml.dll)   abstract class

```
public abstract class XmlLinkedNode : XmlNode {
// Public Instance Properties
   public override XmlNode NextSibling{get; }                          // overrides XmlNode
   public override XmlNode PreviousSibling{get; }                      // overrides XmlNode
}
```

This type of node class is the base class for node types that are not top-level (i.e., nodes that require a parent). For example, XmlCharacterData and XmlElement are derived from XmlLinkedNode.

Hierarchy	System.Object → XmlNode(System.ICloneable, System.Collections.IEnumerable, System.Xml.XPath. IXPathNavigable) → XmlLinkedNode
Subclasses	XmlCharacterData, XmlDeclaration, XmlDocumentType, XmlElement, XmlEntityReference, XmlProcessingInstruction

XmlNamedNodeMap

System.Xml (system.xml.dll)   class

```
public class XmlNamedNodeMap : IEnumerable {
// Public Instance Properties
   public virtual int Count{get; }
// Public Instance Methods
   public virtual IEnumerator GetEnumerator( );                       // implements IEnumerable
   public virtual XmlNode GetNamedItem( string name);
   public virtual XmlNode GetNamedItem( string localName, string namespaceURI);
   public virtual XmlNode Item( int index);
   public virtual XmlNode RemoveNamedItem( string name);
   public virtual XmlNode RemoveNamedItem( string localName, string namespaceURI);
   public virtual XmlNode SetNamedItem( XmlNode node);
}
```

This class represents a collection of nodes accessed by index or name. This is the abstract parent class of XmlAttributeCollection.

Subclasses	XmlAttributeCollection
Returned By	XmlDocumentType.{Entities, Notations}

XmlNamespaceManager

System.Xml (system.xml.dll)   class

```
public class XmlNamespaceManager : IEnumerable {
// Public Constructors
```

```
   public XmlNamespaceManager( XmlNameTable nameTable);
// Public Instance Properties
   public virtual string DefaultNamespace{get; }
   public XmlNameTable NameTable{get; }
// Public Instance Methods
   public virtual void AddNamespace( string prefix, string uri);
   public virtual IEnumerator GetEnumerator( );                                    // implements IEnumerable
   public virtual bool HasNamespace( string prefix);
   public virtual string LookupNamespace( string prefix);
   public virtual string LookupPrefix( string uri);
   public virtual bool PopScope( );
   public virtual void PushScope( );
   public virtual void RemoveNamespace( string prefix, string uri);
}
```

This class represents a collection of namespace prefixes and namespace URIs that are used
to manage and resolve namespace information. The namespace manager is constructed
using an XmlNameTable. XmlNamespaceManager is used internally by XmlReader to resolve namespace
prefixes and track the current scope. XmlNamespaceManager maintains scope in a stack, which
can be manipulated with PopScope( ) and PushScope( ). Namespaces must be added explicitly to
the namespace manager with AddNamespace( ), even if you use an existing XmlNameTable.

Subclasses   System.Xml.Xsl.XsltContext

Returned By   XmlParserContext.NamespaceManager

Passed To   XmlNode.{SelectNodes( ), SelectSingleNode( )}, XmlParserContext.{NamespaceManager,
                   XmlParserContext( )}, System.Xml.XPath.XPathExpression.SetContext( )

XmlNameTable   CF 1.0, ECMA 1.0

System.Xml (system.xml.dll)   abstract class

```
public abstract class XmlNameTable {
// Protected Constructors
  protected XmlNameTable( );
// Public Instance Methods
  public abstract string Add( char[ ] array, int offset, int length);
  public abstract string Add( string array);
  public abstract string Get( char[ ] array, int offset, int length);
  public abstract string Get( string array);
}
```

This class presents a table of string objects (for element and attribute names) used in an
XML document. The XML parser uses these string objects for efficient manipulation of
repeated element and attribute names. An XmlNameTable exists for every XmlDocument you
create. The XmlImplementation class instantiates a new XmlDocument with the XmlNameTable of
another existing XmlDocument.

Subclasses	NameTable
Returned By	XmlDocument.NameTable, XmlNamespaceManager.NameTable, XmlParserContext.NameTable, XmlReader.NameTable, System.Xml.XPath.XPathNavigator.NameTable
Passed To	XmlDocument.XmlDocument( ), XmlNamespaceManager.XmlNamespaceManager( ), XmlParserContext. {NameTable, XmlParserContext( )}, XmlTextReader.XmlTextReader( )

XmlNode
CF 1.0

System.Xml (system.xml.dll)   abstract class

```
public abstract class XmlNode : ICloneable, IEnumerable, System.Xml.XPath.IXPathNavigable {
// Public Instance Properties
  public virtual XmlAttributeCollection Attributes{get; }
  public virtual string BaseURI{get; }
  public virtual XmlNodeList ChildNodes{get; }
  public virtual XmlNode FirstChild{get; }
  public virtual bool HasChildNodes{get; }
  public virtual string InnerText{set; get; }
  public virtual string InnerXml{set; get; }
  public virtual bool IsReadOnly{get; }
  public virtual XmlNode LastChild{get; }
  public abstract string LocalName{get; }
  public abstract string Name{get; }
  public virtual string NamespaceURI{get; }
  public virtual XmlNode NextSibling{get; }
  public abstract XmlNodeType NodeType{get; }
  public virtual string OuterXml{get; }
  public virtual XmlDocument OwnerDocument{get; }
  public virtual XmlNode ParentNode{get; }
  public virtual string Prefix{set; get; }
  public virtual XmlNode PreviousSibling{get; }
  public virtual XmlElement this[ string name ]{get; }
  public virtual XmlElement this[ string localname, string ns ]{get; }
  public virtual string Value{set; get; }
// Public Instance Methods
  public virtual XmlNode AppendChild( XmlNode newChild);
  public virtual XmlNode Clone( );
  public abstract XmlNode CloneNode( bool deep);
  public XPathNavigator CreateNavigator( );                    // implements System.Xml.XPath.IXPathNavigable
  public IEnumerator GetEnumerator( );                         // implements IEnumerable
  public virtual string GetNamespaceOfPrefix( string prefix);
  public virtual string GetPrefixOfNamespace( string namespaceURI);
  public virtual XmlNode InsertAfter( XmlNode newChild, XmlNode refChild);
  public virtual XmlNode InsertBefore( XmlNode newChild, XmlNode refChild);
  public virtual void Normalize( );
  public virtual XmlNode PrependChild( XmlNode newChild);
  public virtual void RemoveAll( );
  public virtual XmlNode RemoveChild( XmlNode oldChild);
```

```
    public virtual XmlNode ReplaceChild( XmlNode newChild, XmlNode oldChild);
    public XmlNodeList SelectNodes( string xpath);
    public XmlNodeList SelectNodes( string xpath, XmlNamespaceManager nsmgr);
    public XmlNode SelectSingleNode( string xpath);
    public XmlNode SelectSingleNode( string xpath, XmlNamespaceManager nsmgr);
    public virtual bool Supports( string feature, string version);
    public abstract void WriteContentTo( XmlWriter w);
    public abstract void WriteTo( XmlWriter w);
}
```

This abstract class represents a node in a document. A node is the basic object described by the DOM for XML. A node can be an element, an element's attributes, the DOCTYPE declaration, a comment, or the entire document itself. Nodes are ordered in a hierarchical tree in which child, parent, and sibling relationships are "known" by each node.

The XmlNode class is the parent object of the specific node type classes. The properties of this class expose the intrinsic values of the node: NamespaceURI, NodeType, parent, child, sibling nodes, etc. The methods allow a node to add to or removed from a node tree (in the context of an XmlDocument or XmlDocumentFragment), with respect to a reference node.

Subclasses	XmlAttribute, XmlDocument, XmlDocumentFragment, XmlEntity, XmlLinkedNode, XmlNotation
Returned By	Multiple types
Passed To	XmlDataDocument.CreateNavigator( ), XmlDocument.ImportNode( ), XmlNamedNodeMap. SetNamedItem( ), XmlNodeReader.XmlNodeReader( )

XmlNodeChangedAction
CF 1.0, serializable

System.Xml (system.xml.dll) enum

```
public enum XmlNodeChangedAction {
    Insert = 0,
    Remove = 1,
    Change = 2
}
```

This simple enumeration that describes the change that has occurred within an XmlDocument instance can be one of the following: Change, which indicates that a node within the document has changed in some way; Insert, which indicates that a node has been inserted into the document; or Remove, which indicates that a node has been removed. This is one of the properties specified in the XmlNodeChangedEventArgs parameter to the XmlNodeChangedEventHandler delegate instance registered with the XmlDocument.

Hierarchy	System.Object → System.ValueType → System.Enum(System.IComparable, System.IFormattable, System.IConvertible) → XmlNodeChangedAction
Returned By	XmlNodeChangedEventArgs.Action

XmlNodeChangedEventArgs

System.Xml (system.xml.dll)

```
public class XmlNodeChangedEventArgs {
// Public Instance Properties
   public XmlNodeChangedAction Action{get; }
   public XmlNode NewParent{get; }
   public XmlNode Node{get; }
   public XmlNode OldParent{get; }
}
```

This type contains information about the changes to a node that are passed when an XmlDocument calls through an XmlNodeChangedEventHandler delegate instance. It contains the changed or changing node, the old and new parents to that node, and an enumeration describing the change (modification, insertion, or removal).

Passed To   XmlNodeChangedEventHandler.{BeginInvoke( ), Invoke( )}

XmlNodeChangedEventHandler

System.Xml (system.xml.dll)

```
public delegate void XmlNodeChangedEventHandler( object sender, XmlNodeChangedEventArgs e);
```

This declared delegate type must be used to receive event notifications from the XmlDocument instance if code wishes to be notified of changes to the document as they occur.

Associated Events XmlDataDocument.{NodeChanged( ), NodeChanging( ), NodeInserted( ), NodeInserting( ),
NodeRemoved( ), NodeRemoving( )}, XmlDocument.{NodeChanged( ), NodeChanging( ), NodeInserted(
), NodeInserting( ), NodeRemoved( ), NodeRemoving( )}

XmlNodeList

System.Xml (system.xml.dll)

```
public abstract class XmlNodeList : IEnumerable {
// Protected Constructors
   protected XmlNodeList( );
// Public Instance Properties
   public abstract int Count{get; }
   public virtual XmlNode this[ int i ]{get; }
// Public Instance Methods
   public abstract IEnumerator GetEnumerator( );                              // implements IEnumerable
   public abstract XmlNode Item( int index);
}
```

This class is an enumerated collection of nodes returned by XmlDocument.GetElementsByTagName( ). Nodes contained in the list can be retrieved by index or iterated through via the IEnumerator

326 | Chapter 16: The System.Xml Namespace

returned by GetEnumerator( ). Changes to the nodes in the list are immediately reflected in the XmlNodeList's properties and methods. For example, if you add a sibling to a node in the list, it appears in the list.

Returned By   XmlDocument.GetElementsByTagName( ), XmlElement.GetElementsByTagName( ), XmlNode.{ChildNodes, SelectNodes( )}

XmlNodeOrder   serializable

System.Xml (system.xml.dll)   enum

```
public enum XmlNodeOrder {
  Before = 0,
  After = 1,
  Same = 2,
  Unknown = 3
}
```

These values describe the position of one node relative to another, with respect to document order.

Hierarchy   System.Object → System.ValueType → System.Enum(System.IComparable, System.IFormattable, System.IConvertible) → XmlNodeOrder

Returned By   System.Xml.XPath.XPathNavigator.ComparePosition( )

XmlNodeReader   CF 1.0

System.Xml (system.xml.dll)   class

```
public class XmlNodeReader : XmlReader {
// Public Constructors
  public XmlNodeReader( XmlNode node);
// Public Instance Properties
  public override int AttributeCount{get; }                              // overrides XmlReader
  public override string BaseURI{get; }                                  // overrides XmlReader
  public override bool CanResolveEntity{get; }                           // overrides XmlReader
  public override int Depth{get; }                                       // overrides XmlReader
  public override bool EOF{get; }                                        // overrides XmlReader
  public override bool HasAttributes{get; }                             // overrides XmlReader
  public override bool HasValue{get; }                                   // overrides XmlReader
  public override bool IsDefault{get; }                                  // overrides XmlReader
  public override bool IsEmptyElement{get; }                            // overrides XmlReader
  public override string LocalName{get; }                               // overrides XmlReader
  public override string Name{get; }                                     // overrides XmlReader
  public override string NamespaceURI{get; }                            // overrides XmlReader
  public override XmlNameTable NameTable{get; }                         // overrides XmlReader
  public override XmlNodeType NodeType{get; }                           // overrides XmlReader
  public override string Prefix{get; }                                   // overrides XmlReader
```

```
  public override char QuoteChar{get; }                                           // overrides XmlReader
  public override ReadState ReadState{get; }                                       // overrides XmlReader
  public override string this[ string name ]{get; }                                // overrides XmlReader
  public override string this[ int i ]{get; }                                      // overrides XmlReader
  public override string this[ string name, string namespaceURI ]{get; }           // overrides XmlReader
  public override string Value{get; }                                              // overrides XmlReader
  public override string XmlLang{get; }                                            // overrides XmlReader
  public override XmlSpace XmlSpace{get; }                                          // overrides XmlReader
// Public Instance Methods
  public override void Close( );                                                   // overrides XmlReader
  public override string GetAttribute( int attributeIndex);                        // overrides XmlReader
  public override string GetAttribute( string name);                               // overrides XmlReader
  public override string GetAttribute( string name, string namespaceURI);          // overrides XmlReader
  public override string LookupNamespace( string prefix);                          // overrides XmlReader
  public override bool MoveToAttribute( string name);                              // overrides XmlReader
  public override bool MoveToAttribute( string name, string namespaceURI);         // overrides XmlReader
  public override void MoveToAttribute( int attributeIndex);                       // overrides XmlReader
  public override bool MoveToElement( );                                           // overrides XmlReader
  public override bool MoveToFirstAttribute( );                                    // overrides XmlReader
  public override bool MoveToNextAttribute( );                                     // overrides XmlReader
  public override bool Read( );                                                    // overrides XmlReader
  public override bool ReadAttributeValue( );                                      // overrides XmlReader
  public override string ReadString( );                                            // overrides XmlReader
  public override void ResolveEntity( );                                           // overrides XmlReader
  public override void Skip( );                                                    // overrides XmlReader
}
```

This class is a non-cached, forward-only reader that accesses the contents of an XmlNode. This class can read a DOM subtree, but doesn't provide full-document support such as validation.

Hierarchy System.Object → XmlReader → XmlNodeReader

XmlNodeType   CF 1.0, ECMA 1.0, serializable

System.Xml (system.xml.dll)   enum

```
public enum XmlNodeType {
  None = 0,
  Element = 1,
  Attribute = 2,
  Text = 3,
  CDATA = 4,
  EntityReference = 5,
  Entity = 6,
  ProcessingInstruction = 7,
  Comment = 8,
  Document = 9,
  DocumentType = 10,
  DocumentFragment = 11,
  Notation = 12,
```

```
    Whitespace = 13,
    SignificantWhitespace = 14,
    EndElement = 15,
    EndEntity = 16,
    XmlDeclaration = 17
}
```

This enumeration contains identifiers for node types. All DOM Core Level 2 types are included.

Hierarchy	System.Object → System.ValueType → System.Enum(System.IComparable, System.IFormattable, System.IConvertible) → XmlNodeType
Returned By	XmlNode.NodeType, XmlReader.{MoveToContent( ), NodeType}
Passed To	XmlDocument.CreateNode( ), XmlTextReader.XmlTextReader( ), XmlValidatingReader. XmlValidatingReader( )

XmlNotation

System.Xml (system.xml.dll)   class

```
public class XmlNotation : XmlNode {
// Public Instance Properties
    public override string InnerXml{set; get; }                                              // overrides XmlNode
    public override bool IsReadOnly{get; }                                                    // overrides XmlNode
    public override string LocalName{get; }                                                  // overrides XmlNode
    public override string Name{get; }                                                       // overrides XmlNode
    public override XmlNodeType NodeType{get; }                                               // overrides XmlNode
    public override string OuterXml{get; }                                                   // overrides XmlNode
    public string PublicId{get; }
    public string SystemId{get; }
// Public Instance Methods
    public override XmlNode CloneNode( bool deep);                                            // overrides XmlNode
    public override void WriteContentTo( XmlWriter w);                                        // overrides XmlNode
    public override void WriteTo( XmlWriter w);                                               // overrides XmlNode
}
```

This class represents a notation declaration (<!NOTATION ...>) in an XML document.

Hierarchy	System.Object → XmlNode(System.ICloneable, System.Collections.IEnumerable, System.Xml.XPath. IXPathNavigable) → XmlNotation

XmlParserContext   CF 1.0, ECMA 1.0

System.Xml (system.xml.dll)   class

```
public class XmlParserContext {
// Public Constructors
    public XmlParserContext( XmlNameTable nt, XmlNamespaceManager nsMgr, string docTypeName, string pubId, string sysId, string
internalSubset, string baseURI, string xmlLang, XmlSpace xmlSpace);
```

public **XmlParserContext**(XmlNameTable *nt*, XmlNamespaceManager *nsMgr*, string *docTypeName*, string *pubId*, string *sysId*, string *internalSubset*, string *baseURI*, string *xmlLang*, XmlSpace *xmlSpace*, System.Text.Encoding *enc*);
  public **XmlParserContext**(XmlNameTable *nt*, XmlNamespaceManager *nsMgr*, string *xmlLang*, XmlSpace *xmlSpace*);
  public **XmlParserContext**(XmlNameTable *nt*, XmlNamespaceManager *nsMgr*, string *xmlLang*, XmlSpace *xmlSpace*, System.Text. Encoding *enc*);
// *Public Instance Properties*
  public string **BaseURI**{set; get; }
  public string **DocTypeName**{set; get; }
  public Encoding **Encoding**{set; get; }
  public string **InternalSubset**{set; get; }
  public XmlNamespaceManager **NamespaceManager**{set; get; }
  public XmlNameTable **NameTable**{set; get; }
  public string **PublicId**{set; get; }
  public string **SystemId**{set; get; }
  public string **XmlLang**{set; get; }
  public XmlSpace **XmlSpace**{set; get; }
}

This class contains document context information normally provided by both the XML declaration and DOCTYPE elements for parsing XML fragments. XmlTextReader and XmlValidatingReader use the XmlParserContext for the base URI, internal subset, public and system identifiers, etc.

Passed To   XmlTextReader.XmlTextReader( ), XmlValidatingReader.XmlValidatingReader( )

XmlProcessingInstruction   CF 1.0

System.Xml (system.xml.dll)   class

public class **XmlProcessingInstruction** : XmlLinkedNode {
// *Protected Constructors*
  protected internal **XmlProcessingInstruction**(string *target*, string *data*, XmlDocument *doc*);
// *Public Instance Properties*
  public string **Data**{set; get; }
  public override string **InnerText**{set; get; }   // *overrides XmlNode*
  public override string **LocalName**{get; }   // *overrides XmlNode*
  public override string **Name**{get; }   // *overrides XmlNode*
  public override XmlNodeType **NodeType**{get; }   // *overrides XmlNode*
  public string **Target**{get; }
  public override string **Value**{set; get; }   // *overrides XmlNode*
// *Public Instance Methods*
  public override XmlNode **CloneNode**(bool *deep*);   // *overrides XmlNode*
  public override void **WriteContentTo**(XmlWriter *w*);   // *overrides XmlNode*
  public override void **WriteTo**(XmlWriter *w*);   // *overrides XmlNode*
}

This class represents a processing instruction in an XML document.

Hierarchy   System.Object → XmlNode(System.ICloneable, System.Collections.IEnumerable, System.Xml.XPath. IXPathNavigable) → XmlLinkedNode → XmlProcessingInstruction

Returned By   XmlDocument.CreateProcessingInstruction( )

XmlQualifiedName CF 1.0

System.Xml (system.xml.dll)class

```
public class XmlQualifiedName {
// Public Constructors
  public XmlQualifiedName( );
  public XmlQualifiedName( string name);
  public XmlQualifiedName( string name, string ns);
// Public Static Fields
  public static readonly XmlQualifiedName Empty;
// Public Instance Properties
  public bool IsEmpty{get; }
  public string Name{get; }
  public string Namespace{get; }
// Public Static Methods
  public static string ToString( string name, string ns);
  public static bool operator !=( XmlQualifiedName a, XmlQualifiedName b);
  public static bool operator ==( XmlQualifiedName a, XmlQualifiedName b);
// Public Instance Methods
  public override bool Equals( object other);                                  // overrides object
  public override int GetHashCode( );                                          // overrides object
  public override string ToString( );                                         // overrides object
}
```

This class represents a namespace-qualified local name. This looks like namespace:name within a document. An XmlQualifiedName object is constructed with the element's name and its namespace as string arguments. The namespace field may be empty, in which case the default namespace of the document is assumed.

XmlReader CF 1.0, ECMA 1.0

System.Xml (system.xml.dll)abstract class

```
public abstract class XmlReader {
// Protected Constructors
  protected XmlReader( );
// Public Instance Properties
  public abstract int AttributeCount{get; }
  public abstract string BaseURI{get; }
  public virtual bool CanResolveEntity{get; }
  public abstract int Depth{get; }
  public abstract bool EOF{get; }
  public virtual bool HasAttributes{get; }
```

```
    public abstract bool HasValue{get; }
    public abstract bool IsDefault{get; }
    public abstract bool IsEmptyElement{get; }
    public abstract string LocalName{get; }
    public abstract string Name{get; }
    public abstract string NamespaceURI{get; }
    public abstract XmlNameTable NameTable{get; }
    public abstract XmlNodeType NodeType{get; }
    public abstract string Prefix{get; }
    public abstract char QuoteChar{get; }
    public abstract ReadState ReadState{get; }
    public abstract string this[ string name, string namespaceURI ]{get; }
    public abstract string this[ int i ]{get; }
    public abstract string this[ string name ]{get; }
    public abstract string Value{get; }
    public abstract string XmlLang{get; }
    public abstract XmlSpace XmlSpace{get; }
// Public Static Methods
    public static bool IsName( string str);
    public static bool IsNameToken( string str);
// Public Instance Methods
    public abstract void Close( );
    public abstract string GetAttribute( int i);
    public abstract string GetAttribute( string name);
    public abstract string GetAttribute( string name, string namespaceURI);
    public virtual bool IsStartElement( );
    public virtual bool IsStartElement( string name);
    public virtual bool IsStartElement( string localname, string ns);
    public abstract string LookupNamespace( string prefix);
    public abstract bool MoveToAttribute( string name);
    public abstract bool MoveToAttribute( string name, string ns);
    public abstract void MoveToAttribute( int i);
    public virtual XmlNodeType MoveToContent( );
    public abstract bool MoveToElement( );
    public abstract bool MoveToFirstAttribute( );
    public abstract bool MoveToNextAttribute( );
    public abstract bool Read( );
    public abstract bool ReadAttributeValue( );
    public virtual string ReadElementString( );
    public virtual string ReadElementString( string name);
    public virtual string ReadElementString( string localname, string ns);
    public virtual void ReadEndElement( );
    public virtual string ReadInnerXml( );
    public virtual string ReadOuterXml( );
    public virtual void ReadStartElement( );
    public virtual void ReadStartElement( string name);
    public virtual void ReadStartElement( string localname, string ns);
    public virtual string ReadString( );
    public abstract void ResolveEntity( );
    public virtual void Skip( );
}
```

This class is a simple reader for XML documents. XmlReader provides a non-cached, forward-only navigation through an XML data stream. It does not provide validation, nor does it expand general entities. Two derived classes provide these features: XmlTextReader and XmlValidatingReader.

The XmlReader class parses XML in a streaming-based approach (exemplified by the SAX specification). This means the XML parser presents "interesting pieces" (elements, attributes, namespace declarations, and so forth) in a linear order. Within XmlReader, this ordering of nodes is done using successive calls to the Read( ) method. An XmlReader is not positioned on a node at first—an initial call to Read( ) is required to move to the root node of a document. Subsequent calls to Read( ) move the reader sequentially through the nodes. The NodeType property tells you which type of node the reader is currently positioned on, returning values from the XmlNodeType enumeration. A special node-type value for XmlReader is EndElement. As Read( ) moves through the stream, it can be positioned on an element's end tag after it has stepped through the element's children. This is not a real node, in the DOM sense, but is required for XmlReader to parse XML data properly. The Skip( ) method steps through data node by node. A call to Skip( ) moves the reader to the next real node, disregarding the current node's children.

XML documents can also be parsed in a tree-based approach, using the XmlDocument type.

Subclasses	XmlNodeReader, XmlTextReader, XmlValidatingReader
Returned By	XmlValidatingReader.Reader, System.Xml.Xsl.XslTransform.Transform( )
Passed To	XmlDocument.{Load( ), ReadNode( )}, XmlValidatingReader.XmlValidatingReader( ), XmlWriter. {WriteAttributes( ), WriteNode( )}, System.Xml.XPath.XPathDocument.XPathDocument( ), System.Xml. Xsl.XslTransform.Load( )

XmlResolver

CF 1.0, ECMA 1.0

System.Xml (system.xml.dll)   abstract class

```
public abstract class XmlResolver {
// Protected Constructors
   protected XmlResolver( );
// Public Instance Properties
   public abstract ICredentials Credentials{set; }
// Public Instance Methods
   public abstract object GetEntity( Uri absoluteUri, string role, Type ofObjectToReturn);
   public virtual Uri ResolveUri( Uri baseUri, string relativeUri);
}
```

This class resolves external resources according to their URIs. This class is used to retrieve an external DTD or Schema in XML documents and also obtains resources from imported stylesheets (xsl:import) and included files (xml:include). This abstract class is implemented by XmlUrlResolver.

Subclasses	XmlSecureResolver, XmlUrlResolver
Passed To	XmlDocument.XmlResolver, XmlSecureResolver.XmlSecureResolver( ), XmlTextReader.XmlResolver, XmlValidatingReader.XmlResolver, System.Xml.Xsl.XslTransform.{Load( ), Transform( ), XmlResolver}

XmlSecureResolver .NET 1.1

System.Xml (system.xml.dll) class

```
public class XmlSecureResolver : XmlResolver {
// Public Constructors
  public XmlSecureResolver( XmlResolver resolver, System.Security.Policy.Evidence evidence);
  public XmlSecureResolver( XmlResolver resolver, System.Security.PermissionSet permissionSet);
  public XmlSecureResolver( XmlResolver resolver, string securityUrl);
// Public Instance Properties
  public override ICredentials Credentials{set; }                              // overrides XmlResolver
// Public Static Methods
  public static Evidence CreateEvidenceForUrl( string securityUrl);
// Public Instance Methods
  public override object GetEntity( Uri absoluteUri, string role, Type ofObjectToReturn);   // overrides XmlResolver
  public override Uri ResolveUri( Uri baseUri, string relativeUri);            // overrides XmlResolver
}
```

This class decorates an XmlResolver instance to provide security restrictions on the normal behavior of an XmlResolver. For example, it can prevent resolving URI references that reference other domains embedded within an XML document. See XmlUrlResolver for the concrete implementation this class will usually wrap around.

Hierarchy	System.Object → XmlResolver → XmlSecureResolver

XmlSignificantWhitespace CF 1.0

System.Xml (system.xml.dll) class

```
public class XmlSignificantWhitespace : XmlCharacterData {
// Protected Constructors
  protected internal XmlSignificantWhitespace( string strData, XmlDocument doc);
// Public Instance Properties
  public override string LocalName{get; }                                      // overrides XmlNode
  public override string Name{get; }                                           // overrides XmlNode
  public override XmlNodeType NodeType{get; }                                   // overrides XmlNode
  public override string Value{set; get; }                                     // overrides XmlCharacterData
// Public Instance Methods
  public override XmlNode CloneNode( bool deep);                               // overrides XmlNode
  public override void WriteContentTo( XmlWriter w);                           // overrides XmlNode
  public override void WriteTo( XmlWriter w);                                  // overrides XmlNode
}
```

This class represents a whitespace node in mixed content data, if whitespace is preserved in the XML document (XmlDocument.PreserveWhitespace is True).

Hierarchy	System.Object → XmlNode(System.ICloneable, System.Collections.IEnumerable, System.Xml.XPath. IXPathNavigable) → XmlLinkedNode → XmlCharacterData → XmlSignificantWhitespace
Returned By	XmlDocument.CreateSignificantWhitespace( )

XmlSpace
CF 1.0, ECMA 1.0, serializable

System.Xml (system.xml.dll)
enum

```
public enum XmlSpace {
  None = 0,
  Default = 1,
  Preserve = 2
}
```

This enumeration provides values for the xml:space scope. Used by XmlParserContext.XmlSpace.

Hierarchy	System.Object → System.ValueType → System.Enum(System.IComparable, System.IFormattable, System.IConvertible) → XmlSpace
Returned By	XmlParserContext.XmlSpace, XmlReader.XmlSpace, XmlWriter.XmlSpace
Passed To	XmlParserContext.{XmlParserContext( ), XmlSpace}, System.Xml.XPath.XPathDocument. XPathDocument( )

XmlText
CF 1.0

System.Xml (system.xml.dll)
class

```
public class XmlText : XmlCharacterData {
// Protected Constructors
  protected internal XmlText( string strData, XmlDocument doc);
// Public Instance Properties
  public override string LocalName{get; }                             // overrides XmlNode
  public override string Name{get; }                                  // overrides XmlNode
  public override XmlNodeType NodeType{get; }                         // overrides XmlNode
  public override string Value{set; get; }                           // overrides XmlCharacterData
// Public Instance Methods
  public override XmlNode CloneNode( bool deep);                      // overrides XmlNode
  public virtual XmlText SplitText( int offset);
  public override void WriteContentTo( XmlWriter w);                  // overrides XmlNode
  public override void WriteTo( XmlWriter w);                         // overrides XmlNode
}
```

This class represents a text node in an XML document. XmlTest is derived from the XmlCharacterData class and contains the text content of an element.

Hierarchy   System.Object → XmlNode(System.ICloneable, System.Collections.IEnumerable, System.Xml.XPath. IXPathNavigable) → XmlLinkedNode → XmlCharacterData → XmlText

Returned By   XmlDocument.CreateTextNode( )

XmlTextReader   CF 1.0, ECMA 1.0
System.Xml (system.xml.dll)   class

```
public class XmlTextReader : XmlReader, IXmlLineInfo {
// Public Constructors
  public XmlTextReader( System.IO.Stream input);
  public XmlTextReader( System.IO.Stream input, XmlNameTable nt);
  public XmlTextReader( System.IO.Stream xmlFragment, XmlNodeType fragType, XmlParserContext context);
  public XmlTextReader( string url);
  public XmlTextReader( string url, System.IO.Stream input);
  public XmlTextReader( string url, System.IO.Stream input, XmlNameTable nt);
  public XmlTextReader( string url, System.IO.TextReader input);
  public XmlTextReader( string url, System.IO.TextReader input, XmlNameTable nt);
  public XmlTextReader( string url, XmlNameTable nt);
  public XmlTextReader( string xmlFragment, XmlNodeType fragType, XmlParserContext context);
  public XmlTextReader( System.IO.TextReader input);
  public XmlTextReader( System.IO.TextReader input, XmlNameTable nt);
// Protected Constructors
  protected XmlTextReader( );
  protected XmlTextReader( XmlNameTable nt);
// Public Instance Properties
  public override int AttributeCount{get; }                                    // overrides XmlReader
  public override string BaseURI{get; }                                        // overrides XmlReader
  public override int Depth{get; }                                             // overrides XmlReader
  public Encoding Encoding{get; }
  public override bool EOF{get; }                                              // overrides XmlReader
  public override bool HasValue{get; }                                         // overrides XmlReader
  public override bool IsDefault{get; }                                        // overrides XmlReader
  public override bool IsEmptyElement{get; }                                   // overrides XmlReader
  public int LineNumber{get; }                                                 // implements IXmlLineInfo
  public int LinePosition{get; }                                               // implements IXmlLineInfo
  public override string LocalName{get; }                                      // overrides XmlReader
  public override string Name{get; }                                          // overrides XmlReader
  public bool Namespaces{set; get; }
  public override string NamespaceURI{get; }                                   // overrides XmlReader
  public override XmlNameTable NameTable{get; }                                // overrides XmlReader
  public override XmlNodeType NodeType{get; }                                  // overrides XmlReader
  public bool Normalization{set; get; }
  public override string Prefix{get; }                                         // overrides XmlReader
  public override char QuoteChar{get; }                                        // overrides XmlReader
  public override ReadState ReadState{get; }                                   // overrides XmlReader
  public override string this[ int i ]{get; }                                  // overrides XmlReader
  public override string this[ string name ]{get; }                            // overrides XmlReader
  public override string this[ string name, string namespaceURI ]{get; }       // overrides XmlReader
  public override string Value{get; }                                          // overrides XmlReader
```

```
  public WhitespaceHandling WhitespaceHandling{set; get; }
  public override string XmlLang{get; }                                          // overrides XmlReader
  public XmlResolver XmlResolver{set; }
  public override XmlSpace XmlSpace{get; }                                        // overrides XmlReader
// Public Instance Methods
  public override void Close( );                                                 // overrides XmlReader
  public override string GetAttribute( int i);                                   // overrides XmlReader
  public override string GetAttribute( string name);                             // overrides XmlReader
  public override string GetAttribute( string localName, string namespaceURI);   // overrides XmlReader
  public TextReader GetRemainder( );
  public override string LookupNamespace( string prefix);                        // overrides XmlReader
  public override bool MoveToAttribute( string name);                            // overrides XmlReader
  public override bool MoveToAttribute( string localName, string namespaceURI);  // overrides XmlReader
  public override void MoveToAttribute( int i);                                  // overrides XmlReader
  public override bool MoveToElement( );                                         // overrides XmlReader
  public override bool MoveToFirstAttribute( );                                  // overrides XmlReader
  public override bool MoveToNextAttribute( );                                   // overrides XmlReader
  public override bool Read( );                                                  // overrides XmlReader
  public override bool ReadAttributeValue( );                                    // overrides XmlReader
  public int ReadBase64( byte[ ] array, int offset, int len);
  public int ReadBinHex( byte[ ] array, int offset, int len);
  public int ReadChars( char[ ] buffer, int index, int count);
  public void ResetState( );
  public override void ResolveEntity( );                                         // overrides XmlReader
}
```

This class is a text-based reader for XML documents derived from XmlReader. XmlTextReader checks for well-formedness and expands entities, but does not validate data according to a DTD or schema.

Hierarchy   System.Object → XmlReader → XmlTextReader(IXmlLineInfo)

XmlTextWriter   CF 1.0, ECMA 1.0

System.Xml (system.xml.dll)   class

```
public class XmlTextWriter : XmlWriter {
// Public Constructors
  public XmlTextWriter( System.IO.Stream w, System.Text.Encoding encoding);
  public XmlTextWriter( string filename, System.Text.Encoding encoding);
  public XmlTextWriter( System.IO.TextWriter w);
// Public Instance Properties
  public Stream BaseStream{get; }
  public Formatting Formatting{set; get; }
  public int Indentation{set; get; }
  public char IndentChar{set; get; }
  public bool Namespaces{set; get; }
  public char QuoteChar{set; get; }
  public override WriteState WriteState{get; }                                   // overrides XmlWriter
  public override string XmlLang{get; }                                          // overrides XmlWriter
  public override XmlSpace XmlSpace{get; }                                       // overrides XmlWriter
```

```
// Public Instance Methods
  public override void Close( );                                                      // overrides XmlWriter
  public override void Flush( );                                                      // overrides XmlWriter
  public override string LookupPrefix( string ns);                                    // overrides XmlWriter
  public override void WriteBase64( byte[ ] buffer, int index, int count);            // overrides XmlWriter
  public override void WriteBinHex( byte[ ] buffer, int index, int count);            // overrides XmlWriter
  public override void WriteCData( string text);                                      // overrides XmlWriter
  public override void WriteCharEntity( char ch);                                     // overrides XmlWriter
  public override void WriteChars( char[ ] buffer, int index, int count);             // overrides XmlWriter
  public override void WriteComment( string text);                                    // overrides XmlWriter
  public override void WriteDocType( string name, string pubid, string sysid, string subset);  // overrides XmlWriter
  public override void WriteEndAttribute( );                                          // overrides XmlWriter
  public override void WriteEndDocument( );                                           // overrides XmlWriter
  public override void WriteEndElement( );                                            // overrides XmlWriter
  public override void WriteEntityRef( string name);                                  // overrides XmlWriter
  public override void WriteFullEndElement( );                                        // overrides XmlWriter
  public override void WriteName( string name);                                       // overrides XmlWriter
  public override void WriteNmToken( string name);                                    // overrides XmlWriter
  public override void WriteProcessingInstruction( string name, string text);         // overrides XmlWriter
  public override void WriteQualifiedName( string localName, string ns);              // overrides XmlWriter
  public override void WriteRaw( char[ ] buffer, int index, int count);               // overrides XmlWriter
  public override void WriteRaw( string data);                                        // overrides XmlWriter
  public override void WriteStartAttribute( string prefix, string localName, string ns);  // overrides XmlWriter
  public override void WriteStartDocument( );                                         // overrides XmlWriter
  public override void WriteStartDocument( bool standalone);                          // overrides XmlWriter
  public override void WriteStartElement( string prefix, string localName, string ns);  // overrides XmlWriter
  public override void WriteString( string text);                                     // overrides XmlWriter
  public override void WriteSurrogateCharEntity( char lowChar, char highChar);        // overrides XmlWriter
  public override void WriteWhitespace( string ws);                                   // overrides XmlWriter
}
```

This class adds basic formatting to the text output and is derived from XmlWriter. The Formatting property uses its values to indicate if the output is to be Indented (None is the default). If Formatting is set to Formatting.Indented, the value of the Indentation property is the number of characters to indent each successive level (or child element) in the output. IndentChar sets the character to use for indentation, which must be a valid whitespace character (the default is space). QuoteChar is the character to use to quote attributes and is either a single or double quote.

Hierarchy   System.Object → XmlWriter → XmlTextWriter

XmlTokenizedType   serializable

System.Xml (system.xml.dll)   enum

```
public enum XmlTokenizedType {
  CDATA = 0,
  ID = 1,
  IDREF = 2,
  IDREFS = 3,
```

```
  ENTITY = 4,
  ENTITIES = 5,
  NMTOKEN = 6,
  NMTOKENS = 7,
  NOTATION = 8,
  ENUMERATION = 9,
  QName = 10,
  NCName = 11,
  None = 12
}
```

This is an enumeration of XML string types based on the XML 1.0 specification.

Hierarchy   System.Object → System.ValueType → System.Enum(System.IComparable, System.IFormattable, System.IConvertible) → XmlTokenizedType

XmlUrlResolver

CF 1.0, ECMA 1.0

System.Xml (system.xml.dll)   class

```
public class XmlUrlResolver : XmlResolver {
// Public Constructors
  public XmlUrlResolver( );
// Public Instance Properties
  public override ICredentials Credentials{set; }                        // overrides XmlResolver
// Public Instance Methods
  public override object GetEntity( Uri absoluteUri, string role, Type ofObjectToReturn);   // overrides XmlResolver
}
```

This class resolves URLs of external resources and retrieves them for parsing. XmlUrlResolver implements XmlResolver and provides methods for retrieving external DTDs, Schemas, and imported stylesheets via a URL. To retrieve resources on a network, the Credentials property can be set to provide usernames and passwords, as well as define authentication schemes. You can set this property by supplying a System.Net.ICredentials object. By default, this property is set for anonymous access to a URI resource.

Hierarchy   System.Object → XmlResolver → XmlUrlResolver

XmlValidatingReader

System.Xml (system.xml.dll)   class

```
public class XmlValidatingReader : XmlReader, IXmlLineInfo {
// Public Constructors
  public XmlValidatingReader( System.IO.Stream xmlFragment, XmlNodeType fragType, XmlParserContext context);
  public XmlValidatingReader( string xmlFragment, XmlNodeType fragType, XmlParserContext context);
  public XmlValidatingReader( XmlReader reader);
// Public Instance Properties
  public override int AttributeCount{get; }                              // overrides XmlReader
```

```
public override string BaseURI{get; }                                                    // overrides XmlReader
public override bool CanResolveEntity{get; }                                              // overrides XmlReader
public override int Depth{get; }                                                          // overrides XmlReader
public Encoding Encoding{get; }
public EntityHandling EntityHandling{set; get; }
public override bool EOF{get; }                                                           // overrides XmlReader
public override bool HasValue{get; }                                                      // overrides XmlReader
public override bool IsDefault{get; }                                                     // overrides XmlReader
public override bool IsEmptyElement{get; }                                                // overrides XmlReader
public override string LocalName{get; }                                                   // overrides XmlReader
public override string Name{get; }                                                        // overrides XmlReader
public bool Namespaces{set; get; }
public override string NamespaceURI{get; }                                                // overrides XmlReader
public override XmlNameTable NameTable{get; }                                             // overrides XmlReader
public override XmlNodeType NodeType{get; }                                               // overrides XmlReader
public override string Prefix{get; }                                                      // overrides XmlReader
public override char QuoteChar{get; }                                                     // overrides XmlReader
public XmlReader Reader{get; }
public override ReadState ReadState{get; }                                                // overrides XmlReader
public XmlSchemaCollection Schemas{get; }
public object SchemaType{get; }
public override string this[ int i ]{get; }                                               // overrides XmlReader
public override string this[ string name ]{get; }                                         // overrides XmlReader
public override string this[ string name, string namespaceURI ]{get; }                    // overrides XmlReader
public ValidationType ValidationType{set; get; }
public override string Value{get; }                                                       // overrides XmlReader
public override string XmlLang{get; }                                                     // overrides XmlReader
public XmlResolver XmlResolver{set; }
public override XmlSpace XmlSpace{get; }                                                   // overrides XmlReader
// Public Instance Methods
public override void Close( );                                                            // overrides XmlReader
public override string GetAttribute( int i);                                              // overrides XmlReader
public override string GetAttribute( string name);                                        // overrides XmlReader
public override string GetAttribute( string localName, string namespaceURI);              // overrides XmlReader
public override string LookupNamespace( string prefix);                                   // overrides XmlReader
public override bool MoveToAttribute( string name);                                       // overrides XmlReader
public override bool MoveToAttribute( string localName, string namespaceURI);             // overrides XmlReader
public override void MoveToAttribute( int i);                                             // overrides XmlReader
public override bool MoveToElement( );                                                    // overrides XmlReader
public override bool MoveToFirstAttribute( );                                             // overrides XmlReader
public override bool MoveToNextAttribute( );                                              // overrides XmlReader
public override bool Read( );                                                             // overrides XmlReader
public override bool ReadAttributeValue( );                                               // overrides XmlReader
public override string ReadString( );                                                     // overrides XmlReader
public object ReadTypedValue( );
public override void ResolveEntity( );                                                    // overrides XmlReader
// Events
public event ValidationEventHandler ValidationEventHandler;
}
```

This class is an XML reader that supports DTD and Schema validation. The type of validation to perform is contained in the ValidationType property, which can be DTD, Schema, XDR, or Auto. Auto is the default and determines which type of validation is required, if any, based on the document. If the DOCTYPE element contains DTD information, that is used. If a schema attribute exists or there is an inline <schema> element, that schema is used.

This class implements an event handler that you can set to warn of validation errors during Read( ) operations. Specifically, a delegate instance of type System.Xml.Schema.ValidationEventHandler can be set for the ValidationEventHandler event in this class. This delegate instance is invoked whenever the XmlValidatingReader finds an schema-invalid construct in the XML document it is reading, giving the delegate a chance to perform whatever error-handling is appropriate. If no event handler is registered, a XmlException is thrown instead on the first error.

Hierarchy   System.Object → XmlReader → XmlValidatingReader(IXmlLineInfo)

XmlWhitespace

CF 1.0

System.Xml (system.xml.dll)   class

```
public class XmlWhitespace : XmlCharacterData {
// Protected Constructors
   protected internal XmlWhitespace( string strData, XmlDocument doc);
// Public Instance Properties
   public override string LocalName{get; }                          // overrides XmlNode
   public override string Name{get; }                               // overrides XmlNode
   public override XmlNodeType NodeType{get; }                      // overrides XmlNode
   public override string Value{set; get; }              // overrides XmlCharacterData
// Public Instance Methods
   public override XmlNode CloneNode( bool deep);                    // overrides XmlNode
   public override void WriteContentTo( XmlWriter w);               // overrides XmlNode
   public override void WriteTo( XmlWriter w);                      // overrides XmlNode
}
```

This class represents whitespace in element content. Whitespace is ignored if XmlDocument. PreserveWhitespace is not set to true.

Hierarchy   System.Object → XmlNode(System.ICloneable, System.Collections.IEnumerable, System.Xml.XPath. IXPathNavigable) → XmlLinkedNode → XmlCharacterData → XmlWhitespace

Returned By   XmlDocument.CreateWhitespace( )

XmlWriter

CF 1.0, ECMA 1.0

System.Xml (system.xml.dll)   abstract class

```
public abstract class XmlWriter {
// Protected Constructors
   protected XmlWriter( );
// Public Instance Properties
```

```
    public abstract WriteState WriteState{get; }
    public abstract string XmlLang{get; }
    public abstract XmlSpace XmlSpace{get; }
// Public Instance Methods
    public abstract void Close( );
    public abstract void Flush( );
    public abstract string LookupPrefix( string ns);
    public virtual void WriteAttributes( XmlReader reader, bool defattr);
    public void WriteAttributeString( string localName, string value);
    public void WriteAttributeString( string localName, string ns, string value);
    public void WriteAttributeString( string prefix, string localName, string ns, string value);
    public abstract void WriteBase64( byte[ ] buffer, int index, int count);
    public abstract void WriteBinHex( byte[ ] buffer, int index, int count);
    public abstract void WriteCData( string text);
    public abstract void WriteCharEntity( char ch);
    public abstract void WriteChars( char[ ] buffer, int index, int count);
    public abstract void WriteComment( string text);
    public abstract void WriteDocType( string name, string pubid, string sysid, string subset);
    public void WriteElementString( string localName, string value);
    public void WriteElementString( string localName, string ns, string value);
    public abstract void WriteEndAttribute( );
    public abstract void WriteEndDocument( );
    public abstract void WriteEndElement( );
    public abstract void WriteEntityRef( string name);
    public abstract void WriteFullEndElement( );
    public abstract void WriteName( string name);
    public abstract void WriteNmToken( string name);
    public virtual void WriteNode( XmlReader reader, bool defattr);
    public abstract void WriteProcessingInstruction( string name, string text);
    public abstract void WriteQualifiedName( string localName, string ns);
    public abstract void WriteRaw( char[ ] buffer, int index, int count);
    public abstract void WriteRaw( string data);
    public void WriteStartAttribute( string localName, string ns);
    public abstract void WriteStartAttribute( string prefix, string localName, string ns);
    public abstract void WriteStartDocument( );
    public abstract void WriteStartDocument( bool standalone);
    public void WriteStartElement( string localName);
    public void WriteStartElement( string localName, string ns);
    public abstract void WriteStartElement( string prefix, string localName, string ns);
    public abstract void WriteString( string text);
    public abstract void WriteSurrogateCharEntity( char lowChar, char highChar);
    public abstract void WriteWhitespace( string ws);
}
```

This class is a fast writer used to output XML data to a stream or file. Two methods work
with input from an XmlReader object to produce output from the currently positioned node.
WriteAttributes( ) outputs all the node's attributes. WriteNode( ) dumps the entire current node to
the output stream and moves the XmlReader to the next node.

The remaining Write* methods of this class take string arguments that are output as properly formed XML markup. For example, WriteComment( ) takes a string and outputs it within <!-- ... --> markup. WriteStartAttribute( ) and WriteStartElement( ) provide some flexibility when writing elements and attributes. These two methods provide the opening contents of each type, given the name, prefix, and namespace. The next call can then provide the value of the element or attribute by other means. For example, you can use WriteString( ) for a simple string value, or another WriteStartElement( ) to begin a child element. WriteEndAttribute( ) and WriteEndElement( ) close the writing.

The derived XmlTextWriter class provides formatting functionality to the output data.

Subclasses   XmlTextWriter

Passed To   XmlDocument.Save( ), XmlNode.{WriteContentTo( ), WriteTo( )}, System.Xml.Xsl.XslTransform.
Transform( )

CHAPTER 17

The System.Xml.Schema Namespace

The System.Xml.Schema namespace is responsible for .NET's implementation of the W3C XML Schema specification, a mechanism for constraining the content of XML documents. In .NET, an XML Schema document (XSD) can also be used to generate classes that know how to serialize themselves to and from XML (see the System.Xml.Serialization namespace for more on serialization). .NET supports Version 1.0 of XML Schema, Section 1 (XML Schemas for Structures), and Section 2 (XML Schemas for Data Types). Documentation for Section 1 is available online at *http://www.w3.org/TR/xmlschema-1*, and documentation for Section 2 is at *http://www.w3.org/TR/xmlschema-2*. For more information about the XML Schema specification, see *XML Schema*, by Eric van der Vlist (O'Reilly).

All types in this namespace that represent an element of an XML Schema document derive from the XmlSchemaObject type, although there are numerous intermediate base classes. Other types in this namespace include those used to collect related XML Schema objects, such as XmlSchemaObjectCollection, and those used to provide additional information about the XML Schema validation process, such as ValidationEventArgs.

Figure 17-1, Figure 17-2, and Figure 17-3 show the many types in this namespace.

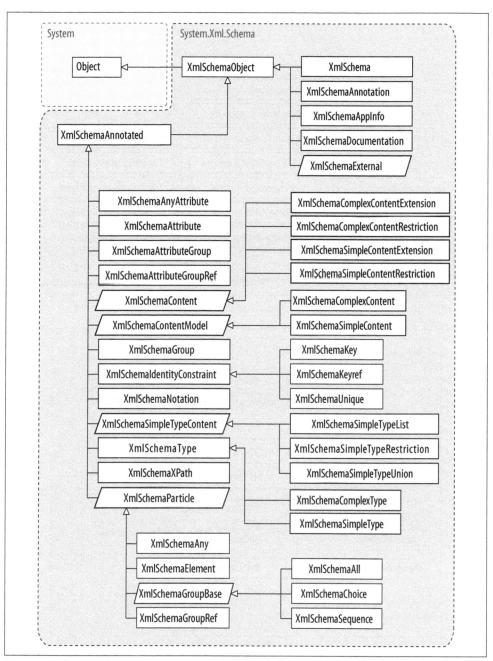

Figure 17-1. XMLSchemaObject and derived types

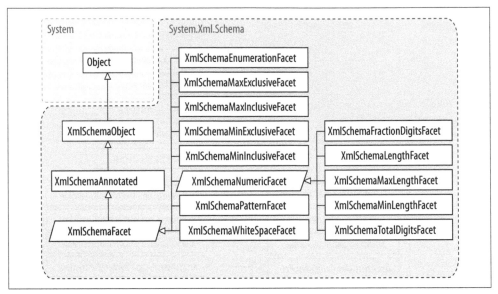

Figure 17-2. More descendants of XMLSchemaObject

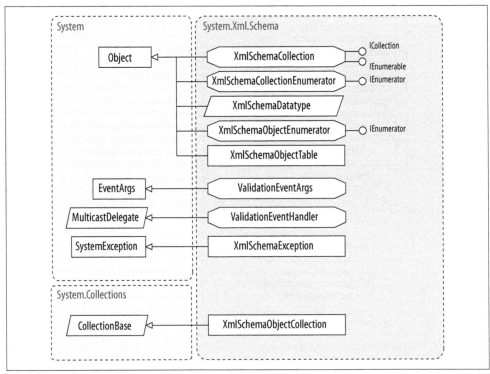

Figure 17-3. Remaining types from System.Xml.Schema

ValidationEventArgs

sealed class

```
public sealed class ValidationEventArgs : EventArgs {
// Public Instance Properties
  public XmlSchemaException Exception{get; }
  public string Message{get; }
  public XmlSeverityType Severity{get; }
}
```

This type gives detailed information about an error reported to the ValidationEventHandler delegate. The Message property may include the line number at which the error occured, and the
Severity property returns an XmlSeverityType enumeration instance indicating the severity of the
validation event.

Hierarchy   System.Object → System.EventArgs → ValidationEventArgs

ValidationEventHandler   serializable

System.Xml.Schema (system.xml.dll)   delegate

```
public delegate void ValidationEventHandler( object sender, ValidationEventArgs e);
```

This declared delegate type is used to receive event notifications from the XmlSchema instance
of XML Schema validation errors as they occur. A delegate of this type may be called for
errors in reading an XML Schema document into an XmlSchema instance using XmlSchema's
Read( ) method as well as when calling XmlSchema's Compile( ) method on an instance in
memory. This delegate may also be called to handle validation of an XML document
instance, when   System.Xml.XmlValidatingReader's   System.Xml.XmlValidatingReader.ValidationEventHandler
event is set to a method of type ValidationEventHandler.

Associated Events System.Xml.XmlValidatingReader.ValidationEventHandler( )

XmlSchema   CF 1.0

System.Xml.Schema (system.xml.dll)   class

```
public class XmlSchema : XmlSchemaObject {
// Public Constructors
  public XmlSchema( );
// Public Static Fields
  public const string InstanceNamespace;                          // =http://www.w3.org/2001/XMLSchema-instance
  public const string Namespace;                                      // =http://www.w3.org/2001/XMLSchema
// Public Instance Properties
  public XmlSchemaForm AttributeFormDefault{set; get; }
  public XmlSchemaObjectTable AttributeGroups{get; }
  public XmlSchemaObjectTable Attributes{get; }
  public XmlSchemaDerivationMethod BlockDefault{set; get; }
```

```
    public XmlSchemaForm ElementFormDefault{set; get; }
    public XmlSchemaObjectTable Elements{get; }
    public XmlSchemaDerivationMethod FinalDefault{set; get; }
    public XmlSchemaObjectTable Groups{get; }
    public string Id{set; get; }
    public XmlSchemaObjectCollection Includes{get; }
    public bool IsCompiled{get; }
    public XmlSchemaObjectCollection Items{get; }
    public XmlSchemaObjectTable Notations{get; }
    public XmlSchemaObjectTable SchemaTypes{get; }
    public string TargetNamespace{set; get; }
    public XmlAttribute[ ] UnhandledAttributes{set; get; }
    public string Version{set; get; }
// Public Static Methods
    public static XmlSchema Read( System.IO.Stream stream, ValidationEventHandler validationEventHandler);
    public static XmlSchema Read( System.IO.TextReader reader, ValidationEventHandler validationEventHandler);
    public static XmlSchema Read( System.Xml.XmlReader reader, ValidationEventHandler validationEventHandler);
// Public Instance Methods
    public void Compile( ValidationEventHandler validationEventHandler);
    public void Compile( ValidationEventHandler validationEventHandler, System.Xml.XmlResolver resolver);
    public void Write( System.IO.Stream stream);
    public void Write( System.IO.Stream stream, System.Xml.XmlNamespaceManager namespaceManager);
    public void Write( System.IO.TextWriter writer);
    public void Write( System.IO.TextWriter writer, System.Xml.XmlNamespaceManager namespaceManager);
    public void Write( System.Xml.XmlWriter writer);
    public void Write( System.Xml.XmlWriter writer, System.Xml.XmlNamespaceManager namespaceManager);
}
```

The XmlSchema type is a subclass of XmlSchemaObject that represents the xs:schema element, and constitutes the top-level element of an instance of an XSD. Its static Read( ) method returns an instance of XmlSchema with data from an XML document via a System.IO.Stream, System.IO. TextReader, or System.Xml.XmlReader, and reports errors in the XML Schema's structure via a ValidationEventHandler delegate instance. Its Write( ) method writes the instance data to a System.IO. Stream, System.IO.TextWriter, or System.Xml.XmlWriter.

The Compile( ) method compiles the XmlSchema instance into a collection of XmlSchemaObjects used for XML validation. Any syntactic or semantic errors in the XML Schema document are reported via a ValidationEventHandler delegate instance passed into the Compile( ) method. The XmlSchemaObjectTables that are the products of compilation may be accessed via the read-only AttributeGroups, Attributes, Elements, Groups, Notations, and SchemaTypes properties. The IsCompiled property indicates whether the instance has been compiled.

The Items property provides access to the XmlSchemaObjectCollection of XmlSchemaAnnotation, XmlSchemaAttribute, XmlSchemaAttributeGroup, XmlSchemaComplexType, XmlSchemaSimpleType, XmlSchemaElement, XmlSchemaGroup, and XmlSchemaNotation objects, which are the xs:schema element's child elements.

The AttributeFormDefault, BlockDefault, ElementFormDefault, FinalDefault, Id, TargetNamespace, and Version properties provide access to the attributes of the xs:schema element.

Hierarchy   System.Object → XmlSchemaObject → XmlSchema

XmlSchemaAll

System.Xml.Schema (system.xml.dll)   class

```
public class XmlSchemaAll : XmlSchemaGroupBase {
// Public Constructors
  public XmlSchemaAll( );
// Public Instance Properties
  public override XmlSchemaObjectCollection Items{get; }                    // overrides XmlSchemaGroupBase
}
```

This type represents the xs:all compositor, which describes an unordered group of optional
elements. Its Items property provides read-only access to the XmlSchemaObjectCollection of its child
elements.

Hierarchy   System.Object → XmlSchemaObject → XmlSchemaAnnotated → XmlSchemaParticle →
                     XmlSchemaGroupBase → XmlSchemaAll

XmlSchemaAnnotated

System.Xml.Schema (system.xml.dll)   class

```
public class XmlSchemaAnnotated : XmlSchemaObject {
// Public Constructors
  public XmlSchemaAnnotated( );
// Public Instance Properties
  public XmlSchemaAnnotation Annotation{set; get; }
  public string Id{set; get; }
  public XmlAttribute[ ] UnhandledAttributes{set; get; }
}
```

This type is the base class for any XmlSchemaObject type that contains an xs:annotation element. In
practice, this makes it the superclass for nearly all the XML Schema types, except for
XmlSchema, documentation elements including XmlSchemaAnnotation, XmlSchemaAppInfo, and XmlSchemaDocumentation, and the types that derive from XmlSchemaExternal. Its Annotation property allows
you to get or set its XmlSchemaAnnotation element, and its UnhandledAttributes property provides
access to an array of System.Xml.XmlAttributes representing the element's attributes from non-
XML Schema namespaces.

Hierarchy   System.Object → XmlSchemaObject → XmlSchemaAnnotated

XmlSchemaAnnotation

System.Xml.Schema (system.xml.dll)   class

```
public class XmlSchemaAnnotation : XmlSchemaObject {
// Public Constructors
  public XmlSchemaAnnotation( );
// Public Instance Properties
```

```
  public string Id{set; get; }
  public XmlSchemaObjectCollection Items{get; }
  public XmlAttribute[ ] UnhandledAttributes{set; get; }
}
```

This type is used to represent an xs:annotation element, which contains additional human- or computer-readable information about an XML Schema element. Its Items property allows access to a XmlSchemaObjectCollection containing its XmlSchemaAppInfo and XmlSchemaDocumentation child elements.

Hierarchy   System.Object → XmlSchemaObject → XmlSchemaAnnotation

XmlSchemaAny

System.Xml.Schema (system.xml.dll)   class

```
public class XmlSchemaAny : XmlSchemaParticle {
// Public Constructors
  public XmlSchemaAny( );
// Public Instance Properties
  public string Namespace{set; get; }
  public XmlSchemaContentProcessing ProcessContents{set; get; }
}
```

This type represents the xs:any XML Schema compositor. The ProcessContents property can be used to get or set a XmlSchemaContentProcessing enumeration representing the value of its processContents attribute. The Namespace attribute, whose value is a System.String, may have the values ##any (the default), ##other, ##targetNamespace, ##local, or a space-delimited list of namespace URIs, and is used to get or set the namespace attribute.

Hierarchy   System.Object → XmlSchemaObject → XmlSchemaAnnotated → XmlSchemaParticle →
                     XmlSchemaAny

XmlSchemaAnyAttribute

System.Xml.Schema (system.xml.dll)   class

```
public class XmlSchemaAnyAttribute : XmlSchemaAnnotated {
// Public Constructors
  public XmlSchemaAnyAttribute( );
// Public Instance Properties
  public string Namespace{set; get; }
  public XmlSchemaContentProcessing ProcessContents{set; get; }
}
```

This type is used to represent the xs:anyAttribute element. Its ProcessContents property can be used to get or set a XmlSchemaContentProcessing enumeration representing the value of its processContents attribute. The Namespace attribute, whose value is a System.String, may have the values ##any (the default), ##other, ##targetNamespace, ##local, or a space-delimited list of namespace URIs, and is used to get or set the namespace attribute.

XmlSchemaAppInfo

System.Xml.Schema (system.xml.dll)   class

```
public class XmlSchemaAppInfo : XmlSchemaObject {
// Public Constructors
  public XmlSchemaAppInfo( );
// Public Instance Properties
  public XmlNode[ ] Markup{set; get; }
  public string Source{set; get; }
}
```

This type represents the xs:appinfo XML Schema element, which is used to provide structured information used by applications to process the XML Schema. Its Source property provides access to the source attribute, which is an optional string containing a URI. The Markup property gets or sets an array of System.Xml.XmlNodes, which represent any child nodes of the xs:appInfo element.

Hierarchy   System.Object → XmlSchemaObject → XmlSchemaAppInfo

XmlSchemaAttribute

System.Xml.Schema (system.xml.dll)   class

```
public class XmlSchemaAttribute : XmlSchemaAnnotated {
// Public Constructors
  public XmlSchemaAttribute( );
// Public Instance Properties
  public object AttributeType{get; }
  public string DefaultValue{set; get; }
  public string FixedValue{set; get; }
  public XmlSchemaForm Form{set; get; }
  public string Name{set; get; }
  public XmlQualifiedName QualifiedName{get; }
  public XmlQualifiedName RefName{set; get; }
  public XmlSchemaSimpleType SchemaType{set; get; }
  public XmlQualifiedName SchemaTypeName{set; get; }
  public XmlSchemaUse Use{set; get; }
}
```

This type represents the xs:attribute element, which is used to define an XML attribute. Its DefaultValue, Form, FixedValue, and Use properties provide access to the default, form, fixed, and use attributes. The Name and RefName properties provide two ways to access the name attribute; either as a string or as a System.Xml.XmlQualifiedName representing the name of an attribute defined in this schema or elsewhere, when given a namespace prefix. The SchemaType and SchemaType-Name properties provide two ways to access the type attribute; either as an XmlSchemaSimpleType instance defined in this schema or as a System.Xml.XmlQualifiedName. After compilation, the

AttributeType property provides read-only access to the CLR type based on the type attribute, and the QualifiedName property provides read-only access to the qualified name of the attribute.

Hierarchy   System.Object → XmlSchemaObject → XmlSchemaAnnotated → XmlSchemaAttribute

XmlSchemaAttributeGroup

System.Xml.Schema (system.xml.dll)   class

```
public class XmlSchemaAttributeGroup : XmlSchemaAnnotated {
// Public Constructors
  public XmlSchemaAttributeGroup( );
// Public Instance Properties
  public XmlSchemaAnyAttribute AnyAttribute{set; get; }
  public XmlSchemaObjectCollection Attributes{get; }
  public string Name{set; get; }
  public XmlSchemaAttributeGroup RedefinedAttributeGroup{get; }
}
```

This type represents an xs:attributeGroup element, as a global definition. It can only be included within a XmlSchema element. Its AnyAttribute property returns the XmlSchemaAnyAttribute child element if present; otherwise the Attributes property can be used to access an XmlSchemaObjectCollection of its child XmlSchemaAttribute and XmlSchemaAttributeGroupRef elements.

Hierarchy   System.Object → XmlSchemaObject → XmlSchemaAnnotated → XmlSchemaAttributeGroup

XmlSchemaAttributeGroupRef

System.Xml.Schema (system.xml.dll)   class

```
public class XmlSchemaAttributeGroupRef : XmlSchemaAnnotated {
// Public Constructors
  public XmlSchemaAttributeGroupRef( );
// Public Instance Properties
  public XmlQualifiedName RefName{set; get; }
}
```

This type represents an xs:attributeGroup element, as a reference to a global attributeGroup definition. Its RefName property can be used to get or set the ref attribute, which contains the qualified name of the xs:attributeGroup XML Schema element to which this element refers.

Hierarchy   System.Object → XmlSchemaObject → XmlSchemaAnnotated → XmlSchemaAttributeGroupRef

XmlSchemaChoice

System.Xml.Schema (system.xml.dll)   class

```
public class XmlSchemaChoice : XmlSchemaGroupBase {
// Public Constructors
  public XmlSchemaChoice( );
// Public Instance Properties
  public override XmlSchemaObjectCollection Items{get; }                    // overrides XmlSchemaGroupBase
}
```

This type represents the xs:choice compositor. Its Items property provides read-only access to an XmlSchemaObjectCollection containing any number of XmlSchemaElement, XmlSchemaGroupRef, XmlSchemaChoice, XmlSchemaSequence, or XmlSchemaAny objects.

Hierarchy   System.Object → XmlSchemaObject → XmlSchemaAnnotated → XmlSchemaParticle → XmlSchemaGroupBase → XmlSchemaChoice

XmlSchemaCollection

System.Xml.Schema (system.xml.dll)   sealed class

```
public sealed class XmlSchemaCollection : ICollection, IEnumerable {
// Public Constructors
  public XmlSchemaCollection( );
  public XmlSchemaCollection( System.Xml.XmlNameTable nametable);
// Public Instance Properties
  public int Count{get; }                                                       // implements ICollection
  public XmlNameTable NameTable{get; }
  public XmlSchema this[ string ns ]{get; }
// Public Instance Methods
  public void Add( XmlSchemaCollection schema);
  public XmlSchema Add( string ns, string uri);
  public XmlSchema Add( string ns, System.Xml.XmlReader reader);
  public XmlSchema Add( string ns, System.Xml.XmlReader reader, System.Xml.XmlResolver resolver);
  public XmlSchema Add( XmlSchema schema);
  public XmlSchema Add( XmlSchema schema, System.Xml.XmlResolver resolver);
  public bool Contains( string ns);
  public bool Contains( XmlSchema schema);
  public void CopyTo( XmlSchema[ ] array, int index);
  public XmlSchemaCollectionEnumerator GetEnumerator( );
// Events
  public event ValidationEventHandler ValidationEventHandler;
}
```

This type provides a collection of XmlSchema objects representing XSD or XML-Data Reduced (XDR) documents. It is used to efficiently validate a document using multiple schemas. Its Add( ) method is used to add an instance of XmlSchema to the collection, to add an XSD or XDR by URI, or to add the contents of an System.Xml.XmlReader. It implements System.

Collections.ICollection and System.Collections.IEnumerable, so the appropriate members are overriden. Its indexer allows access to a particular XmlSchema index by its namespace URI.

Only an XSD is representable by an XmlSchema, so any XDR documents added to the collection are not accessible through members that accept or return an XmlSchema instance.

Returned By   System.Xml.XmlValidatingReader.Schemas

XmlSchemaCollectionEnumerator

System.Xml.Schema (system.xml.dll)   sealed class

```
public sealed class XmlSchemaCollectionEnumerator : IEnumerator {
// Public Instance Properties
  public XmlSchema Current{get; }
// Public Instance Methods
  public bool MoveNext( );                                                         // implements IEnumerator
}
```

This type extends System.Collections.IEnumerator to provide a mechanism to iterate over an XmlSchemaCollection via the Current property and MoveNext( ) method.

XmlSchemaComplexContent

System.Xml.Schema (system.xml.dll)   class

```
public class XmlSchemaComplexContent : XmlSchemaContentModel {
// Public Constructors
  public XmlSchemaComplexContent( );
// Public Instance Properties
  public override XmlSchemaContent Content{set; get; }                     // overrides XmlSchemaContentModel
  public bool IsMixed{set; get; }
}
```

This type represents the complexContent XML Schema element, which allows for the derivation of complex content from a complex type. Its IsMixed property indicates whether the content model is mixed (true) or element only (false). The Content property provides access to its content, in the form of either a XmlSchemaComplexContentRestriction or XmlSchemaComplexContentExtension instance.

Hierarchy   System.Object → XmlSchemaObject → XmlSchemaAnnotated → XmlSchemaContentModel → XmlSchemaComplexContent

XmlSchemaComplexContentExtension

System.Xml.Schema (system.xml.dll)   class

```
public class XmlSchemaComplexContentExtension : XmlSchemaContent {
// Public Constructors
  public XmlSchemaComplexContentExtension( );
// Public Instance Properties
```

```
 public XmlSchemaAnyAttribute AnyAttribute{set; get; }
 public XmlSchemaObjectCollection Attributes{get; }
 public XmlQualifiedName BaseTypeName{set; get; }
 public XmlSchemaParticle Particle{set; get; }
}
```

This type is a subclass of XmlSchemaContent that represents the xs:extension schema element when it is a child of a xs:complexContent element. This provides a mechanism for creating a new complex type by by adding new attributes or child elements to another complex type.

Hierarchy   System.Object → XmlSchemaObject → XmlSchemaAnnotated → XmlSchemaContent → XmlSchemaComplexContentExtension

XmlSchemaComplexContentRestriction

System.Xml.Schema (system.xml.dll)   class

```
public class XmlSchemaComplexContentRestriction : XmlSchemaContent {
// Public Constructors
 public XmlSchemaComplexContentRestriction( );
// Public Instance Properties
 public XmlSchemaAnyAttribute AnyAttribute{set; get; }
 public XmlSchemaObjectCollection Attributes{get; }
 public XmlQualifiedName BaseTypeName{set; get; }
 public XmlSchemaParticle Particle{set; get; }
}
```

This type is a subclass of XmlSchemaContent that represents the xs:restriction schema element when it is a child of a xs:complexContent element. This provides a mechanism for creating a new complex type by the addition of new constraints to another complex type.

Hierarchy   System.Object → XmlSchemaObject → XmlSchemaAnnotated → XmlSchemaContent → XmlSchemaComplexContentRestriction

XmlSchemaComplexType

System.Xml.Schema (system.xml.dll)   class

```
public class XmlSchemaComplexType : XmlSchemaType {
// Public Constructors
 public XmlSchemaComplexType( );
// Public Instance Properties
 public XmlSchemaAnyAttribute AnyAttribute{set; get; }
 public XmlSchemaObjectCollection Attributes{get; }
 public XmlSchemaObjectTable AttributeUses{get; }
 public XmlSchemaAnyAttribute AttributeWildcard{get; }
 public XmlSchemaDerivationMethod Block{set; get; }
 public XmlSchemaDerivationMethod BlockResolved{get; }
 public XmlSchemaContentModel ContentModel{set; get; }
```

```
public XmlSchemaContentType ContentType{get; }
public XmlSchemaParticle ContentTypeParticle{get; }
public bool IsAbstract{set; get; }
public override bool IsMixed{set; get; }                              // overrides XmlSchemaType
public XmlSchemaParticle Particle{set; get; }
}
```

This type represents a xs:complexType element. The Block property allows access to the XmlSchemaDerivationMethod enumeration, which overrides the blockDefault attribute of the parent XmlSchema. The IsAbstract and IsMixed properties provide access to the abstract and mixed attributes. The content of the element can be accessed through the AnyAttribute, Attributes, and Particle properties.

Hierarchy   System.Object → XmlSchemaObject → XmlSchemaAnnotated → XmlSchemaType → XmlSchemaComplexType

XmlSchemaContent

System.Xml.Schema (system.xml.dll)   abstract class

```
public abstract class XmlSchemaContent : XmlSchemaAnnotated {
// Protected Constructors
  protected XmlSchemaContent( );
}
```

This type is an abstract base class for all XML Schema elements that represent schema content (xs:extension and xs:restriction).

Hierarchy   System.Object → XmlSchemaObject → XmlSchemaAnnotated → XmlSchemaContent

XmlSchemaContentModel

System.Xml.Schema (system.xml.dll)   abstract class

```
public abstract class XmlSchemaContentModel : XmlSchemaAnnotated {
// Protected Constructors
  protected XmlSchemaContentModel( );
// Public Instance Properties
  public abstract XmlSchemaContent Content{set; get; }
}
```

This type is an abstract base class for all schema elements that represent schema content model (xs:complexContent and simpleContent). Its abstract Content property provides access to the XmlSchemaContent instance that represents the content.

Hierarchy   System.Object → XmlSchemaObject → XmlSchemaAnnotated → XmlSchemaContentModel

XmlSchemaContentProcessing

System.Xml.Schema (system.xml.dll)

serializable

enum

```
public enum XmlSchemaContentProcessing {
  None = 0,
  Skip = 1,
  Lax = 2,
  Strict = 3
}
```

This enumeration is used to specify the value of the processContents attribute in xs:any and xs: anyAttribute schema elements. Its value indicates how the content of the element or attribute is validated. When set to Lax, the validator will validate any items it can find definitions for, and skip the rest; the ValidationEventHandler will be called with a severity of XmlSeverityType.Warning to notify the client of any skipped items. When set to None, the items will not be validated at all. When set to Skip, the items will be checked for well-formedness but will not be validated; the ValidationEventHandler will be called with a severity of XmlSeverityType.Warning to notify the client that no validation was performed. When set to Strict, the items will be validated. In any case, if validation fails, the ValidationEventHandler will be called with an appropriate severity to notify the client of the error. If no ValidationEventHandler is assigned, an XmlSchemaException will be thrown.

Hierarchy   System.Object → System.ValueType → System.Enum(System.IComparable, System.IFormattable, System.IConvertible) → XmlSchemaContentProcessing

XmlSchemaContentType

serializable

System.Xml.Schema (system.xml.dll)

enum

```
public enum XmlSchemaContentType {
  TextOnly = 0,
  Empty = 1,
  ElementOnly = 2,
  Mixed = 3
}
```

This enumeration is used to provide information about the content model of a complex type.

Hierarchy   System.Object → System.ValueType → System.Enum(System.IComparable, System.IFormattable, System.IConvertible) → XmlSchemaContentType

XmlSchemaDatatype

System.Xml.Schema (system.xml.dll)

abstract class

```
public abstract class XmlSchemaDatatype {
// Protected Constructors
  protected XmlSchemaDatatype( );
```

```
// Public Instance Properties
  public abstract XmlTokenizedType TokenizedType{get; }
  public abstract Type ValueType{get; }
// Public Instance Methods
  public abstract object ParseValue( string s, System.Xml.XmlNameTable nameTable, System.Xml.XmlNamespaceManager nsmgr);
}
```

This abstract type is used to map XML Schema data types to .NET Framework types. The TokenizedType property returns an System.Xml.XmlTokenizedType for the data type, which allows the type to be referenced as an XML type. The ValueType property returns a System.Type object corresponding to the data type.

XmlSchemaDerivationMethod

serializable, flag

System.Xml.Schema (system.xml.dll)

enum

```
public enum XmlSchemaDerivationMethod {
  Empty = 0x00000000,
  Substitution = 0x00000001,
  Extension = 0x00000002,
  Restriction = 0x00000004,
  List = 0x00000008,
  Union = 0x00000010,
  All = 0x000000FF,
  None = 0x00000100
}
```

This enumeration is used to provide methods for preventing derivation of an XML Schema type. Its values can be logically combined through bitwise operators. XmlSchemaElement.Block can be set to Empty, Substitution, Extension, Restriction, or All, while XmlSchemaComplexType.Block can be set to None, Extension, Restriction, or All.

Hierarchy   System.Object → System.ValueType → System.Enum(System.IComparable, System.IFormattable, System.IConvertible) → XmlSchemaDerivationMethod

XmlSchemaDocumentation

System.Xml.Schema (system.xml.dll)

class

```
public class XmlSchemaDocumentation : XmlSchemaObject {
// Public Constructors
  public XmlSchemaDocumentation( );
// Public Instance Properties
  public string Language{set; get; }
  public XmlNode[ ] Markup{set; get; }
  public string Source{set; get; }
}
```

This type is used to represent the xs:documentation XML Schema element, which provides human-readable information about the XML Schema element it decorates. It is only valid as a child of a XmlSchemaAnnotation element. Since any content is valid within the xs:documentation element, the content is accessible through the Markup property, which returns an array of System.Xml.XmlNodes.

Hierarchy System.Object → XmlSchemaObject → XmlSchemaDocumentation

XmlSchemaElement

System.Xml.Schema (system.xml.dll) class

```
public class XmlSchemaElement : XmlSchemaParticle {
// Public Constructors
  public XmlSchemaElement( );
// Public Instance Properties
  public XmlSchemaDerivationMethod Block{set; get; }
  public XmlSchemaDerivationMethod BlockResolved{get; }
  public XmlSchemaObjectCollection Constraints{get; }
  public string DefaultValue{set; get; }
  public object ElementType{get; }
  public XmlSchemaDerivationMethod Final{set; get; }
  public XmlSchemaDerivationMethod FinalResolved{get; }
  public string FixedValue{set; get; }
  public XmlSchemaForm Form{set; get; }
  public bool IsAbstract{set; get; }
  public bool IsNillable{set; get; }
  public string Name{set; get; }
  public XmlQualifiedName QualifiedName{get; }
  public XmlQualifiedName RefName{set; get; }
  public XmlSchemaType SchemaType{set; get; }
  public XmlQualifiedName SchemaTypeName{set; get; }
  public XmlQualifiedName SubstitutionGroup{set; get; }
}
```

This type represents the xs:element element as a global or local definition, as a reference, or within xs:all, although in each of these cases, the valid values of its properties can differ. It provides the definition of an element. Its Block, DefaultValue, Final, FixedValue, Form, IsAbstract, IsNillable, Name, RefNameSchemaType, and SubstitutionGroup properties provide access to the block, default, final, fixed, form, abstract, nillable, name, ref, type, and substitutionGroup attributes, respectively. Constraints returns an XmlSchemaObjectCollection of XmlSchemaIdentityConstraint instances for the element. The ElementType property returns the CLR object instance that corresponds to the post-compilation type of the element. The other properties hold post-compilation (read-only) values of these attributes and derived information.

Hierarchy System.Object → XmlSchemaObject → XmlSchemaAnnotated → XmlSchemaParticle → XmlSchemaElement

XmlSchemaEnumerationFacet

System.Xml.Schema (system.xml.dll)   class

```
public class XmlSchemaEnumerationFacet : XmlSchemaFacet {
// Public Constructors
  public XmlSchemaEnumerationFacet( );
}
```

This XmlSchemaFacet subclass represents an xs:enumeration facet, which is used to restrict the possible values of a simple type. Its Value property contains one of the accepted values of the enumeration.

Hierarchy   System.Object → XmlSchemaObject → XmlSchemaAnnotated → XmlSchemaFacet → XmlSchemaEnumerationFacet

XmlSchemaException   CF 1.0, serializable

System.Xml.Schema (system.xml.dll)   class

```
public class XmlSchemaException : SystemException {
// Public Constructors
  public XmlSchemaException( string message, Exception innerException);
// Protected Constructors
  protected XmlSchemaException( System.Runtime.Serialization.SerializationInfo info,
      System.Runtime.Serialization.StreamingContext context);
// Public Instance Properties
  public int LineNumber{get; }
  public int LinePosition{get; }
  public override string Message{get; }                                        // overrides Exception
  public XmlSchemaObject SourceSchemaObject{get; }
  public string SourceUri{get; }
// Public Instance Methods
  public override void GetObjectData( System.Runtime.Serialization.SerializationInfo info,
      System.Runtime.Serialization.StreamingContext context);                  // overrides Exception
}
```

This class contains the error thrown by XML Schema validation operations. The LineNumber and LinePosition properties store the location of the error in the source document, and SourceUri property reports the location of the file used to load the XML Schema.

Hierarchy   System.Object → System.Exception(System.Runtime.Serialization.ISerializable) → System.SystemException → XmlSchemaException

XmlSchemaExternal

System.Xml.Schema (system.xml.dll)   abstract class

```
public abstract class XmlSchemaExternal : XmlSchemaObject {
// Protected Constructors
```

```
    protected XmlSchemaExternal( );
// Public Instance Properties
    public string Id{set; get; }
    public XmlSchema Schema{set; get; }
    public string SchemaLocation{set; get; }
    public XmlAttribute[ ] UnhandledAttributes{set; get; }
}
```

This is the abstract type from which the xs:import, xs:include, and xs:redefine schema elements are derived. Its SchemaLocation property is used to access the schemaLocation attribute.

Hierarchy   System.Object → XmlSchemaObject → XmlSchemaExternal

XmlSchemaFacet

System.Xml.Schema (system.xml.dll)   abstract class

```
public abstract class XmlSchemaFacet : XmlSchemaAnnotated {
// Protected Constructors
    protected XmlSchemaFacet( );
// Public Instance Properties
    public virtual bool IsFixed{set; get; }
    public string Value{set; get; }
}
```

This is the abstract base type from which all schema facets are derived. All facets have a Value property that accesses the value attribute, and a IsFixed property that accesses the fixed attribute.

Hierarchy   System.Object → XmlSchemaObject → XmlSchemaAnnotated → XmlSchemaFacet

XmlSchemaForm   serializable

System.Xml.Schema (system.xml.dll)   enum

```
public enum XmlSchemaForm {
    None = 0,
    Qualified = 1,
    Unqualified = 2
}
```

This enumeration is used to indicate whether element and attribute names must be qualified, or can be left unqualified.

Hierarchy   System.Object → System.ValueType → System.Enum(System.IComparable, System.IFormattable, System.IConvertible) → XmlSchemaForm

XmlSchemaFractionDigitsFacet

System.Xml.Schema (system.xml.dll)   class

```
public class XmlSchemaFractionDigitsFacet : XmlSchemaNumericFacet {
// Public Constructors
  public XmlSchemaFractionDigitsFacet( );
}
```

This type represents the xs:fractionDigits facet. Its Value property represents the maximum number of digits to maintain after a decimal point in an xs:decimal datatype.

Hierarchy   System.Object → XmlSchemaObject → XmlSchemaAnnotated → XmlSchemaFacet → XmlSchemaNumericFacet → XmlSchemaFractionDigitsFacet

XmlSchemaGroup

System.Xml.Schema (system.xml.dll)   class

```
public class XmlSchemaGroup : XmlSchemaAnnotated {
// Public Constructors
  public XmlSchemaGroup( );
// Public Instance Properties
  public string Name{set; get; }
  public XmlSchemaGroupBase Particle{set; get; }
}
```

This type represents the definition of an xs:group schema element. Its Name property allows access to its name attribute, and its Particle property allows access to the XmlSchemaGroupBase instance that represents its content.

Hierarchy   System.Object → XmlSchemaObject → XmlSchemaAnnotated → XmlSchemaGroup

XmlSchemaGroupBase

System.Xml.Schema (system.xml.dll)   abstract class

```
public abstract class XmlSchemaGroupBase : XmlSchemaParticle {
// Protected Constructors
  protected XmlSchemaGroupBase( );
// Public Instance Properties
  public abstract XmlSchemaObjectCollection Items{get; }
}
```

This type is the base class from which the xs:all, xs:choice, and xs:sequence schema elements derive. Its Items property returns an XmlSchemaObjectCollection of XmlSchemaElement that constitutes its content.

Hierarchy   System.Object → XmlSchemaObject → XmlSchemaAnnotated → XmlSchemaParticle → XmlSchemaGroupBase

XmlSchemaGroupRef

System.Xml.Schema (system.xml.dll)   class

```
public class XmlSchemaGroupRef : XmlSchemaParticle {
// Public Constructors
  public XmlSchemaGroupRef( );
// Public Instance Properties
  public XmlSchemaGroupBase Particle{get; }
  public XmlQualifiedName RefName{set; get; }
}
```

This type represents the xs:group when used as a reference to a globally defined group. Its RefName property contains the System.Xml.XmlQualifiedName of the xs:group element being referenced.

Hierarchy   System.Object → XmlSchemaObject → XmlSchemaAnnotated → XmlSchemaParticle → XmlSchemaGroupRef

XmlSchemaIdentityConstraint

System.Xml.Schema (system.xml.dll)   class

```
public class XmlSchemaIdentityConstraint : XmlSchemaAnnotated {
// Public Constructors
  public XmlSchemaIdentityConstraint( );
// Public Instance Properties
  public XmlSchemaObjectCollection Fields{get; }
  public string Name{set; get; }
  public XmlQualifiedName QualifiedName{get; }
  public XmlSchemaXPath Selector{set; get; }
}
```

This type is used as the base for all identity constraints, XmlSchemaKey, XmlSchemaKeyref, and XmlSchemaUnique. Its Selector property contains an XmlSchemaXPath instance that represents the XPath expression for the constraint.

Hierarchy   System.Object → XmlSchemaObject → XmlSchemaAnnotated → XmlSchemaIdentityConstraint

XmlSchemaImport

System.Xml.Schema (system.xml.dll)   class

```
public class XmlSchemaImport : XmlSchemaExternal {
// Public Constructors
  public XmlSchemaImport( );
// Public Instance Properties
  public XmlSchemaAnnotation Annotation{set; get; }
  public string Namespace{set; get; }
}
```

This type is used to represent the xs:import schema element, which is used to import another XML Schema's content for use in the current schema. Its Namespace property provides access to the namespace attribute, which indicates the namespace URI of the items to import. The SourceUri property, inherited from XmlSchemaObject, maps to the schemaLocation attribute and indicates the location of the schema to import.

Hierarchy   System.Object → XmlSchemaObject → XmlSchemaExternal → XmlSchemaImport

XmlSchemaInclude

System.Xml.Schema (system.xml.dll)   class

```
public class XmlSchemaInclude : XmlSchemaExternal {
// Public Constructors
  public XmlSchemaInclude( );
// Public Instance Properties
  public XmlSchemaAnnotation Annotation{set; get; }
}
```

This type represents the xs:include schema element, which is used to include the contents of another XML schema for use in the current schema. The difference between xs:import and xs:include is that the former requires a namespace, while the latter does not. All definitions are included in the current schema's target namespace.

Hierarchy   System.Object → XmlSchemaObject → XmlSchemaExternal → XmlSchemaInclude

XmlSchemaKey

System.Xml.Schema (system.xml.dll)   class

```
public class XmlSchemaKey : XmlSchemaIdentityConstraint {
// Public Constructors
  public XmlSchemaKey( );
}
```

This type represents the xs:key XML schema element, which is used to define a simple or compound key. Like all subclasses of XmlSchemaIdentityConstraint, it uses XPath to define the unique key for an element.

Hierarchy   System.Object → XmlSchemaObject → XmlSchemaAnnotated → XmlSchemaIdentityConstraint → XmlSchemaKey

XmlSchemaKeyref

System.Xml.Schema (system.xml.dll)   class

```
public class XmlSchemaKeyref : XmlSchemaIdentityConstraint {
// Public Constructors
  public XmlSchemaKeyref( );
```

```
// Public Instance Properties
  public XmlQualifiedName Refer{set; get; }
}
```

This type is used to represent the xs:keyref schema element. Its Refer property contains the qualified name of the xs:key element to which it refers.

Hierarchy System.Object → XmlSchemaObject → XmlSchemaAnnotated → XmlSchemaIdentityConstraint → XmlSchemaKeyref

XmlSchemaLengthFacet

System.Xml.Schema (system.xml.dll) class

```
public class XmlSchemaLengthFacet : XmlSchemaNumericFacet {
// Public Constructors
  public XmlSchemaLengthFacet( );
}
```

This type represents the xs:length facet. Its Value property should contain a non-negative integer representing the logical length of a restriction type's value.

Hierarchy System.Object → XmlSchemaObject → XmlSchemaAnnotated → XmlSchemaFacet → XmlSchemaNumericFacet → XmlSchemaLengthFacet

XmlSchemaMaxExclusiveFacet

System.Xml.Schema (system.xml.dll) class

```
public class XmlSchemaMaxExclusiveFacet : XmlSchemaFacet {
// Public Constructors
  public XmlSchemaMaxExclusiveFacet( );
}
```

This type represents the xs:maxExclusive facet. Its Value property should contain the string representation of the exclusive maximum value of the restriction type.

Hierarchy System.Object → XmlSchemaObject → XmlSchemaAnnotated → XmlSchemaFacet → XmlSchemaMaxExclusiveFacet

XmlSchemaMaxInclusiveFacet

System.Xml.Schema (system.xml.dll) class

```
public class XmlSchemaMaxInclusiveFacet : XmlSchemaFacet {
// Public Constructors
  public XmlSchemaMaxInclusiveFacet( );
}
```

This type is used to represent the xs:maxInclusive facet, which specifies the inclusive minimum value of the restriction type.

Hierarchy   System.Object → XmlSchemaObject → XmlSchemaAnnotated → XmlSchemaFacet → XmlSchemaMaxInclusiveFacet

XmlSchemaMaxLengthFacet

System.Xml.Schema (system.xml.dll)   class

```
public class XmlSchemaMaxLengthFacet : XmlSchemaNumericFacet {
// Public Constructors
  public XmlSchemaMaxLengthFacet( );
}
```

This type represents the xs:maxLength facet. This facet allows you to specify the maximum length of a restriction type. xs:maxLength and xs:length are mutually exclusive within a given restriction step.

Hierarchy   System.Object → XmlSchemaObject → XmlSchemaAnnotated → XmlSchemaFacet → XmlSchemaNumericFacet → XmlSchemaMaxLengthFacet

XmlSchemaMinExclusiveFacet

System.Xml.Schema (system.xml.dll)   class

```
public class XmlSchemaMinExclusiveFacet : XmlSchemaFacet {
// Public Constructors
  public XmlSchemaMinExclusiveFacet( );
}
```

This type represents the xs:minExclusive facet, which determines the exclusive minimum value of the restriction type.

Hierarchy   System.Object → XmlSchemaObject → XmlSchemaAnnotated → XmlSchemaFacet → XmlSchemaMinExclusiveFacet

XmlSchemaMinInclusiveFacet

System.Xml.Schema (system.xml.dll)   class

```
public class XmlSchemaMinInclusiveFacet : XmlSchemaFacet {
// Public Constructors
  public XmlSchemaMinInclusiveFacet( );
}
```

This type is used to represent the xs:minInclusive facet. This facet allows you to specify the inclusive minimum value of the restriction type.

Hierarchy   System.Object → XmlSchemaObject → XmlSchemaAnnotated → XmlSchemaFacet → XmlSchemaMinInclusiveFacet

XmlSchemaMinLengthFacet

System.Xml.Schema (system.xml.dll)   class

```
public class XmlSchemaMinLengthFacet : XmlSchemaNumericFacet {
// Public Constructors
  public XmlSchemaMinLengthFacet( );
}
```

This type is used to represent the xs:minLength facet. This facet specifies the minimum length of the restriction type's value. xs:minLength and xs:length are mutually exclusive within a given restriction step.

Hierarchy   System.Object → XmlSchemaObject → XmlSchemaAnnotated → XmlSchemaFacet → XmlSchemaNumericFacet → XmlSchemaMinLengthFacet

XmlSchemaNotation

System.Xml.Schema (system.xml.dll)   class

```
public class XmlSchemaNotation : XmlSchemaAnnotated {
// Public Constructors
  public XmlSchemaNotation( );
// Public Instance Properties
  public string Name{set; get; }
  public string Public{set; get; }
  public string System{set; get; }
}
```

This type represents the xs:notation element. Its Name, Public, and System properties provide access to the name, public, and system attributes. The xs:notation element allows you to declare an external unparsed entity.

Hierarchy   System.Object → XmlSchemaObject → XmlSchemaAnnotated → XmlSchemaNotation

XmlSchemaNumericFacet

System.Xml.Schema (system.xml.dll)   abstract class

```
public abstract class XmlSchemaNumericFacet : XmlSchemaFacet {
// Protected Constructors
  protected XmlSchemaNumericFacet( );
}
```

This base type is used to represent any of the numeric facet elements, xs:fractionDigits, xs:length, xs:maxLength, xs:minLength, and xs:totalDigits.

Hierarchy   System.Object → XmlSchemaObject → XmlSchemaAnnotated → XmlSchemaFacet →
                       XmlSchemaNumericFacet

```
public abstract class XmlSchemaObject {
// Protected Constructors
  protected XmlSchemaObject( );
// Public Instance Properties
  public int LineNumber{set; get; }
  public int LinePosition{set; get; }
  public XmlSerializerNamespaces Namespaces{set; get; }
  public string SourceUri{set; get; }
}
```

This abstract type is the base for all of the types that represent XML Schema elements. Its LineNumber and LinePosition properties provide information about the location of the element within the XML Schema document, and its SourceUri property provides information about the location of the source document itself. Although all the XML Schema types extend XmlSchemaObject, only XmlSchema and the three documentation types XmlSchemaAnnotation, XmlSchemaDocumentation, and XmlSchemaAppInfo do so directly; the rest extend the intermediate base types XmlSchemaAnnotated or XmlSchemaExternal.

XmlSchemaObjectCollection

System.Xml.Schema (system.xml.dll)

class

```
public class XmlSchemaObjectCollection : CollectionBase {
// Public Constructors
  public XmlSchemaObjectCollection( );
  public XmlSchemaObjectCollection( XmlSchemaObject parent);
// Public Instance Properties
  public virtual XmlSchemaObject this[ int index ]{set; get; }
// Public Instance Methods
  public int Add( XmlSchemaObject item);
  public bool Contains( XmlSchemaObject item);
  public void CopyTo( XmlSchemaObject[ ] array, int index);
  public XmlSchemaObjectEnumerator GetEnumerator( );
  public int IndexOf( XmlSchemaObject item);
  public void Insert( int index, XmlSchemaObject item);
  public void Remove( XmlSchemaObject item);
// Protected Instance Methods
  protected override void OnClear( );                                    // overrides System.Collections.CollectionBase
  protected override void OnInsert( int index, object item);             // overrides System.Collections.CollectionBase
  protected override void OnRemove( int index, object item);            // overrides System.Collections.CollectionBase
  protected override void OnSet( int index, object oldValue, object newValue);  // overrides System.Collections.CollectionBase
}
```

This type extends System.Collections.CollectionBase to provide an ordered list of XmlSchemaObject instances. The Add( ) and Insert( ) methods allow you to add XmlSchemaObject instances to the collection, and the indexer allows you to retrieve items by integral index. The GetEnumerator( ) method returns a XmlSchemaObjectEnumerator that can be used to iterate over the collection.

Hierarchy   System.Object → System.Collections.CollectionBase(System.Collections.IList, System.Collections.ICollection, System.Collections.IEnumerable) → XmlSchemaObjectCollection

XmlSchemaObjectEnumerator

System.Xml.Schema (system.xml.dll)   sealed class

```
public sealed class XmlSchemaObjectEnumerator : IEnumerator {
// Public Instance Properties
  public XmlSchemaObject Current{get; }
// Public Instance Methods
  public bool MoveNext( );                                                              // implements IEnumerator
  public void Reset( );                                                                 // implements IEnumerator
}
```

This type, which implements the IEnumerator interface, is returned by the GetEnumerator( ) methods of XmlSchemaObjectCollection and XmlSchemaObjectTable and provides a mechanism to iterate over their elements. The MoveNext( ) method moves the enumerator to the next element, and the Current property returns the instance of XmlSchemaObject at the enumerator's current location.

XmlSchemaObjectTable

System.Xml.Schema (system.xml.dll)   class

```
public class XmlSchemaObjectTable {
// Public Instance Properties
  public int Count{get; }
  public ICollection Names{get; }
  public XmlSchemaObject this[ System.Xml.XmlQualifiedName name ]{get; }
  public ICollection Values{get; }
// Public Instance Methods
  public bool Contains( System.Xml.XmlQualifiedName name);
  public IDictionaryEnumerator GetEnumerator( );
}
```

This type represents a dictionary of XML Schema objects contained within other XML Schema objects. Its Item property, the indexer, provides access to an XmlSchemaObject by its XmlQualifiedName. The Names property returns an ICollection of XmlSchemaObjects representing the names of the elements of the collection, and the Values property returns an ICollection of XmlSchemaObjects representing the values. The GetEnumerator( ) method returns an IDictionaryEnumerator suitable for iterating over the values.

XmlSchemaParticle

```
public abstract class XmlSchemaParticle : XmlSchemaAnnotated {
// Protected Constructors
  protected XmlSchemaParticle( );
// Public Instance Properties
  public decimal MaxOccurs{set; get; }
  public string MaxOccursString{set; get; }
  public decimal MinOccurs{set; get; }
  public string MinOccursString{set; get; }
}
```

This abstract type is the base type for all XML Schema particle types, including XmlSche-maAny, XmlSchemaElement, XmlSchemaGroup, and XmlSchemaGroupBase. Its properties MaxOccurs and MinOccurs represent the maxOccurs and minOccurs attributes, respectively, as decimal values, and the MaxOccursString and MinOccursString properties provide access to the same attributes as string values.

Hierarchy   System.Object → XmlSchemaObject → XmlSchemaAnnotated → XmlSchemaParticle

XmlSchemaPatternFacet

```
public class XmlSchemaPatternFacet : XmlSchemaFacet {
// Public Constructors
  public XmlSchemaPatternFacet( );
}
```

This type represents the xs:pattern XML Schema facet. Its Value property should contain a regular expression used to constrain the value of the simple type to which the facet applies.

Hierarchy   System.Object → XmlSchemaObject → XmlSchemaAnnotated → XmlSchemaFacet →
                     XmlSchemaPatternFacet

XmlSchemaRedefine

```
public class XmlSchemaRedefine : XmlSchemaExternal {
// Public Constructors
  public XmlSchemaRedefine( );
// Public Instance Properties
  public XmlSchemaObjectTable AttributeGroups{get; }
  public XmlSchemaObjectTable Groups{get; }
  public XmlSchemaObjectCollection Items{get; }
  public XmlSchemaObjectTable SchemaTypes{get; }
}
```

This type provides the .NET implementation of the xs:redefine XML Schema element. Similar to xs:include, it allows you to include the contents of another XML Schema in the current schema, and redefine types defined in the external schema.

Hierarchy   System.Object → XmlSchemaObject → XmlSchemaExternal → XmlSchemaRedefine

XmlSchemaSequence

System.Xml.Schema (system.xml.dll)   class

```
public class XmlSchemaSequence : XmlSchemaGroupBase {
// Public Constructors
  public XmlSchemaSequence( );
// Public Instance Properties
  public override XmlSchemaObjectCollection Items{get; }                              // overrides XmlSchemaGroupBase
}
```

This type represents the xs:sequence XML Schema compositor. This type is used to specify an ordered list of other schema elements, an XmlSchemaObjectCollection of which is accessible through its Items property.

Hierarchy   System.Object → XmlSchemaObject → XmlSchemaAnnotated → XmlSchemaParticle → XmlSchema-
              GroupBase → XmlSchemaSequence

XmlSchemaSimpleContent

System.Xml.Schema (system.xml.dll)   class

```
public class XmlSchemaSimpleContent : XmlSchemaContentModel {
// Public Constructors
  public XmlSchemaSimpleContent( );
// Public Instance Properties
  public override XmlSchemaContent Content{set; get; }                              // overrides XmlSchemaContentModel
}
```

This type is used to represent the xs:simpleContent XML Schema element. Its Content property, whose value must be of a type that extends XmlSchemaContent, represents the definition of a simple content model.

Hierarchy   System.Object → XmlSchemaObject → XmlSchemaAnnotated → XmlSchemaContentModel →
              XmlSchemaSimpleContent

XmlSchemaSimpleContentExtension

System.Xml.Schema (system.xml.dll)   class

```
public class XmlSchemaSimpleContentExtension : XmlSchemaContent {
// Public Constructors
```

```
   public XmlSchemaSimpleContentExtension( );
// Public Instance Properties
   public XmlSchemaAnyAttribute AnyAttribute{set; get; }
   public XmlSchemaObjectCollection Attributes{get; }
   public XmlQualifiedName BaseTypeName{set; get; }
}
```

This type is the subclass of XmlSchemaContent that represents the XML Schema xs:extension element for simple content. This element is used to extend a simple type or complex type with simple content into a complex type with simple content, by adding attributes. The BaseTypeName property is used to access the System.Xml.XmlQualifiedName of the type being extended, and the Attributes property returns an XmlSchemaObjectCollection of attributes as XmlSchemaAttributes and XmlSchemaAttributeGroupRefs.

Hierarchy   System.Object → XmlSchemaObject → XmlSchemaAnnotated → XmlSchemaContent → XmlSchemaSimpleContentExtension

XmlSchemaSimpleContentRestriction

System.Xml.Schema (system.xml.dll)   class

```
public class XmlSchemaSimpleContentRestriction : XmlSchemaContent {
// Public Constructors
   public XmlSchemaSimpleContentRestriction( );
// Public Instance Properties
   public XmlSchemaAnyAttribute AnyAttribute{set; get; }
   public XmlSchemaObjectCollection Attributes{get; }
   public XmlSchemaSimpleType BaseType{set; get; }
   public XmlQualifiedName BaseTypeName{set; get; }
   public XmlSchemaObjectCollection Facets{get; }
}
```

This type represents the xs:restriction XML Schema type for simple content, which allows for the creation of a new simple type with additional constraints on its attributes and on its text content. The BaseTypeName property is used to access the System.Xml.XmlQualifiedName of the type being extended, and the Attributes property returns an XmlSchemaObjectCollection of attributes as XmlSchemaAttributes and XmlSchemaAttributeGroupRefs. The Facets property returns an XmlSchemaObjectCollection of the XmlSchemaFacets that restrict its text content.

Hierarchy   System.Object → XmlSchemaObject → XmlSchemaAnnotated → XmlSchemaContent → XmlSchemaSimpleContentRestriction

XmlSchemaSimpleType

System.Xml.Schema (system.xml.dll)   class

```
public class XmlSchemaSimpleType : XmlSchemaType {
// Public Constructors
   public XmlSchemaSimpleType( );
```

```
// Public Instance Properties
  public XmlSchemaSimpleTypeContent Content{set; get; }
}
```

This type represents the xs:simpleType XML Schema element, which is used to define a type
that can be referenced in the values of attributes and text nodes. Its Content property
contains an XmlSchemaSimpleTypeContent representing the content of the schema element.

Hierarchy   System.Object → XmlSchemaObject → XmlSchemaAnnotated → XmlSchemaType →
                     XmlSchemaSimpleType

XmlSchemaSimpleTypeContent

System.Xml.Schema (system.xml.dll)   abstract class

```
public abstract class XmlSchemaSimpleTypeContent : XmlSchemaAnnotated {
// Protected Constructors
  protected XmlSchemaSimpleTypeContent( );
}
```

This type is the abstract type that serves as the base type for all simple type content classes,
representing xs:list, xs:restriction, and xs:union.

Hierarchy   System.Object → XmlSchemaObject → XmlSchemaAnnotated → XmlSchemaSimpleTypeContent

XmlSchemaSimpleTypeList

System.Xml.Schema (system.xml.dll)   class

```
public class XmlSchemaSimpleTypeList : XmlSchemaSimpleTypeContent {
// Public Constructors
  public XmlSchemaSimpleTypeList( );
// Public Instance Properties
  public XmlSchemaSimpleType ItemType{set; get; }
  public XmlQualifiedName ItemTypeName{set; get; }
}
```

This type is used to represent the xs:list schema element, which is used to derive a new
simple type whose value is a whitespace-delimited list of values of the base type. The Item-
Type property contains the XmlSchemaSimpleType whose value the type is based on, and the
ItemTypeName property contains the System.Xml.XmlQualifiedName of the base simple type.

Hierarchy   System.Object → XmlSchemaObject → XmlSchemaAnnotated → XmlSchemaSimpleTypeContent →
                     XmlSchemaSimpleTypeList

XmlSchemaSimpleTypeRestriction

System.Xml.Schema (system.xml.dll)   class

```
public class XmlSchemaSimpleTypeRestriction : XmlSchemaSimpleTypeContent {
// Public Constructors
  public XmlSchemaSimpleTypeRestriction( );
// Public Instance Properties
  public XmlSchemaSimpleType BaseType{set; get; }
  public XmlQualifiedName BaseTypeName{set; get; }
  public XmlSchemaObjectCollection Facets{get; }
}
```

This type represents the xs:restriction XML Schema element for simple types. It is used to
derive a new simple type by adding new facets to restrict its value. The Facets property
returns an XmlSchemaObjectCollection containing the XmlSchemaFacets used to restrict the value.

Hierarchy   System.Object → XmlSchemaObject → XmlSchemaAnnotated → XmlSchemaSimpleTypeContent →
                    XmlSchemaSimpleTypeRestriction

XmlSchemaSimpleTypeUnion

System.Xml.Schema (system.xml.dll)   class

```
public class XmlSchemaSimpleTypeUnion : XmlSchemaSimpleTypeContent {
// Public Constructors
  public XmlSchemaSimpleTypeUnion( );
// Public Instance Properties
  public XmlSchemaObjectCollection BaseTypes{get; }
  public XmlQualifiedName[ ] MemberTypes{set; get; }
}
```

This type is used to represent the xs:union schema element. This element is used to derive a
new simple type from the union of other simple types. The MemberTypes property returns an
array of XmlQualifiedNames of the simple types whose union makes up the definition.

Hierarchy   System.Object → XmlSchemaObject → XmlSchemaAnnotated → XmlSchemaSimpleTypeContent →
                    XmlSchemaSimpleTypeUnion

XmlSchemaTotalDigitsFacet

System.Xml.Schema (system.xml.dll)   class

```
public class XmlSchemaTotalDigitsFacet : XmlSchemaNumericFacet {
// Public Constructors
  public XmlSchemaTotalDigitsFacet( );
}
```

This type represents the xs:totalDigits facet. Its Value property is used to get or set the total
number of digits in a numeric datatype, including digits before and after a decimal point,
but not including the decimal point itself.

XmlSchemaType

System.Xml.Schema (system.xml.dll)   class

```
public class XmlSchemaType : XmlSchemaAnnotated {
// Public Constructors
  public XmlSchemaType( );
// Public Instance Properties
  public object BaseSchemaType{get; }
  public XmlSchemaDatatype Datatype{get; }
  public XmlSchemaDerivationMethod DerivedBy{get; }
  public XmlSchemaDerivationMethod Final{set; get; }
  public XmlSchemaDerivationMethod FinalResolved{get; }
  public virtual bool IsMixed{set; get; }
  public string Name{set; get; }
  public XmlQualifiedName QualifiedName{get; }
}
```

This is the type used as the base for all simple and complex types. its Final, IsMixed, and Name properties provide access to the final, mixed, and name attributes. The other properties hold post-compilation (read-only) values.

Hierarchy   System.Object → XmlSchemaObject → XmlSchemaAnnotated → XmlSchemaType

XmlSchemaUnique

System.Xml.Schema (system.xml.dll)   class

```
public class XmlSchemaUnique : XmlSchemaIdentityConstraint {
// Public Constructors
  public XmlSchemaUnique( );
}
```

This type represents the xs:unique schema element, which is use to define a unique constraint for an element. Like xs:key, the Selector property contains the XmlSchemaXPath instance that defines the constraint.

Hierarchy   System.Object → XmlSchemaObject → XmlSchemaAnnotated → XmlSchemaIdentityConstraint → XmlSchemaUnique

XmlSchemaUse   serializable

System.Xml.Schema (system.xml.dll)   enum

```
public enum XmlSchemaUse {
  None = 0,
  Optional = 1,
```

```
    Prohibited = 2,
    Required = 3
}
```

This enumeration is returned by XmlSchemaAttribute.Use to indicate whether the attribute is prohibited, required, or optional. The default is Optional.

Hierarchy   System.Object → System.ValueType → System.Enum(System.IComparable, System.IFormattable, System.IConvertible) → XmlSchemaUse

XmlSchemaWhiteSpaceFacet

System.Xml.Schema (system.xml.dll)   class

```
public class XmlSchemaWhiteSpaceFacet : XmlSchemaFacet {
// Public Constructors
  public XmlSchemaWhiteSpaceFacet( );
}
```

This type represents the xs:whiteSpace facet, which is used to describe how whitespace is to be treated in the content of the type being defined. Its Value property can contain any of the string literals "preserve", "replace", or "collapse".

Hierarchy   System.Object → XmlSchemaObject → XmlSchemaAnnotated → XmlSchemaFacet → XmlSchemaWhiteSpaceFacet

XmlSchemaXPath

System.Xml.Schema (system.xml.dll)   class

```
public class XmlSchemaXPath : XmlSchemaAnnotated {
// Public Constructors
  public XmlSchemaXPath( );
// Public Instance Properties
  public string XPath{set; get; }
}
```

This type is used to represent the xs:selector schema element. Its XPath property is used to access the xpath attribute as a string, which represents the relative XPath expression whose result is an element on which the uniqueness constraint is based. The xs:field schema element is represented as an XmlSchemaObjectCollection of XmlSchemaXPath instances.

Hierarchy   System.Object → XmlSchemaObject → XmlSchemaAnnotated → XmlSchemaXPath

XmlSeverityType

serializable

System.Xml.Schema (system.xml.dll)

enum

```
public enum XmlSeverityType {
  Error = 0,
  Warning = 1
}
```

This type is used to indicate the severity of a validation event handled by the ValidationEventHandler.

Hierarchy   System.Object → System.ValueType → System.Enum(System.IComparable, System.IFormattable, System.IConvertible) → XmlSeverityType

CHAPTER 18

The System.Xml.Serialization Namespace

The System.Xml.Serialization namespace contains classes that are used to control the serialization of .NET types to XML. Serialization refers to the process of encoding an object as a series of bytes, which can then be decoded by another program in order to replicate the original object. The System.Xml.Serialization namespace supports *XML serialization*, the serialization of objects to arbitrary XML formats, including SOAP. For serialization to binary and user-defined formats, as well as to specific SOAP formats used for the transmission of objects between instances of .NET applications, collectively known as *runtime serialization*, see the System.Runtime.Serialization namespace.

SOAP, which formerly stood for *Simple Object Access Protocol*, defines a standard mechanism for encoding objects as XML. The specification for SOAP 1.1 is available at *http://www.w3.org/TR/SOAP*. For more information about SOAP, see *Programming Web Services with SOAP*, by Doug Tidwell, James Snell, and Pavel Kulchenko (O'Reilly). SOAP Version 1.2 recently became a W3C Recommendation.

To serialize an object instance to XML, create an instance of XmlSerializer for that type by passing the type as a parameter to XmlSerializer's constructor. Then use the XmlSerializer. Serialize() method to serialize the object to a System.IO.Stream, System.IO.TextWriter, or System. Xml.XmlWriter. To deserialize an object from XML, use the staticXmlSerializer.Deserialize() method, which returns an instance of System.Object that you can cast to the appropriate type. XmlSerializer.Deserialize() also allows you to read XML from a System.IO.Stream, System.IO. TextReader, or System.Xml.XmlReader.

To serialize an object instance to SOAP, get an instance of XmlTypeMapping by constructing a new SoapReflectionImporter and calling its SoapReflectionImporter.ImportTypeMapping() method with the System.Type you want to serialize. The details of how an object is serialized to XML and SOAP, including the names of elements and attributes and the handling of nested elements, can be specified either by attaching attributes to types and fields in the source code, or at runtime by adding attributes to a XmlAttributeOverrides or SoapAttributeOverrides object, which can be passed to the XmlSerializer or SoapReflectionImporter constructor, respectively.

This namespace contains numerous classes that, although public, are reserved for internal use by the .NET Framework. No documentation is included in this quick reference for those classes. Figure 18-1, Figure 18-2, and Figure 18-3 show the types in this namespace.

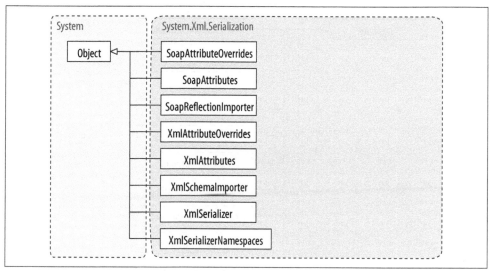

Figure 18-1. The System.Xml.Serialization namespace

SoapAttributeAttribute

CF 1.0

System.Xml.Serialization (system.xml.dll)   class

```
public class SoapAttributeAttribute : Attribute {
// Public Constructors
  public SoapAttributeAttribute( );
  public SoapAttributeAttribute( string attrName);
// Public Instance Properties
  public string AttributeName{set; get; }
  public string DataType{set; get; }
  public string Namespace{set; get; }
}
```

This attribute is used to indicate that the field it is attached to should be serialized as a SOAP attribute by the XmlSerializer. Its AttributeName property specifies the name of the attribute, and its DataType property specifies its XML Schema datatype. The Namespace property can be used to set the namespace of the attribute. Like all the SOAP attributes, it can be applied in code or via the SoapAttributeOverrides object.

Hierarchy   System.Object → System.Attribute → SoapAttributeAttribute

Valid On   Property, Field, Parameter, ReturnValue

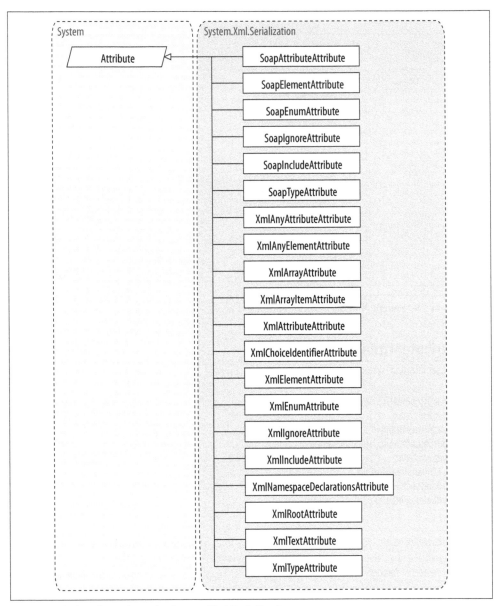

Figure 18-2. Attributes from the System.Xml.Serialization namespace

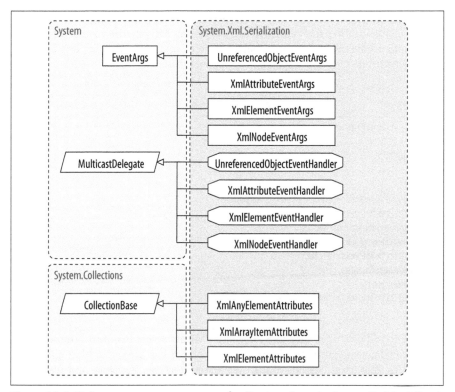

Figure 18-3. Delegates, event arguments, and collections from the System.Xml.Serialization namespace

SoapAttributeOverrides

System.Xml.Serialization (system.xml.dll)   class

```
public class SoapAttributeOverrides {
// Public Constructors
  public SoapAttributeOverrides( );
// Public Instance Properties
  public SoapAttributes this[ Type type, string member ]{get; }
  public SoapAttributes this[ Type type ]{get; }
// Public Instance Methods
  public void Add( Type type, SoapAttributes attributes);
  public void Add( Type type, string member, SoapAttributes attributes);
}
```

This type represents a collection of SoapAttributes instances, which allows you to customize the way the XmlSerializer serializes objects to SOAP. It is used in conjunction with the XmlTypeMapping class at runtime to override the serialization attributes attached to an object, such as changing SoapAttributeAttribute to SoapElementAttribute so that a particular field is serialized as an XML element rather than an XML attribute. The Add() method is used to add a SoapAttributes instance to the collection for a specific type or member, and indexers are used to retrieve a SoapAttributes instance for a specific type or member.

SoapAttributes

System.Xml.Serialization (system.xml.dll)   class

```
public class SoapAttributes {
// Public Constructors
  public SoapAttributes( );
  public SoapAttributes( System.Reflection.ICustomAttributeProvider provider);
// Public Instance Properties
  public SoapAttributeAttribute SoapAttribute{set; get; }
  public object SoapDefaultValue{set; get; }
  public SoapElementAttribute SoapElement{set; get; }
  public SoapEnumAttribute SoapEnum{set; get; }
  public bool SoapIgnore{set; get; }
  public SoapTypeAttribute SoapType{set; get; }
}
```

This type is used to add new attributes to a SoapAttributeOverrides object to control the serialization of an object instance at runtime. The SoapAttributes object has properties that allow you to set the attributes SoapAttribute, SoapDefaultValue, SoapElement, SoapEnum, SoapIgnore, and SoapType of a type or member.

SoapElementAttribute   CF 1.0

System.Xml.Serialization (system.xml.dll)   class

```
public class SoapElementAttribute : Attribute {
// Public Constructors
  public SoapElementAttribute( );
  public SoapElementAttribute( string elementName);
// Public Instance Properties
  public string DataType{set; get; }
  public string ElementName{set; get; }
  public bool IsNullable{set; get; }
}
```

This attribute is used to indicate that the field it is attached to should be serialized as a SOAP element by the XmlSerializer. Its ElementName property specifies the name of the element, and its DataType property specifies its XML Schema datatype. The IsNullable property can be used to set the element's xsi:nil attribute, which indicates a null value for the element. Like all the SOAP attributes, it can be applied in code or via the SoapAttributeOverrides object.

Hierarchy	System.Object → System.Attribute → SoapElementAttribute
Valid On	Property, Field, Parameter, ReturnValue

SoapEnumAttribute

CF 1.0

System.Xml.Serialization (system.xml.dll)   class

```
public class SoapEnumAttribute : Attribute {
// Public Constructors
  public SoapEnumAttribute( );
  public SoapEnumAttribute( string name);
// Public Instance Properties
  public string Name{set; get; }
}
```

This attribute is used to change the name of an enumeration values that should be serialized as SOAP. Its Name property specifies the name that should be serialized rather than using the name of the enumeration value. Like all the SOAP attributes, it can be applied in code or via the SoapAttributeOverrides object.

Hierarchy	System.Object → System.Attribute → SoapEnumAttribute
Valid On	Field

SoapIgnoreAttribute

CF 1.0

System.Xml.Serialization (system.xml.dll)   class

```
public class SoapIgnoreAttribute : Attribute {
// Public Constructors
  public SoapIgnoreAttribute( );
}
```

This attribute is used to indicate that the field to which it is attached should not be serialized to SOAP. If an element with the same name is found in an XML stream being deserialized it will be ignored. Like all the SOAP attributes, it can be applied in code or via the SoapAttributeOverrides object.

Hierarchy	System.Object → System.Attribute → SoapIgnoreAttribute
Valid On	Property, Field, Parameter, ReturnValue

SoapIncludeAttribute

System.Xml.Serialization (system.xml.dll)   class

```
public class SoapIncludeAttribute : Attribute {
// Public Constructors
   public SoapIncludeAttribute( Type type);
// Public Instance Properties
   public Type Type{set; get; }
}
```

This attribute is used to change the type of an object that is serialized to SOAP to a specific subclass. For example, a type specified as a System.Object in the code may be serialized as a specific subclass such as System.String by setting the Type property to typeof(System.String). Like all the SOAP attributes, it can be applied in code or via the SoapAttributeOverrides object.

Hierarchy   System.Object → System.Attribute → SoapIncludeAttribute

Valid On   Class, Struct, Method

SoapReflectionImporter

System.Xml.Serialization (system.xml.dll)   class

```
public class SoapReflectionImporter {
// Public Constructors
   public SoapReflectionImporter( );
   public SoapReflectionImporter( SoapAttributeOverrides attributeOverrides);
   public SoapReflectionImporter( SoapAttributeOverrides attributeOverrides, string defaultNamespace);
   public SoapReflectionImporter( string defaultNamespace);
// Public Instance Methods
   public XmlMembersMapping ImportMembersMapping( string elementName, string ns, XmlReflectionMember[ ] members);
   public XmlMembersMapping ImportMembersMapping( string elementName, string ns, XmlReflectionMember[ ] members,
      bool hasWrapperElement, bool writeAccessors);
   public XmlMembersMapping ImportMembersMapping( string elementName, string ns, XmlReflectionMember[ ] members,
      bool hasWrapperElement, bool writeAccessors, bool validate);
   public XmlTypeMapping ImportTypeMapping( Type type);
   public XmlTypeMapping ImportTypeMapping( Type type, string defaultNamespace);
   public void IncludeType( Type type);
   public void IncludeTypes( System.Reflection.ICustomAttributeProvider provider);
}
```

Although this type is mostly used internally by the .NET Framework, you may create an instance of it in order to call its ImportTypeMapping() method to obtain an instance of XmlTypeMapping, which can be passed to the XmlSerializer constructor to serialize an object to SOAP.

SoapTypeAttribute

System.Xml.Serialization (system.xml.dll)   class

```
public class SoapTypeAttribute : Attribute {
// Public Constructors
   public SoapTypeAttribute( );
   public SoapTypeAttribute( string typeName);
   public SoapTypeAttribute( string typeName, string ns);
// Public Instance Properties
   public bool IncludeInSchema{set; get; }
   public string Namespace{set; get; }
   public string TypeName{set; get; }
}
```

This type is used to control the XML Schema that is generated when an object is serialized to XML. The TypeName property can be used to set the name of the XSD type, and the Namespace property can be used to set its namespace. The IncludeInSchema property is used to indicate whether the type will be included in the generated XML Schema. Like all the SOAP attributes, it can be applied in code or via the SoapAttributeOverrides object.

Hierarchy   System.Object → System.Attribute → SoapTypeAttribute

Valid On   Class, Struct, Enum, Interface

UnreferencedObjectEventArgs

System.Xml.Serialization (system.xml.dll)   class

```
public class UnreferencedObjectEventArgs : EventArgs {
// Public Constructors
   public UnreferencedObjectEventArgs( object o, string id);
// Public Instance Properties
   public string UnreferencedId{get; }
   public object UnreferencedObject{get; }
}
```

This type is sent as a parameter to the UnreferencedObjectEventHandler when an unreferenced object is detected in the XML stream. Its UnreferencedId property contains the id attribute of the unreferenced object, the its UnreferencedObject property contains the actual unreferenced object, which can be cast to its known type if you wish to examine its properties directly.

Hierarchy   System.Object → System.EventArgs → UnreferencedObjectEventArgs

UnreferencedObjectEventHandler

serializable

System.Xml.Serialization (system.xml.dll)

delegate

public delegate void **UnreferencedObjectEventHandler**(object *sender*, UnreferencedObjectEventArgs *e*);

This declared delegate type is used to receive event notifications from an XmlSerializer instance of unreferenced objects in the XML data stream. An unreferenced object is an element that occurs in a SOAP envelope but whose id attribute is not referenced by any other element's href attribute. When this callback is invoked, you have the opportunity to examine the unreferenced object through the UnreferencedObjectEventArgs.

XmlAnyAttributeAttribute

CF 1.0

System.Xml.Serialization (system.xml.dll)

class

public class **XmlAnyAttributeAttribute** : Attribute {
// *Public Constructors*
  public **XmlAnyAttributeAttribute**( );
}

This attribute is used to indicate that the member it is applied to can contain any attribute. The member it is applied to must return an array of System.Xml.XmlAttribute or System.Xml.XmlNode objects. When the XmlSerializer.Deserialize( ) method is called, any attributes that do not have a corresponding member already assigned will be placed in the array. You can then deal with them individually by iterating through the array.

Hierarchy   System.Object → System.Attribute → XmlAnyAttributeAttribute

Valid On   Property, Field, Parameter, ReturnValue

XmlAnyElementAttribute

CF 1.0

System.Xml.Serialization (system.xml.dll)

class

public class **XmlAnyElementAttribute** : Attribute {
// *Public Constructors*
  public **XmlAnyElementAttribute**( );
  public **XmlAnyElementAttribute**(string *name*);
  public **XmlAnyElementAttribute**(string *name*, string *ns*);
// *Public Instance Properties*
  public string **Name**{set; get; }
  public string **Namespace**{set; get; }
}

This attribute is used to indicate that the member it is applied to can contain any element. The member it is applied to must return an array of System.Xml.XmlElement or System.Xml.XmlNode objects, or a System.Xml.XmlElement. When the XmlSerializer.Serialize( ) method is called, all members of the array will be serialized as elements in the XML stream. If the Name property of XmlAnyElementAttribute has been set, all of the elements in the array must have the same name. If the Namespace property has been set, the Name property must also be set, and all of the elements in the array must have the same namespace.

When the XmlSerializer.Deserialize( ) method is called, any elements that do not have a corresponding member already assigned will be placed in the array. If the Name property has been set, only those elements that have that name will be placed in the array. If the Namespace property is set, only those elements having that namespace will be placed in the array. You can apply XmlAnyElementAttribute to multiple members of an object, as long as each of them has a different Name/Namespace pair.

If the member XmlAnyElementAttribute is applied to returns an instance of System.Xml.XmlElement, you can use the System.Xml.XmlElement's properties and methods to iterate through the deserialized elements.

Hierarchy   System.Object → System.Attribute → XmlAnyElementAttribute

Valid On   Property, Field, Parameter, ReturnValue

XmlAnyElementAttributes

System.Xml.Serialization (system.xml.dll)   class

```
public class XmlAnyElementAttributes : CollectionBase {
// Public Constructors
  public XmlAnyElementAttributes( );
// Public Instance Properties
  public XmlAnyElementAttribute this[ int index ]{set; get; }
// Public Instance Methods
  public int Add( XmlAnyElementAttribute attribute);
  public bool Contains( XmlAnyElementAttribute attribute);
  public void CopyTo( XmlAnyElementAttribute[ ] array, int index);
  public int IndexOf( XmlAnyElementAttribute attribute);
  public void Insert( int index, XmlAnyElementAttribute attribute);
  public void Remove( XmlAnyElementAttribute attribute);
}
```

This type is used to represent a collection of XmlAnyElementAttribute objects. Multiple instances of XmlAnyElementAttribute with different Name properties may be applied to the same member, so they are collected in the XmlAttributes.XmlAnyElements property.

Hierarchy   System.Object → System.Collections.CollectionBase(System.Collections.IList, System.Collections.ICollection, System.Collections.IEnumerable) → XmlAnyElementAttributes

XmlArrayAttribute

System.Xml.Serialization (system.xml.dll)

```
public class XmlArrayAttribute : Attribute {
// Public Constructors
  public XmlArrayAttribute( );
  public XmlArrayAttribute( string elementName);
// Public Instance Properties
  public string ElementName{set; get; }
  public XmlSchemaForm Form{set; get; }
  public bool IsNullable{set; get; }
  public string Namespace{set; get; }
}
```

This attribute is used to specify how the XmlSerializer should serialize a member that returns an array to XML. The ElementName property indicates the name of the element that holds the array, when it is different from the member name. The Form property can be used to set the System.Xml.Schema.XmlSchemaForm for the element name. The IsNullable property indicates whether the element will be written with the attribute xsi:nil="true" if the array is empty. The Namespace property contains the namespace for the array element.

Hierarchy   System.Object → System.Attribute → XmlArrayAttribute

Valid On   Property, Field, Parameter, ReturnValue

XmlArrayItemAttribute

System.Xml.Serialization (system.xml.dll)

```
public class XmlArrayItemAttribute : Attribute {
// Public Constructors
  public XmlArrayItemAttribute( );
  public XmlArrayItemAttribute( string elementName);
  public XmlArrayItemAttribute( string elementName, Type type);
  public XmlArrayItemAttribute( Type type);
// Public Instance Properties
  public string DataType{set; get; }
  public string ElementName{set; get; }
  public XmlSchemaForm Form{set; get; }
  public bool IsNullable{set; get; }
  public string Namespace{set; get; }
  public int NestingLevel{set; get; }
  public Type Type{set; get; }
}
```

This attribute is used to specify how the XmlSerializer should deserialize individual elements of a member that returns an array. The ElementName property contains the name of the XML element for each element of the array, when it is different from the name of the type. The DataType property allows you to set the XML Schema data type for the array elements. The

Form property can be used to set the System.Xml.Schema.XmlSchemaForm for the element name. The IsNullable property indicates whether the element will be written with the attribute xsi:nil="true" if the array element is null. The Namespace property contains the namespace for the XML element. When the array is two-dimensional, the NestingLevel property indicates the depth of the XML tree at which the XmlArrayItemAttribute applies. The Type property indicates the System. Types of elements that can be inserted into the array, if there is more than one, and if the concrete type differs from the declared type of the array elements.

Hierarchy System.Object → System.Attribute → XmlArrayItemAttribute

Valid On Property, Field, Parameter, ReturnValue

XmlArrayItemAttributes

System.Xml.Serialization (system.xml.dll)   class

```
public class XmlArrayItemAttributes : CollectionBase {
// Public Constructors
   public XmlArrayItemAttributes( );
// Public Instance Properties
   public XmlArrayItemAttribute this[ int index ]{set; get; }
// Public Instance Methods
   public int Add( XmlArrayItemAttribute attribute);
   public bool Contains( XmlArrayItemAttribute attribute);
   public void CopyTo( XmlArrayItemAttribute[ ] array, int index);
   public int IndexOf( XmlArrayItemAttribute attribute);
   public void Insert( Int index, XmlArrayItemAttribute attribute);
   public void Remove( XmlArrayItemAttribute attribute);
}
```

This type extends System.Collections.CollectionBase to provide a collection of XmlArrayItemAttribute instances. This collection is used to specify the concrete types that can be elements of the array returned by the member to which the attribute is applied.

Hierarchy System.Object → System.Collections.CollectionBase(System.Collections.IList, System.Collections.ICollection, System.Collections.IEnumerable) → XmlArrayItemAttributes

XmlAttributeAttribute   CF 1.0

System.Xml.Serialization (system.xml.dll)   class

```
public class XmlAttributeAttribute : Attribute {
// Public Constructors
   public XmlAttributeAttribute( );
   public XmlAttributeAttribute( string attributeName);
   public XmlAttributeAttribute( string attributeName, Type type);
   public XmlAttributeAttribute( Type type);
// Public Instance Properties
   public string AttributeName{set; get; }
```

```
public string DataType{set; get; }
public XmlSchemaForm Form{set; get; }
public string Namespace{set; get; }
public Type Type{set; get; }
}
```

This attribute is used to indicate that the member to which it is applied should be serialized as an XML attribute. The AttributeName element holds the name of the attribute, the DataType property holds the XML Schema datatype of the attribute, and the Form property holds the System.Xml.Schema.XmlSchemaForm of the attribute name.

Hierarchy	System.Object → System.Attribute → XmlAttributeAttribute

Valid On	Property, Field, Parameter, ReturnValue

XmlAttributeEventArgs

System.Xml.Serialization (system.xml.dll)   class

```
public class XmlAttributeEventArgs : EventArgs {
// Public Instance Properties
  public XmlAttribute Attr{get; }
  public int LineNumber{get; }
  public int LinePosition{get; }
  public object ObjectBeingDeserialized{get; }
}
```

An object of this type is passed to the XmlAttributeEventHandler callback when an unknown attribute is encountered while deserializing an object from XML. Its Attr property returns the System.Xml.XmlAttribute being deserialized, and its LineNumber and LinePosition properties give more information about the attribute's location in the XML stream. The ObjectBeingDeserialized property returns the object being deserialized.

Hierarchy	System.Object → System.EventArgs → XmlAttributeEventArgs

XmlAttributeEventHandler   serializable

System.Xml.Serialization (system.xml.dll)   delegate

```
public delegate void XmlAttributeEventHandler( object sender, XmlAttributeEventArgs e);
```

This declared delegate type is used to receive event notifications from the XmlSerializer instance when an unknown attribute is encountered. The XmlSerializer.UnknownAttribute event is fired after the XmlSerializer.UnknownNode event. If no XmlAttributeEventHandler is assigned, any unknown attributes will be ignored.

XmlAttributeOverrides

```
public class XmlAttributeOverrides {
// Public Constructors
  public XmlAttributeOverrides( );
// Public Instance Properties
  public XmlAttributes this[ Type type, string member ]{get; }
  public XmlAttributes this[ Type type ]{get; }
// Public Instance Methods
  public void Add( Type type, string member, XmlAttributes attributes);
  public void Add( Type type, XmlAttributes attributes);
}
```

This type contains a collection of XmlAttributes objects, which are used to customize the way the XmlSerializer serializes an object to XML. Its Add( ) method has two overrides, one that takes a System.Type indicating the type of object it applies to and the XmlAttribute instance containing the attributes, and one that takes those two parameters plus a System.String containing the name of the member of the type to which the attributes apply.

The XmlAttributeOverrides instance is passed to the XmlSerializer constructor to create the serializer with the overriden attributes.

XmlAttributes

```
public class XmlAttributes {
// Public Constructors
  public XmlAttributes( );
  public XmlAttributes( System.Reflection.ICustomAttributeProvider provider);
// Public Instance Properties
  public XmlAnyAttributeAttribute XmlAnyAttribute{set; get; }
  public XmlAnyElementAttributes XmlAnyElements{get; }
  public XmlArrayAttribute XmlArray{set; get; }
  public XmlArrayItemAttributes XmlArrayItems{get; }
  public XmlAttributeAttribute XmlAttribute{set; get; }
  public XmlChoiceIdentifierAttribute XmlChoiceIdentifier{get; }
  public object XmlDefaultValue{set; get; }
  public XmlElementAttributes XmlElements{get; }
  public XmlEnumAttribute XmlEnum{set; get; }
  public bool XmlIgnore{set; get; }
  public bool XmlNs{set; get; }
  public XmlRootAttribute XmlRoot{set; get; }
  public XmlTextAttribute XmlText{set; get; }
  public XmlTypeAttribute XmlType{set; get; }
}
```

This type is used in conjunction with the XmlAttributeOverrides class to customize the serialization of an object at runtime. It has a property for each type of XML serialization attribute, which allows you to set the attributes at runtime.

XmlChoiceIdentifierAttribute

System.Xml.Serialization (system.xml.dll)   class

```
public class XmlChoiceIdentifierAttribute : Attribute {
// Public Constructors
  public XmlChoiceIdentifierAttribute( );
  public XmlChoiceIdentifierAttribute( string name);
// Public Instance Properties
  public string MemberName{set; get; }
}
```

This type is used to indicate to the XmlSerializer that the member to which it is applied should be serialized as defined by an XML Schema xsi:choice compositor.

Hierarchy   System.Object → System.Attribute → XmlChoiceIdentifierAttribute

Valid On   Property, Field, Parameter, ReturnValue

XmlElementAttribute

System.Xml.Serialization (system.xml.dll)   class

```
public class XmlElementAttribute : Attribute {
// Public Constructors
  public XmlElementAttribute( );
  public XmlElementAttribute( string elementName);
  public XmlElementAttribute( string elementName, Type type);
  public XmlElementAttribute( Type type);
// Public Instance Properties
  public string DataType{set; get; }
  public string ElementName{set; get; }
  public XmlSchemaForm Form{set; get; }
  public bool IsNullable{set; get; }
  public string Namespace{set; get; }
  public Type Type{set; get; }
}
```

This attribute indicates that the member to which it is applied should be serialized as an XML element. The ElementName property indicates the name of the element, the DataType property holds the XML Schema datatype of the element, and the Form property holds the System.Xml.Schema.XmlSchemaForm of the element name. If the member returns a System.Collections. ArrayList, the Type property holds the System.Type of the object to be added to the member;

several XmlElementAttributes may be applied to the member in such a case. An element may additionally have its IsNullable property set to true to set the xsi:nil attribute to true, and the Namespace property can be used to set the element's namespace.

Hierarchy   System.Object → System.Attribute → XmlElementAttribute

Valid On   Property, Field, Parameter, ReturnValue

XmlElementAttributes

System.Xml.Serialization (system.xml.dll)   class

```
public class XmlElementAttributes : CollectionBase {
// Public Constructors
  public XmlElementAttributes( );
// Public Instance Properties
  public XmlElementAttribute this[ int index ]{set; get; }
// Public Instance Methods
  public int Add( XmlElementAttribute attribute);
  public bool Contains( XmlElementAttribute attribute);
  public void CopyTo( XmlElementAttribute[ ] array, int index);
  public int IndexOf( XmlElementAttribute attribute);
  public void Insert( int index, XmlElementAttribute attribute);
  public void Remove( XmlElementAttribute attribute);
}
```

This type provides a collection of XmlElementAttribute objects, which allows you to customize the serialization of a member as an XML element. An instance of XmlElementAttributes is returned by the XmlAttributes.XmlElements property of XmlAttributes.

Hierarchy   System.Object → System.Collections.CollectionBase(System.Collections.IList, System.Collections.ICol-
                   lection, System.Collections.IEnumerable) → XmlElementAttributes

XmlElementEventArgs

System.Xml.Serialization (system.xml.dll)   class

```
public class XmlElementEventArgs : EventArgs {
// Public Instance Properties
  public XmlElement Element{get; }
  public int LineNumber{get; }
  public int LinePosition{get; }
  public object ObjectBeingDeserialized{get; }
}
```

An object of this type is passed to the XmlElementEventHandler callback when an unknown element is encountered while deserializing an object from XML. Its Element property returns the System.Xml.XmlElement being deserialized, and its LineNumber and LinePosition properties give more information about the element's location in the XML stream. The ObjectBeingDeserialized property returns the object being deserialized.

Hierarchy   System.Object → System.EventArgs → XmlElementEventArgs

XmlElementEventHandler   serializable

System.Xml.Serialization (system.xml.dll)   delegate

public delegate void **XmlElementEventHandler**(object *sender*, XmlElementEventArgs *e*);

This declared delegate type is used to receive event notifications from the XmlSerializer instance when an unknown element is encountered. The XmlSerializer.UnknownElement event is fired after the XmlSerializer.UnknownNode event. If no XmlElementEventHandler is assigned, any unknown elements will be ignored.

XmlEnumAttribute   CF 1.0

System.Xml.Serialization (system.xml.dll)   class

```
public class XmlEnumAttribute : Attribute {
// Public Constructors
  public XmlEnumAttribute( );
  public XmlEnumAttribute( string name);
// Public Instance Properties
  public string Name{set; get; }
}
```

This type is used to indicate that the enumeration member to which it is applied should be serialized with the name specified in its Name property.

Hierarchy   System.Object → System.Attribute → XmlEnumAttribute

Valid On   Field

XmlIgnoreAttribute   CF 1.0

System.Xml.Serialization (system.xml.dll)   class

```
public class XmlIgnoreAttribute : Attribute {
// Public Constructors
  public XmlIgnoreAttribute( );
}
```

This type is used to indicate that the member to which it is applied should not be serialized to XML or deserialized from XML.

Valid On   Property, Field, Parameter, ReturnValue

XmlIncludeAttribute   CF 1.0

System.Xml.Serialization (system.xml.dll)   class

```
public class XmlIncludeAttribute : Attribute {
// Public Constructors
  public XmlIncludeAttribute( Type type);
// Public Instance Properties
  public Type Type{set; get; }
}
```

This type is used to specify the concrete System.Type of the object to be created when deserializing an object from XML.

Hierarchy   System.Object → System.Attribute → XmlIncludeAttribute

Valid On   Class, Struct, Method

XmlNamespaceDeclarationsAttribute   CF 1.0

System.Xml.Serialization (system.xml.dll)   class

```
public class XmlNamespaceDeclarationsAttribute : Attribute {
// Public Constructors
  public XmlNamespaceDeclarationsAttribute( );
}
```

This is used to specify the namespaces used in an XML document, and their prefixes. It can only be applied to one member that returns an instance of XmlSerializerNamespaces per class.

Hierarchy   System.Object → System.Attribute → XmlNamespaceDeclarationsAttribute

Valid On   Property, Field, Parameter, ReturnValue

XmlNodeEventArgs

System.Xml.Serialization (system.xml.dll)   class

```
public class XmlNodeEventArgs : EventArgs {
// Public Instance Properties
  public int LineNumber{get; }
  public int LinePosition{get; }
  public string LocalName{get; }
  public string Name{get; }
```

```
  public string NamespaceURI{get;}
  public XmlNodeType NodeType{get;}
  public object ObjectBeingDeserialized{get;}
  public string Text{get;}
}
```

An object of this type is passed to the XmlNodeEventHandler callback when an unknown node is encountered while deserializing an object from XML. Its Name, LocalName, and NamespaceURI properties return the name, local name, and namespace URI of the node, respectively, and the NodeType property returns its System.Xml.XmlNodeType. The Text property returns the text of the XML node, if any. The LineNumber and LinePosition properties give more information about the node's location in the XML stream. The ObjectBeingDeserialized property returns the object being deserialized.

Hierarchy   System.Object → System.EventArgs → XmlNodeEventArgs

XmlNodeEventHandler   serializable

System.Xml.Serialization (system.xml.dll)   delegate

```
public delegate void XmlNodeEventHandler( object sender, XmlNodeEventArgs e);
```

This declared delegate type is used to receive event notifications from the XmlSerializer instance when an unknown node is encountered. The UnknownNode() event is fired before the UnknownAttribute() or UnknownElement() event. If no XmlNodeEventHandler is assigned to the XmlSerializer. UnknownNode event, any unknown nodes will be handled by the appropriate XmlAttributeEventHandler or XmlElementEventHandler, if one is assigned.

XmlRootAttribute   CF 1.0

System.Xml.Serialization (system.xml.dll)   class

```
public class XmlRootAttribute : Attribute {
// Public Constructors
  public XmlRootAttribute( );
  public XmlRootAttribute( string elementName);
// Public Instance Properties
  public string DataType{set; get;}
  public string ElementName{set; get;}
  public bool IsNullable{set; get;}
  public string Namespace{set; get;}
}
```

This type is used to indicate the class that will be serialized to XML as the root element. Its ElementName property indicates the name of the element to be serialized.

Hierarchy   System.Object → System.Attribute → XmlRootAttribute

Valid On   Class, Struct, Enum, Interface, ReturnValue

XmlSerializer

```
public class XmlSerializer {
// Public Constructors
  public XmlSerializer( Type type);
  public XmlSerializer( Type type, string defaultNamespace);
  public XmlSerializer( Type type, Type[ ] extraTypes);
  public XmlSerializer( Type type, XmlAttributeOverrides overrides);
  public XmlSerializer( Type type, XmlAttributeOverrides overrides, Type[ ] extraTypes, XmlRootAttribute root, string defaultNamespace);
  public XmlSerializer( Type type, XmlRootAttribute root);
  public XmlSerializer( XmlTypeMapping xmlTypeMapping);
// Protected Constructors
  protected XmlSerializer( );
// Public Static Methods
  public static XmlSerializer[ ] FromMappings( XmlMapping[ ] mappings);
  public static XmlSerializer[ ] FromTypes( Type[ ] types);
// Public Instance Methods
  public virtual bool CanDeserialize( System.Xml.XmlReader xmlReader);
  public object Deserialize( System.IO.Stream stream);
  public object Deserialize( System.IO.TextReader textReader);
  public object Deserialize( System.Xml.XmlReader xmlReader);
  public void Serialize( System.IO.Stream stream, object o);
  public void Serialize( System.IO.Stream stream, object o, XmlSerializerNamespaces namespaces);
  public void Serialize( System.IO.TextWriter textWriter, object o);
  public void Serialize( System.IO.TextWriter textWriter, object o, XmlSerializerNamespaces namespaces);
  public void Serialize( System.Xml.XmlWriter xmlWriter, object o);
  public void Serialize( System.Xml.XmlWriter xmlWriter, object o, XmlSerializerNamespaces namespaces);
// Protected Instance Methods
  protected virtual XmlSerializationReader CreateReader( );
  protected virtual XmlSerializationWriter CreateWriter( );
  protected virtual object Deserialize( XmlSerializationReader reader);
  protected virtual void Serialize( object o, XmlSerializationWriter writer);
// Events
  public event XmlAttributeEventHandler UnknownAttribute;
  public event XmlElementEventHandler UnknownElement;
  public event XmlNodeEventHandler UnknownNode;
  public event UnreferencedObjectEventHandler UnreferencedObject;
}
```

This type provides the core functionality of the System.Xml.Serialization namespace. Various constructors are used to create an instance based on a System.Type or a XmlTypeMapping, and some include parameters to provide extra information on how the object is to be serialized. The static FromTypes( ) method will create an array of XmlSerializer instances suitable for serializing and deserializing an array of System.Type instances passed in.

The Serialize( ) method does the work of encoding to XML an instance of an object of the type the XmlSerializer is made for. The serialization is performed according to the attributes placed on the object and its members, as well as any XmlAttributeOverrides passed into the constructor. An object can be serialized to any System.IO.Stream, System.IO.TextWriter, or System.Xml. XmlWriter instance.

The static Deserialize() method decodes an object from XML into an instance of the object in memory. The XML object can be deserialized from any System.IO.Stream, System.IO.TextReader, or System.Xml.XmlReader instance that contains XML. Additionally, if using a System.Xml.XmlReader, the CanDeserialize() method indicates whether the data in the XML stream is of the proper type to be deserialized by this instance of XmlSerializer.

During deserialization, the XmlSerializer may fire one or more of four events. The UnreferencedObject event is fired if an object deserialized from a SOAP stream has no other object referencing it. If an unknown node is encountered in the XML stream, the UnknownNode event is fired, followed by the UnknownAttribute event if the node is a System.Xml.XmlAttribute, or the UnknownElement event if the node is a System.Xml.XmlElement.

An XmlSerializer instance is created specifically to provide XML serialization for one particular type of object. At the time the XmlSerializer is instantiated, the .NET Framework generates a private assembly to perform the serialization. Because of this, the first time you create a serializer for a particular type, there may be some performance degradation.

XmlSerializerNamespaces
CF 1.0

System.Xml.Serialization (system.xml.dll)
class

```
public class XmlSerializerNamespaces {
// Public Constructors
  public XmlSerializerNamespaces( );
  public XmlSerializerNamespaces( System.Xml.XmlQualifiedName[ ] namespaces);
  public XmlSerializerNamespaces( XmlSerializerNamespaces namespaces);
// Public Instance Properties
  public int Count{get; }
// Public Instance Methods
  public void Add( string prefix, string ns);
  public XmlQualifiedName[ ] ToArray( );
}
```

This type provides a collection of XML namespaces and namespace prefixes that the XmlSerializer uses to determine the qualified names of nodes when serializing an object to an XML document. To assign a namespace to a node, set the XmlElementAttribute.Namespace or XmlAttributeAttribute.Namespace property. This can be done either by attaching the attribute to a member in the code, or by assigning the attribute in the XmlAttributeOverrides class.

XmlTextAttribute
CF 1.0

System.Xml.Serialization (system.xml.dll)
class

```
public class XmlTextAttribute : Attribute {
// Public Constructors
  public XmlTextAttribute( );
  public XmlTextAttribute( Type type);
// Public Instance Properties
  public string DataType{set; get; }
  public Type Type{set; get; }
}
```

This type is used to indicate that the member should be serialized to XML as text. Only one member per class can be serialized as text. The member to which XmlTextAttribute is applied must return a primitive or enumeration type, a System.Xml.XmlNode, an array of System.Strings, or an array of System.Objects, the latter only if the individual array elements are of one of the former types. The DataType property determines the XML Schema type serialized, and the Type property determines the System.Type of the member.

Hierarchy System.Object → System.Attribute → XmlTextAttribute

Valid On Property, Field, Parameter, ReturnValue

XmlTypeAttribute

CF 1.0

System.Xml.Serialization (system.xml.dll) class

```
public class XmlTypeAttribute : Attribute {
// Public Constructors
  public XmlTypeAttribute( );
  public XmlTypeAttribute( string typeName);
// Public Instance Properties
  public bool IncludeInSchema{set; get; }
  public string Namespace{set; get; }
  public string TypeName{set; get; }
}
```

This type is used to specify the name and namespace of an XML Schema xs:complexType element when an XML Schema definition is generated for the class by the XSD tool. The TypeName property holds the XML Schema type name, and the Namespace property holds its namespace. The IncludeInSchema property indicates whether the type should be included in the generated XML Schema definition.

Hierarchy System.Object → System.Attribute → XmlTypeAttribute

Valid On Class, Struct, Enum, Interface

XmlTypeMapping

System.Xml.Serialization (system.xml.dll) class

```
public class XmlTypeMapping : XmlMapping {
// Public Instance Properties
  public string ElementName{get; }
  public string Namespace{get; }
  public string TypeFullName{get; }
  public string TypeName{get; }
}
```

This type is passed to the XmlSerializer constructor when serializing an object type to SOAP. The XmlTypeMapping instance is obtained by instantiating a SoapReflectionImporter and calling its SoapReflectionImporter.ImportTypeMapping() method. The serialization can be further customized using the SoapAttributeOverrides class.

XmlTypeMapping's ElementName and Namespace properties return the element name and namespace, respectively. The TypeName and TypeFullName properties return the name and full name, respectively, of the mapped type.

Hierarchy   System.Object → XmlMapping → XmlTypeMapping

The System.Xml.XPath Namespace

XPath is a W3C specification for locating nodes in an XML document. It provides an expression syntax that can determine a node based on its type, location, and relation to other nodes in a document. XPath is generally not useful alone, but works in conjunction with other tools, especially XSLT. Figure 19-1 shows the types in this namespace.

System.Xml.XPath provides types that evaluate expressions and match nodes in XML documents. XPathDocument is a document object designed to provide fast document navigation through XPath and is used by the System.Xml.Xsl classes for XSLT transformations. XPathNavigator is the core entry point for doing XPath expressions; it is abstract, allowing for more than just XML documents to be XPath-navigated. For example, an ADO.NET provider could, if it desired, implement the IXPathNavigable interface and return an XPathNavigator that translated XPath queries into a SQL SELECT statement.

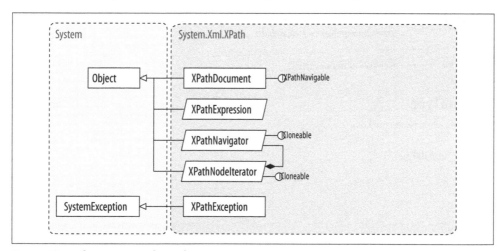

Figure 19-1. The System.Xml.XPath namespace

IXPathNavigable

System.Xml.XPath (system.xml.dll)   interface

```
public interface IXPathNavigable {
// Public Instance Methods
  public XPathNavigator CreateNavigator( );
}
```

This is an interface to XPathNavigator implemented by XPathDocument, System.Xml.XmlNode, and derived classes. It implements one method, CreateNavigator(), which creates an XPathNavigator instance for the document object.

Implemented By   XPathDocument, System.Xml.XmlNode

Passed To   System.Xml.Xsl.XslTransform.{Load( ), Transform( )}

XmlCaseOrder   serializable

System.Xml.XPath (system.xml.dll)   enum

```
public enum XmlCaseOrder {
  None = 0,
  UpperFirst = 1,
  LowerFirst = 2
}
```

This enumeration specifies how nodes are sorted with respect to case. A value of None indicates that case is to be ignored when ordering nodes.

Hierarchy   System.Object → System.ValueType → System.Enum(System.IComparable, System.IFormattable, System.IConvertible) → XmlCaseOrder

Passed To   XPathExpression.AddSort( )

XmlDataType   serializable

System.Xml.XPath (system.xml.dll)   enum

```
public enum XmlDataType {
  Text = 1,
  Number = 2
}
```

This enumeration specifies whether to sort node values by type as numeric value (Number) or alphabetically (Text).

Hierarchy   System.Object → System.ValueType → System.Enum(System.IComparable, System.IFormattable, System.IConvertible) → XmlDataType

Passed To   XPathExpression.AddSort( )

XmlSortOrder

serializable

System.Xml.XPath (system.xml.dll)

enum

```
public enum XmlSortOrder {
  Ascending = 1,
  Descending = 2
}
```

This enumeration specifies how nodes are sorted by numerical value, either ascending or descending.

Hierarchy   System.Object → System.ValueType → System.Enum(System.IComparable, System.IFormattable, System.IConvertible) → XmlSortOrder

Passed To   XPathExpression.AddSort( )

XPathDocument

System.Xml.XPath (system.xml.dll)

class

```
public class XPathDocument : IXPathNavigable {
// Public Constructors
  public XPathDocument( System.IO.Stream stream);
  public XPathDocument( string uri);
  public XPathDocument( string uri, System.Xml.XmlSpace space);
  public XPathDocument( System.IO.TextReader reader);
  public XPathDocument( System.Xml.XmlReader reader);
  public XPathDocument( System.Xml.XmlReader reader, System.Xml.XmlSpace space);
// Public Instance Methods
  public XPathNavigator CreateNavigator( );                              // implements IXPathNavigable
}
```

This class is a concrete implementation of IXPathNavigable for creating an XPathNavigator that knows how to scan through an XML document. There are overloaded forms of the constructor designed to pull an XML document from various sources—a System.IO.Stream, a string, a System.IO.TextReader (which presumably is pulling from some other valid data source), or a System.Xml.XmlReader. Note that if the XmlReader is currently positioned on top of a particular node within a document, the constructed XPathDocument instance is only valid for that element and its children. This allows partial XPath scans of a given document.

This class serves no other purpose than as a factory for producing XPathNavigator instances.

XPathException

serializable

System.Xml.XPath (system.xml.dll)

class

```
public class XPathException : SystemException {
// Public Constructors
  public XPathException( string message, Exception innerException);
// Protected Constructors
```

```
    protected XPathException( System.Runtime.Serialization.SerializationInfo info,
        System.Runtime.Serialization.StreamingContext context);
// Public Instance Properties
    public override string Message{get; }                                        // overrides Exception
// Public Instance Methods
    public override void GetObjectData( System.Runtime.Serialization.SerializationInfo info,
        System.Runtime.Serialization.StreamingContext context);                  // overrides Exception
}
```

This exception indicates a problem with an XPathExpression, such as an invalid prefix.

Hierarchy System.Object → System.Exception(System.Runtime.Serialization.ISerializable) → System.SystemException → XPathException

XPathExpression

System.Xml.XPath (system.xml.dll)   abstract class

```
public abstract class XPathExpression {
// Public Instance Properties
  public abstract string Expression{get; }
  public abstract XPathResultType ReturnType{get; }
// Public Instance Methods
  public abstract void AddSort( object expr, System.Collections.IComparer comparer);
  public abstract void AddSort( object expr, XmlSortOrder order, XmlCaseOrder caseOrder, string lang, XmlDataType dataType);
  public abstract XPathExpression Clone( );
  public abstract void SetContext( System.Xml.XmlNamespaceManager nsManager);
}
```

This class represents a compiled XPath expression. An XPathExpression is returned by the
Compile( ) method of XPathNavigator from an XPath expression string. The AddSort( ) method
allows you to specify the order of returned nodes from the expression. SetContext( ) sets the
namespace to use in the evaluation of the expression.

Returned By XPathNavigator.Compile( )

Passed To XPathNavigator.{Evaluate( ), Matches( ), Select( )}

XPathNamespaceScope   serializable

System.Xml.XPath (system.xml.dll)   enum

```
public enum XPathNamespaceScope {
  All = 0,
  ExcludeXml = 1,
  Local = 2
}
```

This enumeration defines the namespace scope for certain XPathNavigator operations. All
includes all namespaces within the scope of the current node (including the xmlns:xml

namespace, whether defined explicitly or not). ExcludeXml includes all namespaces within the scope of the current node, *except* the xmlns:xml namespace. Local includes all locally defined namespaces within the scope of the current node.

Hierarchy   System.Object → System.ValueType → System.Enum(System.IComparable, System.IFormattable, System.IConvertible) → XPathNamespaceScope

Passed To   XPathNavigator.{MoveToFirstNamespace( ), MoveToNextNamespace( )}

XPathNavigator

System.Xml.XPath (system.xml.dll)   abstract class

```
public abstract class XPathNavigator : ICloneable {
// Protected Constructors
  protected XPathNavigator( );
// Public Instance Properties
  public abstract string BaseURI{get; }
  public abstract bool HasAttributes{get; }
  public abstract bool HasChildren{get; }
  public abstract bool IsEmptyElement{get; }
  public abstract string LocalName{get; }
  public abstract string Name{get; }
  public abstract string NamespaceURI{get; }
  public abstract XmlNameTable NameTable{get; }
  public abstract XPathNodeType NodeType{get; }
  public abstract string Prefix{get; }
  public abstract string Value{get; }
  public abstract string XmlLang{get; }
// Public Instance Methods
  public abstract XPathNavigator Clone( );
  public virtual XmlNodeOrder ComparePosition( XPathNavigator nav);
  public virtual XPathExpression Compile( string xpath);
  public virtual object Evaluate( string xpath);
  public virtual object Evaluate( XPathExpression expr);
  public virtual object Evaluate( XPathExpression expr, XPathNodeIterator context);
  public abstract string GetAttribute( string localName, string namespaceURI);
  public abstract string GetNamespace( string name);
  public virtual bool IsDescendant( XPathNavigator nav);
  public abstract bool IsSamePosition( XPathNavigator other);
  public virtual bool Matches( string xpath);
  public virtual bool Matches( XPathExpression expr);
  public abstract bool MoveTo( XPathNavigator other);
  public abstract bool MoveToAttribute( string localName, string namespaceURI);
  public abstract bool MoveToFirst( );
  public abstract bool MoveToFirstAttribute( );
  public abstract bool MoveToFirstChild( );
  public bool MoveToFirstNamespace( );
  public abstract bool MoveToFirstNamespace( XPathNamespaceScope namespaceScope);
  public abstract bool MoveToId( string id);
```

```
public abstract bool MoveToNamespace( string name);
public abstract bool MoveToNext( );
public abstract bool MoveToNextAttribute( );
public bool MoveToNextNamespace( );
public abstract bool MoveToNextNamespace( XPathNamespaceScope namespaceScope);
public abstract bool MoveToParent( );
public abstract bool MoveToPrevious( );
public abstract void MoveToRoot( );
public virtual XPathNodeIterator Select( string xpath);
public virtual XPathNodeIterator Select( XPathExpression expr);
public virtual XPathNodeIterator SelectAncestors( string name, string namespaceURI, bool matchSelf);
public virtual XPathNodeIterator SelectAncestors( XPathNodeType type, bool matchSelf);
public virtual XPathNodeIterator SelectChildren( string name, string namespaceURI);
public virtual XPathNodeIterator SelectChildren( XPathNodeType type);
public virtual XPathNodeIterator SelectDescendants( string name, string namespaceURI, bool matchSelf);
public virtual XPathNodeIterator SelectDescendants( XPathNodeType type, bool matchSelf);
public override string ToString( );                                            // overrides object
}
```

This class is a read-only representation of an XPathDocument based on the IXPathNavigable interface. It provides an easy-to-use data object for quick XPath-based navigation, particularly for XSLT transformations.

An XPathNavigator instance maintains its state with the current node position to provide the proper context for any XPath expression evaluation. Initially, the current node is the root node. The current node is changed by using the Select() method or the various MoveTo* methods. If the XPath expression evaluates to a set of nodes, the first node of the set is the current node for the XPathNavigator. All the Select* methods return an XPathNodeIterator object containing the set of nodes returned by the function. Except for plain-old Select(), the Select* functions do not change the current node of the XPathNavigator they are used on. Any actions on the XPathNodeIterator objects that they return also do not affect the originating object.

The Compile() method takes an XPath expression string and encapsulates it into a compiled XPathExpression object. XPathExpression objects are used by Select(), Evaluate(), and Matches() as input to search a node list.

Returned By	System.Xml.XmlDataDocument.CreateNavigator( ), System.Xml.XmlNode.CreateNavigator( ), IXPathNavigable.CreateNavigator( ), XPathDocument.CreateNavigator( ), XPathNodeIterator.Current
Passed To	System.Xml.Xsl.IXsltContextFunction.Invoke( ), System.Xml.Xsl.XsltContext.PreserveWhitespace( ), System.Xml.Xsl.XslTransform.{Load( ), Transform( )}

XPathNodeIterator

System.Xml.XPath (system.xml.dll)   abstract class

```
public abstract class XPathNodeIterator : ICloneable {
// Protected Constructors
  protected XPathNodeIterator( );
// Public Instance Properties
  public virtual int Count{get; }
```

```
  public abstract XPathNavigator Current{get; }
  public abstract int CurrentPosition{get; }
// Public Instance Methods
  public abstract XPathNodeIterator Clone( );
  public abstract bool MoveNext( );
}
```

This class is a node-set constructed from a compiled XPath expression. This type is returned by the Select* methods of XPathNavigator. The MoveNext( ) method moves to the next node of the node set in document order and does not affect the XPathNavigator on which the Select( ) was called.

Returned By   XPathNavigator.{Select( ), SelectAncestors( ), SelectChildren( ), SelectDescendants( )}

Passed To   XPathNavigator.Evaluate( )

XPathNodeType   serializable

System.Xml.XPath (system.xml.dll)   enum

```
public enum XPathNodeType {
  Root = 0,
  Element = 1,
  Attribute = 2,
  Namespace = 3,
  Text = 4,
  SignificantWhitespace = 5,
  Whitespace = 6,
  ProcessingInstruction = 7,
  Comment = 8,
  All = 9
}
```

This enumeration contains the types of nodes that can be listed with the XPathNavigator.Node-Type property.

Hierarchy   System.Object → System.ValueType → System.Enum(System.IComparable, System.IFormattable, System.IConvertible) → XPathNodeType

Returned By   XPathNavigator.NodeType

Passed To   XPathNavigator.{SelectAncestors( ), SelectChildren( ), SelectDescendants( )}

XPathResultType   serializable

System.Xml.XPath (system.xml.dll)   enum

```
public enum XPathResultType {
  Number = 0,
  String = 1,
  Navigator = 1,
```

```
    Boolean = 2,
    NodeSet = 3,
    Any = 5,
    Error = 6
}
```

This enumeration contains the result types used by the XPathExpression.ReturnType property.

Hierarchy   System.Object → System.ValueType → System.Enum(System.IComparable, System.IFormattable, System.IConvertible) → XPathResultType

Returned By   XPathExpression.ReturnType, System.Xml.Xsl.IXsltContextFunction.{ArgTypes, ReturnType}, System.Xml.Xsl.IXsltContextVariable.VariableType

Passed To   System.Xml.Xsl.XsltContext.ResolveFunction( )

CHAPTER 20

The System.Xml.Xsl Namespace

The **System.Xml.Xsl** namespace provides support for Extensible Stylesheet Language Transformations (XSLT). XSLT is a W3C specification that describes how to transform one XML document into another with the use of stylesheet templates. For example, a common use of XSLT is to transform an XML document into standard HTML by transforming the specific elements of the input XML document into comparable HTML elements. XSLT templates use XPath expression syntax to specify which nodes of the input XML are transformed.

The **XslTransform** class constructs the transform object. It loads a stylesheet and applies its templates to an XML document to output the transformed data. The **XsltArgumentList** class creates objects for XSLT parameters that can be loaded into the stylesheet at runtime. **XsltContext** provides the XSLT processor with the current context node information used for XPath expression resolution. Figure 20-1 shows the types in this namespace.

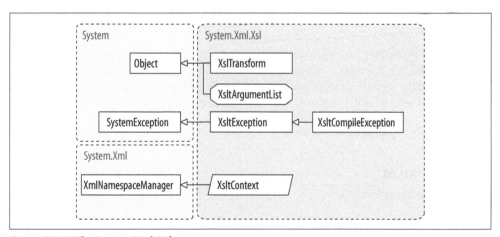

Figure 20-1. The System.Xml.Xsl namespace

IXsltContextFunction

System.Xml.Xsl (system.xml.dll)   interface

```
public interface IXsltContextFunction {
// Public Instance Properties
  public XPathResultType[ ] ArgTypes{get; }
  public int Maxargs{get; }
  public int Minargs{get; }
  public XPathResultType ReturnType{get; }
// Public Instance Methods
  public object Invoke( XsltContext xsltContext, object[ ] args, System.Xml.XPath.XPathNavigator docContext);
}
```

The Microsoft .NET XSLT engine, like many other XSLT engines, allows custom functions inside of an XSLT stylesheet document. By providing an "extension object" to an XsltArgumentList instance, an XSLT stylesheet can "call out" to methods in the CLR. See the XsltArgumentList description for an example.

Returned By   XsltContext.ResolveFunction( )

IXsltContextVariable

System.Xml.Xsl (system.xml.dll)   interface

```
public interface IXsltContextVariable {
// Public Instance Properties
  public bool IsLocal{get; }
  public bool IsParam{get; }
  public XPathResultType VariableType{get; }
// Public Instance Methods
  public object Evaluate( XsltContext xsltContext);
}
```

As with IXsltContextFunction, this interface is used to help the XSLT engine resolve data objects bound into the XSLT engine's executing context while processing an XML document. See the XsltArgumentList method description for an example of how context functions and variables are used with an XSLT instance.

Returned By   XsltContext.ResolveVariable( )

XsltArgumentList

System.Xml.Xsl (system.xml.dll)   sealed class

```
public sealed class XsltArgumentList {
// Public Constructors
  public XsltArgumentList( );
// Public Instance Methods
```

```
  public void AddExtensionObject( string namespaceUri, object extension);
  public void AddParam( string name, string namespaceUri, object parameter);
  public void Clear( );
  public object GetExtensionObject( string namespaceUri);
  public object GetParam( string name, string namespaceUri);
  public object RemoveExtensionObject( string namespaceUri);
  public object RemoveParam( string name, string namespaceUri);
}
```

The XsltArgumentList class constructs lists of parameters and node fragment objects that can be called from stylesheets. This type is called as the second argument to the Transform( ) method of XslTransform. Parameters are associated with namespace-qualified names, and objects are associated with their namespace URIs.

The XsltArgumentList can also be used to bind functions and variables into the XSLT engine's execution space—commonly called the XSLT context—for use by the XSLT stylesheet during processing.

Passed To   XslTransform.Transform( )

XsltCompileException   serializable

System.Xml.Xsl (system.xml.dll)   class

```
public class XsltCompileException : XsltException {
// Public Constructors
  public XsltCompileException( Exception inner, string sourceUri, int lineNumber, int linePosition);
// Protected Constructors
  protected XsltCompileException( System.Runtime.Serialization.SerializationInfo info,
      System.Runtime.Serialization.StreamingContext context);
// Public Instance Properties
  public override string Message{get; }                                  // overrides XsltException
// Public Instance Methods
  public override void GetObjectData( System.Runtime.Serialization.SerializationInfo info,
      System.Runtime.Serlalization.StreamingContext context);            // overrides XsltException
}
```

The XslTransform.Load( ) method throws this exception when it encounters an error in an XSLT document.

Hierarchy   System.Object → System.Exception(System.Runtime.Serialization.ISerializable) → System.SystemException → XsltException → XsltCompileException

XsltContext

System.Xml.Xsl (system.xml.dll)   abstract class

```
public abstract class XsltContext : System.Xml.XmlNamespaceManager {
// Public Constructors
  public XsltContext( );
```

```
  public XsltContext( System.Xml.NameTable table);
// Public Instance Properties
  public abstract bool Whitespace{get; }
// Public Instance Methods
  public abstract int CompareDocument( string baseUri, string nextbaseUri);
  public abstract bool PreserveWhitespace( System.Xml.XPath.XPathNavigator node);
  public abstract IXsltContextFunction ResolveFunction( string prefix, string name, System.Xml.XPath.XPathResultType[ ] ArgTypes);
  public abstract IXsltContextVariable ResolveVariable( string prefix, string name);
}
```

This class provides a way to resolve namespaces and determine the current context for XPath variables and expressions. It inherits System.Xml.XmlNamespaceManager and its namespace functions. Additional methods defined for this class resolve variables (ResolveVariable( )) as well as references to XPath functions invoked during execution (ResolveFunction( )).

Hierarchy   System.Object → System.Xml.XmlNamespaceManager(System.Collections.IEnumerable) → XsltContext

Passed To   IXsltContextFunction.Invoke( ), IXsltContextVariable.Evaluate( )

XsltException   serializable

System.Xml.Xsl (system.xml.dll)   class

```
public class XsltException : SystemException {
// Public Constructors
  public XsltException( string message, Exception innerException);
// Protected Constructors
  protected XsltException( System.Runtime.Serialization.SerializationInfo info, System.Runtime.Serialization.StreamingContext context);
// Public Instance Properties
  public int LineNumber{get; }
  public int LinePosition{get; }
  public override string Message{get; }                                       // overrides Exception
  public string SourceUri{get; }
// Public Instance Methods
  public override void GetObjectData( System.Runtime.Serialization.SerializationInfo info,
    System.Runtime.Serialization.StreamingContext context);                   // overrides Exception
}
```

This class returns XSLT exception errors thrown by XslTransform.Transform( ).

Hierarchy   System.Object → System.Exception(System.Runtime.Serialization.ISerializable) → System.SystemException → XsltException

Subclasses   XsltCompileException

XslTransform

System.Xml.Xsl (system.xml.dll)   sealed class

```
public sealed class XslTransform {
// Public Constructors
  public XslTransform( );
// Public Instance Properties
  public XmlResolver XmlResolver{set; }                                                                         // obsolete
// Public Instance Methods
  public void Load( System.Xml.XPath.IXPathNavigable stylesheet);                                              // obsolete
  public void Load( System.Xml.XPath.IXPathNavigable stylesheet, System.Xml.XmlResolver resolver);            // obsolete
  public void Load( System.Xml.XPath.IXPathNavigable stylesheet, System.Xml.XmlResolver resolver,
    System.Security.Policy.Evidence evidence);
  public void Load( string url);
  public void Load( string url, System.Xml.XmlResolver resolver);
  public void Load( System.Xml.XmlReader stylesheet);                                                          // obsolete
  public void Load( System.Xml.XmlReader stylesheet, System.Xml.XmlResolver resolver);                        // obsolete
  public void Load( System.Xml.XmlReader stylesheet, System.Xml.XmlResolver resolver, System.Security.Policy.Evidence evidence);
  public void Load( System.Xml.XPath.XPathNavigator stylesheet);                                               // obsolete
  public void Load( System.Xml.XPath.XPathNavigator stylesheet, System.Xml.XmlResolver resolver);             // obsolete
  public void Load( System.Xml.XPath.XPathNavigator stylesheet, System.Xml.XmlResolver resolver,
    System.Security.Policy.Evidence evidence);
  public void Transform( System.Xml.XPath.IXPathNavigable input, XsltArgumentList args, System.IO.Stream output);        // obsolete
  public void Transform( System.Xml.XPath.IXPathNavigable input, XsltArgumentList args, System.IO.Stream output,
    System.Xml.XmlResolver resolver);
  public void Transform( System.Xml.XPath.IXPathNavigable input, XsltArgumentList args, System.IO.TextWriter output);    // obsolete
  public void Transform( System.Xml.XPath.IXPathNavigable input, XsltArgumentList args, System.IO.TextWriter output,
    System.Xml.XmlResolver resolver);
  public void Transform( System.Xml.XPath.IXPathNavigable input, XsltArgumentList args, System.Xml.XmlWriter output);    // obsolete
  public void Transform( System.Xml.XPath.IXPathNavigable input, XsltArgumentList args, System.Xml.XmlWriter output,
    System.Xml.XmlResolver resolver);
  public void Transform( string inputfile, string outputfile);                                                 // obsolete
  public void Transform( string inputfile, string outputfile, System.Xml.XmlResolver resolver);
  public void Transform( System.Xml.XPath.XPathNavigator input, XsltArgumentList args, System.IO.Stream output);         // obsolete
  public void Transform( System.Xml.XPath.XPathNavigator input, XsltArgumentList args, System.IO.Stream output,
    System.Xml.XmlResolver resolver);
  public void Transform( System.Xml.XPath.XPathNavigator input, XsltArgumentList args, System.IO.TextWriter output);     // obsolete
  public void Transform( System.Xml.XPath.XPathNavigator input, XsltArgumentList args, System.IO.TextWriter output,
    System.Xml.XmlResolver resolver);
  public void Transform( System.Xml.XPath.XPathNavigator input, XsltArgumentList args, System.Xml.XmlWriter output);     // obsolete
  public void Transform( System.Xml.XPath.XPathNavigator input, XsltArgumentList args, System.Xml.XmlWriter output,
    System.Xml.XmlResolver resolver);
  public XmlReader Transform( System.Xml.XPath.IXPathNavigable input, XsltArgumentList args);                  // obsolete
  public XmlReader Transform( System.Xml.XPath.IXPathNavigable input, XsltArgumentList args, System.Xml.XmlResolver resolver);
  public XmlReader Transform( System.Xml.XPath.XPathNavigator input, XsltArgumentList args);                   // obsolete
  public XmlReader Transform( System.Xml.XPath.XPathNavigator input, XsltArgumentList args, System.Xml.XmlResolver resolver);
}
```

This object uses the **Load( )** method to input a stylesheet from either a URL, an **XPathNavigator** object, an object implementing **IXPathNavigable**, or an **XmlReader** object (remember, an XSL stylesheet is an XML document itself). The **Transform( )** method takes a URL, an **XPathNavigator** object, or an object implementing **IXPathNavigable** as its first argument, which contains the XML document to transform. The second argument is an **XsltArgumentList** object; see **XsltArgumentList** for an example of using bound functions and/or variables.

The transformed result is output to an **XmlReader** object by default, or you can specify either a **System.IO.Stream**, **XmlWriter**, or **XmlTextWriter** object in the third argument for the output.

Note that in the .NET 1.1 release, any method or constructor of this class that does not take an **XmlResolver** instance has been marked obsolete, in favor of overloads that take an **XmlResolver** instance to resolve external entities (DTD references, entity references, and so on). Change any legacy code (pre-1.1) using those methods to take an **XmlResolver** instance in the method or constructor call, as these obsolete methods could disappear in a future version of the framework.

Type, Method, Property, and Field Index

Use this index to look up a type or member and see where it is defined. For a type (a class or interface), you can find the enclosing namespace. If you know the name of a member (a method, property, event, or field), you can find all the types that define it.

Action: XmlNodeChangedEventArgs

Add( ): CodeIdentifiers, NameTable, SoapAttribute-Overrides, XmlAnyElementAttributes, XmlArrayItemAttributes, XmlAttributeOverrides, XmlElementAttributes, XmlNameTable, XmlSchemaCollection, XmlSchemaObjectCollection, XmlSchemas, XmlSerializerNamespaces

AddExtensionObject( ): XsltArgumentList

AddFixup( ): XmlSerializationReader

AddMappingMetadata( ): SoapCodeExporter, XmlCodeExporter

AddNamespace( ): XmlNamespaceManager

AddParam( ): XsltArgumentList

AddReadCallback( ): XmlSerializationReader

AddReserved( ): CodeIdentifiers

AddSort( ): XPathExpression

AddTarget( ): XmlSerializationReader

AddUnique( ): CodeIdentifiers

AddWriteCallback( ): XmlSerializationWriter

After: XmlNodeOrder

Algorithm: XmlDiff

All: WhitespaceHandling, XmlSchema-DerivationMethod, XPathNamespaceScope, XPath-NodeType

Annotation: XmlSchemaAnnotated, XmlSchema-Import, XmlSchemaInclude

Any: XmlMemberMapping, XPathResultType

AnyAttribute: XmlSchemaAttributeGroup, XmlSchemaComplexContentExtension, XmlSchema-ComplexContentRestriction, XmlSchemaComplex-Type, XmlSchemaSimpleContentExtension, XmlSchemaSimpleContentRestriction

Append( ): XmlAttributeCollection

AppendChild( ): XmlNode

AppendData( ): XmlCharacterData

AppSettings: ConfigurationSettings

AppSettingsReader: System.Configuration

ArgTypes: IXsltContextFunction

Ascending: XmlSortOrder

Attr: XmlAttributeEventArgs

Attribute: WriteState, XmlNodeType, XPathNodeType

AttributeCount: XmlNodeReader, XmlReader, XmlTextReader, XmlValidatingReader

AttributeFormDefault: XmlSchema

AttributeGroups: XmlSchema, XmlSchemaRedefine

AttributeName: SoapAttributeAttribute, XmlAttributeAttribute

Attributes: XmlElement, XmlNode, XmlSchema, XmlSchemaAttributeGroup, XmlSchema-ComplexContentExtension, XmlSchemaComplex-ContentRestriction, XmlSchemaComplexType, XmlSchemaSimpleContentExtension, XmlSchema-SimpleContentRestriction

AttributeType: XmlSchemaAttribute

AttributeUses: XmlSchemaComplexType

AttributeWildcard: XmlSchemaComplexType

Auto: ValidationType, XmlDiffAlgorithm

BareMessage: ConfigurationException

BaseSchemaType: XmlSchemaType

BaseStream: XmlTextWriter

BaseType: XmlSchemaSimpleContentRestriction, XmlSchemaSimpleTypeRestriction

BaseTypeName: XmlSchemaComplexContent-Extension, XmlSchemaComplexContentRestriction, XmlSchemaSimpleContentExtension, XmlSchema-SimpleContentRestriction, XmlSchemaSimpleType-Restriction

BaseTypes: XmlSchemaSimpleTypeUnion

BaseURI: XmlAttribute, XmlDocument, XmlEntity, XmlEntityReference, XmlNode, XmlNodeReader, XmlParserContext, XmlReader, XmlTextReader, XmlValidatingReader, XPathNavigator

Before: XmlNodeOrder

BeginInvoke( ): UnreferencedObjectEventHandler, ValidationEventHandler, XmlAttributeEvent-Handler, XmlElementEventHandler, XmlNode-ChangedEventHandler, XmlNodeEventHandler, XmlSerializationCollectionFixupCallback, XmlSerializationFixupCallback, XmlSerialization-ReadCallback, XmlSerializationWriteCallback

Block: XmlSchemaComplexType, XmlSchemaElement

BlockDefault: XmlSchema

BlockResolved: XmlSchemaComplexType, XmlSchemaElement

Boolean: XPathResultType

CanDeserialize( ): XmlSerializer

CanResolveEntity: XmlNodeReader, XmlReader, XmlValidatingReader

CDATA: XmlNodeType, XmlTokenizedType

Change: XmlNodeChangedAction

CheckSpecified: XmlMemberMapping

ChildNodes: XmlNode

Clean( ): XmlDiffPerf

Clear( ): CodeIdentifiers, XsltArgumentList

Clone( ): XmlNode, XPathExpression, XPathNavigator, XPathNodeIterator

CloneNode( ): XmlAttribute, XmlCDataSection, XmlComment, XmlDataDocument, XmlDeclaration, XmlDocument, XmlDocumentFragment, XmlDocumentType, XmlElement, XmlEntity, XmlEntityReference, XmlNode, XmlNotation,

XmlProcessingInstruction, XmlSignificant-Whitespace, XmlText, XmlWhitespace

Close( ): XmlNodeReader, XmlReader, XmlTextReader, XmlTextWriter, XmlValidatingReader, XmlWriter

Closed: ReadState, WriteState

CodeIdentifier: System.Xml.Serialization

CodeIdentifiers: System.Xml.Serialization

Comment: XmlNodeType, XPathNodeType

Compare( ): XmlDiff

CompareDocument( ): XsltContext

ComparePosition( ): XPathNavigator

Compile( ): XmlSchema, XPathNavigator

ConfigurationException: System.Configuration

ConfigurationSettings: System.Configuration

ConfigXmlDocument: System.Configuration

Constraints: XmlSchemaElement

Contains( ): XmlAnyElementAttributes, XmlArray-ItemAttributes, XmlElementAttributes, XmlSchema-Collection, XmlSchemaObjectCollection, XmlSchemaObjectTable, XmlSchemas

Content: WriteState, XmlSchemaComplexContent, XmlSchemaContentModel, XmlSchemaSimple-Content, XmlSchemaSimpleType

ContentModel: XmlSchemaComplexType

ContentType: XmlSchemaComplexType

ContentTypeParticle: XmlSchemaComplexType

CopyTo( ): XmlAnyElementAttributes, XmlArray-ItemAttributes, XmlAttributeCollection, XmlElementAttributes, XmlSchemaCollection, XmlSchemaObjectCollection, XmlSchemas

Count: XmlMembersMapping, XmlNamedNodeMap, XmlNodeList, XmlSchemaCollection, XmlSchema-ObjectTable, XmlSerializerNamespaces, XPathNode-Iterator

Create( ): DictionarySectionHandler, IConfigurationSectionHandler, IgnoreSection-Handler, NameValueFileSectionHandler, Name-ValueSectionHandler, SingleTagSectionHandler

CreateAbstractTypeException( ): XmlSerializationReader

CreateAttribute( ): ConfigXmlDocument, XmlDocument

CreateCDataSection( ): ConfigXmlDocument, XmlDocument

CreateChoiceIdentifierValueException( ): XmlSerializationWriter

CreateComment( ): ConfigXmlDocument, XmlDocument

CreateCtorHasSecurityException( ): XmlSerializationReader

CreateDocument( ): XmlImplementation

CreateDocumentFragment( ): XmlDocument

CreateDocumentType( ): XmlDocument

CreateElement( ): ConfigXmlDocument, XmlData-Document, XmlDocument

CreateEntityReference( ): XmlDataDocument, XmlDocument

CreateEvidenceForUrl( ): XmlSecureResolver

CreateInaccessibleConstructorException( ): XmlSerializationReader

CreateInvalidCastException( ): XmlSerializationReader

CreateInvalidChoiceIdentifierValueException( ): XmlSerializationWriter

CreateMismatchChoiceException( ): XmlSerializationWriter

CreateNavigator( ): IXPathNavigable, XmlData-Document, XmlNode, XPathDocument

CreateNode( ): XmlDocument

CreateProcessingInstruction( ): XmlDocument

CreateReader( ): XmlSerializer

CreateReadOnlyCollectionException( ): XmlSerializationReader

CreateSignificantWhitespace( ): ConfigXml-Document, XmlDocument

CreateTextNode( ): ConfigXmlDocument, XmlDocument

CreateUnknownAnyElementException( ): XmlSerializationWriter

CreateUnknownConstantException( ): XmlSerializationReader

CreateUnknownNodeException( ): XmlSerializationReader

CreateUnknownTypeException( ): XmlSerializationReader, XmlSerializationWriter

CreateWhitespace( ): ConfigXmlDocument, XmlDocument

CreateWriter( ): XmlSerializer

CreateXmlDeclaration( ): XmlDocument

Credentials: XmlResolver, XmlSecureResolver, XmlUrlResolver

Current: XmlSchemaCollectionEnumerator, XmlSchemaObjectEnumerator, XPathNodeIterator

CurrentPosition: XPathNodeIterator

Data: XmlCharacterData, XmlProcessingInstruction

DataSet: XmlDataDocument

Datatype: XmlSchemaType

DataType: SoapAttributeAttribute, SoapElement-Attribute, XmlArrayItemAttribute, XmlAttribute-Attribute, XmlElementAttribute, XmlRootAttribute, XmlTextAttribute

DecodeName( ): XmlConvert

Default: XmlSpace

DefaultNamespace: XmlNamespaceManager

DefaultValue: XmlSchemaAttribute, XmlSchema-Element

DeleteData( ): XmlCharacterData

Depth: XmlNodeReader, XmlReader, XmlTextReader, XmlValidatingReader

DerivedBy: XmlSchemaType

Descending: XmlSortOrder

Deserialize( ): XmlSerializer

DictionarySectionHandler: System.Configuration

DocTypeName: XmlParserContext

Document: XmlNodeType

DocumentElement: XmlDocument

DocumentFragment: XmlNodeType

DocumentType: XmlDocument, XmlNodeType

DTD: ValidationType

Element: WriteState, XmlElementEventArgs, XmlNodeType, XPathNodeType

ElementFormDefault: XmlSchema

ElementName: SoapElementAttribute, XmlArray-Attribute, XmlArrayItemAttribute, XmlElement-Attribute, XmlMemberMapping, XmlMembers-Mapping, XmlRootAttribute, XmlTypeMapping

ElementOnly: XmlSchemaContentType

Elements: XmlSchema

ElementType: XmlSchemaElement

Empty: XmlQualifiedName, XmlSchemaContentType, XmlSchemaDerivationMethod

EncodeLocalName( ): XmlConvert

EncodeName( ): XmlConvert

EncodeNmToken( ): XmlConvert

Encoding: XmlDeclaration, XmlParserContext, XmlTextReader, XmlValidatingReader

EndElement: XmlNodeType

EndEntity: XmlNodeType

EndInvoke( ): UnreferencedObjectEventHandler, ValidationEventHandler, XmlAttributeEvent-Handler, XmlElementEventHandler, XmlNode-ChangedEventHandler, XmlNodeEventHandler, XmlSerializationCollectionFixupCallback, XmlSerializationFixupCallback, XmlSerialization-ReadCallback, XmlSerializationWriteCallback

EndOfFile: ReadState

EnsureArrayIndex( ): XmlSerializationReader

Entities: XmlDocumentType

ENTITIES: XmlTokenizedType

Entity: XmlNodeType

ENTITY: XmlTokenizedType

EntityHandling: System.Xml, XmlValidatingReader

EntityReference: XmlNodeType

ENUMERATION: XmlTokenizedType

EOF: XmlNodeReader, XmlReader, XmlTextReader, XmlValidatingReader

Equals( ): XmlQualifiedName

Error: ReadState, XmlSeverityType, XPathResultType

Evaluate( ): IXsltContextVariable, XPathNavigator

Exception: ValidationEventArgs

ExcludeXml: XPathNamespaceScope

ExpandCharEntities: EntityHandling

ExpandEntities: EntityHandling

ExportAnyType( ): XmlSchemaExporter

ExportMembersMapping( ): SoapCodeExporter, SoapSchemaExporter, XmlCodeExporter, XmlSchemaExporter

ExportTypeMapping( ): SoapCodeExporter, Soap-SchemaExporter, XmlCodeExporter, XmlSchema-Exporter

Expression: XPathExpression

Extension: XmlSchemaDerivationMethod

Facets: XmlSchemaSimpleContentRestriction, XmlSchemaSimpleTypeRestriction

Fast: XmlDiffAlgorithm

Fields: XmlSchemaIdentityConstraint

Filename: ConfigurationException, ConfigXml-Document

Final: XmlSchemaElement, XmlSchemaType

FinalDefault: XmlSchema

FinalResolved: XmlSchemaElement, XmlSchemaType

Find( ): XmlSchemas

FirstChild: XmlNode

FixedValue: XmlSchemaAttribute, XmlSchemaElement

FixupArrayRefs( ): XmlSerializationReader

Flush( ): XmlTextWriter, XmlWriter

Form: XmlArrayAttribute, XmlArrayItemAttribute, XmlAttributeAttribute, XmlElementAttribute, XmlSchemaAttribute, XmlSchemaElement

Formatting: System.Xml, XmlTextWriter

FromByteArrayBase64( ): XmlSerializationWriter

FromByteArrayHex( ): XmlSerializationWriter

FromChar( ): XmlSerializationWriter

FromDate( ): XmlSerializationWriter

FromDateTime( ): XmlSerializationWriter

FromEnum( ): XmlSerializationWriter

FromMappings( ): XmlSerializer

FromTime( ): XmlSerializationWriter

FromTypes( ): XmlSerializer

FromXmlName( ): XmlSerializationWriter

FromXmlNCName( ): XmlSerializationWriter

FromXmlNmToken( ): XmlSerializationWriter

FromXmlNmTokens( ): XmlSerializationWriter

FromXmlQualifiedName( ): XmlSerializationWriter

Get( ): NameTable, XmlNameTable

GetArrayLength( ): XmlSerializationReader

GetAttribute( ): XmlElement, XmlNodeReader, XmlReader, XmlTextReader, XmlValidatingReader, XPathNavigator

GetAttributeNode( ): XmlElement

GetConfig( ): ConfigurationSettings, IConfiguration-System

GetElementById( ): XmlDataDocument, XmlDocument

GetElementFromRow( ): XmlDataDocument

GetElementsByTagName( ): XmlDocument, XmlElement

GetEntity( ): XmlResolver, XmlSecureResolver, XmlUrlResolver

GetEnumerator( ): XmlNamedNodeMap, XmlNamespaceManager, XmlNode, XmlNodeList, XmlSchemaCollection, XmlSchemaObjectCollection, XmlSchemaObjectTable

GetExtensionObject( ): XsltArgumentList

GetHashCode( ): XmlQualifiedName

GetNamedItem( ): XmlNamedNodeMap

GetNamespace( ): XPathNavigator

GetNamespaceOfPrefix( ): XmlNode

GetNode( ): IHasXmlNode

GetNullAttr( ): XmlSerializationReader

GetObjectData( ): ConfigurationException, XmlException, XmlSchemaException, XPath-Exception, XsltCompileException, XsltException

GetParam( ): XsltArgumentList

GetPrefixOfNamespace( ): XmlNode

GetRemainder( ): XmlTextReader

GetRowFromElement( ): XmlDataDocument

GetSchema( ): IXmlSerializable

GetTarget( ): XmlSerializationReader

GetValue( ): AppSettingsReader

GetXmlNodeFilename( ): ConfigurationException

GetXmlNodeLineNumber( ): ConfigurationException

GetXsiType( ): XmlSerializationReader

Groups: XmlSchema, XmlSchemaRedefine

HasAttribute( ): XmlElement

HasAttributes: XmlElement, XmlNodeReader, XmlReader, XPathNavigator

HasChildNodes: XmlNode

HasChildren: XPathNavigator

HasFeature( ): XmlImplementation

HasLineInfo( ): IXmlLineInfo

HasNamespace( ): XmlNamespaceManager

HasValue: XmlNodeReader, XmlReader, XmlText-Reader, XmlValidatingReader

IConfigurationSectionHandler: System.Configuration

IConfigurationSystem: System.Configuration

Id: XmlSchema, XmlSchemaAnnotated, XmlSchemaAnnotation, XmlSchemaExternal

ID: XmlTokenizedType

IDREF: XmlTokenizedType

IDREFS: XmlTokenizedType

IgnoreChildOrder: XmlDiff, XmlDiffOptions

IgnoreComments: XmlDiff, XmlDiffOptions

IgnoreDtd: XmlDiff, XmlDiffOptions

IgnoreNamespaces: XmlDiff, XmlDiffOptions

IgnorePI: XmlDiff, XmlDiffOptions

IgnorePrefixes: XmlDiff, XmlDiffOptions

IgnoreSectionHandler: System.Configuration

IgnoreWhitespace: XmlDiff, XmlDiffOptions

IgnoreXmlDecl: XmlDiff, XmlDiffOptions

IHasXmlNode: System.Xml

Implementation: XmlDocument

ImportAnyType( ): XmlSchemaImporter

ImportDerivedTypeMapping( ): SoapSchema-Importer, XmlSchemaImporter

ImportMembersMapping( ): SoapReflection-Importer, SoapSchemaImporter, XmlReflection-Importer, XmlSchemaImporter

ImportNode( ): XmlDocument

ImportTypeMapping( ): SoapReflectionImporter, XmlReflectionImporter, XmlSchemaImporter

IncludeInSchema: SoapTypeAttribute, XmlType-Attribute

IncludeMetadata: SoapCodeExporter, XmlCode-Exporter

Includes: XmlSchema

IncludeType( ): SoapReflectionImporter, XmlReflectionImporter

IncludeTypes( ): SoapReflectionImporter, XmlReflectionImporter

Indentation: XmlTextWriter

IndentChar: XmlTextWriter

Indented: Formatting

IndexOf( ): XmlAnyElementAttributes, XmlArray-ItemAttributes, XmlElementAttributes, XmlSchema-ObjectCollection, XmlSchemas

Init( ): IConfigurationSystem

InitCallbacks( ): XmlSerializationReader, XmlSerializationWriter

Initial: ReadState

InitIDs( ): XmlSerializationReader

InnerText: XmlAttribute, XmlCharacterData, XmlDeclaration, XmlElement, XmlEntity, XmlNode, XmlProcessingInstruction

InnerXml: XmlAttribute, XmlDocument, XmlDocumentFragment, XmlElement, XmlEntity, XmlNode, XmlNotation

Insert: XmlNodeChangedAction

Insert( ): XmlAnyElementAttributes, XmlArrayItem-Attributes, XmlElementAttributes, XmlSchema-ObjectCollection, XmlSchemas

InsertAfter( ): XmlAttributeCollection, XmlNode

InsertBefore( ): XmlAttributeCollection, XmlNode

InsertData( ): XmlCharacterData

InstanceNamespace: XmlSchema

Interactive: ReadState

InternalSubset: XmlDocumentType, XmlParserContext

InternalValidationEventHandler: XmlValidating-Reader

Invoke( ): IXsltContextFunction, Unreferenced-ObjectEventHandler, ValidationEventHandler, XmlAttributeEventHandler, XmlElementEvent-Handler, XmlNodeChangedEventHandler, XmlNode-EventHandler, XmlSerializationCollectionFixup-Callback, XmlSerializationFixupCallback, XmlSerializationReadCallback, XmlSerialization-WriteCallback

IsAbstract: XmlSchemaComplexType, XmlSchema-Element

IsCompiled: XmlSchema

IsDataSet( ): XmlSchemas

IsDefault: XmlNodeReader, XmlReader, XmlText-Reader, XmlValidatingReader

IsDescendant( ): XPathNavigator

IsEmpty: XmlElement, XmlQualifiedName

IsEmptyElement: XmlNodeReader, XmlReader, XmlTextReader, XmlValidatingReader, XPath-Navigator

IsFixed: XmlSchemaFacet

IsInUse( ): CodeIdentifiers

IsLocal: IXsltContextVariable

IsMixed: XmlSchemaComplexContent, XmlSchemaComplexType, XmlSchemaType

IsName( ): XmlReader

IsNameToken( ): XmlReader

IsNillable: XmlSchemaElement

IsNullable: SoapElementAttribute, XmlArrayAttribute, XmlArrayItemAttribute, XmlElementAttribute, XmlRootAttribute

IsParam: IXsltContextVariable

IsReadOnly: XmlDocument, XmlDocumentType, XmlEntity, XmlEntityReference, XmlNode, XmlNotation

IsReturnValue: XmlReflectionMember

IsSamePosition( ): XPathNavigator

IsStartElement( ): XmlReader

IsXmlnsAttribute( ): XmlSerializationReader

Item: SoapAttributeOverrides, XmlAnyElement-Attributes, XmlArrayItemAttributes, XmlAttribute-Overrides, XmlElementAttributes, XmlMembersMapping, XmlNode, XmlNodeReader, XmlReader, XmlSchemaCollection, XmlSchema-ObjectCollection, XmlSchemaObjectTable, XmlSchemas, XmlTextReader, XmlValidatingReader

Item( ): XmlNamedNodeMap, XmlNodeList

ItemOf: XmlAttributeCollection, XmlNodeList

Items: XmlSchema, XmlSchemaAll, XmlSchema-Annotation, XmlSchemaChoice, XmlSchemaGroup-Base, XmlSchemaRedefine, XmlSchemaSequence

ItemType: XmlSchemaSimpleTypeList

ItemTypeName: XmlSchemaSimpleTypeList

IXmlLineInfo: System.Xml

IXmlSerializable: System.Xml.Serialization

IXPathNavigable: System.Xml.XPath

IXsltContextFunction: System.Xml.Xsl

IXsltContextVariable: System.Xml.Xsl

Language: XmlSchemaDocumentation

LastChild: XmlNode

Lax: XmlSchemaContentProcessing

Length: XmlCharacterData

Line: ConfigurationException

LineNumber: ConfigXmlDocument, IXmlLineInfo, XmlAttributeEventArgs, XmlElementEventArgs, XmlException, XmlNodeEventArgs, XmlSchema-Exception, XmlSchemaObject, XmlTextReader, Xslt-Exception

LinePosition: IXmlLineInfo, XmlAttributeEventArgs, XmlElementEventArgs, XmlException, XmlNode-EventArgs, XmlSchemaException, XmlSchema-Object, XmlTextReader, XsltException

List: XmlSchemaDerivationMethod

Load( ): ConfigXmlDocument, XmlDataDocument, XmlDocument, XslTransform

LoadSingleElement( ): ConfigXmlDocument

LoadXml( ): XmlDocument

Local: XPathNamespaceScope

LocalName: XmlAttribute, XmlCDataSection, XmlComment, XmlDeclaration, XmlDocument, XmlDocumentFragment, XmlDocumentType, XmlElement, XmlEntity, XmlEntityReference, XmlNode, XmlNodeEventArgs, XmlNodeReader, XmlNotation, XmlProcessingInstruction, XmlReader, XmlSignificantWhitespace, XmlText, XmlText-Reader, XmlValidatingReader, XmlWhitespace, XPathNavigator

LookupNamespace( ): XmlNamespaceManager, XmlNodeReader, XmlReader, XmlTextReader, XmlValidatingReader

LookupPrefix( ): XmlNamespaceManager, XmlTextWriter, XmlWriter

LowerFirst: XmlCaseOrder

MakeCamel( ): CodeIdentifier

MakePascal( ): CodeIdentifier

MakeRightCase( ): CodeIdentifiers

MakeUnique( ): CodeIdentifiers

MakeValid( ): CodeIdentifier

Markup: XmlSchemaAppInfo, XmlSchema-
Documentation

Matches( ): XPathNavigator

Maxargs: IXsltContextFunction

MaxOccurs: XmlSchemaParticle

MaxOccursString: XmlSchemaParticle

MemberName: SoapSchemaMember, XmlChoice-
IdentifierAttribute, XmlMemberMapping,
XmlReflectionMember

MemberType: SoapSchemaMember,
XmlReflectionMember

MemberTypes: XmlSchemaSimpleTypeUnion

Message: ConfigurationException, ValidationEvent-
Args, XmlException, XmlSchemaException, XPath-
Exception, XsltCompileException, XsltException

Minargs: IXsltContextFunction

MinOccurs: XmlSchemaParticle

MinOccursString: XmlSchemaParticle

Mixed: XmlSchemaContentType

MoveNext( ): XmlSchemaCollectionEnumerator,
XmlSchemaObjectEnumerator, XPathNodeIterator

MoveTo( ): XPathNavigator

MoveToAttribute( ): XmlNodeReader, XmlReader,
XmlTextReader, XmlValidatingReader, XPath-
Navigator

MoveToContent( ): XmlReader

MoveToElement( ): XmlNodeReader, XmlReader,
XmlTextReader, XmlValidatingReader

MoveToFirst( ): XPathNavigator

MoveToFirstAttribute( ): XmlNodeReader,
XmlReader, XmlTextReader, XmlValidatingReader,
XPathNavigator

MoveToFirstChild( ): XPathNavigator

MoveToFirstNamespace( ): XPathNavigator

MoveToId( ): XPathNavigator

MoveToNamespace( ): XPathNavigator

MoveToNext( ): XPathNavigator

MoveToNextAttribute( ): XmlNodeReader,
XmlReader, XmlTextReader, XmlValidatingReader,
XPathNavigator

MoveToNextNamespace( ): XPathNavigator

MoveToParent( ): XPathNavigator

MoveToPrevious( ): XPathNavigator

MoveToRoot( ): XPathNavigator

Name: SoapEnumAttribute, XmlAnyElementAttribute,
XmlAttribute, XmlCDataSection, XmlComment,
XmlDeclaration, XmlDocument, XmlDocument-
Fragment, XmlDocumentType, XmlElement,
XmlEntity, XmlEntityReference, XmlEnumAttribute,
XmlNode, XmlNodeEventArgs, XmlNodeReader,
XmlNotation, XmlProcessingInstruction,
XmlQualifiedName, XmlReader, XmlSchema-
Attribute, XmlSchemaAttributeGroup, XmlSchema-
Element, XmlSchemaGroup, XmlSchemaIdentity-
Constraint, XmlSchemaNotation, XmlSchemaType,
XmlSignificantWhitespace, XmlText, XmlText-
Reader, XmlValidatingReader, XmlWhitespace,
XPathNavigator

Names: XmlSchemaObjectTable

Namespace: SoapAttributeAttribute, SoapType-
Attribute, XmlAnyElementAttribute, XmlArray-
Attribute, XmlArrayItemAttribute, XmlAttribute-
Attribute, XmlElementAttribute,
XmlMemberMapping, XmlMembersMapping,
XmlQualifiedName, XmlRootAttribute, XmlSchema,
XmlSchemaAny, XmlSchemaAnyAttribute,
XmlSchemaImport, XmlTypeAttribute, XmlType-
Mapping, XPathNodeType

NamespaceManager: XmlParserContext

Namespaces: XmlSchemaObject, XmlTextReader,
XmlTextWriter, XmlValidatingReader

NamespaceUri: XmlDiff

NamespaceURI: XmlAttribute, XmlElement, XmlNode,
XmlNodeEventArgs, XmlNodeReader, XmlReader,
XmlTextReader, XmlValidatingReader, XPath-
Navigator

NameTable: System.Xml, XmlDocument,
XmlNamespaceManager, XmlNodeReader,
XmlParserContext, XmlReader, XmlSchema-
Collection, XmlTextReader, XmlValidatingReader,
XPathNavigator

NameValueFileSectionHandler: System.Configura-
tion

NameValueSectionHandler: System.Configuration

Navigator: XPathResultType

NCName: XmlTokenizedType

NestingLevel: XmlArrayItemAttribute

NewParent: XmlNodeChangedEventArgs

NextSibling: XmlElement, XmlLinkedNode, XmlNode

NMTOKEN: XmlTokenizedType

NMTOKENS: XmlTokenizedType

Node: XmlNodeChangedEventArgs

NodeChanged: XmlDocument

NodeChanging: XmlDocument

NodeInserted: XmlDocument

NodeInserting: XmlDocument

NodeRemoved: XmlDocument

NodeRemoving: XmlDocument

NodeSet: XPathResultType

NodeType: XmlAttribute, XmlCDataSection, XmlComment, XmlDeclaration, XmlDocument, XmlDocumentFragment, XmlDocumentType, XmlElement, XmlEntity, XmlEntityReference, XmlNode, XmlNodeEventArgs, XmlNodeReader, XmlNotation, XmlProcessingInstruction, XmlReader, XmlSignificantWhitespace, XmlText, XmlTextReader, XmlValidatingReader, XmlWhitespace, XPathNavigator

None: Formatting, ValidationType, WhitespaceHandling, XmlCaseOrder, XmlDiffOptions, XmlNodeType, XmlSchemaContentProcessing, XmlSchemaDerivationMethod, XmlSchemaForm, XmlSchemaUse, XmlSpace, XmlTokenizedType

Normalization: XmlTextReader

Normalize( ): XmlNode

Notation: XmlNodeType

NOTATION: XmlTokenizedType

NotationName: XmlEntity

Notations: XmlDocumentType, XmlSchema

Number: XmlDataType, XPathResultType

ObjectBeingDeserialized: XmlAttributeEventArgs, XmlElementEventArgs, XmlNodeEventArgs

OldParent: XmlNodeChangedEventArgs

OnClear( ): XmlSchemaObjectCollection, XmlSchemas

OnInsert( ): XmlSchemaObjectCollection, XmlSchemas

OnRemove( ): XmlSchemaObjectCollection, XmlSchemas

OnSet( ): XmlSchemaObjectCollection, XmlSchemas

Optional: XmlSchemaUse

Options: XmlDiff

OuterXml: XmlEntity, XmlNode, XmlNotation

OverrideIsNullable: XmlReflectionMember

OwnerDocument: XmlAttribute, XmlDocument, XmlDocumentFragment, XmlElement, XmlNode

OwnerElement: XmlAttribute

ParentNode: XmlAttribute, XmlDocumentFragment, XmlNode

ParseOptions( ): XmlDiff

ParseValue( ): XmlSchemaDatatype

ParseWsdlArrayType( ): XmlSerializationReader

Particle: XmlSchemaComplexContentExtension, XmlSchemaComplexContentRestriction, XmlSchemaComplexType, XmlSchemaGroup, XmlSchemaGroupRef

Patch( ): XmlPatch

PopScope( ): XmlNamespaceManager

Precise: XmlDiffAlgorithm

Prefix: XmlAttribute, XmlElement, XmlNode, XmlNodeReader, XmlReader, XmlTextReader, XmlValidatingReader, XPathNavigator

Prepend( ): XmlAttributeCollection

PrependChild( ): XmlNode

Preserve: XmlSpace

PreserveWhitespace: XmlDocument

PreserveWhitespace( ): XsltContext

PreviousSibling: XmlLinkedNode, XmlNode

ProcessContents: XmlSchemaAny, XmlSchemaAnyAttribute

ProcessingInstruction: XmlNodeType, XPathNodeType

Prohibited: XmlSchemaUse

Prolog: WriteState

Public: XmlSchemaNotation

PublicId: XmlDocumentType, XmlEntity, XmlNotation, XmlParserContext

PushScope( ): XmlNamespaceManager

QName: XmlTokenizedType

Qualified: XmlSchemaForm

QualifiedName: XmlSchemaAttribute, XmlSchemaElement, XmlSchemaIdentityConstraint, XmlSchemaType

QuoteChar: XmlNodeReader, XmlReader, XmlTextReader, XmlTextWriter, XmlValidatingReader

Read( ): XmlNodeReader, XmlReader, XmlSchema, XmlTextReader, XmlValidatingReader

ReadAttributeValue( ): XmlNodeReader, XmlReader, XmlTextReader, XmlValidatingReader

ReadBase64( ): XmlTextReader

ReadBinHex( ): XmlTextReader

ReadChars( ): XmlTextReader

ReadElementQualifiedName( ): XmlSerializationReader

ReadElementString( ): XmlReader

ReadEndElement( ): XmlReader,
XmlSerializationReader

Reader: XmlValidatingReader

ReadInnerXml( ): XmlReader

ReadNode( ): XmlDocument

ReadNull( ): XmlSerializationReader

ReadNullableQualifiedName( ):
XmlSerializationReader

ReadNullableString( ): XmlSerializationReader

ReadOuterXml( ): XmlReader

ReadReference( ): XmlSerializationReader

ReadReferencedElement( ): XmlSerializationReader

ReadReferencedElements( ): XmlSerializationReader

ReadReferencingElement( ): XmlSerializationReader

ReadSerializable( ): XmlSerializationReader

ReadStartElement( ): XmlReader

ReadState: System.Xml, XmlNodeReader, XmlReader,
XmlTextReader, XmlValidatingReader

ReadString( ): XmlNodeReader, XmlReader,
XmlSerializationReader, XmlValidatingReader

ReadTypedPrimitive( ): XmlSerializationReader

ReadTypedValue( ): XmlValidatingReader

ReadXml( ): IXmlSerializable

ReadXmlDocument( ): XmlSerializationReader

ReadXmlNode( ): XmlSerializationReader

RedefinedAttributeGroup: XmlSchema-
AttributeGroup

Refer: XmlSchemaKeyref

Referenced( ): XmlSerializationReader

RefName: XmlSchemaAttribute, XmlSchema-
AttributeGroupRef, XmlSchemaElement,
XmlSchemaGroupRef

Remove: XmlNodeChangedAction

Remove( ): CodeIdentifiers, XmlAnyElement-
Attributes, XmlArrayItemAttributes, XmlAttribute-
Collection, XmlElementAttributes, XmlSchema-
ObjectCollection, XmlSchemas

RemoveAll( ): XmlAttributeCollection, XmlElement,
XmlNode

RemoveAllAttributes( ): XmlElement

RemoveAt( ): XmlAttributeCollection

RemoveAttribute( ): XmlElement

RemoveAttributeAt( ): XmlElement

RemoveAttributeNode( ): XmlElement

RemoveChild( ): XmlNode

RemoveExtensionObject( ): XsltArgumentList

RemoveNamedItem( ): XmlNamedNodeMap

RemoveNamespace( ): XmlNamespaceManager

RemoveParam( ): XsltArgumentList

RemoveReserved( ): CodeIdentifiers

ReplaceChild( ): XmlNode

ReplaceData( ): XmlCharacterData

Required: XmlSchemaUse

Reset( ): XmlSchemaObjectEnumerator

ResetState( ): XmlTextReader

ResolveEntity( ): XmlNodeReader, XmlReader,
XmlTextReader, XmlValidatingReader

ResolveFunction( ): XsltContext

ResolveUri( ): XmlResolver, XmlSecureResolver

ResolveVariable( ): XsltContext

Restriction: XmlSchemaDerivationMethod

ReturnType: IXsltContextFunction, XPathExpression

Root: XPathNodeType

Same: XmlNodeOrder

Save( ): XmlDocument

Schema: ValidationType, XmlSchemaExternal

SchemaLocation: XmlSchemaExternal

Schemas: XmlValidatingReader

SchemaType: XmlSchemaAttribute, XmlSchema-
Element, XmlValidatingReader

SchemaTypeName: XmlSchemaAttribute,
XmlSchemaElement

SchemaTypes: XmlSchema, XmlSchemaRedefine

Select( ): XPathNavigator

SelectAncestors( ): XPathNavigator

SelectChildren( ): XPathNavigator

SelectDescendants( ): XPathNavigator

SelectNodes( ): XmlNode

Selector: XmlSchemaIdentityConstraint

SelectSingleNode( ): XmlNode

Serialize( ): XmlSerializer

SetAttribute( ): XmlElement

SetAttributeNode( ): XmlElement

SetContext( ): XPathExpression

SetNamedItem( ): XmlAttributeCollection,
XmlNamedNodeMap

Severity: ValidationEventArgs

ShrinkArray( ): XmlSerializationReader

Significant: WhitespaceHandling

SignificantWhitespace: XmlNodeType, XPath-
NodeType

Index

Symbols

& (ampersand), 55, 225
<> (angle brackets), 48, 312
* (asterisk), 112
@ (at sign)
   C# and, 14
   prefix, 244
   reserved character, 225
   selecting attributes, 112
   WebService directive, 217
   XDL paths, 280
\ (backslash), 14
: (colon), 225
$ (dollar sign), 154
:: (double colon), 110
.. (double period axis), 111
</> end tag, 54
= (equal), 225
> (greater than), 55, 113
- (hyphen), 52, 55, 58, 69, 280
< (less than), 55
() parentheses, 52, 54, 55, 58, 68, 69
| (pipe), 112, 280
+ (plus sign), 24, 225
? (question mark), 52, 55, 69, 225
<= relational operator, 113
[] (square brackets), 66, 110
/ (slash), 109, 110, 111, 225, 280
// (double slash), 110, 111

A

A prefix character, 52, 55
accessPoint element (UDDI), 232
ACID properties (relational database), 237,
     238
activation, 183
Actor attribute (SOAP-ENV:Header), 185
Add( ) method
   DataColumnCollection, 247
   DataRelationCollection, 248
   SoapAttributeOverrides class, 381
   XmlAttributeOverrides class, 391
   XmlSchemaCollection class, 168, 353
   XmlSchemaObjectCollection class, 368
AddExtensionObject( ) method
     (XsltArgumentList), 155
AddNameSpace( ) method
     (XmlNameSpaceManager), 323
add_publisherAssertions method (UDDI
     API), 234
AddressElementToString( ) method
     (XmlTextReader), 27
AddSort( ) method (XPathExpression), 117,
     404
ADO.NET
   overview, 238–246
   System.Data namespace and, 175
   XmlConvert class, 314
   (see also DataSet class)
Algorithm property (XmlDiff), 285
America Online, 17

We'd like to hear your suggestions for improving our indexes. Send email to *index@oreilly.com*.

Z

About the Author

Niel M. Bornstein has worked as a software developer for over ten years in such diverse areas as corporate information systems, client-server application development, and web-hosted applications. A graduate of the Georgia Institute of Technology, he has worked for companies in an impressively random set of industries, including publishing, financial services, geographic information systems, lodging, and theatrical entertainment. Niel lives in Marietta, Georgia, with his wife, Dawn; their son, Nicholas; their English Springer Spaniel, Wil-Orion's Angus Highlander; and their domestic short-haired cat, Sir Winston Butler.

Colophon

Our look is the result of reader comments, our own experimentation, and feedback from distribution channels. Distinctive covers complement our distinctive approach to technical topics, breathing personality and life into potentially dry subjects.

The animal on the cover of *.NET and XML* is a Canada goose (*Branta canadensis*). The Canada goose can be easily recognized by its black head, long neck, and whitish cheek patches. The underparts of the goose vary in color from light pearl gray, to chestnut, to blackish brown. There are at least 40, and possibly more, types of Canada geese. These groups also range in size. The largest Canada geese have a very deep honking voice, while the smallest have a high-pitched cackle. Males and females look similar, with the males being larger. The weights of the various types can range from 1.1 to 8 kilograms, and they can grow to a length of 43 inches, attaining a wingspan of 68 inches.

When geese migrate, they often fly at a considerable altitude. Long-distance flying by the flock is in a "V" formation. Flying just off the wing tips of the leader cuts turbulence, and creates a slipstream and a suction that lets the geese fly with less energy expended. The goose pilots take turns; one will drop back in the "V" to rest while another takes over.

Breeding season is from April to June. The pairs wait until the snow and ice melt before they begin nesting. Canada geese mate in their third year and pairs usually remain together as long as both birds are alive. There is a tendency for females to return to their own birth site to nest, and nesting areas are usually in marshes along sloughs or lakeshores. Both males and females collect debris for the nest. The female wiggles back and forth in the debris to shape the nest to her liking; she also plucks her down to line the nest. The female lays between 2 and 11 cream-colored eggs, and incubates them for 25 to 30 days while the male stands guard nearby. Both parents tend to the newborns, who are able to fly at about 8 weeks. The family bonds are strong, and the young remain with their parents on migration and throughout their first winter.

Reg Aubry was the production editor and copyeditor, and Sarah Sherman was the proofreader for *.NET and XML*. Marlowe Shaeffer and Claire Cloutier provided quality control. Jamie Peppard provided production assistance. Lucie Haskins wrote the index.

Ellie Volckhausen designed the cover of this book, based on a series design by Edie Freedman. The cover image is an original illustration created by Susan Hart. Emma Colby produced the cover layout with QuarkXPress 4.1 using Adobe's ITC Garamond font.

David Futato designed the interior layout. This book was converted by Julie Hawks to FrameMaker 5.5.6 with a format conversion tool created by Erik Ray, Jason McIntosh, Neil Walls, and Mike Sierra that uses Perl and XML technologies. The text font is Linotype Birka; the heading font is Adobe Myriad Condensed; and the code font is LucasFont's TheSans Mono Condensed. The illustrations that appear in the book were produced by Robert Romano and Jessamyn Read, using Macromedia FreeHand 9 and Adobe Photoshop 6. The tip and warning icons were drawn by Christopher Bing. This colophon was written by Janet Santackas.

Get even more for your money.

Join the O'Reilly Community, and register the O'Reilly books you own. It's free, and you'll get:

- $4.99 ebook upgrade offer
- 40% upgrade offer on O'Reilly print books
- Membership discounts on books and events
- Free lifetime updates to ebooks and videos
- Multiple ebook formats, DRM FREE
- Participation in the O'Reilly community
- Newsletters
- Account management
- 100% Satisfaction Guarantee

Signing up is easy:

1. Go to: oreilly.com/go/register
2. Create an O'Reilly login.
3. Provide your address.
4. Register your books.

Note: English-language books only

To order books online:
oreilly.com/store

For questions about products or an order:
orders@oreilly.com

To sign up to get topic-specific email announcements and/or news about upcoming books, conferences, special offers, and new technologies:
elists@oreilly.com

For technical questions about book content:
booktech@oreilly.com

To submit new book proposals to our editors:
proposals@oreilly.com

O'Reilly books are available in multiple DRM-free ebook formats. For more information:
oreilly.com/ebooks

O'REILLY®

Spreading the knowledge of innovators   oreilly.com

Have it your way.

Lightning Source UK Ltd.
Milton Keynes UK
UKHW031813110319
338925UK00004B/176/P